The Politics of Knowledge

The Politics of Knowledge

*Area Studies
and the Disciplines*

Edited by David Szanton

UNIVERSITY OF CALIFORNIA PRESS
Berkeley • Los Angeles • London

UCIAS is a partnership of the University of California Press, the California Digital Library (CDL), and internationally oriented research units on eight UC campuses. The Digital Collection publishes articles, monographs, and edited volumes that are peer-reviewed according to standards set by an interdisciplinary UCIAS Editorial Board and approved by the University of California Press. UCIAS makes digital versions of these works available free of charge to a global network of scholars and encourages international intellectual exchange and research collaboration.

University of California Press
Berkeley and Los Angeles, California

University of California Press, Ltd.
London, England

Library of Congress Cataloging-in-Publication Data available upon request

ISBN 0-520-24536-9

Manufactured in the United States of America

This book is a print-on-demand volume. It is manufactured using toner in place of ink. Type and images may be less sharp than the same material seen in traditionally printed University of California Press editions.

Contents

Acknowledgments

This volume began in a 1996 conversation with Toby Volkman, then new at the Ford Foundation, and charged to rethink the Foundation's long support for Area Studies in US universities and related institutions. At the time, Area Studies was under attack from scholars in several fields who in general argued that Area Studies had been an invention of the Cold War, reflected US political interests and Euro-centric prejudices, and now that the Cold War was over that Area Studies had lost its rationale and value. Some also charged that Area Studies scholarship was merely descriptive and of less intellectual power than the theoretical or universal claims of their own disciplines.

At the time, Toby and I had recently competed many years staffing the South Asia and Southeast Asia Joint Committees of the Social Science Research Council and the American Council of Learned Societies. We knew well the work of those committees and a good deal about the other SSRC based Area Studies committees. What was clear to us was that all of these committees had long abandoned Cold War related agendas, and were driven by empirical and theoretical issues and debates, quite as much, and quite as varied, as other academic communities. The scholars on the various Council committees, and the area fields generally, had long taken the initiative and constructed their own intellectual and academic agendas. Furthermore, those agendas were extremely diverse. Thus, for example, the questions being studied and debated by the Committee on Latin American Studies looked little like those of the Committees on Southeast Asia, on Africa, or on Japan. Scholars on the Committees, and in the fields at large, were, for numerous reasons, doing research, writing, teaching, and theorizing on very different kinds of issues. In effect, while external critics tended to present Area Studies fields as homogeneous, narrowly political, and were largely irrelevant, from the inside they appeared intellectually diverse, individually distinctive, and highly productive.

Nevertheless, the striking social, economic, and political transformations of the 1990s, certainly seemed to call for some "rethinking" of Area Studies. But it also seemed clear that any such rethinking should be grounded in reasonably accurate and quite concrete understandings of the distinctive character, debates, past and present trajectories, and continuing contributions of the various Area Studies fields.

This volume is an attempt to provide that grounding. The authors are specialists in each area, chosen for their depth of knowledge and interests in its intellectual history. With funding from the Ford Foundation, we began with a two-day workshop at the University of California, Berkeley, in May 1997. The workshop was structured as a series of area panels including the authors in the volume plus two members of the Berkeley faculty who also worked in that region but who approached from different disciplines and perspectives. Time was also allotted for general discussion, comparisons, and to identify common themes and issues. Aside from the authors in this volume, I must give special thanks to the other panelists: for Latin America, David Collier and Gwen Kirkpatrick; for Soviet/CIS studies, Michael Burawoy and Reginald Zelnick; for Southeast Asia, Nancy Peluso and Peter Zinoman; for Japan, Andrew Barshay and Elizabeth Berry; for Eastern Europe, Ronelle Alexander and Andrew Janos; for China, Thomas Gold and Wen-hsin Yeh; for Africa, Gillian Hart and Richard Roberts (Stanford); for the Middle East, Nezar AlSayyad, Stefania Pandolfo and Michael Gilsenan (NYU) standing in for volume author Timothy Mitchell; and for South Asia, Lawrence Cohen and Priya Joshi. In addition, although they did not lead to chapters in this volume, there were also panels on Western Europe with Manuel Castells and Jan de Vries, on the United States with Michael Johns, Emily Martin, and Aih-wa Ong, and a preliminary statement of key themes by Randolph Starn.

On the following day, the authors met again to specify issues and themes to be addressed in draft papers for a second workshop, looking towards the publication of this collective volume. Many of those issues and themes are at least mentioned in the Introduction, and then discussed more fully in the chapters that follow.

The second workshop was held at New York University in May 1998 with the authors and their draft papers, as well as eight discussants, each of whom played an active and important role in shaping the discussions and the eventual chapters. The discussants were Thomas Bender, Sara Berry, Craig Calhoun, Michael Gilsenan, Ira

Katznelson, David Ludden, James C. Scott, and Toby Volkman. Their contributions were substantial and are deeply appreciated.

Both workshops were also immensely aided by the presence, interventions, and excellent summaries of the proceedings by two doctoral student rapporteurs, David Engerman at UC Berkeley, and Sophia C. Anninos at NYU. Their contributions to the substance and coherence of the discussions were invaluable. Likewise, the logistical and organizational finesse of Caverlee Cary at Berkeley and Jake Kreilkamp at NYU were central to the success of both workshops.

Even before formal peer review and attendant revisions, drafts of the chapters in this volume were made available, gratis, on-line, by a new University of California International and Area Studies Publications Program maintained by the University's California Digital Library. Indeed, the Program has agreed to retain the entire volume, in perpetuity, on its website: http://repositories.cdlib.org/uciaspubs/editedvolumes/3/. The goal of this Program is to provide easy access to such materials to scholars elsewhere in the world who might otherwise have difficulty obtaining hard copies of the volume, or even learning of its existence. Numerous people contributed to the development of the new Program. I myself was involved at the beginning, but special thanks must go to Catherine Candee, Charles Faulhaber, David Leonard, Jerry Lubenow, Karla Neilson, Roy Tennant, and Lynne Withey (and no doubt others I am unaware of) who over the years since then, struggled with the conceptual, organizational, technical, and legal issues involved in establishing this innovative web-based Program.

My final thanks must go to the authors of the chapters in this volume. They agreed to the initial uncertainties of electronic publication of their work, waited patiently for the resolution of the numerous problems and glitches such a new program inevitably generates. They have again waited patiently for the volume's hard copy publication. Still more important, their chapters are major contributions to understanding the substance, differentiation, and evolution of the various Area Studies fields. They also provide essential foundations for indeed "rethinking" Area Studies past trajectories, new directions, and future contributions to a post 9/11 world.

Introduction

The Origin, Nature, and Challenges of Area Studies in the United States

David L. Szanton

In his essay that follows, Alan Tansman notes that Area Studies is a form of translation; "an enterprise seeking to know, analyze, and interpret foreign cultures through a multidisciplinary lens." "To know, analyze, and interpret" another culture—whether an American seeking to understand China, or an Angolan seeking to understand India—is inevitably an act of translation. It is primarily an effort to make the assumptions, meanings, structures, and dynamics of another society and culture comprehensible to an outsider. But it also creates reflexive opportunities to expand, even challenge by the contrast, the outsider's understanding of his or her own society and culture. The "multidisciplinary lens" is essential because no single academic discipline is capable of capturing and conveying a full understanding of another society or culture.

Good translations of any text—whether a poem, a speech, a social event, or a culture—must begin with a serious attempt to understand the text's structures, meanings, and dynamics. The text must be set in its own language and history, in its prior texts and current contexts to avoid simply imposing one's own meanings or expectations on it. Perfect translations are rarely possible, something is almost always lost in translation; rough or partial translations are the best we can expect. Inevitably, translations from or of even very distant languages and cultures will produce some familiar ideas and images, and will support some familiar concepts and propositions. But they will also almost certainly generate some surprises. Merely finding or imposing our own selves, structures, or dynamics in another culture—in effect, reading it as a Rorschach inkblot onto which we project our

1

own experience—only tells us about ourselves. It also probably means that we have missed whatever we might have learned from it. Such failures to understand—or projections onto—other societies and cultures often result from forms of ethnocentrism. This seems a particular danger in the US given its powerful and now seemingly hegemonic socio-economic and political position. All too often US social scientists and humanists have proclaimed universals or imposed on other parts of the world concepts, theories, models, and analytic fashions derived from West European or US experience. At one level this is readily understandable; seriously seeking the diverse and alternative knowledges and experiences of other cultures and societies can be deeply challenging, decentering, and threatening. But doing so can also help deparochialize understandings, and illuminate the world, the other, and ultimately, one's own society and self.

This volume argues that the fundamental role of Area Studies in the United States has been—and continues to be—to deparochialize US- and Euro-centric visions of the world in the core social science and humanities disciplines, among policy makers, and in the public at large. Within the US university, Area Studies scholarship attempts to document the existence, internal logic, and theoretical implications of the distinctive social and cultural values, expressions, structures, and dynamics that shape the societies and nations beyond Europe and the United States. The broad goals are twofold. One, to generate new knowledge and new forms of knowledge for their intrinsic and practical value. Two, and more reflexively, to historicize and contextualize—in effect, to de-naturalize—the formulations and universalizing tendencies of the US social science and humanities disciplines which continue to draw largely on US and European experience. When successful, Area Studies research and teaching demonstrates the limitations of fashioning analyses based largely on the particular and contingent histories, structures, power formations, and selective, and often idealized, narratives of "the West." Still more ambitiously, Area Studies can provide the materials and ideas to help reconstruct the disciplines so that they become more inclusive and more effective tools for social and cultural analysis.

Area Studies communities have not always succeeded in this;

there have been many failures, and other agendas as well. As an intellectual movement, Area Studies has been heterogeneous and itself must be historicised, contextualized, and continually reconstructed to meet the changing dynamics of the world. But the deparochialization of the US social sciences and humanities has been a central concern from the beginning.[1] Furthermore, given post-1989 Western triumphalism, intertwined with current processes and claims of economic, social and cultural "globalization," reinvigorating and recasting Area Studies to meet its original goal of translating back to us the continuing diversities of the world is an ever more complex and challenging intellectual and political enterprise.

Within the universities of the United States Area Studies represents a major social invention. Area Studies research and teaching on Africa, Asia, Latin America, the Middle East, and the Soviet Union has repeatedly challenged the institutional and the intellectual hegemony of the US and Euro-centric social science and humanities disciplines. By generating new kinds of data, questions, and insights into social formations, political dynamics, and cultural constructions (e.g. Anderson's "Imagined Communities," The Rudolphs' "Modernity of Tradition," Geertz' "Theatre State," O'Donnell's "Bureaucratic Authoritarianism", Scott's "Weapons of the Weak" Turner's "Liminal Spaces"), Area Studies scholars have frequently undermined received wisdom and established theories, replacing them with more context sensitive formulations. By creating new interdisciplinary academic programs, and developing close collaborations with colleagues overseas rooted in different national and intellectual cultures, Area Studies scholars press the social science and humanities disciplines in the US to look beyond, even sometimes recast unstated presumptions and easy interpretations.

At times the challenges to the disciplines have often involved sharp intellectual, institutional, and political struggles. Despite, or perhaps because of, its successes, tensions between Area Studies and certain disciplines continue over intellectual issues, economic resources, and the structure of academic programs. The debates over the appropriate content and organization of internationally oriented university-based teaching and research rise and fall, and never quite seem to be resolved, though over time they do shift ground.

To complicate matters, the individual Area Studies fields are neither internally homogeneous, nor are they similar to each other. Indeed examined up close, they are strikingly distinctive in their political, institutional, and intellectual histories, and in their relationships with the disciplines. This volume then is an effort to illuminate the divergent trajectories, agendas, strengths, and weaknesses of the individual fields in order to provide a concrete sense of their intellectual substance, a framework for defining their contributions, limits, and relations to the core disciplines (themselves changing over time), and a fresh basis for thinking about—even attem-pting to shape—where Area Studies might be headed.

As the nine chapters that follow suggest, "Area Studies" is best understood as a cover term for a family of academic fields and activities joined by a common commitment to: (1) intensive language study; (2) in-depth field research in the local language(s); (3) close attention to local histories, viewpoints, materials, and interpretations; (4) testing, elaborating, critiquing, or developing grounded theory against detailed observation; and (5) multi-disciplinary conversations often crossing the boundaries of the social sciences and humanities. Most Area Studies scholars concentrate their own research and teaching on one or a number of related countries, but generally try to contextualize their efforts in large regions of the world (e.g., Africa, Latin America, Southeast Asia), beyond the US and Western Europe. Scholars working on the three one-country Area Studies fields (China, Japan, and Korea), often engage in at least implicit comparisons among them, and often command literatures in languages from two or more of these countries.[2] As the essays will demonstrate, the boundaries of the Area Studies fields—and especially the African, East European, Soviet, and Southeast Asian fields—are historically contingent, pragmatic, and highly contestable. The conventional boundaries have often been intellectually generative, but they clearly have limits as well.

Always controversial for the challenges it poses to the disciplines, recently Area Studies has itself been challenged from various directions as a vestigial remnant of the Cold War, as politically tainted, as a-theoretical exotica, or as increasingly irrelevant in the face of hegemonic and homogenizing globalization and transnational forces. This volume responds to and rejects these charges by laying out the divergent and productive intellectual and institutional trajectories of the major fields over the last several decades, and many of the most significant debates in and around them. The nine essays that follow—on the African, Chinese, Eastern European, Japanese, Latin American, Middle Eastern, South Asian, Southeast Asian, and the Soviet studies fields[3]—are varied in approach and style. The authors were selected for their interest in and knowledge of the intellectual history of their own specific area studies field, and were charged to write freely from their own particular vantage point. As part of the collective enterprise, they all attempt to describe the key issues, contributions, and controversies within their field and its engagements and interactions with the core social science and humanities disciplines. They also deal with their fields' relationships to the private foundations, US government agencies, national and international politics, generational changes, new domestic constituencies, and colleagues and institutions overseas. At the same time, coming from a wide range of disciplines and intellectual perspectives, they vary in their emphases. Read together, and comparatively, they should provide a reasonable sense of the heterogeneity, multiple trajectories, tensions, problems, and productivity of US area studies.

This Introduction summarizes some key issues and conclusions from the essays. It begins with a brief account of their political, intellectual, and institutional roots in US universities. It then turns to both the critiques of Area Studies and the challenges and contributions they have brought to the disciplines, to the universities, and to the structure and generation of knowledge. It closes with some suggestions regarding their future evolution as the various fields engage with social science and humanities scholarship in the US and abroad.

THE ASTONISHING GROWTH OF AREA STUDIES
From the beginning of the Twentieth Century through the Second

World War, internationally-oriented teaching and research in US colleges and universities rarely went beyond European History and Literature, Classics, and Comparative Religion. Up to 1940, US universities had produced no more than 60 PhDs on the contemporary non-western world and most dealt with antiquity.[4] Today, thousands of college and university faculty regularly teach on the history, literature, contemporary affairs, and international relations of Africa, Asia, Latin America, the Middle East, and the former Soviet Union. Freshman seminars on "South Africa Today," large undergraduate lecture courses on the Middle East or Latin America, specialized graduate seminars on "Indonesian Gamelan," or "The Nineteenth Century Indian Novel," are now standard components of contemporary higher education. Topical courses in the social sciences, humanities, and professional schools now use examples, readings, ideas, and case materials from all across the world.

At the same time, US universities and colleges now host over two hundred thousand foreign students every year as well as tens of thousands of visiting scholars from overseas.[5] Vast numbers of students from recent immigrant families are now studying in US colleges and universities and tens of thousands of US students annually study or conduct research overseas. International workshops and conferences, publication programs and journals abound, increasingly facilitated by the new electronic media. Area Studies and internationally oriented courses, research, and collaboration are now central components of higher education in the United States, and many campuses have programs or plans to facilitate their "internationalization."

In general, Area Studies has been institutionalized in US universities in two distinct types of units; (1) Area Studies Departments, and (2) Area Studies Centers, Institutes, or Programs. Area Studies Departments—for example, South Asian Studies at the University of Chicago, Middle East Studies at Princeton University, or East Asian Languages and Literatures at the University of California, Berkeley—usually offer undergraduate degrees combining course work in the language, literature, history, religion, and sometimes the politics of the particular region. While these departments are multi-disciplinary they generally tilt to the humanities. At the graduate level, Area Studies Departments tend to concentrate on literature and history. In the 1940s and 1950s, when Area Studies were just starting to take root in US universities, these departments were considered crucial to training area specialists. However, during the 1960s, and clearly by the 1970s, the overwhelming majority of MA and PhD students specializing on the non-Western world were being trained in, and then hired to teach in, the core social science and humanities departments; anthropology, art history, geography, history, language and literature, music, sociology, political science, etc.[6] One result is that nearly all Area Studies faculty have at least double identities, e.g., as an historian and as a China scholar, as a sociologist but also as a Latin Americanist. Institutionally, this has meant that Area Studies departments have often shrunk and become increasingly marginalized and embattled. They continue to produce small numbers of MAs and PhDs, but provide many fewer employment opportunities in the university and beyond than internationally oriented degrees in the social science and humanities disciplines. As a result many Area Studies departments—the hope and key means for developing Area Studies in the 1940s and 1950s—were by the 1980s and 1990s, struggling to maintain their students and status within their universities.

In contrast, Area Studies Centers, Institutes, and Programs have been institutionally far more successful. US universities now house hundreds of these units dealing with every region and all the major countries of the world. These Centers and Institutes may sponsor a few courses, but they do not usually grant degrees. However, they draw in and on faculty and graduate students from all across the social sciences, humanities, and professional schools by organizing or supporting multi-disciplinary lecture series, workshops, conferences, research and curriculum development projects, advanced language and topical courses, publication and library collection programs, and a wide variety of public outreach activities. By these various means, they often become active intellectual and programmatic focal points for both new and established scholars concerned with a particular area of the world.

Despite this dramatic growth of area and other international studies in US colleges and universities debates continue on whether there is enough international and foreign language content in the curriculum; whether it is the right content; how it should be related to undergraduate majors or advanced degree programs. In recent years there has been growing attention to the role and interests of diasporic populations in the student body; the appropriate relationships to current concerns for diversity and "multiculturalism;" and the teaching of foreign languages beyond the traditional French, Spanish, German, and Italian. Equally debated, both in universities and in funding agencies, are the most valued topics, theories, intellectual perspectives, and methods for faculty and graduate student research.

Even if still a debated domain, the extraordinary growth and worldwide coverage of Area Studies scholarship and teaching in the US has no equivalent elsewhere in the world. Paris and London have gathered numerous intellectuals from other parts of the globe, and many European universities have, or have had, comparable centers or programs but they are mostly focused on their colonial or ex-colonial possessions. Likewise, Japanese and Australian universities have active research and training centers concerned with their immediate neighbors in East and Southeast Asia, but they support relatively little scholarship on more distant regions, such as the Middle East, Africa, or Latin America. Elsewhere in the world only a few universities have sizeable programs or centers that go beyond their own region—and the study of the US or North America. Only the US has numerous universities with multiple Area Studies Centers, Institutes, and Programs dealing simultaneously with several regions of the world. Overlapping and competitive, they jointly provide global coverage.

How did this dramatic internationalization of US higher education come about? What prompted or provoked it? How has it been organized and what effects has it had on the overall shape and activities of the US university?

As suggested above and as documented by the essays that follow, prior to the Second World War American universities had only a few scattered faculty who taught or conducted research on the non-Western world. Shortly before the War small numbers of scholars of Latin America and of the Soviet Union began to encourage more coordinated research on their respective regions. During the War, many of the few US specialists on other regions of the world—mostly at Ivy League universities—became intelligence analysts in the Office of Strategic Services (OSS) and helped train officers for overseas commands and postwar occupation forces. Post War, some initiated careers in the several new US government security and intelligence agencies. Most returned to university life.

For the vast majority of Americans at the time, Western Europe was the only familiar area of the world beyond the US.[7] Most Americans had studied something of Europe in secondary school, some had traveled there, and many had recently fought there. Likewise, nearly all the faculty and students in US colleges and universities came from families of European background. European institutions, politics, economies, cultures, and social formations were at least somewhat familiar from the media and they were often similar or even sources for their US counterparts. Thus although the US was helping to rebuild Europe with Marshall Plan aid, increasing US academic expertise on Europe did not seem of the highest priority.

In contrast, US ignorance of the rest of the world was striking. At the same time, both liberal and conservative elites in US universities and foundations perceived direct challenges and threats from the Soviet Union, China, the emerging Cold War, but also in the passions and prospects of decolonization in Africa and Asia. In the this context, the Ford and Rockefeller foundations and the Carnegie Endowment convened a series of meetings producing a broad consensus that the US had to increase sharply its ability to understand and act effectively in previously unfamiliar nations and societies all across the globe.[8] To this end, the US seemed to need internationally oriented economists and political scientists able to construct programs that would encourage capitalist development, "modernization," and democracy both to achieve social and political stability and to secure US interests.

Although many presumed that the adoption of US institutions

and procedures in other countries would bring about their rapid development, at least some academics and foundation staff were aware that the largely American and Euro-centric forms of knowledge and experience of most US economists and political scientists might not be adequate for understanding or acting effectively in the non-Western world. They argued that the direct application of Western models, examples, and techniques in societies of very different character and history might not work at all, and that more culturally and historically contextualized knowledge of the nations of Africa, Asia, Central Europe, Latin America, and the Middle East would be essential if the US was to assist their economic development, modernization, and political stability—as well as to compete effectively for their loyalty with the Soviet Union.[9] From their perspective, the US would need not just economists and political scientists, but also other social scientists as well as humanists who focused on the basic structures and dynamics of these societies; their social organization, demography, social psychology, cultural and moral values, aesthetics, religious traditions, cosmologies and philosophies, etc. Indeed, such knowledge would be useful not just for policy analysts, diplomats, and development specialists, but in business, the media, primary and secondary education, and the foundations. And it seemed especially needed in higher education where it could be generated, mobilized, directed towards overseas projects, but also broadly disseminated to wider populations.

The lead to develop these capacities was taken by a set of major US research universities; Berkeley, Chicago, Columbia, Cornell, Harvard, Michigan, Pennsylvania, Princeton, Wisconsin, and Yale. In various ways, and with varying foci, each began to make large long-term investments in faculty, student fellowships, foreign language facilities and courses, libraries, research funding, etc. A small Fulbright overseas teaching and exchange program had begun in 1946. But in 1950, The Ford Foundation established the prestigious Foreign Area Fellowship Program (FAFP), the first large-scale national competition in support of Area Studies training in the US. The initial FAFP awards provided two years of inter-disciplinary and language training on a selected country or region of the world, plus two years of

funding for in-depth overseas dissertation research and write-up. The
FAFP made its first awards in 1951, and by 1972 had supported
training and research in nearly every corner of the accessible world of
some 2,050 doctoral students in the social sciences and humanities. In
1972, the Ford Foundation turned over the FAFP to the
interdisciplinary (humanities and social sciences) Area Studies
Committees jointly sponsored by Social Science Research Council
(SSRC) and the American Council of Learned Societies (ACLS). Over
the next 30 years, and primarily with continuing Ford Foundation
support, the two Councils funded approximately nearly another 3,000
area studies dissertation fellowships, and with funds from other
foundations as well, another 2,800 postdoctoral area studies research
grants. The Ford Foundation also provided the joint area studies
committees of the two Councils several million dollars for the field
development workshops, conferences, and publication programs.[10]
During this same period, the foundation also provided $120 million
in grants directly to some 15 major US research universities to
establish interdisciplinary Area Studies Centers. Altogether,
between 1951 and 1966, the Ford Foundation invested more than $270
million in Area Studies training, research, and related programs.[11]

Although it built on earlier initiatives, and other funders joined in
along the way, The Ford Foundation was the single most important
force and source of external funding for the institutionalization of
multi-disciplinary Area Studies as a core component of higher
education in the US. Other large and important programs followed.
Precipitated by Sputnik, the variously , amended National Defense
Education Act of 1957 established the Department of Education's
program that now partially funds the primarily administrative,
language teaching and public service (outreach) costs of some 125
university-based Area Studies units as National Resource Centers.
The Fulbright Program for "Mutual Education and Cultural
Exchange," was much expanded in 1961, ultimately funding 1000s of
dissertation and postdoctoral research and teaching projects in
selected countries around the world. Likewise, the National Science
Foundation and the National Endowment for the Humanities
developed national competitions to fund international research

projects, workshops, conferences, exchanges, and related activities. Private foundations (e.g. Mellon, Henry Luce, Tinker), have also provided major support for Area Studies programs dealing with particular countries or regions of the world, while still others (e.g., The Rockefeller Foundation, Carnegie Endowment for International Peace, the John D. and Katherine T. MacArthur Foundation), both funded and have drawn on numerous Area Studies scholars for their own topically focused international programs. But it was the long term commitment and massive support of training and scholarship by the Ford Foundation at key research universities, and through the SSRC/ACLS joint area committees, that established Area Studies as a powerful and academically legitimate approach to generating knowledge about the non-Western world. Still today, the Foundation continues to play a major role in funding the continuing evolution of Area Studies, now in a very different international context.[12]

Clearly, Cold War concerns, and a view of US elites that the country would need to play a vastly expanded international role in the second half of the century were the major impetus in founding and funding US Area Studies in the late 1940s and early 1950s. The CIA and other government intelligence and security agencies often tried to draw on academics and to shape research agendas—with few known successes, and some spectacular failures.[13] However, as documented in the essays that follow, within a very few years the scholars in the universities and SSRC/ACLS area studies committees re-captured the initiative with broader academic agendas specifically including the humanities, history, and other fields far from immediate political concerns. As Bonnell and Breslauer demonstrate in their essay, even the Soviet field, dealing with the Cold War enemy, expanded in these directions. And while this led Reuben Frodin, a key Ford Foundation official, to exclaim repeatedly, "not another study of Pushkin?!" he fought to keep Ford Foundation funds flowing to Area Studies programs all across the country.

Indeed, from the 1960s onwards, many Area Studies scholars were publicly and passionately critical of the US government's definition of "the national interest," and its policies and actions in the region of the world they were studying. This was most dramatically evident in the Southeast Asia field during the Vietnam War—though the war in fact triggered intellectual and political dissent all across the area studies fields. At the same time, numerous Latin Americanists—often personally and intellectually close to their counterparts in Latin America—were becoming publicly and deeply critical of US policies towards Cuba, the Caribbean, and Latin America. Likewise, large numbers of South Asia scholars vigorously protested the US government's "tilt towards Pakistan" during the Indo-Pakistan conflict of 1965. As Bonnell and Breslauer, and Walder demonstrate, even the Soviet and China Studies fields quickly came to include many scholars sharply critical of US policies towards those "enemy" countries. And numerous Area Studies scholars and organizations attacked US government sponsored "development" and "modernization" programs in the Third World as variously ill-conceived, unworkable, counter-productive (if not simply counter-insurgency), self-serving, elite oriented, and of limited value to the poor of the countries they were claiming to aid.

In effect, while international political considerations were at the root of the initial investments in Area Studies in the 1940s and 1950s, charges that Area Studies have simply been a function of or handmaiden to US Cold War concerns, have been grossly inaccurate for at least the last 40 years. Clearly, some scholars stayed close to the initial political concerns and continue to use US lenses and models to interpret other regions of the world. However, as the essays in this volume demonstrate, all of the Area Studies fields quickly broadened and took on much more varied and distinctive intellectual and research agendas, debates, and trajectories. By the mid-1970s they were sharply differentiated from each other. For example, as John R. Bowen points out in his essay, US research on Southeast Asia began with heavy emphasis on political issues and the social sciences but has since become heavily "cultural" (though still not humanistic) in orientation. In Latin American Studies, as Paul W. Drake and Lisa Hilbank illustrate, a variety of political economy frameworks have spiraled through the field over the past four decades—heavily influencing Political Science, Sociology, and theories of development generally, far beyond Latin America. As Victoria Bonnell and George Breslauer emphasize in their essay, the key debates in the Soviet Studies field since the late 1960s turned around whether the USSR could evolve towards more "rational" socio-political forms, or would necessarily degenerate. Pearl T. Robinson's essay on African Studies points to the sharply conflicting definitions of Africa and consequently divergent research agendas among African-American scholars, mainstream (white) Africanists, and their counterparts in African universities. In contrast, the South Asia field in the US was initially built on 19th century European humanistic studies of Sanskrit and South Asian religion and philosophy. In the past 25 years however, as Nicholas B. Dirks points out, the intellectual life of the field has been re-directed if not dominated by the "Subaltern" movement and broader epistemological debate over the position of the scholar and appropriate categories and subjects for the study of post-colonial societies.

As these abbreviated examples begin to suggest, and the essays that follow elaborate, multiple factors account for the dispersion of intellectual interests and trajectories among the various Area Studies fields. These include:

- the evolving political relations of the US to the countries in question
- the changing interests of public and private funders
- the academic disciplines and personal and political commitments of the academics in each field
- the shifting mix of disciplines, and thus of methods and debates, that have dominated research in the field
- evolving relations, debates, and collaborations with scholars within the country or region of study
- the age of the field (that is, newly invented in the US, or building on literature from within the region, or by European colonial scholars)
- the difficulty of learning the languages of the region
- dramatic events or conflicts (revolutions, wars, insurgencies) within the area
- the intellectual and political demands of populations from the region residing in the US
- ease of access for field, archival, or collaborative research

Given all these dimensions along which the Area Studies fields vary, and have varied still more over time, it is not surprising that the fields now have highly distinctive characters and have diverged in very different directions.

But the development of Area Studies in US universities has meant more than simply the addition of new research agendas or idiosyncratic scholarly communities in US universities. Thanks to their diverse disciplinary bases and the continuing evolution of the fields, Area Studies scholars have been developing and legitimating new understandings and forms of knowledge which their Euro-centric or Americanist colleagues in the social sciences and humanities are not likely to have imagined. By generating new data, new concepts, new approaches to key issues, and new units of analysis, by legitimating the intrinsic and analytic value of the perspectives of the "native" or the "other," as well as more culturally rooted interpretations and explanations, and by creating new types of multi-disciplinary academic units, they have intellectually and politically challenged, and even in varying degrees transformed, US universities and the social science and humanities disciplines.

As Immanuel Wallerstein et al. have pointed out in "Open the Social Sciences," (1996), the current disciplinary division of labor in the social sciences was established in the last decades of the 19th century. At that time, drawing on European models, American universities established the major social science departments for research and teaching to match the then current understandings and categorizations of the world. Economics was to deal with the Market, Government (later, Political Science) with the State, Sociology with Society, Psychology with the Individual, History with the Past, and Anthropology with "the Other." The Humanities were likewise divided into distinct Departments of English, the literatures of various other languages (French, German, Italian, etc.), Philosophy, Classics, Religion, Art History, Music, etc. Each of these departments, and real world domains, and disciplines were perceived as essentially well-bounded unitary wholes that could appropriately and usefully be studied independently from the others. A domain in the world, an academic department, and an intellectual discipline were perceived as mutually defining. Equated with, and legitimating each other, they became the fundamental building blocks of US universities.

Either individually or clustered in Schools or Colleges within a university, departments compete for resources from the central administrations. However, at least in the major research universities, it has long been the disciplinary departments that have made the primary decisions to hire and fire, give tenure and promote, set research agendas and curricula, determined what is useful and valuable knowledge, and what and where to publish. Over time, each discipline has developed its own distinctive agendas, concepts, curricula, jargon, research methods, internal debates, subfields and specializations, standards of evidence, journals, national organizations, and intellectual and institutional hierarchies. In this context, cross-disciplinary or multi-disciplinary training and research have long been at best looked on askance, and often denigrated. At the same time, as early as the 1920s there was a growing recognition that the rigid 19th century compartmentalization of the world still reflected in these disciplinary *cum* departmental structures no longer fit current understandings of how societies and cultures actually operate. Not only were increasingly sharp divisions and specializations within departments reducing their integrity and coherence, but numerous scholars were pointing out that the market, polity, society, culture, etc.—the domains that justified the 19th century division of academic labor and departmental and disciplinary boundaries—all penetrate, interact, and shape each other and cannot be studied in isolation. For at least the last 30 years, scholars have often been seeking out intellectual colleagues in other departments, and there are now constant pleas and proposals for greater interdisciplinarity. Institutionally, however, despite—or perhaps because of—these critiques of their constrained intellectual foundations, the walls between the disciplines have only become higher and more difficult. Given the power to hire and recommend or deny tenure, buttressed by exclusionary discourses or jargons, and in competition with each other for the resources of the university, most social science departments have become, if anything, more sharply bounded. Indeed, Timothy Mitchell argues in his essay that follows that the resulting tensions and contradictions, and the critiques they engender, have created a "crisis in the disciplines" far more problematic than the debates surrounding Area Studies.

In effect, the core social science and humanities departments can be thought of as a set of vertical columns forming the core of the US university, linked at the top by administrators who have risen through this departmental structure but now charged to oversee the institution as a whole. Internally, departments may be increasingly fragmented, with individual faculty often finding more common cause and intellectual companionship with scholars in other disciplines entirely. But the organizational and political response has been overwhelmingly defensive; using increasingly heavy bindings to fend off reorganization and keep the department intact.[14]

By calling for multi-disciplinary approaches and a variety of research methods to understand non-Western societies or cultures, area studies scholars, communities, and funders were arguing that new forms of knowledge call for new structures of knowledge generation. In doing so, they directly challenged the disciplinary departments' insistence on maintaining their preferred and limited methods, traditional intellectual and organizational boundaries, their stylized narratives of "the West," their frequent "universalization" of Western experience, and the vertical organization of the US university.[15] The efforts in the 1950s to create Area Studies departments defined *ab initio* as multi-disciplinary seemed a way to avoid this conflict; they were attempts to slip the multi-disciplinary Area Studies approach into a traditional departmental structure. But without a conventional disciplinary framework, Area Studies departments have been subject to disparagement and attack from other faculty and administrators. Subtly or overtly, Area Studies departments frequently were (and other later multi-disciplinary departments often still are) denigrated as deriving from external, "more political" agendas, and thus less intellectually legitimate and lower status in the university community. Trying to be both multi-disciplinary and departmental—challenging the traditional notion that a department equated with a discipline—was more than the older elements of the university would easily tolerate.

In contrast, Area Studies Centers, which made no claim to being departments or disciplines, but instead were structured and understood as venues for cross-disciplinary discussion, debate, programs, and projects, were much less of a threat. They fit more readily into the culture and structures of the university, and have been far more accepted and successful.[16] In this context, Area Studies units are not about to replace the disciplines, no less attain institutional equivalency. At least for the moment—and short of an unlikely intellectual and institutional revolution and the reconstruction of the social science and humanities departments along some unimagined new lines—Area Studies needs these disciplines for the concepts and methods they can contribute to understanding and translating another society or culture. At the same time, the disciplines need Area Studies to continually challenge their US- or Euro-centric assumptions and for the construction of alternative social and cultural processes and understandings. As the essays that follow indicate, Area Studies and the disciplines have historically stood and continue to stand in productive tension with each other.

Beyond these structural considerations, Area Studies has also paved the way for many other multi-disciplinary academic movements. By demonstrating that there are intellectually, politically, and socially important forms of knowledge, and legitimate modes of generating knowledge that require interdisciplinary collaboration which the traditional disciplines are unlikely to produce on their own, Area Studies has laid the institutional basis for the subsequent establishment of Women's Studies, Gender Studies, African-American Studies, Ethnic Studies, Asian-American Studies, Cultural Studies, Agrarian Studies, and numerous other interdisciplinary centers, and programs since the 1970s. Indeed, there are now growing efforts and calls to draw on Area Studies models in order to counter "American exceptionalism," to "internationalize" American Studies, and to set research on the US into comparative contexts.[17] The core disciplines are still central to the university and are maintaining their institutional and intellectual power; Area Studies and the other multi-disciplinary enterprises are not leading to the dissolution of the disciplines. However, they now function as a countervailing force in US universities, a set of venues for cross-disciplinary conversations increasingly recognized as essential for understanding the mutually constitutive elements of any society.

THE CRITIQUES OF AREA STUDIES

Despite the relative success of Area Studies Centers in legitimating intellectual and organizational innovations in the US university, Area Studies continue to be critiqued by scholars who define themselves solely or largely in terms of a disciplinary affiliation. Strikingly, attitudes towards Area Studies and the frequency and severity of the critiques vary with the discipline or sub-field they come from. Economists were key actors in Area Studies in the early decades when modernization theory and development economics were at their peak. But now having been captured by quantitative techniques and formal modeling—and more recently by the presumed power of so-called free markets to dissolve or render superfluous other cultural, historical, and institutional influences—few US economists, and certainly no mainstream departments, pay any attention to Area Studies at all. The data from the non-Western world is rarely adequate for their quantitative models, and particular locations can hardly matter when universal and convergent processes are presumed to be at work. In contrast, scholars in Political Science, attempting to adopt the rational actor and formal modeling of Economics, have been the most active source of criticism, followed by some more positivistic elements of Sociology.[18] On the other hand, anthropologists, historians, and linguists representing disciplines in which contextualization is fundamental, manifest fewer qualms about Area Studies. In the Humanities, Cultural and Postmodern Studies, though on different grounds that will be described below, have turned out to be a more productive source of critiques of Area Studies. Ironically, the academics most resistant to Area Studies are often un-selfconscious area studies specialists themselves—their "area" being the United States. By focusing on the US and treating it as a natural unit of analysis, thus making the US the universal measure for other societies, and not subject to the international scrutiny, comparisons, or contextualizations which Area Studies scholars conducting research in other areas of the world cannot avoid. These various critiques of non-US Area Studies are sometimes contradictory and may be aggressive or defensive. But because they are sufficiently common, institutionally powerful, and in some cases intellectually serious, they do need to be addressed. Four major themes have been sounded.

First, as noted earlier, various scholars have charged that Area Studies was simply a political movement, essentially an effort to "know the enemy," and a function of the United States' effort to win the Cold War. In that light, although perhaps useful for understanding and dealing with the Communist world and the threats it posed up to 1991, with the collapse of the Soviet Union and the end of the Cold War, they argue Area Studies is now obsolete. This critique is most frequently heard from within Political Science, the discipline most excited by rational choice theories and most directly engaged with the political rivalries of the Cold War, its termination, and the transitions that have followed. But another version is heard from the scholars on the left opposed to US foreign policy and international activities who view Area Studies as a component of and support to US hegemony, and as opposed to progressive change elsewhere in the world. We have already suggested that such narrow political views and representations are grossly inaccurate; they will be deconstructed in detail in the essays that follow. In fact, as the essays on Chinese, East European, and Soviet Studies all point out, the fields were already highly diversified during the Cold War. With its termination in 1991, access to scholars, archives, field studies, and collaboration, research agendas have expanded further to include post-socialist transitions, civil society, ethnic resurgence, cultural change, etc.

Second, and somewhat in contradiction, others in the positivist tradition have charged Area Studies with being merely "ideographic," primarily concerned with description, as opposed to the "nomothetic" or the theory building and generalizing character of the core social science disciplines. At its worst, this dismisses Area Studies as simply generating exotica, which, however intrinsically interesting, cannot add up to a convincing or more broadly useful theory or narrative. At best, this view sees Area Studies as a source of data and information, fodder for useful and more universal theories by scholars in the disciplines with broader visions, more sophisticated techniques, and greater intellectual skills. Again, this critique is largely heard from academics committed to rational choice theories and the formal modeling of social and political processes.

As the essays that follow demonstrate, however, there is no reason to believe that Area Studies research has been any less systematic or theory-driven—or, indeed, has contributed less to the refinement or development of new theory—than social science and humanistic research on the US and Western Europe. Perhaps quite the contrary. It is certainly true that few scholars anywhere ever propose grand new theoretical statements and proofs. Most, more modestly, see themselves as analyzing an interesting issue or topic, in the process testing, critiquing, confirming, or marginally elaborating or refining, some larger (possibly theoretical) generalizations. This is equally true of scholars writing on the politics of Bangkok or the politics of Washington DC, on Russian novels or US novels. More fundamentally, all social and cultural research is inevitably rooted in some kind of theory or theories, however explicit or implicit, intended to make sense of significant relationships among selected but intensely examined elements of a society, a poem, a history or religious movement, etc. As Drake and Hilbink underscore in their essay on Latin American Studies, data collection and theory development are inextricably intertwined and inter-active.[19] Without a reasonably coherent theoretical structure or narrative in mind—that is, parts fitting together in some plausible logic—a researcher would not know what to look for, how to interpret it, or how to write it up as a publishable article, essay, or book.

The issue, then, is not the presence or absence of theory, but what kinds of theory are being used, and how explicit or implicit, ambitious or modest, scholars are in articulating their theoretical assumptions and concerns. Here, of course, there is vast room for variation and debate as theories come and go, attract attention, are tried out against diverse data, materials, and concerns, and are then rejected, refined, celebrated, or absorbed into disciplinary (or common) knowledge. As the essays on Africa, Latin America, South Asia, and the Soviet field in this volume document, not only have the Area Studies fields been thick with theory and theoretical debates, but they have also regularly generated theoretical developments and debates within the disciplines as well. In fact this should not be surprising, for as previously noted, the vast majority of Area Studies scholars are located in the core social science and humanities departments. Privileging (or worse, universalizing) theory derived from accounts or analysis of US experience or phenomena alone overlooks the fact that the US is, although "unmarked" by US scholars who work on it, as much a contingent, historically shaped and particular, if not peculiar, "area" as China, or India, or Latin America. Indeed, on many dimensions, the US is probably one of the more unusual and least "representative" societies in the world—and thus a particularly problematic case from which to build generalizing theory. In addition, Area Studies scholars working on societies and cultures outside the US usually recognize, at least implicitly (and often explicitly), both the comparative value and the limits of their research arenas. In contrast, US scholars working on similar issues at home often seem to treat the US as the "natural" society, theorize, universalize, and advise others freely, and see no bounds to their findings. A classic, and perhaps most egregious case would be the 1994 claim by Shepsle and Weingast that the study of the US Congress provides the template for understanding comparative politics and the political systems of other parts of the world, ignoring differences in institutional forms, norms, values, histories, and the contexts they might exhibit.[20]

A third and more subtle set of critiques of Area Studies scholars argues that they have absorbed and have continued to use uncritically the politically biased categories, perspectives, commitments, and theories of their colonialist scholar-administrator predecessors—or indeed, of contemporary US or Western leaders attempting to maintain or expand hegemonic control over the rest of the world. The claim, dramatically put forward by Edward Said (1987), and echoed across Subaltern and Cultural Studies generally, is that despite Area Studies scholars' evident personal interest and specialized knowledge of the area of the world they are studying, the conceptualization of their projects, their research agendas, and what they have taken as appropriate units of analysis and relevant models of society and social change, have been fundamentally and consistently US- or Euro-centric.

In effect, there are two different charges here. One is that Area Studies scholars have sometimes or often failed to study other societies in their own terms, as social and cultural life and processes are experienced and might be construed, constructed, analyzed, and critiqued from the inside. The second is that they have failed to extract themselves from their conscious or unconscious political biases and therefore have not adequately framed their analyses in some purportedly more universal theory, whether neo-liberal, neo-Marxist, post-modern, etc. Instead, Area Studies scholars are accused of—at best, naively, at worst, intentionally—imposing their own personal and/or national agendas and variously idealized or mythologized formulations of the historical experience of "the West," both to explain, and most often in the process, to denigrate, other societies that have almost always been in one way of another, politically and economically subordinated.

There is certainly some truth to these charges. As Michel Foucault has repeatedly reminded us, political power and position and the generation of knowledge are inevitably entwined. Area Studies, however, has no monopoly on this. As Alan Tansman and Timothy Mitchell in this volume stress, it is true of essentially all social science and humanistic research, whether conducted by insiders or outsiders. All scholars in the US or elsewhere, including the critics of Area Studies, are influenced by their political context and political commitments. The imposition of politically freighted categories and theories is unavoidable and always shapes how issues are framed, what kinds of questions are raised, what equally valid questions are ignored, and who benefits from the research. Choosing the interesting question, which elements to emphasize, how to balance them, and how to decide which is more important, will always be a matter of judgement based on the values and interests of the observer. (Indeed, as Timothy Mitchell notes in his essay, for many years the Middle East Studies Association would not allow panels on Arab-Israeli relations because no one could be expected to "be objective" about the issues.) But this is equally true for the insider, or the outsider looking in; power and perspective will always shape the generation of social knowledge.

Given, however, the current economic and political hegemony of the US as the world's sole "superpower," the research assumptions, concepts, procedures and funding of US scholars, often seem overbearing or irresistible. They also often provoke deep cultural and political resentments (and sometimes alternative analytic formulations) in other parts of the world. Nevertheless, Area Studies scholars have perhaps one advantage in dealing with this problem. Intensive, research conducted outside of one's home country, in a setting which in various ways is unfamiliar, is at least somewhat more conducive to disruptive self-consciousness about these issues than research conducted in the familiar and seemingly "natural" US. And a self-conscious attempt to articulate as clearly as possible the commitments, perspectives, and power relations one brings to one's research, is perhaps the best that any scholar can do.

A fourth critique of Area Studies derives from the current fascination with "globalization." Although there is huge debate on how to define it, how new it really is, and how to study it, globalization, in one form or another (as financial, population, media, or cultural flows, as networks, "deterritorialization," etc.), is broadly seen as erasing boundaries, and forcing the homogenization of localities, cultures, and social and economic practices. From this viewpoint, an Area Studies focus on the residual and presumably diminishing specificities or unique dynamics of particular localities, is seen as beside the point; an outdated concern for a world that no longer exists, or at best, that is rapidly fading away.

In fact, globalization, however defined, when closely examined in particular places is rarely a homogenizing force or erasing all other social or cultural forms and processes. Not only is globalization producing increased disparities in power and wealth—both nodes of rapid accumulation and large zones of exploitation and poverty—but its particular manifestations are always mediated and shaped by local histories, structures, and dynamics. Likewise, the recent growth and virulence of divisive ethnic movements, identity politics, fundamentalisms, and now terrorist networks as well, often seem both a consequence of, and a reaction to, elements of globalization. Growing concern with these phenomena is certainly increasing the number of Area Studies projects examining the complex interaction of global and local economic, political, and cultural forces. But while the specifics vary place to place, this approach to globalization only makes the intensive multidisciplinary and broadly contextualized analysis of particular locations and areas—the hallmark of Area Studies—even more essential.

But still more dramatic changes in the conceptualization, procedures, and to some extent, the programmatic organization, of Area Studies are now resulting from increased recognition of the importance of processes of transnationalism, as an element of globalization. At its origins in the 1950s, the geographic regions into which the Area Studies world was divided—South Asia, Sub-Saharan Africa, Latin America, etc.—were conventional, politically inspired, and in culture-historical terms sometimes quite arbitrary and always debatable. (Is Afghanistan part of South Asia, the Middle East, or Central Asia? Why should the study of Africa be divided between the Sub-Saharan countries and those of North Africa? What common features unite Burma and the Philippines as parts of Southeast Asia? Should the Baltic nations be included in Europe, or Eastern (or Central) Europe, or the Former Soviet Union? Is Eurasia a meaningful unit?) With the collapse of the Soviet Union and the bi-polar world, several of these conventional categorizations are now deeply questioned and old boundaries are being redrawn. Still more to the point, recent attention to a variety of transnational diasporas and networks is emphasizing the importance of new social and cultural formations cross cutting previous nation-state and area boundaries. Al-Qaeda, as a transnational terrorist network, is almost too obvious to mention. Of deeper history, the millions of Indians, Pakistanis, Bangladeshis now scattered all across the globe and interacting simultaneously with their new host countries and their original homelands in complex and deeply significant ways have

made it increasingly implausible to study South Asia, or the
individual countries within that region, as bounded geo-political
communities. Likewise, African-Americans, and many residents of
the Caribbean are now engaged with Africa in ways that are
reshaping the cultures and politics of their current homelands. And
despite the US Border Patrol, Mexico, Central America, California,
and Texas are increasingly becoming an integrated social and
economic region. In another way, recognition is growing that England,
France, Portugal, and the Netherlands as past metropoles of world-
spanning empires, have been—and continue to be—deeply shaped by
their ex-colonial activities and subjects. The reality and analytic
value of the old geo-political Area Studies units has not completely
disappeared. But many boundaries have become much more
permeable, and the importance of sometimes new, sometimes
longstanding, transnational social, economic, and cultural formations
and networks are increasingly being recognized, studied, and becoming
the basis for new institutional support and organizational
arrangements.

One immediate response to the questioning of the traditional
boundaries of the Area Studies fields was to suggest that more
comparative and thematic research across areas should be encouraged
to, among other things, help determine exactly how different and/or
interconnected the areas really are. With this in mind, the Social
Science Research Council (SSRC) in 1986 established the Committee
on the Comparative Study of Muslim Societies to focus attention on
the variations and continuities across Islamic world, stretching from
Southeast Asia, South and Central Asia, to the Middle East, Africa,
Europe and the United States. In 1994 the SSRC developed a new
Mellon Foundation-funded Dissertation Fellowship Program giving
priority to cross-area comparative research seeking broad
generalizations and cross-culturally robust theory. This sort of
comparative research is clearly valuable and likely to grow,
constrained though it is by the need to learn at least two languages,
two histories, and two cultures, the contextualizing features and
processes essential to make sense of comparative cases.
Unfortunately, not many scholars at the dissertation stage (or
beyond) are able to manage this with ease.

SOME FUTURE DIRECTIONS

The new geo-politics and the softening of national and area boundaries are already being reflected in the new attention population diasporas. Once one could comfortably study Southeast Asia, or countries within it, e.g., the Philippines, Vietnam, Thailand, as relatively bounded units. Today, there is growing recognition of the value—indeed the necessity—of studying the flows of people from such areas, or the countries within them, as they spread around the world. The analytic reasons are several; diasporized populations have numerous feedback effects on the dynamics of their homelands. They may drain off educational investments, alter the age structure, and reduce population and sometimes political pressures. But diasporas also send back remittances, and political ideas, sometimes provide new investments or entrepreneurial skills, and can reshape, even globalize the world views, opportunities, and networks of those remaining at home. Diasporized populations also often affect the political and diplomatic relations between their host country and original homeland. German relations with Turkey, US relations with Cuba, Chinese relations with Indonesia, etc., are all affected by the migrant populations from those countries. In addition, viewed in the new setting of a host country, immigrant communities may reveal previously unremarked elements of their homeland society and culture—or of the host society and culture. Thus a previously unnoticed strain of racism in Swedish society is now evident thanks to the presence of African and Middle East populations in that country.[21] In the US, the children of historic and current diasporas constitute increasingly large proportions of college and university students. As such they are demanding new kinds of courses, not just on the language, culture, and history of their ex-homeland, but also on their own diaspora, as well as critical courses on their homeland's relationship to the United States. Likewise, the growing numbers of scholars from other regions of the world—especially South Asia—now teaching in US universities have generated a vast array of new intellectual approaches, theories, and interpretive schemes.

More broadly, the expanding attention of Area Studies scholars to diasporas and transnational populations is raising questions about and recontextualizing the prior focus on the nation-state as the primary actor and ultimate natural unit of international analysis. The nation-state was clearly one of the great social inventions of the 19th century and over the last 150 years it has spread across the globe as the seemingly natural macro-political unit for organizing societies and inter-state relations. Yet public and scholarly interest in the development and character of nation-states has tended to draw attention away from other powerful world shaping macro institutions and processes ranging from the numerous diasporas now coming into focus, to the rapid transmission of cultural forms, to the multiple forms of global capitalism, to the various world-girdling political and social institutions and movements ranging from transnational NGOs and the United Nations and its international conventions, to the Bretton Woods institutions, to the environmental, feminist, and peace movements. These alternative macro-foci to the nation-state vary in strength, salience, and manifestations in different world areas, but are all in one way or another challenging traditional nation-state and area boundaries. Their significance, however, can only be understood by close analysis of particular manifestations and processes in diverse parts of the world, the classic role of Area Studies scholarship.

Area Studies' particular leverage for the study of global and transnational phenomena has forced a new recognition of the necessity of serious and ethical collaboration with scholars elsewhere in the world. Well trained Area Studies scholars, as outsiders, may discern significant elements of a society or culture that insiders tend to take for granted. But as outsiders they will still inevitably miss some key internal understandings and dynamics. Scholars and intellectuals rooted in those cultures will have different research agendas, perspectives, experiences, and priorities than their US counterparts and can answer questions, redirect or reframe straying analyses, and open unanticipated doors and domains that the most well trained area scholar might not even imagine existed. To usefully translate these key elements back to US audiences almost always requires the active assistance of insiders.

Russian scholars are now working with US, European, and other counterparts to clarify the multiple transitions their society is going through. The theoretical generativity of Latin America studies, a field long marked by high levels of collaboration, only underscores this point. And humanists in other regions of the world who command the local languages, literatures, philosophies, and cosmologies are now especially well placed to challenge and redirect Western formulations and presumptions. More broadly still, the future evolution of social theory will almost certainly derive from efforts to take into account social experience and understandings in a much wider variety of societies than has been the case up to now.

There is also a more fundamental reason value to cross-national collaboration. More reflexively, collaborators abroad enable US scholars to begin to see the particularities and limitations of their own society, agendas, perspectives, and theories. Collaboration and complementarity, the insider's view and the outsider's, joined together, can provide a much fuller and more analytically rich and useful account of other societies and our own, than either view alone. Unfortunately, while this may be easy to assert in principal, it is often difficult to achieve in the current global context. As Timothy Mitchell points out in his essay, we now live in a world increasingly dominated, economically, politically, culturally, and militarily by "a new US Imperium." European social theorists (Bourdieu, Foucault, Giddens, Gramsci, Habermas, Hall, etc.) and South Asian and other "Subalterns" continue to provide important new perspectives and intellectual frameworks, but US scholars and universities nevertheless shape much world-wide academic (and public policy) discourse. US views tend to define the key questions, approaches, and methods, and US universities train large numbers of scholars from all over the world, socializing them into the particular assumptions and perspectives of the US disciplines. As Andrew Walder points out in his essay this has facilitated joint projects with Chinese sociologists trained in the US, but it has also reduced the salience in social and cultural analyses of perspectives, understandings, and issues emerging from Chinese experience. Genuinely collaborative relationships, drawing equally on multiple national perspectives, will be increasingly important if US scholars are not simply going to read into other societies the presumptions of their own. Given continuing imbalances in political and economic power, institutional strength, and research funding between the US and most other societies, such balanced relationships are often difficult to construct.

In general, although Area Studies in the United States as an institutionalized form of generating new knowledge may have started from relatively narrow view of US "national interest," the character and intellectual agendas of the individual Area Studies fields have diverged dramatically over the past 50 years. While the end of the Cold War in some quarters reduced the seeming significance and support Area Studies and its concern for understanding the internal dynamics of other societies, 9/11 has selectively re-stimulated support for the study of "less commonly taught" languages (e.g., Arabic), and parts of the world (e.g., Central Asia), once thought exotic and irrelevant to US national interests. However, the context has changed dramatically since the 1940s and 1950s, and the beginning of the Cold War. Large, diverse, and critical Area Studies communities are now in place, and while additional support for international training and research is usually (though not always) welcomed[22], scholars in these fields today are even less likely to be swayed in their research and teaching by short term government agendas. Instead, individually and collectively, the Area Studies fields and the scholars who constitute them continue to focus on de-parochializing the humanities and social sciences. At the same time, they continue to contribute to the diversity and flexibility of the US university, to innovative approaches to the generation of social theory, to at least rough translations and greater knowledge of other societies and cultures, and in the best of cases, to a new basis for deeper comparative understandings of US society and culture as well.

David L. Szanton worked for many years at the Ford Foundation and the Social Science Research Council before coming to the University of California at Berkeley where he served as the Executive Director of International and Area Studies. He received his Ph.D. in Anthropology from the University of Chicago.

Notes

1. Robert B. Hall, Area Studies: With Special Reference to Their Implications for Research in the Social Sciences, 1947.

2. Scholars with any historical interest in Japan and Korea must read Chinese. Likewise, serious scholars of China must be able to read the vast literature on that country in Japanese.

3. Several of the smaller area studies fields (Canada, Korea, Australia, New Zealand, and the Pacific) have been left out of the volume, because the contributions they have made and the issues they face are reasonably similar to those of the larger fields that are addressed. It was also a pragmatic matter of leaving sufficient room in a single volume for adequate discussion of the larger and more influential fields.

Western European Area Studies has also been omitted from this volume because it is of a very different character than the other Area Studies fields. West European experience, and West Europe scholars, languages, and literatures have historically been central subjects in US universities and intellectual life generally. Vast numbers of US scholars have written and taught about England, France, Germany, Italy, Spain, Scandinavia, etc.; their cultures, histories, and institutions are at the core of our own, and are even taught in US primary and secondary schools. Western Europe is therefore vastly more familiar, and has a very different status in our educational system and lives than Area Studies fields dealing with the more distant societies and cultures discussed in this volume.

4. Thomas Bender, "International Studies in the United States: the Twentieth Century." International Rectors Conference, New York University, February 22, 1997.

5. Open Doors, Institute of International Education, 1999.

6. At the University of California, Berkeley, for example, since 1946, over 90 percent of the advanced degrees dealing with Southeast Asia were granted from the core disciplines or professional schools. Across the country, however, Psychology was always absent, and Economics has now essentially stopped producing area specialists. Through the early 1970s small numbers of economists working on Third World development issues counted themselves, and were often regarded as, area specialists. But as the problems of Third World development turned out to be more intractable than imagined in the years following the Second World War and decolonization, and as Economics has increasingly moved towards quantitative analyses and formal modelling, the sub-field of development economics has lost status in the discipline, and very few US economists now claim to be, train others to be, or indeed, engage intellectually or programmatically with area studies scholars.

In contrast, very few psychologists ever became involved in area studies. The discipline seems content to derive universal psychological principles largely from the study of US high school students and college sophomores.

7. In 1949, the SSRC sponsored a meeting of all the people in US universities, government, foundations, the professions, and journalism with and expertise on any country in South Asia and Southeast Asia. Altogether, only 50 such people could be found. [citation].

8. Hall, Area Studies.

9. In his Western Economists and Eastern Societies: Agents of Change in South Asia, 1950–1970 (Baltimore: John Hopkins University Press, 1985)] George Rosen provides a fascinating and compelling account of the agonies and failures of MIT and Harvard economists attempting to suggest or impose decontextualized economic development strategies in India and Pakistan during the 1950s and early 1960s.

10. The eleven joint committees of the two Councils and their year of formation are as follows: Slavic 1948, Latin American Studies 1959, Near and Middle East Studies 1951, Contemporary China 1959, African Studies 1960, Japanese Studies 1967, Korean Studies 1967, Eastern Europe 1971, South Asia 1975, Western Europe 1975, Southeast Asia 1976. They were all terminated in 1997, and replaced by Regional Advisory Panels for essentially those same areas.

11. Beresford in Volkman, Ford Foundation, 1999.

12. 1997 $25 million Crossing Borders initiative.

13. E.g., the 1964–65 Project Camelot, the 1967 Advanced Research Projects Administration (ARPA) Thailand Study Group.

14. There have of course been exceptions. An early brief success, and then total failure, was Harvard's Department of Social Relations formed in the 1950s by faculty from Anthropology, Psychology, and Sociology, and disbanded in the 1970s. Likewise, the University of California at Santa Cruz attempted to forgo disciplinary departments and organize instead around themes or issues, but that too only lasted a brief while before the disciplinary structures reemerged as dominant. At the University of California, Berkeley, the Life Sciences managed to reconfigure, integrate, and collapse ("decant" was term of art) 37 departments and units into 17 new units which made intellectual sense. However, it took them five years of debate and the promise of substantial new facilities to achieve that goal; there seem no comparable prospects for the social sciences and humanities.

15. Indeed, the Center for Southeast Asian Studies at Cornell was explicitly intended by its founder, Lauriston Sharp, to become a model for subverting the departmental structure of the university. [Personal communication 1978].

16. In founding the Center for Southeast Asian Studies at Cornell University in 1950, Lauriston Sharp quite explicitly hoped to create a model that would be the basis for radically reorienting Cornell into a set of multidisciplinary topically focused units. He obviously did not succeed, but Cornell did develop many such centers and programs earlier than most other US universities.

17. Thomas Bender, "An Institute on Internationalizing the Study of

American History" 1996; Desmond and Dominguez, "Resituating American Studies in a Critical Internationalism," *American Quarterly*, vol. 48, no. 3, 1996.

18. These have been largely, though not entirely, Americanists. Political Scientists and Sociologists who have had to learn Chinese, Japanese, Russian, Eastern European languages, and even Spanish, in order to conduct their research have been much more supportive of Area Studies approaches.

19. Donald Stokes (1997) makes a similar point in insisting on the mutual dependence or dialectical relationship of basic and applied research.

20. American Political Science Association Comparative Politics Newsletter, 1994.

21. Allan Pred, *Even in Sweden*, (Berkeley: University of California Press, 2000).

22. There has been huge debate in the Area Studies communities and associations around the National Security Education Program because of its close connections with US intelligence agencies.

Chapter 1

Latin American Studies
Theory and Practice

Paul W. Drake and Lisa Hilbink

INTRODUCTION

Latin Americanists have developed and/or contributed to some of the most important and influential theories and debates in the social sciences and humanities in recent history[1]. From dependency to democratization, from studies on the state to research on social movements, scholars of Latin America have been at the forefront of theoretical development in a variety of disciplines. Despite these achievements, Latin American studies in the United States, along with all foreign-area studies, is suffering from a decline in intellectual and material support. The possibility of specialization in the region, which demands field work and sustained dialogue with Latin American scholars, is threatened. It has therefore become necessary to turn our analytical lenses inward to examine critically the past and future trajectory of Latin American studies and to evaluate and respond to criticisms of the field.

As a contribution to this effort, this essay traces the institutional and intellectual history of Latin American studies, principally in the United States, and, with this in mind, addresses contemporary criticisms of area studies. It contends that scholarly work under the umbrella of Latin American studies has been and will be innovative and important in a variety of disciplines. The mid-level theorizing which has been the hallmark of Latin American studies offers a healthy balance between problem-driven research and causal analysis. Moreover, the crossnational collaboration and inter-disciplinary cross-fertilization which characterize Latin American studies are precisely the sorts of practices which should be encouraged in the emerging era of global cooperation and production.

34

INSTITUTIONAL HISTORY OF LATIN AMERICAN STUDIES

The origins and characteristics of Latin American studies differ somewhat from those of other world areas. To begin, the study of Latin America did not originate in an "Orientalist" tradition, such as that which initiated the study of Asia and the Middle East. In other words, present-day Latin American studies is not rooted in colonial scholarship, heavily oriented toward ancient history and language.[2] While some scholars of the region have always focused on Amer-Indian cultures and institutions, and while the influence of postmodernism has brought the region's cultural heterogeneity to the forefront of contemporary concerns, most U.S. researchers have traditionally followed the Latin American lead in defining the region as primarily New World and predominantly mestizo (mixed-race peoples exercising some combination of indigenous and European cultural practices). Partly because of this mixing of peoples and cultures, claims of uniqueness or exceptionalism—e.g., Ecuador is so unusual that it can be understood only on its own terms and only by Ecuadoreans or by those deeply immersed in Ecuadorian culture—have been less common in Latin American studies than in studies of some other areas, such as the United States, China, Japan, India, etc.[3]

Secondly, and relatedly, Latin American studies has become a cooperative endeavor between U.S. scholars and their counterparts south of the border. That is, Latin American studies is something that North Americans do *with* Latin Americans, not *to* Latin Americans. Indeed, much of the knowledge production about the region has always come from the Latin Americans. This is as it should be, since the internationalization of knowledge production through dialogue with researchers around the globe is today a keystone of not only the social sciences and humanities but also the natural sciences and all scholarly pursuits. A reciprocal and free flow of questions, ideas, and information is essential to all scientific inquiries, whether in physics or anthropology. Perhaps due to the geographic, linguistic, religious, and historico-political ties between the United States and Latin America, there have been fewer cultural barriers to such scholarly collaboration than there might be between U.S. and African or East Asian scholars. Moreover, many Latin American scholars have come to the United States either in exile or for education, and political obstacles have diminished over the years.[4]

Interactions between national and foreign analysts of Latin America have been beneficial to both sides. Fruitful interdisciplinary work has been fostered, partly because disciplinary boundaries are less rigid in Latin America, and new questions have been generated. For example, the content of scholarly debate in Latin America compelled North American scholarship to address issues such as class inequality and class conflict, both domestically and internationally, while North Americans have brought to the table concerns about democratic stability and gender inequities.

Cross-fertilization occurred between the approaches of the generally more qualitative, theoretical, often Marxist Latin Americans and the frequently more quantitative, empirical, often liberal North Americans. Such interchange tested theories, whether modernization from the north or dependency from the south. Both sides helped each other see beyond their biases. These interactions also produced some unfortunate intellectual distortions, including the imposition of U.S. Cold War research concerns on Latin America, the uninhibited imbibing of U.S. economic models by some Latin Americans, and the uncritical consumption of dependency theory by many North Americans.[5] Yet gradually, the two sides have converged around key issues, methods, theories, and even policies, especially with the end of the Cold War and the seeming triumph of classic liberal economics and politics in the 1980s.

Although relations between the colossus of the north and its neighbors to the south have long been asymmetrical, examples of inter-American scholarly cooperation abound. From 1969 to 1989, nearly half of all of the Social Science Research Council's Joint Committee on Latin American Studies (JCLAS, jointly sponsored by the American Council of Learned Societies) advanced research grants were awarded to Latin American investigators. In addition, before its closure, Latin American researchers came to constitute approximately half of the membership of the JCLAS,[6] and Argentine sociologist Jorge Balan once served as Chair of the Committee. Heavy Latin American participation has also been the norm at conventions and on committees of the Latin American Studies Association (LASA), as well as on the editorial boards of the major area journals.[7] Thus, while there have always been segments of Latin American populations suspicious of the *yanquis*, and while there are certainly some very real reasons justifying these suspicions, the production of knowledge about Latin America has been a transnational enterprise for at least three decades.[8]

Of course, this is not to dispute that Latin American studies, as all area studies in the United States, acquired its present-day stature as the result, at least in part, of U.S. foreign policy and especially Cold War reasoning.[9] While programs on Latin America developed in the 1920s, they got their first big boost with the announcement of Franklin Roosevelt's "Good Neighbor Policy" in the late 1930s, the creation of the Office of the Coordinator of Inter-American Affairs (headed by Nelson D. Rockefeller) in 1940, and the founding of the SSRC's Joint Committee on Latin American Studies in 1942.[10] However, because policy-makers did not deem Latin America a national security priority, and because they viewed Spanish as an "easy" language with bountiful practitioners, they did not see specialized knowledge of Latin America as a major investment in the late forties and early fifties.[11]

Only with the Cuban Revolution of 1959 did Latin America once again become a strategic priority, and it remained so through the end of the Cold War.[12] From 1959 to 1989, the JCLAS funded the research for 488 dissertations, provided advanced research grants to 762 U.S., Latin American, and west European scholars, and sponsored nearly 80 workshops and conferences involving more than 2,000 leading researchers (50% of them Latin American). In addition, between 1949 and 1985, the Fulbright and USIA faculty exchange programs brought 12,881 Latin Americans to the United States and sponsored 4, 589 North Americans in Latin America.[13]

Meanwhile, area studies centers throughout the United States benefited from federal government grants given under Title VI of the National Defense Education Act, created in response to the launching of the first Sputnik in October of 1957.[14] "By the 1970s, more than 150 organized Latin American studies programs were offering courses and enrolling students at U.S. colleges and universities."[15] A significant number of research projects were also funded over the years by the Ford Foundation, the Inter-American Foundation, the Woodrow Wilson International Center for Scholars, the Tinker Foundation, the Henry L. and Grace Doherty Charitable Foundation, Inc., the John

Simon Guggenheim Memorial Foundation, the Hewlett and Mellon foundations, and the MacArthur Foundation.[16] As a result of this support, Latin American studies became arguably "the largest, most intellectually vibrant, and influential of the area studies communities in the United States."[17]

Notwithstanding the Cold War "national interest" incentives for funding U.S. scholarship on Latin American, many tensions arose over the years between the Latin American Studies community and the foreign policy, defense, and intelligence circles of the U.S. government.[18] Interestingly, and perhaps somewhat ironically, "Title VI programs actually resulted in a democratization of foreign area intelligence that fueled opposition to cold war policies of the government."[19] The first serious conflict emerged around the "Operation Camelot" scandal in 1964. Project Camelot was a U.S. Army-funded initiative of the Special Operations Research Office of American University that sought to use area scholars to gather information relevant to the counterinsurgency program of the U.S. government. The operation turned scandal when a Norwegian sociologist working in Chile was invited to participate, but instead publicized the goals of the project to his Chilean colleagues. This was "enough to arouse considerable discussion in Chile, an intervention by the president of Chile with the U.S. State Department, debate in the U.S. Congress, and cancellation of the project worldwide."[20] It also led to fear on the part of the Latin American studies community that their scholarship would be tainted, appropriated for improper purposes, and even made impossible by anti-U.S. security agency suspicions on the part of Latin Americans.[21]

In the years that followed, scholars of the hemisphere criticized a wide array of U.S. policies, including those toward Cuba, multinational corporations, Brazil, Central America, and especially Chile.[22] As Gilbert Merkx explains, "U.S. Latin Americanists of all persuasions felt deep sympathy and support for professional colleagues suffering under dictatorship. [The] Latin American Studies Association achieved a certain fame (or notoriety) for the frequency and rigor of its criticisms of U.S. actions in the hemisphere."[23] This passionate engagement of U.S. Latin Americanists with policy issues in the region was one outcome of their collaboration with their counterparts to the south, most of whom were sharply critical of U.S. imperialism, interventionism, capitalism, conservatism, and association with dictators.

The conservative drift of U.S. public opinion and Capitol Hill politics in the 1980s and 1990s is one of the factors contributing to the present decline in support for area studies. Yet cuts to area studies programs began even earlier—in the 1970s—due to economic recessions and stagflation, the contraction of the academic market in the United States, the war in Vietnam, and the turn from revolutionary expectations to right-wing authoritarianism in Latin America, where repression severely damaged the social sciences. Total Title VI Fellowships for Latin Americanist graduate students plunged from an average of around 170 per year in the 1960s to a low of 54 in 1975, and by 1979, U.S. government investment in exchange programs had fallen proportionately beneath that of France, Great Britain, the Federal Republic of Germany, Japan, China, and the Soviet Union.[24]

At the same time, previous foundation support for Latin American studies dried up. Some, like Rockefeller, withdrew almost completely. Most importantly, Ford Foundation funding for advanced training and research in international affairs and foreign areas fell from approximately $27 million per year in the 1960s to $4 million per annum in the 1970s. Its direct grants to U.S. area studies centers faded away and its Foreign Area Fellowship Program for graduate students was passed on a smaller scale to the JCLAS. Nevertheless, Ford continued to have a smaller, less direct impact through its crucial support for thematic U.S. university programs, for the Latin American Studies Association, for conferences, and, above all, for Latin American social scientists, whether at home or in exile.[25]

The 1980s witnessed a resurgence of course enrollments, graduate training, and public interest in Latin America. As always, many trends in Latin American studies followed international events. Several factors were at work: turmoil in Central America, the movement of migrants and narcotics across borders, the wave of democratization throughout the hemisphere, the international debt crisis, the revival of the U.S. economy and the decline of inflation, and the reawakening of the academic marketplace in the United States. However, funding continued to lag behind the swelling need for new researchers and research, despite the emergence of some new—albeit small—private benefactors of Latin American studies (e.g., the Helen Kellogg Institute for International Studies at Notre Dame, the Howard Heinz Endowment, and the Gildred Foundation). In 1987, the Tinker Foundation terminated its Postdoctoral Fellowships, and the Henry L. and Grace Doherty Charitable Foundation, Inc., which had produced the dissertations of many of the leaders in the field, shut down. Consequently, by 1989 the total available awards per year for U.S. faculty to conduct extended research in Latin America were only sufficient to cover 7% of the existing pool of approximately 1,800 active researchers.[26]

As historian John Coatsworth noted in 1989, this lack of institutional support means that the number of active researchers working on Latin America has stagnated since the 1970s, that graduate students increasingly find themselves unable to obtain funding for research in the region, and that young scholars in both Latin America and the United States have become isolated from one another, and hence less able to benefit from the collaboration which has been so fruitful in the past.[27] In the 1990s, this disturbing trend has continued. In 1993, the Ford and Mellon foundations reduced their funding of regionally-focused scholars and projects and inaugurated a joint "globalization" project.[28] In 1997, the Social Science Research Council terminated its area studies committees, the JCLAS among them, replacing them with less powerful "regional advisory panels." These panels no longer control significant funds for fellowships or research projects. This comes at a time when restricted public funds for education and general economic hardship have made it extremely difficult for most Latin Americans to pursue academic careers in their own countries. Given the past success of Latin American studies in terms of the strengthening of ties between scholars in North and South America and the advancement of research agendas in both hemispheres, this weakening of support should be of great concern to all those interested in the future terms and quality of intellectual inquiry.

INTELLECTUAL HISTORY OF LATIN AMERICAN STUDIES

As discussed above, the collaborative research fostered under the umbrella of Latin American studies has had many general benefits for scholarly work, including the generation of new questions, the testing of theories, and the challenging of national biases. This section discusses the evolution of particular topics, theories, and approaches which have tied the field of Latin American studies together, and which have contributed to the understanding of issues of common concern to scholars in different academic disciplines. The emphasis is on transdisciplinary trends, especially in the United States. No attempt is made to map all the key intradisciplinary debates and patterns, although Political Science receives some extra attention.[29]

The earliest U.S. works on Latin America were concentrated in History and Literature.[30] The first journal specific to the area, the *Hispanic-American Historical Review,* began publication in 1918.[31] In Language and Literature, journals such as *Hispania,* the *Hispanic Review,* and the *Revista Hispánica Moderna,* appeared on the scene. Anthropologists and archaeologists also became early leaders in Latin American studies, specializing in native cultures.[32]

Since the 1960s, however, and with support from the SSRC, the social sciences, and especially Political Science, have come to rival History for dominance in the major area journals. In 1974–75, submissions to the *Latin American Research Review,*[33] the most prominent area journal, were dominated by History and Political Science. By 1979, Political Science submissions had taken the lead, rising from 1/4 to 1/3 of the total. In the 1980s and 1990s, this flow of articles from Political Science continued unabated. Meanwhile, History submissions remained solidly in second place in most years, and Languages/Literature and Anthropology submissions were displaced by those from Economics and Sociology.[34] The *Journal of Latin American Studies,* founded in 1969 and published in England, has featured articles primarily in History and Political Science, with none in Literature or the Arts. The bulk of these articles in both journals focused on Mexico, Brazil, Argentina, Central America or individual Central American countries, Chile, and Peru.[35]

In general, the nature of such social scientific studies has tended to be more qualitative than quantitative, and generally (and not surprisingly) more oriented towards a transdisciplinary audience. What characterizes the field of Latin American studies is methodological diversity, a fact which may be partially explained by the significant percentage of Latin American contributions made to these journals (30–40% to *LARR* in recent years[36]). *LARR* regularly solicits and includes manuscripts from Latin American scholars and reports on the activities of research centers in the region. It also incorporates Latin American colleagues into the editorial process.[37] Such collaboration demands greater openness to different approaches and methods, since Latin American disciplinary norms and boundaries differ from those of the United States.

This is a very positive development, since some Latin Americans have had harsh words for scholars trained to think exclusively in North American terms. As one Brazilian researcher argued in 1975:

> All too often the attitude of the visiting North American scholar was that all he had to do was collect the data, take them home, and analyze them. He looked at Latin America from his own theoretical and existential perspective. He was closed to local intellectual inputs and often found local criticism and points of view difficult to understand. Unfamiliarity with the history of the country, regions, and institutions involved, as well as the with the data sources, has placed narrow intellectual constraints on the outcome of this type of research.[38]

With Latin Americans themselves influencing the research agenda in the United States, this unfortunate situation has changed for the better.[39]

Such influence has not been unidirectional, however. While Latin Americans may challenge North Americans to pay greater attention to historical and structural variables, U.S. scholars have begun to persuade their Latin American counterparts of the value of new types of empirical research. For example, survey research has become a virtual cottage industry in Latin America.[40] By the same token, the study of institutions and institutional change has become a central focus for many Latin American as well as U.S. scholars.[41]

What specifically have been the contributions of Latin Americanists to scholarship in the United States? While the most important contributions have been made in the past thirty or forty years, it is useful to begin with a historical discussion of the intellectual trajectory of the field. The first North American university to accept a dissertation on a Pan-American topic was Yale in 1869. From 1869–1960, 103 North American institutions accepted some 2,000 theses on some topic involving one or more Latin American countries.[42]

Today, the prevailing view of these early works (especially those of the pre-1950s) is that they were largely narrative, parochial, and atheoretical. Indeed, many early historical and political studies tended to be more descriptive than analytical, and very legalistic and elitist in approach.[43] However, many authors of the 19th and early 20th centuries did work with implicit or explicit theories, albeit theories which have since been dismissed due to their proven inaccuracy and general unpalatability. One such discredited theory is climatic determinism, or "tropicalism," which suggested that the tropical setting of many Latin American countries inhibits economic growth, debilitates sickly and enervated populations, and foments hot-headed, violent politics. The fact, however, is that the majority of Latin Americans live in temperate zones, either far from the equator or up in the mountains. Moreover, the tropical zones exhibit a wide variety of experiences and achievements: from a revolution and long-standing socialist government in Cuba to flourishing British-style parliamentary governments in the English-speaking Caribbean. Although climate and geography present challenges in Latin America, we now know that they do not determine national development.

A second school of thought was based on racial determinism. According to racist ways of thinking, Latin America is made up of poor, backward, inequitable, and politically volatile or dictatorial countries because of the large number of darker peoples, especially Indians and Africans. Latin American intellectuals themselves imbibed Social Darwinism in the closing decades of the 19th century, blaming their lagging behind northern Europe on the prevalence of the offspring and admixtures of "inferior" races.[44] Racism most certainly played a part in the exploitation of Latin America by richer western nations. Today, however, all educated people know that racial characteristics do not determine prosperity, productivity, class relations, or political beliefs or behavior. Moreover, after centuries of miscegenation in Latin America, it is futile to try to categorize the region's people precisely by genotype or phenotype.[45]

Following World War II, these theories were definitively abandoned by serious scholars, but the metahistorical determinism which characterized them was not.[46] The two major paradigms which dominated social scientific inquiry on Latin America in the 1950s, 1960s and 1970s, modernization theory and the dependency approach, were both holistic interpretations grounded in economic determinism. In addition, arguments based on cultural determinism, which were not really new to the field, emerged (or re-emerged) to complement or challenge these perspectives.

Modernization theory arose in the context of decolonization in Africa and Asia and the early years of the Cold War. It grew out of efforts to understand how recently independent nations and other "Third World" countries might achieve economic and political development similar to that of the United States and northern Europe, which were viewed as the products of a linear and potentially universal process of rationalization and progress.[47] The theory was developed largely by specialists on Africa and Asia, but Latin Americanists in all the social scientific disciplines fell in line to offer supporting evidence.[48] Following the spread of U.S. interest in the region from the Caribbean basin towards the larger, industrializing countries, scholarly attention turned towards Mexico, and the Southern Cone of Latin America.[49]

The main argument of modernization theory was that industrialization and economic growth, and/or the value orientations associated with them, were the engines of social and political progress.[50] This was a vision rooted in classic, Western liberal economic and political thought. In order to develop, Third World societies needed to embrace ideas, values, techniques, and organizations commensurate with urbanization, a complex division of labor, increased social mobility, and a rational-legal, impersonal economic and political system. As countries overcame feudal, semifeudal, precapitalist, or at least inefficient behavior patterns and institutions from the past, new urban social groups, particularly the middle classes, would emerge, and these groups would in turn push for social equality and political democracy. The appropriate subjects for social science research were thus the social groups and institutions that would implement and reflect these changes, and as noted above, plenty of funding was forthcoming for extensive studies involving scholars from many disciplines.[51]

In Economics, the structuralist school within the U.N.'s Economic Commission on Latin America (ECLA) supported the strategy of import substitution industrialization which had begun in Latin America in the 1930s and 1940s and had launched several Latin

American countries into what many hoped would be the "take-off stage," as theorized by Walt Rostow.[52] Rostow argued that Third World countries could replicate the industrialization and economic growth of Western Europe and the United States by adopting policies to increase capital accumulation and investment and to promote entrepreneurial values.[53] Central to the structuralist strategy was land reform, a policy which was advocated by the United States in the "Alliance for Progress,"[54] and which enlisted the support of many anthropologists who specialized in community studies and understood well the dynamics of the countryside in Latin American countries.[55] Structuralist policies, by creating an industrial bias in the economy, "enhanced the power and prestige of the urban industrialists vis-à-vis the rural oligarchy,"[56] and urban industrialists, it was believed, would direct the social and political changes integral to modernization.

This change in value orientations was a central concern of modernization theorists within Political Science and Sociology, who focused on issues such as elite and mass education, mobilization of the popular classes, interest articulation, and institutional development. Political scientists produced valuable studies on "key institutions such as the military and the Church, and about the political role of urban dwellers, peasants, and students, all of which were studied as interest groups—that is, as actors within a political process of competing groups at different levels of modernization."[57] Meanwhile, sociologists in both the United States and Latin America studied emerging social groups and boasted "grand visions of guiding or at least aiding major processes of societal change," focusing on "the [generalizable] forces that produced sustained economic growth and improvements in mass standards of living."[58] Historians, too, were brought on board to offer historical perspectives on the "geographic, demographic, social, and . . . even social-psychological preconditions and consequences" of economic and social change.[59] This increased contact between historians and social scientists definitively changed the study of Latin American history, as historians were exposed to and increasingly embraced the methodological and analytical tools of social science.[60]

Quickly, however, critics assailed the main tenets of modernization theory based on evidence and perspectives from Latin

America itself. Economic growth in most countries did not meet expectations, social inequalities were rarely reduced, and military dictatorships became the norm in the region. Scholars thus began to take issue with many of the underlying assumptions of modernization theory. They challenged the idea of a linear, evolutionary developmental continuum, the conception of preindustrial societies as homogeneous and static, the assumption of the Western European capitalist experience as generalizable and desirable, the faith that new urban social sectors would be democratic and progressive, and the neglect of constraining factors exogenous to Third World societies.

While alternative theories were advanced to explain Latin American patterns,[61] the primary challenge to modernization theory, and that which bridged all the disciplines within Latin American studies, was the dependency approach. The dependency school accepted modernization's economic determinism, but turned it on its head: The adoption of U.S. and European-style economic policies had not and would not lead to healthy economic and political development, but rather to skewed and highly limited development, or "underdevelopment." Rather than the cure for underdevelopment, capitalism was seen as the cause. The dependency approach, developed mainly by Latin Americans but also by foreign Latin Americanists, and highly influential outside the region, "called for a broad inter-disciplinary perspective to explain the major themes of Latin American reality: economic underdevelopment, social inequality, political instability, and authoritarianism."[62] It emphasized the need to go beyond the examination of individual societies to understand the international historical process of development.

Within the dependency paradigm, economists, sociologists, and political scientists argued that a country's "position within the international system is determinant of internal class behavior."[63] Because Latin American countries occupied an inferior position in the international division of labor, producing mainly raw materials and cheap workers, they were the victims of unequal terms of trade and exploitation by foreign investors.[64] Local entrepreneurial classes and political leaders were captives of the international market and had only limited opportunities to steer the development of their own economies and societies. In addition, the copying of consumption patterns characteristic of the advanced industrialized countries led to severe distortions within Latin American economies. According to the more radical dependency writers, foreign and national capitalists siphoned off Latin America's surplus, leaving the vast majority of people sunk in poverty and oppressed by authoritarian regimes.

By implication, the solution to inequality between the center and the periphery was to break out of the capitalist network, or at least renegotiate the terms of participation, for example raising taxes on or expropriating multinational corporations. The first solution was touted by radical *dependentistas* who extrapolated from Marxist ideas to conceptualize the international division of labor as a struggle between bourgeois and proletarian nations, pointing to the Cuban revolution as an attractive alternative.[65] The second solution was advocated by economists identified with ECLA who contended that unequal exchange could be overcome through protected industrialization and controls on foreign capital. Dependency ideas spread throughout the third world and beyond.[66] For example, an influential global vision of center-periphery relations was elaborated by an Africanist, Immanuel Wallerstein, who added the concept of a semi-periphery of middle-income countries between the rich and the poor, not unlike the Marxian category of the petty bourgeoisie.[67]

Building on the these general points, anthropologists developed the theory of internal colonialism, focusing particularly on the relation of domination between the European/mestizo elites and indigenous peoples.[68] Meanwhile, historians began to critique the methods and concepts which many had adopted in the heyday of modernization theory. They thus shifted their perspective to economic and social history, and began to examine the role of external exploiters and subordinate sectors in both the colonial and post-independence periods. Some historians argued that capitalist relations of production stretched all the way back to the conquest and accounted for Latin America's inferior position in the world system. Others focused on disadvantaged groups, a research agenda which eventually fed into the international interest in subaltern studies.[69]

Within Political Science, the most important theoretical contribution to come out of the dependency paradigm was bureaucratic-authoritarianism.[70] This theory argued that the bureaucratic-authoritarian state which emerged in the most economically advanced Latin American countries was "a necessary political stage, dictated by an alliance of political forces intent on overcoming economic stagnation with a strategy of deepening industrialization in alliance with foreign capital."[71] In other words, continued economic growth depended on the repression of the working classes, whose demand for higher wages and other guarantees would otherwise fuel inflation and drive out foreign investment. Contrary to the explanation offered by modernization theorists, then, "repressive regimes did not emerge despite Latin America's economic development; they emerged because of it."[72]

Dependency arguments held sway into the late 1970s, when Latin American countries began a wave of transitions to formally democratic regimes. Already, dependency-related economic theories had been displaced by international monetarism in many countries, increasingly so as the 1980s unfolded. Both import substituting industrialization and socialism seemed to have failed to overcome underdevelopment. Governments began slashing trade barriers and encouraging comparative advantage, while they pruned the bloated public sector. Moreover, foreign investment and loans were "welcomed to compensate for the scarcity of national capital and to bring domestic interest rates into parity with international levels," particularly in the wake of the debt crisis.[73] These changes towards a model of export-led growth were supported by historical research, which showed that growth, structural changes like urbanization and industrialization, social mobility, and political liberalization could occur during periods of great reliance on the international market, such as the 1880s-1920s heyday of laissez-faire.[74] The examples of export-led development in East Asia, namely South Korea and Taiwan, also cast heavy doubt on the pessimistic tenets of the *dependentistas*.[75]

By the 1980s, sociologists in Latin America had been hard hit by authoritarian persecution and were thus "compelled to aim at increasingly more modest goals" than rapid modernization or revolution.[76] Instead of engaging in broad ideological and philosophical debates characteristic of the dependency era, they began to focus on more practical problems, such as household strategies for economic survival among low-income groups, the position of women in the family and society, and the emergence and dynamics of grass-roots organizations in poor urban settlements. "High hopes for egalitarian and anti-imperialist processes of change" were abandoned, and focused field research became the norm. Just as the Latin American middle classes had failed to carry out the progressive transformations expected by the modernization theorists, so the workers and peasants had failed to bring about the revolutions awaited by some dependency thinkers.[77]

Also in the 1980s, political scientists turned their attention to the analysis of the politics of liberalization and transition from authoritarian regimes.[78] Like their counterparts in Sociology, they gradually abandoned the grand theorizing and structural determinism which had characterized both the modernization and dependency eras. Instead, they focused on the dynamics of agency, the role of ideology, the issue of political will, and the application of game theory. "Democracy came to be viewed as the achievement of courageous leaders and/or civil society, rather than an automatic consequence of economic performance."[79]

Meanwhile, many anthropologists and historians were challenging the totalizing logic of both modernization and dependency theories, which they claimed "subsumed difference into the service of a greater machinery that set limits, extracted surpluses, established hierarchies, and shaped identities." Like political scientists, these scholars sought to "break down reifications and restore agency to the historical narrative." However, in contrast to political scientists, who tended to focus on the agency of the political elite within formal state structures, these anthropologists and historians sought to expand notions of the political. Under the influence of neo-Gramscian theory, they began to examine the intersection of culture and power, and to emphasize the social construction of political life. They advanced gendered, ethnic, and linguistic analyses of imperial-subaltern encounters, and highlighted the contributions to community and national life of traditionally marginalized groups.

All of this does not mean that either modernization or dependency was swept definitively into the dustbin of history. Like most good theories in the social sciences, both bequeathed a legacy of important lessons and middle-level hypotheses, shorn of their more grandiose pretensions. Both theories contributed an abiding concern with underlying structural conditions, especially with dependency's emphasis on historical structuralism, although most social scientists now insist that we must focus on institutions, agents, identities and/or choices as well as structures. Dependency thinking was moderated and adapted to explain persuasively instances of "dependent development," not only in Latin America but in other regions of the globe as well. In addition, it left its mark in terms of a general awareness of the important role of external factors to the internal economic and political systems of Latin America.[80] Remnants of modernization theory are evident in some recent analyses which attempt to establish pre-requisites, economic and/or cultural, of political democracy.[81]

Many Latin Americanists are now analyzing, if not celebrating, the current coincidence of liberal economics and politics in the region. Economists are hailing the growth achieved by free-market models, though some worry about the lack of equity. Political scientists are studying the potential for consolidation and/or the quality of the new democracies, the functioning of new institutions, and the trend toward decentralization; many of them believe that the challenge today is to synchronize and sustain relatively free economic and political markets, while realizing that progress may not be linear, that structural conditions are not sufficient for success, and that fortuitous combinations of agents, institutions, and actions will be required. Sociologists and anthropologists are concerned about the fate of disadvantaged groups as the state pulls back from social welfare and about the ability of new actors—such as social movements and non-governmental organizations—to fill the gap. Historians draw parallels with previous periods of market-oriented economics and elitist democracies with low levels of participation and contestation. Few scholars are venturing predictions about the future.

In the 1980s and 1990s, despite the cross-disciplinary attention to the resurgence of classical liberalism, Latin American studies has been characterized by the absence of a prevailing paradigm.[82] From the perspective of many, the resultant eclecticism is healthy and promising. As one prominent political scientist has put it, "In the absence of an overarching conceptual framework, scholars may [now] turn their focus toward empirical hypothesis-testing and examination of questions at the so-called middle range of social science theory." The same could be said for sociologists and anthropologists, and many historians are more comfortable not having to prove or disprove some all-encompassing theory of development.[83] This is important because "[t]he resilient pillars of development studies are not works of grand theory, but rather detailed studies of historical and contemporary processes."[84]

Of course, Latin American studies has not been unaffected by the more recent trends toward theory-driven analysis, whether shaped by world-systems theory (mainly in Sociology), rational choice theory (Economics and Political Science), or post-modernism (Literature, Anthropology, and History). However, for the time being, studies within these paradigms must share the intellectual terrain with an abundance of middle-level theories. In Political Science, such theories have emerged on topics ranging from the specific forms that democracy has assumed in Latin America, to the sources and political effects of different institutional structures, to the emergence and effectiveness of social movements, to changing constructions of gender and citizenship.[85] In the realm of Economics, nearly everyone emphasizes market mechanisms and free trade more than in the past, but not everyone embraces the canon of neoliberal, Chicago-school orthodoxy. In Latin America, despite the apparent hegemony of neoliberalism, "a pragmatic neostructuralism appears to be gaining influence throughout the region," with emphasis on a reduced but flexible and non-negligible role for the state in economic development.[86] In Anthropology, recent studies examine such subjects as ethnohistory, workers, women, the middle class, urban social movements, Indian ethnic militancy, and communities participating in international migration.[87] And in Sociology, thematic comparative studies have emerged on the flow of capital and technology across the center-periphery divide, the reproduction of cultural forms on a global scale, the elaboration of social networks, the causes of rebellion and revolution, the evolution of social movements, and the uses and control of labor in different parts of the world economy.[88] While no overarching paradigms link these studies today, fruitful cooperation continues on themes which cross both disciplinary and geographic boundaries, such as political economy, social movements, gender, and immigration. Throughout the social sciences, scholars are studying the interactions between globalizing forces and local conditions.

This boundary-crossing trend is also evident in the bridging, or even merging, of Latin American and Latina/o Studies. An increasing number of scholars and institutions are now combining approaches from these two intellectual traditions in creative ways, building a new curriculum and pursuing research on the "Latin/oAmericas."

A survey of the main area journals confirms the general topical and theoretical developments discussed above. To complement our narrative account of the intellectual trajectory of Latin American studies since the 1960s, we surveyed all the issues (through 1996) of the five most important interdisciplinary Latin American studies journals: the *Latin American Research Review*, the *Journal of Latin American Studies, Latin American Perspectives*, the *Journal of Inter-American Studies and World Affairs*, and *The Americas*. While there were numerous important journals published in Latin America and consulted frequently by Latin Americanists, it would be a monumental task to appropriately survey all of them. We have thus limited ourselves to the main inter-disciplinary area journals published in the United States and Great Britain.

The *Latin American Research Review*, as noted above, began publication in 1965. During the first five years (1965–69), it featured mainly "state of research" articles on such grand themes of modernization as urbanization, agrarian problems and change, and sources of political instability. Such articles tended to be interdisciplinary in focus, and largely social scientific. In the next five years (1970–74), central issues were students, guerrillas, and political violence, topics in social history, and the quantitative history debate. The first article on women, entitled "The Female in Ibero-America," appeared in 1972. During the 1975–79 period, the influence of the dependency approach was fully evident as articles focused on issues such as U.S. policy towards Latin America, foreign investment, and income distribution. Urban and rural social relations and problems were still a focus and two articles on women appeared.

Analyses of Chile spiked following the 1973 military coup, and the journal offered a greater representation of articles from literature and the arts. From 1980–84, critiques and modifications of dependency theory appeared, but many articles continued to focus on issues of political economy, both international and national. In the wake of the triumph of the Sandinistas in Nicaragua, revolutions, both the recent Nicaraguan (1979) and the earlier Mexican (1910), became a focus topic. Gender received increased attention, and Literature and the Arts maintained a steady representation. In the late 1980s (1985–89), the journal featured a marked diversity of articles, with debt, democratization, and policy making in specific areas as leading subjects. In the 1990s, this diversity has continued, with articles ranging from the examination of changing patterns of religiosity in the region, dissections of the effects of neoliberal economics, globalization, and democratization, discourse analyses, and histories of agrarian relations and peasant rebellion. Gender and ethnicity, and more generally, identity, have become central analytical categories.

The *Journal of Latin American Studies*, surveyed from 1969–1995, was more heavily dominated by articles in History, especially social history. From the start, the journal emphasized topics on foreign influences in the region, both military and economic. From 1969 to 1983,[89] entries on political organizations and movements, topics in economics, and militarism and military institutions appeared most frequently after articles in history and social history. From 1984–1995, common subjects were economic history, especially the history of particular sectors and/or industries, foreign relations, urban and rural labor history, and the Church or religion. Gender received only limited treatment, appearing as a central category in only three articles over both periods. Literature and the arts remained completely outside the purview of the journal.

Latin American Perspectives began publication in 1974. Its first issue made clear its leftist mission: "While the many bourgeois journals and scholarly associations dealing with Latin America prefer to disguise their support of the capitalist system behind a facade of 'academic neutrality,' *Latin American Perspectives* has no such abstract pretensions. We explicitly declare that nothing academic can ever be neutral and that all scholarship has a political function."[90] The development of leftist thought on the region can be traced through the issue titles and themes. In the 1970s, these included dependency, imperialism, the process of underdevelopment, class struggle, and revolution. Interestingly, significant attention was paid to issues of gender in these early issues, albeit in the context of class analysis.[91] In the 1980s, while class remained a central organizational category, race and ethnicity, along with gender, also received attention. The state, hegemony, and popular protest and resistance became the main themes in articles on most countries, although revolution was still the focus for the many articles on Nicaragua and Central America. In the 1990s, several issues have been devoted to the Left in the post-Marxist era, and ethnicity and gender have become central categories of analysis. As in other journals, global restructuring, social movements, and democratization have received significant attention. Over the years, Literature and the Arts received some, albeit limited, attention within the context of the journal's political focus.

The *Journal of Inter-American Studies and World Affairs* began publication in 1959 under an editorial policy which embraced all aspects of Latin American culture and life, including Literature and the Arts. Until 1971, it featured inter-disciplinary articles in Spanish, Portuguese, and French as well as English, and while these articles covered history as far back as the colonial period, the emphasis was on the post-World War II era. From 1971–83, the journal became increasingly social scientific in orientation, and in 1983 began focusing exclusively on issues relevant to contemporary international relations, especially U.S.-Latin American relations. From 1959–1989, then, the journal's major focus topics, in order of frequency, were politics and political violence, international relations, developmental economics, demographic issues, intellectual thought, literature, and culture and society.[92] Since 1989, almost all the articles appearing in the journal have been on topics in international relations, political economy, and democratization, with special focus on such issues as NAFTA and the drug trade.

Finally, the oldest of the inter-disciplinary area journals, *The Americas*, deserves mention. A publication of the Academy of American Franciscan History, the quarterly journal first went to press in 1944. Early issues were devoted almost exclusively to the history of the Franciscan order, the Church, and religion. However, over time, the journal's subtitle, "A Quarterly Review of Inter-American Cultural History," took on broader meaning, with featured articles covering intellectual history, literary analysis, some political and economic history, and in the 1970s and 80s, increasing social history. Many essays traced the historical influence of political and economic concepts and/or the impact of a given individual on events of a given period. Articles on U.S.-Latin American relations and on contributions of Indians and Afro-Americans to the region's cultural history also appeared quite frequently. And as noted in the forward to the 1991 cumulative index, the most notable change in the journal's content over time was the increased number of contributions by and on women, a trend which began in the 1980s.

CONTEMPORARY CHALLENGES TO LATIN AMERICAN STUDIES

Despite all of the noteworthy contributions discussed above, Latin American studies still comes under attack, as do most area studies, for "ghettoizing" itself from the disciplines of the North American academy. This is particularly the case within Economics, Political Science, and Sociology, which tend to be the boldest in making universal claims about human behavior based on United States and European observations. Sociologist Alejandro Portes notes that "sociology in the United States has never regarded the Third World studies as a priority area or particularly encouraged its practitioners."[93] Sociologists specializing in Latin America have thus foregone economic and professional rewards. Economists, for their part, have in general steered clear of all inter-disciplinary endeavors, "both fearing the anarchy that (doubtless) reigns there and cherishing how much has been learned by pushing ahead with the canonical principles. [W]hat trade in ideas there has been between economics and the other social sciences has largely been one way, through missions established to sociology, political science, and the academic discipline of law."[94]

Within Political Science, few articles on Latin America (or on other "developing regions") have graced the pages of disciplinary journals, and we suspect that the same is true in the leading venues in

the other disciplines. As John Martz has shown, from 1960–1987, only
2.3% of the articles appearing in the top five U.S. Political Science
journals dealt with Latin American politics.[95] Instead, most of the
works mentioned above were published as chapters in edited
volumes, as collaborative multi-authored books, and/or as articles in
area or alternative thematic journals. Perhaps as a result, a debate
has been raging in the pages of major Political Science journals and
newsletters regarding the quality of contributions by area
specialists.[96]

This is not to say, however, that Latin America area scholars are
somehow second-rate. The paucity of area-studies articles in the most
prestigious disciplinary journals could conceivably be a reflection of
the parochialism or even low quality of those journals. An SSRC
survey of its 1970–1985 JCLAS postdoctoral grantees revealed that
the 220 respondents (in a variety of disciplines) "had published a
total of 866 books, 5,527 articles and book chapters, and 5,774 other
works including reports, papers published in conference proceedings,
and the like."[97] In addition, "they enjoyed a large measure of success
in their careers, as measured by the large proportion of the non-
tenured who achieved tenured positions after receiving the award."[98]
Thus, while there may be a gulf between some Latin Americanists and
the agenda-setters of their respective disciplines, it is clearly not a
gulf of competence, creativity, or productivity. Why, then, the
assault on area studies?

Probably the most basic characteristic of all area studies is that,
in emphasizing extensive knowledge of cases gained through field
work, they group social scientists and humanists together and
encourage cross-fertilization. Although "the heavy disciplinary
focus of much of American graduate education" means that "few
students [including area specialists] actually distribute the courses in
their training very far from their major discipline," and while even
"the set of scholars who have a long-term professional concern with a
particular part of the world" tend to have a "perspective bound by
[their] discipline," area specialists will often choose topics in
"domains where the methodological and conceptual superstructure of
disciplines is less intrusive."[99] Because "area specialists who are in
the social sciences are likely to have a great deal more contact and
shared intellectual activity [via field work and conferences] with
humanists than do most of their non area-oriented disciplinary

colleagues," their work tends to be at the non-technical or so-called "soft" end of the social scientific spectrum.[100] While this is viewed as "immensely enriching" by area scholars themselves, for those social scientists "at the 'hard' end of the spectrum, the close ties of area studies with the humanities reinforces their perception that area studies is not a scientific activity."[101]

The latest such critique has been launched by Harvard political scientist and noted Africanist Robert Bates, who argues that comparative political scientists should follow the lead of many specialists in U.S. politics who use rational choice and game theoretic models to produce testable hypotheses and strive for universalizable conclusions. He and those who share his convictions view area studies in the same way their behavioralist predecessors did: as primarily descriptive, largely atheoretical, and (above all), methodologically soft and hence unanalytical or unscientific.[102] Given that Political Science has become one of the dominant disciplines within Latin American studies, this latest attack is particularly troubling for Latin Americanists.

Moreover, this iteration of the "war on area studies" is complicated by the emergence of a comprehensive critique of area studies from within the humanities as well, specifically from the postmodernist (or "cultural studies") camp. In an attempt to challenge prevailing terms and categories, and to "decenter" the Western, white, male, colonialist/imperialist subject, postmodernist analysts pose such questions as: Why are "areas" our objects? What defines an "area?" How can "we" presume to understand "them" given our cultural biases and the politics that drive theorizing? Who, really, are "we" and "them?"[103] Such a critique is usually driven by empathy with historically subordinated and marginalized groups, and is often part of a more general attack on positivist social science which has objectified these groups and defined the terms by which they are studied by scholars and understood by society at large (the state, the nation, development, modernity, nature, etc.).[104]

This postmodernist critique is also connected to what Immanuel Wallerstein identifies as the emergence of a "new form of 'area studies'," namely of women's studies and ethnic studies programs.[105] "Women's studies and the multiple variants of 'ethnic' studies had bottom-up origins. The represented the (largely post-1969) revolt of those whom the university had 'forgotten.' Theirs was a claim to be heard, and to be heard not merely as describers of particular groups that were marginal, but as revisers of the central theoretical premises of social science."[106]

While these movements and the programs they produced represent a welcome and necessary innovation within the university, they add a new dynamic to the debate over area studies. On the one hand, they pose a challenge to the traditional disciplines in terms of theoretical and epistemological differences. Their interdisciplinary thrust and methodological openness thus render them in many ways intellectual allies of more traditional area studies scholars. Indeed, it could be argued that the vigor of the present attacks from the hardcore disciplinary specialists is a reaction to the critiques made by postmodernists and the threat that the "new form" of area studies poses to the mainstream of the disciplines. On the other hand, the more extreme postmodern critiques of scientific inquiry and academic standards frequently do not sit well with more traditional area experts, who maintain extensive interests in and loyalties to their respective disciplines.

Moreover, it remains unclear what effect the expansion of the new programs will have on traditional area studies in the competition for university resources. For example, as more students become interested in Latino studies, demand for more traditional Latin American studies may decline; on the other hand, as we suggested above, synergies with ethnic studies might cause it to rise. Indeed, in some places, the melding of Latina/o Studies and Latin American Studies is arguably succeeding at revitalizing and reshaping the field for the 21st century.

This may be a crucial development, since traditional area studies is facing strong challenges from outside the academy. The end of the Cold War has meant the demise of the general "national interest" justification for funding area studies programs. The issues that affect U.S. security interests are increasingly understood as global problems, better handled by issue experts rather than area experts.[107] In such a scenario, Latin American studies may be particularly vulnerable, given the low tendency of Latin Americanists to pursue studies with clear policy relevance, or, perhaps more accurately, the (not undeserved) association of Latin American specialists with causes often at odds with those of the Washington policy community.[108]

Relatedly, the global expansion of U.S. power in the 1990s, both economic and political, as well as the great leaps in communications technology of the last decade, have fed the notion that the world is becoming increasingly homogeneous. English has become the lingua franca of the international business and political worlds, and more and more countries have accepted and even embraced the "Washington consensus" on neoliberal economics and procedural democracy. As a result, emphasizing dissimilarities and urging an understanding of differences among the cultures, histories, and languages of the countries that make up "the global village" is regarded as passé in many powerful circles in the United States. More appropriate, from this perspective, is the development and exportation of universal theories and "tool-kits" which can be applied uniformly around the globe, irrespective of historical and cultural differences.[109]

IN DEFENSE OF AREA STUDIES

Despite these challenges, we contend that there are still strong intellectual and practical reasons to nurture area studies. To begin, the kind of mid-level theorizing[110] which has become the hallmark of Latin American and most area studies should not become the victim of "social science wars."[111] As noted above, the present round of attacks on area studies from within the Academy comes from two sides: from the hard social science camp which views area studies as overly ideographic, on the one hand; and from the post-modern camp which sees area studies as too closely tied to the totalizing and (falsely) "scientific" discourse of the traditional disciplines, on the other. The former lauds abstract, deductive models and large cross-national studies, while the latter "doubt[s] the value of causal explanations altogether and thus of conventional social science theorizing. . . . "[112] For opposite reasons, then, both perspectives dismiss (and at times disparage) the kind of analysis most common to area studies scholars: a mid-level, theoretically informed empirical study of one or more countries.

It is precisely such analysis, however, which is the great strength and contribution of research fostered by area studies programs and/or area specialization. Within Latin American studies, for example, it was the familiarity of Latin Americanists with particular historical and structural features of Latin American societies which allowed the universalist assumptions of modernization theory to be challenged and produced the highly influential dependency approach in the 1970s. As dependency itself came under fire, it was a close empirical analysis by Latin America area experts which produced the concept of "dependent development" and led to the elaboration of theories of state-led development around the world. In the fields of democratization and social movement theory, it has been transcontinental and transdisciplinary cooperation by Latin America experts which have produced some of the most significant recent works.

For those who believe in science, then, we would argue that area studies is fully justifiable on its scientific merits. Area studies is not an agenda of research; rather it is an intellectual and institutional construct which supports deep knowledge of cases through field work and encourages inter-disciplinary cross-fertilization. As noted above, most "area studies" scholars are strongly anchored in their respective disciplines. Without area studies, however, we could not capture the universe of cases to test the validity of discipline-specific theories. In addition, we would lose sight of new empirical puzzles that require theoretical explanations and that generate hypotheses. Exhaustive data collection and comparative analysis are at the heart of the scientific method, since in their absence, generalizations are difficult to make and hard to sustain. For those who are suspicious of the scientific project, we ask simply whether channeling resources away from language-learning, field research, and transnational cooperation is really the solution to promoting better understanding of and empathy with the "other?" Indeed, if the fruitful ties established over the past thirty years between U.S. and Latin American scholars are not nourished, we risk returning to the kind of isolated and parochial theorizing which is so much the subject of postmodernist critique.

As regards the broader challenge posed by a change in the priorities of funding agencies in the post Cold War era, we contend that support for area specialization is still a good investment. While globalization may mean that many different countries face similar problems, it does not mean that similar solutions will work everywhere. Local and regional traditions and politics will continue to influence events and outcomes in all parts of the world, and knowledge of those traditions and politics will continue to be essential for policy makers and academic theorists. In acquiring such knowledge, we should not allow nativism and xenophobia to blind and deafen us to alternative ways of viewing the world, nor can we expect foreign scholars to cooperate in data collection on international cases while refusing to let them question or "pollute" our models. If we honestly believe in "the global village," then U.S.-based institutions must accept and encourage the participation of foreigners on an equal basis and foster, ideologically and financially, a true exchange of ideas. Only this way will we produce a global community of scholars, whose perspectives can be respected and embraced both in the United States and abroad.

The great advantages of such programs as Title VI and Fulbright, as well as many of the leading private endeavors, have been their support for basic research and teaching. They have nourished a broad, heterogeneous array of area expertise, thus democratizing the marketplace of ideas. All scientific inquiry is enriched by having a multitude of competing researchers and perspectives. In contrast, more specific or targeted research programs, especially for security or corporate purposes, are arguably at greater risk of manipulation, bias, and perversion and can thus breed mistrust among researchers and between researchers and their subjects. As manifest in "Operation Camelot," as well as in debates surrounding more recent U.S. government initiatives to fund area studies through security agencies, international cooperation in research of questionable scientific intent is difficult to come by.

Moreover, the end of the Cold War actually presents an excellent opportunity for less politicized, less policy-driven, or less ethnocentric research. Scholars no longer operate in a climate in which their work tends to be categorized by many colleagues as serving either right-wing or left-wing purposes. Instead, they are freer to re-examine methodological and theoretical issues and make decisions based more on intellectual than political grounds.[113] In addition, area studies associations and journals have come of age, such that their professional norms and criteria are much clearer than they were in the 1960s and 70s.[114] As noted in the intellectual history section above, most scholars of Latin America have abandoned the grandiose theories of the past, have become more methodologically sophisticated, and have grown closer to the mainstream of their disciplines.

All of this is not to say that scholars should be required to limit their studies to one area, or that foundations should not encourage cross-regional studies. In fact, it is entirely reasonable for some funding institutions to switch their focus to topic areas, such as democratization/regime change, economic development, ethnic conflict, citizenship, gender relations, social movements, diasporic literatures, popular culture, etc. However, it would then be necessary and important to ensure the fair representation of diverse societies of the world (i.e., making sure that entire continents or sub-continents were not systematically excluded), to provide sufficient support to allow those studying one or more foreign countries to learn the relevant language(s) well and to conduct thorough field research, and to continue to encourage and support cross-national cooperation.[115]

For if there is not a somewhat 'level playing field' in terms of case selection and professional rewards, resource-poor students and scholars will seldom choose those cases which require a greater investment and/or sacrifice, and many cases will go unstudied, if not by the generation of established scholars, then certainly by their successors. This would be most troublesome, for as political scientist Gabriel Almond has argued, "The depth and distribution of detailed and accurate knowledge of foreign countries and cultures around the world is the best single indicator of our capacity to confront and solve our urgent international problems constructively. Knowledge does not guarantee that we will solve them constructively, but lack of it makes it likely that we will not."[116]

Paul Drake is a Professor of Political Science and Dean of the Division of Social Science at the University of California, San Diego. Lisa Hilbink is an Assistant Professor of Political Science at the University of Minnesota.

Notes

For comments on earlier drafts of this essay, we are grateful to Sonia Alvarez, Victor Bulmer-Thomas, David Collier, Carlos Ivan De Gregori, Eric Hershberg, Evelyne Huber, Elizabeth Jelín, Gilbert Joseph, Ira Katznelson, Gwen Kirkpatrick, Gerardo Munck, Peter Smith, Doris Sommer, Carlos Waisman, and two anonymous reviewers.

1. The authors, two political scientists, acknowledge the emphasis, perhaps inescapable, placed on the social sciences, and especially political science, in this chapter. A reasonable attempt was made to discuss the increasingly important contributions of scholars in the humanities to debates in Latin American Studies, but the authors recognize that there remain many worthy ideas and works that they were unable to cover in this short essay.

2. As Richard Lambert explains, "for a scholar studying China or India, the classical civilization is part of everyday life. Serious scholars, even social scientists, must master it to make sense of the contemporary society." See Richard Lambert, "Blurring the Disciplinary Boundaries: Area Studies in the United States," *American Behavioral Scientist* 33:6 (July/August 1990): 712–732, at 724.

3. This is not to say that claims of exceptionalism are completely absent in Latin America.

4. Two caveats to this generally positive cooperative scenario are in order. First, there have always been huge inequalities between U.S. and Latin American scholars in terms of the resources, both financial and scholarly, to which they have access. These inequalities have worsened since the continent-wide depression of the 1980s in Latin America. Second, the developmental heterogeneity of the region has also produced inequalities among Latin American scholars themselves, such that scholars from the larger, middle-income countries, particularly Argentina, Brazil, and Mexico, have always assumed a larger role in the field of Latin American Studies than their counterparts in poorer countries such as Bolivia, Paraguay, or the Caribbean states.

5. Fernando Henrique Cardoso, "The Consumption of Dependency Theory in the United States," *Latin American Research Review* 12:3 (Fall 1977): 7–24.

6. John H. Coatsworth, "International Collaboration in the Social Sciences: The ACLS/SSRC Joint Committee on Latin American Studies" (Paper presented at the SSRC/CLACSO conference on "International Scholarly Relations in the Social Sciences," Montevideo, Uruguay, August 15–17, 1989), 31.

7. Europeans have also been active in the programs of the JCLAS and LASA.

8. On Latin American attitudes toward the United States, see Carlos Rangel, *Latin Americans: Their Love-Hate Relationship with the U.S.* (New York: Harcourt Brace, 1977).

9. See Immanuel Wallerstein, "The Unintended Consequences of Cold War Area Studies," in Noam Chomsky et al., *The Cold War and the University: Toward an Intellectual History of the Postwar Years* (New York: The New Press, 1997),esp. p. 202; Vicente L. Rafael, "The Cultures of Area Studies in the United

States," *Social Text* (Winter 1994): 91–111; Paul Drake, "From Retrogression to Resurgence: International Scholarly Relations with Latin America in U.S. Universities, 1970s-1980s" (Paper presented at the SSRC/CLACSO conference on "International Scholarly Relations in the Social Sciences," Montevideo, Uruguay, August 15–17, 1989).

10. See Charles Wagley, ed., *Social Science Research on Latin America* (New York: Columbia University Press, 1964).

11. In fact, the JCLAS was disbanded from 1947–1959. Nonetheless, during this period some Latin Americanists did serve as consultants to the U.S. State Department. See Michael Jiménez, "In the Middle of the Mess: Rereading John J. Johnson's *Political Change in Latin America* Thirty Years Later" (Paper presented at the Latin American Studies Association XV Annual Conference, Miami, Florida, December 6, 1989).

12. See Thomas C. Wright, *Latin America in the Era of the Cuban Revolution* (New York: Praeger, 1991).

13. Thus, in cumulative totals, Latin America outranked Africa (5,066), Eastern Europe (6,638), and Near East and South Asia (13,873), but not East Asia and Pacific (20,487) or Western Europe (88,837). Board of Foreign Scholarships, *Fulbright Program Exchanges, 1984–85* (Washington, DC, 1985).

14. Wallerstein , "Unintended Consequences," p. 209 . Latin America was incorporated into the Title VI mission in 1960. It should be noted, however, that "The legislative debate [over the NDEA] had less to do with the cold war than with whether the federal government should fund higher education. ... The bill was strongly contested by conservatives who argued that the NDEA would open the floodgates of federal assistance to higher education" (Gilbert Merkx, "Editor's Foreword," *Latin American Research Review* 30:1 (1995), 4).

15. Gilbert Merkx, "Editor's Foreword," *Latin American Research Review* 29:1 (1994), 4–5.

16. Coatsworth, "International Collaboration," 2.

17. Ibid. As Merkx ("Editor's Foreword," 1994) notes, "in 1985, the Library of Congress's *National Directory of Latin Americanists* identified some 5,000 professionals working as specialists on the region" and judging by student enrollments, subscriptions to *LARR* , and attendance at LASA conferences, the field is now even larger (p. 5).

18. Coatsworth, "International Collaboration," 15. See also Mark T. Berger, *Under Northern Eyes: Latin American Studies and U.S. Hegemony in the Americas, 1898–1990* (Bloomington, IN: Indiana University Press, 1995).

19. Merkx, "Editor's Foreword," 1995, 4.

20. Wallerstein, "Unintended Consequences," p.223.

21. On this issue see Irving Louis Horowitz, The Rise and Fall of Project Camelot: Studies in the Relationship between Social Science and Practical Politics (Cambridge: MIT Press, 1967); and Sigmund Diamond, Compromised Campus: The Collaboration of Universities with the Intelligence Community, 1945–1955 (New York: Oxford University Press, 1992).

22. Christopher Mitchell, "Introduction," *Changing Perspectives in Latin American Studies* (Stanford: Stanford University Press, 1988), 10–11. See also Robert Packenham, *The Dependency Movement* (Cambridge: Harvard University Press, 1992).

23. Merkx, "Editor's Foreword," 1994, 4. Indeed, in his contribution to Samuels and Weiner's (1992) edited volume on the political culture of area studies, Gabriel Almond notes that the politicization of area studies, which the volume discusses as a general problem, has been "the most marked in Latin American studies." See Gabriel A. Almond, "The Political Culture of Foreign Area Research: Methodological Reflections," in Richard J. Samuels and Myron Weiner, eds., *The Political Culture of Foreign Area and International Studies* (New York: Brassey's, 1992).

24. Drake, "Retrogression to Resurgence," 3.

25. President's Commission on Foreign Language and International Studies, *Strength through Wisdom* (Washington , D.C., 1979), 8–9, 101–103.

26. Drake, "Retrogression to Resurgence," 28.

27. Coatsworth, "International Collaboration," 8–9.

28. Jacob Heilbrunn, "The News from Everywhere: Does Global Thinking Threaten Local Knowledge?", *Lingua Franca,* May / June 1996, 49–56 at 52.

29. Because the study of Latin American Literature followed a slightly different path, we do not treat developments in that discipline below. However, interested readers can consult the following essays for discussions of the developments in the region's Literature and Literary Criticism during the same period: Jean Franco, "From Modernism to Resistance: Latin American Literature 1959–1976," *Latin American Perspectives* 5:1 (Winter 1978): 77–97; Saúl Sosnowski, "Spanish-American Literary Criticism: The State of the Art," in Christopher Mitchell, ed., *Changing Perspectives in Latin American Studies* (Stanford: Stanford University Press, 1988): 163–182; Paul B. Dixon, "'Decentering' a Discipline: Recent Trends in Latin American Literary Studies," *Latin American Research Review* 31:3 (1996): 203–217; and essays in Leslie Bethell, ed., *The Cambridge History of Latin America* Vol. X (New York: Cambridge University Press, 1995).

30. See Wagley, *Social Science Research.* For other surveys of work done under the umbrella of Latin American studies see Bryce Wood and Manuel Diegues Junior, eds., *Social Science in Latin America: Papers Presented at the Conference on Latin American Studies Held at Rio de Janeiro, March 29–31, 1965* (New York: Columbia University Press, 1967); Roberto Esquenazi-Mayo and Michael C. Mayer, *Latin American Scholarship since WWII* (Lincoln, NE: University of Nebraska Press, 1971); and Gláucio Ary Dillon Soares, "Latin American Studies in the United States," *LARR* 11:2 (1976): 51–69.

31. Howard F. Cline, "Latin American History: Development of Its Study and Teaching in the United States Since 1898," in Howard Cline, ed., *Latin American History* Vol. I (Austin: University of Texas Press, 1967), pp. 6–16. The *Handbook of Latin American Studies* began publication in 1936.

32. Lewis Hanke, "The Development of Latin-American Studies in the

United States, 1939–1945," *The Americas* 4:1 (July 1947): 32–64, at 58–9.

33. The *Latin American Research Review (LARR)* was founded in 1965 as the official publication of the Latin American Studies Association (LASA), established in 1964.

34. John D. Martz, "Political Science and Latin American Studies," *Latin American Research Review* 25:1 (1990): 67–86, at 75; Gilbert Merkx, "Editor's Foreword," for *Latin American Research Review* volumes 28:1, 29:1, 30:1, and 31:1 (1993, 1994, 1995, 1996).

35. From 1965–95 *LARR* featured 191 entries on Mexico, 136 on Brazil, 112 on Argentina, 80 on Central America or individual Central American countries, 64 on Chile, and 58 on Peru. From 1969–95, JLAS published 62 articles on Brazil, 57 on Mexico, 50 on Argentina, 37 on Central America or individual Central American countries, 32 on Peru, and 28 on Chile.

36. Merkx, "Editor's Foreword," 1993, 1994, 1995, 1996.

37. Joseph Tulchin, "Emerging Patterns of Research in the Study of Latin America," *Latin American Research Review* 18:1 (1983), 86.

38. Soares, "Latin American Studies," 52.

39. However, the current crisis in Latin American academia has meant that the possibility for such influence has diminished significantly. As a result, the social scientific research agenda in the U.S. is increasingly shaped by narrow theoretical debates which are specific to U.S. disciplines and divorced from Latin American concerns. We thank Eric Hershberg for this insight.

40. Examples are Edgardo Catterberg, "Attitudes towards Democracy in Argentina During the Transition Period," *International Journal of Public Opinion Research* 2:2 (Summer 1990): 155–68; Catherine M Conaghan, "Polls, Political Discourse, and the Public Sphere," and Miguel Basáñez, "Public Opinion Research in Mexico," in Peter H. Smith, *Latin America in Comparative Perspective* (Boulder: Westview Press, 1995), 227–274. See also the uses of survey material in Juan J. Linz and Alfred Stepan, *Problems of Democratic Transition and Consolidation: Southern Europe, South America, and Post-Communist Europe* (Baltimore: Johns Hopkins University Press, 1996).

41. See for example Juan J. Linz and Arturo Valenzuela, eds., *The Failure of Presidential Democracy* (Baltimore: Johns Hopkins University Press, 1994); Arend Lijphart and Carlos H. Waisman, *Institutional Design in New Democracies: Eastern Europe and Latin America* (Boulder: Westview Press, 1996).

42. Allen D. Bushong, "Doctoral Dissertations on Pan-American Topics Accepted by United States and Canadian Colleges and Universities," *Latin American Research Review Supplement* 2:2 (Spring 1967).

43. Charles W. Bergquist, "Recent U.S. Studies in Latin American History: Trends since 1965," *Latin American Research Review* 9:1 (Spring 1974): 3–35; Arturo Valenzuela, "Political Science and the Study of Latin America," in Christopher Mitchell, ed., *Changing Perspectives in Latin American Studies* (Stanford: Stanford University Press, 1988): 63–86.

44. See Albert O. Hirschmann, "Ideologies of Economic Development in Latin America," in Hirschmann, ed., *Latin American Issues: Essays and Comments* (New York: The Twentieth Century Fund, 1961), 3–42.

45. Paul Drake, "Latin America in the Changing World Order: 1492–1992," in Roberto G. Rabel, ed., *Latin America in a Changing World Order* (Dunedin, New Zealand: University of Otago Press, 1992).

46. On the continuity in theorizing, see Hirschmann, "Ideologies of Economic Development."

47. As Peter Klarén explains, modernization theory evolved, via Talcott Parson's structural-functionalism, from Max Weber's polar conception of traditional versus modern and Auguste Comte's theory of social evolution via stages (See Peter F. Klarén, "Lost Promise: Explaining Latin American Underdevelopment," in Peter F. Klarén and Thomas J. Bossert, *Promise of Development: Theories of Change in Latin America* (Boulder: Westview Press, 1986), 9.

48. See for example Gabriel A. Almond and James S. Coleman, *The Politics of Developing Areas* (Princeton: Princeton University Press,1960); Seymour Martin Lipset and Aldo Solari, eds., *Elites in Latin America* (New York: Oxford University Press, 1967); Jacques Lambert, *Latin America: Social Structure and Political Institutions* (Berkeley: University of California Press, 1967). Latin America was also used as the point of comparison for Seymour Martin Lipset's classic work in this paradigm, *Political Man : The Social Bases of Politics* (Garden City, NY: Doubleday, 1960).

49. Jiménez, "Middle of the Mess," 24.

50. Classic works in modernization theory are W. A. Lewis, *The Theory of Economic Growth* (London: Allen and Unwin, 1955); W.W. Rostow, *The Stages of Economic Growth* (New York: Cambridge University Press, 1960); Cyril Black, *The Dynamics of Modernization* (New York: Harper and Row, 1966).

51. See Lipset and Solari, *Elites in Latin America* ; Lambert, *Latin America: Social Structure and Political Institutions;* and John J. Johnson, *Political Change in Latin America* (Stanford: Stanford University Press, 1958).

52. See Albert Fishlow, "The State of Latin American Economics," in Christopher Mitchell, ed., *Changing Perspectives in Latin American Studies* (Stanford: Stanford University Press, 1988): 87–119, and Rostow, *The Stages of Economic Growth* . On the general evolution of economic thought in Latin America after 1930, see Joseph L. Love, "Economic Ideas and Ideologies in Latin America since 1930," in Leslie Bethell, ed., *The Cambridge History of Latin America* , Vol. XI (New York: Cambridge University Press, 1994), 393–460; Joseph Love, *Crafting the Third World: Theorizing Underdevelopment in Rumania and Brazil* (Stanford: Stanford University Press, 1996); E.V.K. Fitzgerald, "ECLA and the Formation of Latin American Economic Doctrine," in David Rock, ed. *Latin American in the 1940s: War and Postwar Transitions* (Berkeley: University of California Press, 1994), 89–108.

53. It should be noted that while the driving idea behind modernization theory was that Latin America could and should replicate U.S. development,

modernization theory was not based in the same (neo-)liberal economic theory that drives U.S. policy toward Latin America (and the world) in the 1990s. Structuralism called for an explicit and leading role for the state in economic affairs.

54. The Alliance for Progress was a $22.3 billion program launched by the Kennedy administration to attack the social ills (poverty, illiteracy, inequality) which might breed support for communism in the region. See Tony Smith, "The Alliance for Progress: the 1960s," in Abraham F. Lowenthal, *Exporting Democracy: The U.S. and Latin America* (Baltimore: Johns Hopkins University Press, 1991), 71–89.

55. Lourdes Arizpe, "Anthropology in Latin America: Old Boundaries, New Contexts," in Christopher Mitchell, ed., *Changing Perspectives in Latin American Studies* (Stanford: Stanford University Press, 1988): 143–161 at 145 and 156.

56. Fishlow, "Latin American Economics," 92.

57. Valenzuela, "Political Science and the Study of Latin America," 67–68.

58. Alejandro Portes, "Latin American Sociology in the Mid-1980's: Learning from Hard Experience," in Christopher Mitchell, ed., *Changing Perspectives in Latin American Studies* (Stanford: Stanford University Press, 1988): 121–142, at 123 and 131.

59. Tulio Halperín Donghi, "The State of Latin American History," in Christopher Mitchell, ed., *Changing Perspectives in Latin American Studies* (Stanford: Stanford University Press, 1988): 13–62, at 13. On historians' participation in the modernization school, see Cristóbal Kay, *Latin American Theories of Development and Underdevelopment* (London: Routledge, 1989) and Frederick Cooper et al., *Confronting Historical Paradigms: Peasants, Labor, and the Capitalist World System in Africa and Latin America* (Madison, WI: University of Wisconsin Press, 1993).

60. Bergquist, "Recent U.S. Studies," 4.

61. One holistic theory developed to explain Latin American development patterns was corporatism, which held that Latin American societies had inherited a distinct Iberian tradition, featuring feudalistic social relations, anti-capitalist preferences and incentives, patrimonial extended families, hierarchical Roman Catholic religious affinities, corporatist and organic links between the state and society, and authoritarian, verticalist governing structures. From this perspective, such characteristics were not necessarily undesirable or destined to vanish with economic development, as modernization theorists would have it, but were part of Latin America's unique developmental path. Accordingly, powerful, activist, and interventionist states within the essentially Catholic cultural and philosophical framework of the Latin American tradition would direct Latin American societies on a noncapitalist, non-Marxist path to modernity and development. (See Klarén, "Lost Promise," 26–8.) The most influential works on the corporatist tradition were Richard M. Morse, "The Heritage of Latin America," in Louis Hartz, ed., *The Founding of*

New Societies (New York: Harcourt, Brace and World, 1964); Howard J. Wiarda, ed., *Politics and Social Change in Latin America: The Distinct Tradition* (Amherst: University of Massachusetts Press, 1974); and Claudio Veliz, *The Centralist Tradition of Latin America* (Princeton: Princeton University Press, 1979). It should be noted that other analysts of Latin America had employed the concept of corporatism to describe the monopolistic, hierarchical, state-structured form of interest group politics common in the region, but did not accept the broader cultural explanation developed therefrom. See for example Philippe C. Schmitter, *Interest Conflict and Political Change in Brazil* (Stanford: Stanford University Press, 1971) and "Still the Century of Corporatism?" *The Review of Politics* 36:1 (January 1974): 85–132. For an excellent summary of the literature on corporatism in Latin America, see David Collier, "Trajectory of a Concept: "Corporatism" in the Study of Latin American Politics," in Peter H. Smith, *Latin America in Comparative Perspective* (Boulder, CO: Westview Press, 1995), 135–162. We do not discuss corporatism further in this essay because it did not have as broad an interdisciplinary impact as did modernization and dependency.

62. Valenzuela, "Political Science and the Study of Latin America," 71.

63. Fishlow, "Latin American Economics," 97–8. See for example Paul Baran, *The Political Economy of Growth* (New York: Monthly Review Press, 1957); Fernando Henrique Cardoso and Enzo Faletto, *Dependencia y Desarrollo en América Latina* (Mexico City: Siglo Veintiuno, 1969); Theotonio dos Santos, *Dependencia y Cambio Social* (Santiago: CESO, Universidad de Chile, 1970); Andre Gunder Frank, *Capitalism and Underdevelopment in Latin America* (New York: Monthly Review Press, 1967); Celso Furtado, *Economic Development of Latin America* (New York: Cambridge University Press, 1970); Osvaldo Sunkel, "Transnational Capitalism and National Disintegration in Latin America," *Social and Economic Studies* 22:1 (March 1973): 132–76.

64. See Raúl Prebisch, *The Economic Development of Latin America and Its Principle Problems* (New York: United Nations, 1950), placed in historical context in Joseph L. Love, "Raúl Prebisch and the Origins of the Doctrine of Unequal Exchange," *Latin American Research Review* 15:1 (1980): 45–72.

65. Baran, The Political Economy of Growth; Frank, Capitalism and Underdevelopment in Latin America.

66. See Samir Amin, *Imperialism and Unequal Development* (New York: Monthly Review Press, 1977); Cardoso, "Consumption of Dependency Theory;" Love, *Crafting the Third World*; Packenham, *Dependency Movement*;. Most economists in the United States did not subscribe to dependency thinking, however.

67. See Immanuel Wallerstein, *The Capitalist World-Economy* (New York: Cambridge University Press, 1979),*The Politics of the World-Economy: The States, the Movements, and the Civilizations* (New York: Cambridge University Press, 1984), and *The Modern World-System III: the Second Era of Great Expansion of the Capitalist World Economy, 1730–1840s* (New York: Academic Press, 1989).

68. Arizpe, "Anthropology in Latin America."

69. For example, see Stanley J. and Barbara H. Stein, The Colonial Heritage of Latin America; Essays on Economic Dependence in Perspective (New York: Oxford University Press, 1970).

70. See Guillermo O'Donnell, Modernization and Bureaucratic-Authoritarianism: Studies in South American Politics (Berkeley: Institute of International Studies, University of California 1973), and David Collier, ed., The New Authoritarianism in Latin America (Princeton: Princeton University Press, 1979).

71. Valenzuela, "Political Science and the Study of Latin America," 72.

72. Peter H. Smith, "The Changing Agenda for Social Science Research on Latin America," in Peter H. Smith, Latin America in Comparative Perspective (Boulder: Westview Press, 1995): 1–29, at 9.

73. Fishlow, "Latin American Economics," 101.

74. Jonathan Brown, A Socioeconomic History of Argentina, 1776–1860 (New York: Cambridge University Press, 1979); Paul Drake, The Money Doctor in the Andes : The Kemmerer Missions, 1923–1933 (Durham: Duke University Press, 1989); Joseph L. Love and Nils Jacobsen, eds., Guiding the Invisible Hand: Economic Liberalism and the State in Latin American History (New York: Praeger, 1988).

75. See articles on this topic in Frederic C. Deyo, ed., The Political Economy of the New Asian Industrialism (Ithaca: Cornell University Press, 1987).

76. Portes, "Latin American Sociology," 123. As Portes further explains, "Military regimes, in particular those of the Southern Cone countries, took aim at the discipline as one of their major intellectual adversaries. The career of sociology was abolished in several universities ... [and] many of the best thinkers and researchers were compelled to seek refuge either abroad or in private centers supported by foreign foundations."

77. Ibid, 125.

78. See for example Guillermo O'Donnell and Philippe C. Schmitter, Transitions from Authoritarian Rule: Tentative Conclusions about Uncertain Democracies (Baltimore: Johns Hopkins University Press, 1986); Adam Przeworski, Democracy and the Market: Political and Economic Reforms in Eastern Europe and Latin America (New York: Cambridge University Press, 1991).

79. Smith, "Changing Agenda," 9.

80. Political-economists specializing in Latin America produced noteworthy and enduring works explaining the variable patterns of development that had occurred in peripheral countries. See for example Peter Evans, Dependent Development: The Alliance of Multinational, State, and Local Capital in Brazil (Princeton: Princeton University Press, 1979) and Embedded Autonomy: States and Industrial Transformation (Princeton: Princeton University Press, 1995; Gary Gereffi and Donald L. Wyman, Manufacturing Miracles: Paths of Industrialization in Latin America and East Asia (Princeton:

Princeton University Press, 1990); Stephan Haggard, *Pathways from the Periphery: The Politics of Growth in the Newly Industrializing Countries* (Ithaca: Cornell University Press, 1990); Stephan Haggard and Robert R. Kaufman, eds., *The Politics of Economic Adjustment: International Constraints, Distributive Conflicts, and the State* (Princeton: Princeton University Press, 1992).

81. See for example Kenneth Bollen and Robert W Jackman, "Political Democracy and the Size Distribution of Income," *American Sociological Review* 50 (1985): 438–57; Francis Fukuyama, *The End of History and the Last Man* (New York: Free Press, 1992);Samuel Huntington, *The Third Wave: Democratization in the Late Twentieth Century* (Norman, OK: University of Oklahoma Press, 1991); Mitchell A. Seligson, "Democratization in Latin America: The Current Cycle," in James M. Malloy and Mitchell A. Seligson, eds., *Authoritarians and Democrats: Regime Transition in Latin America* (Pittsburgh, PA: University of Pittsburgh Press, 1987).

82. Portes, "Latin American Sociology in the Mid-1980's," 127, speaking specifically of Sociology, but this can surely be applied to Political Science and Anthropology, as well. See Daniel H. Levine, "Paradigm Lost: Dependence to Democracy," *World Politics* 40 (April 1988): 377–95.

83. Smith, "Changing Agenda," 10; Halperín, "Latin American History."

84. Alejandro Portes and A. Douglas Kincaid, "Sociology and Development in the 1990s: Critical Challenges and Empirical Trends," *Sociological Forum* 4:4 (1989): 479–503 at 499.

85. For examples, see Guillermo O'Donnell, "Delegative Democracy," *Journal of Democracy* 5:1 (January 1994): 55–69; Linz and Stepan, *Problems of Democratic Transition and Consolidation;* David Collier and Ruth Berins Collier, *Shaping the Political Arena* (Princeton: Princeton University Press, 1991); Scott Mainwaring and Timothy R. Scully, *Building Democratic Institutions: Party Systems in Latin America* (Stanford: Stanford University Press, 1995); Scott Mainwaring and Matthew S. Shugart, *Presidentialism and Democracy in Latin America* (New York: Cambridge University Press, 1997); Joe Foweraker and Ann L. Craig, eds., *Popular Movements and Political Change in Mexico* (Boulder: Lynne Rienner, 1990); Arturo Escobar and Sonia E. Alvarez, *The Making of Social Movements in Latin America* (Boulder: Westview Press, 1992); Sonia E. Alvarez, *Engendering Democracy in Brazil: Women's Movements in Transition Politics* (Princeton: Princeton University Press, 1990); Jane S. Jacquette, *The Women's Movement in Latin America: Participation and Democracy* (Boulder: Westview Press, 1994); Elizabeth Jelín and Eric Hershberg, eds., *Constructing Democracy: Human Rights, Citizenship, and Society in Latin America* (Boulder: Westview Press, 1996).

86. Fishlow, "Latin American Economics," 111.

87. For specifics see Arizpe, "Anthropology in Latin America."

88. See Portes, "Latin American Sociology," pp. 136–7 and related citations; Peter Evans, *Embedded Autonomy;* Susan Eckstein, ed., *Power and Popular Protest: Latin American Social Movements* (Berkeley: University of California

Press, 1988); Elizabeth Jelin, ed., *Los nuevos movimientos sociales* (Buenos Aires: Centro Editor de America Latina, 1985); Elizabeth Jelin, ed., *Women and Social Change in Latin America* (London: Zed, 1990); Alejandro Portes, *The Economic Sociology of Immigration: Essays on Networks, Ethnicity, and Entrepreneurship* (New York: Russell Sage Foundation, 1995); Alejandro Portes, Manuel Castells, and Lauren A. Benton, eds., *The Informal Economy: Studies in Advanced and Less Developed Countries* (Baltimore: Johns Hopkins University Press, 1989).

89. A useful cumulative index was published in 1984 for these years.

90. *Latin American Perspectives* 1:1 (1974), 2.

91. In 1977, for example, an entire double issue was devoted to women and class struggle.

92. See the cumulative index for 1959–1989.

93. Portes, "Latin American Sociology," 126.

94. David M. Kreps, "Economics—The Current Position," *Daedalus* 126:1 (Winter 1997): 59–85 at 59–60.

95. Martz, "Political Science and Latin American Studies," 69.

96. For a summary of this debate, see Christopher Shea, "Political Scientists Clash Over Value of Area Studies," *Chronicle of Higher Education* , January 10, 1997, A13.

97. Coatsworth, "International Collaboration," 38.

98. Ibid, 39.

99. Lambert, "Blurring Disciplinary Boundaries," 718, 727, and 729. Lambert notes that the core disciplines in area studies are Anthropology, History, Literature, and Political Science, and that "it is precisely at their juncture point—a kind of historically informed political anthropology, using materials in the local languages—that much of the genuinely interdisciplinary work in area studies occurs. History operates as a swing discipline, facing both the humanities and the social sciences, and the principal thrust of a particular research theme determines where in the spectrum it will lie" (p. 730).

100. Ibid, 731.

101. Ibid.

102. See Robert H. Bates, "Area Studies and Political Science: Rupture and Possible Synthesis," Ms. 1997 and "Letter from the President: Area Studies and the Discipline," APSA-CP: Newsletter of the APSA Organized Section in Comparative Politics 7:1 (Winter 1996): 1–2, as well as Christopher Shea, "Political Scientists Clash."

103. For an example, see Rafael, "Cultures of Area Studies."

104. As Fernando Coronil explains, these scholars "reject ... master narratives of modernism and opt for the more modest goal of illuminating social reality through partial glimpses, attentiveness to localized context, and sensitivity to multiple stories and protean symbolic systems" ("Foreword," Joseph et al., Close Encounters of Empire, 3). See for example Florencia E. Mallon, "The Promise and Dilemma of Subaltern Studies: Perspectives from Latin American History," *American Historical Review* 99 (Dec. 1995):

1491–1515; Arturo Escobar, Encountering Development: The Making and Unmaking of the Third World (Princeton: Princeton University Press, 1995).

105. Wallerstein, "Unintended Consequences," p.227.

106. Ibid.

107. See Heilbrunn, "News from Everywhere," 50.

108. One study revealed that Latin Americanists, of all area specialists, authored the lowest percentage of publications with any clear policy relevance: 11% compared to a high typically of 22% among East Asian scholars. (Lambert, Beyond, 156–167, 363–364.)

109. Such an attitude is particularly salient within the international economic and financial community. See discussions in Paul Drake, ed., Money Doctors, Foreign Debts, and Economic Reforms in Latin America from the 1890s to the Present (Wilmington: SR Books, 1994); Adam Przeworski et al., Sustainable Development (New York: Cambridge University Press, 1995); J. Sirowiecki, "Dr. Shock: Jeffrey Sachs has a cure for every sick economy. Is he coming to a country near you?" Lingua Franca 7:5 (Jun-Jul 1997): 61–73.

110. On mid-level theorizing, see Rogers Smith, "Still Blowing in the Wind: A Quest for a Democratic, Scientific Political Science," Daedalus 126:1 (Winter 1997): 253–287.

111. Here we make reference to an analogous debate currently raging over the study of the (hard) sciences. See for example Paul R. Gross and Norman Levitt, Higher Superstition: The Academic Left and Its Quarrels with Science (Baltimore, MD: Johns Hopkins University Press, 1994); Alan Sokal, "Transgressing the Boundaries: Toward a Transformative Hermeneutics of Quantum Gravity," Social Text 46/47 (Spring/Summer 1996): 217–252; and Andrew Ross, ed., Science Wars (Durham, NC: Duke University Press, 1996).

112. Atul Kohli, in his introduction to the symposium, "The Role of Theory in Comparative Politics," World Politics 48 (October 1995): 1–49 at 1.

113. Gabriel A. Almond, "The Political Culture of Foreign Area Research: Methodological Reflections," in Richard J. Samuels and Myron Weiner, eds., The Political Culture of Foreign Area and International Studies (New York: Brassey's, 1992), 205–6.

114. Ibid, 212.

115. Similar concerns are noted in Coatsworth, "International Collaboration," at 50.

116. Almond, "Political Culture of Foreign Area Research," 200.

Chapter 2

The Middle East in the Past and Future of Social Science

Timothy Mitchell

The founding of the Middle East Institute in Washington D.C. in May 1946 seems a convenient event to mark the arrival of Middle Eastern area studies in the United States. In January 1947 the Institute launched *The Middle East Journal,* the first American quarterly devoted to the contemporary Middle East. The journal's inaugural issue declared that the region was now "very near" the United States, both in point of time-distance and with respect to the United States' new involvement there in "questions of power politics." Yet the Middle East remained to all except a very few Americans "essentially *terra incognita.*"[1] The principal purpose of the journal was not to analyze the attitudes and policies of the Western powers, which had shaped the countries of the region in the past. Its aim was to set forth and evaluate the forces shaping the region today, namely "forces and factors engendered in and among these countries themselves—their national consciousness, urge for economic self-determination, cultural conditions, population pressures, regional understandings."[2] Since these countries shared a common Islamic heritage and experience of European expansionism, moreover, a proper understanding of one country could be acquired "only though a proper knowledge of all." The journal would therefore present particular conditions and problems in the Middle East "as facets of the whole."[3]

Fifty years later, in 1996, the Institute assessed the success of this ambition with an article in the journal entitled "The Study of Middle East Politics 1946–1996: A Stocktaking."[4] The assessment was not a positive one. Its author, James Bill, a senior academic in the field, concluded that "we have learned disturbingly little after fifty years of heavy exertion." He gave a list of major political developments in the region that scholars had failed to interpret or foresee, and devoted the rest of the article to listing possible reasons for these failures.

Such acknowledgments of failure have been a regular feature of

Middle Eastern area studies. Almost a quarter of a century earlier, in August 1973, the Research and Training Committee of the Middle East Studies Association of North America (MESA) convened a conference in Palo Alto, funded by the Ford Foundation, to assess the state of the field. In his introduction to the subsequent volume of conference papers, Leonard Binder stated: "The fact is that Middle East studies are beset by subjective projections, displacements of affect, ideological distortion, romantic mystification, and religious bias, as well as by a great deal of incompetent scholarship."[5] Twelve years earlier, in another essay on the state of Middle Eastern studies, Manfred Halpern complained that despite the great expansion of the field over the preceding decade, "we have been devoting ourselves to a kind of stamp collecting," filling in pieces of information, country by country, but "neglecting to identify essential structures and relationships or to essay preliminary syntheses." Given the present situation in the region, he said, "[i]t may even be that we are losing ground."[6]

These regular statements of failure have always shared another feature: their optimism that the field has turned a corner and that the failures they diagnose belong to the past. "The new Orientalist" emerging from of the combination of area studies and the social sciences, Halpern predicted in 1962, would produce "a sense of the whole" that was lost in the division of labor among the disciplines. Despite the distortions and incompetence of their youth, said Binder hopefully in 1974, "Middle East studies have come of age." The book he was introducing on the state of the field, he suggested, "marks the rites of passage." Although the field's record of achievements was undistinguished, wrote Bill in 1995, "the future seems brighter, partly because of the increasing recognition of the problems of the past."[7]

Given this pattern, there seems no point in writing yet another assessment of the state of the field. It would not be difficult to reproduce the pattern, equally pessimistic about past accomplishments, equally optimistic about the appearance of a new dawn. Instead, I want to pose two related questions. First, what structures and possibilities of knowledge shape the field of Middle Eastern area studies, in ways that make the Middle East seem knowable and yet not? What intellectual strategies make it possible to see the Middle East "as a whole" yet render the resulting pictures so disappointing? More specifically, how has the changing relationship between the local expertise of area studies and the general questions asked by social science disciplines governed the forms of knowledge? Second, by way of introduction to these first questions, how should we understand the relationship between the "questions of power politics" that make the Middle East seem so near and the production of this academic knowledge? The organizers of post-war area studies in the United States almost always invoked the expansion of U.S. power in World War II and in the Cold War crises that ensued. Calls for the dismantling or remodeling of area studies in the 1990s also referred to the passing of the Cold War as signaling the end of area studies' usefulness.[8] Yet if area studies never produced much in the way of useful knowledge, how exactly did it serve the needs of the expansion of U.S. power? The fact that both defenders and critics of area studies always tell us that it did so is not in itself evidence of a direct relationship between the construction of knowledge and the exercise of power.

The genealogy of area studies must be understood in relation to the wider structuring of academic knowledge and to the struggles not of the Cold War but of science—and social science in particular—as a twentieth-century political project. This project has been closely connected with structuring the global power of the United States, but the relationship is not the simple one that is often assumed in discussions of area studies. The social sciences took their modern form in the same period as area studies and were themselves created as a kind of area study. The development of the two kinds of study was interrelated and so were their subsequent difficulties. The so-called crisis of area studies over the last quarter of the twentieth century was also a crisis in the project of creating a general science of society. The question of the future of area studies is therefore a question about the future of the social science project rather than simply an issue of how best to learn about foreign parts.

PRE-WAR AREA STUDIES

World War II and the ensuing crises of the Cold War did not give birth to area studies. One could argue on the contrary, as Robert Hall argued in 1947 and Vicente Rafael recently proposed again, that they may have postponed its development.[9] The conventional story is that area studies developed thanks to the passing of the National Defense Education Act (NDEA) in 1958, in response to the Sputnik crisis and the escalation of the Cold War. Yet as Barbara Clowse has shown, the NDEA was related more to domestic political battles than Cold War agendas. The significance of Sputnik and its attendant hysteria "was not that it produced initial interest in such bills but that it disarmed opposition to federal aid."[10] The opposition reflected two domestic concerns: the possibility that unrestricted federal aid to states might be used for sectarian schools and breach the first-amendment separation of church and state; and the fear that following the 1954 Brown v. Board of Education decision, federal aid would be used to enforce the racial integration of schools.[11] These domestic battles delayed the funding of area studies programs in the United States, setting back developments that were already under way. The focus on the NDEA also obscures the role of the foundations, especially Ford and Rockefeller, which dates back to the 1930s and was of larger significance.[12]

The concerns of area studies first emerged, at least in the Middle East case, in the inter war period, and were related to developments that were simultaneously political and intellectual. As Edward Said argues, the period between the wars was characterized by a civilizational anxiety, especially in Europe, which turned in response to the study of oriental civilizations. Borrowing new ideas of total humanistic knowledge fostered by classical studies and histories of civilizations, scholars began to see in the idea of another civilization a way of exploring the contemporary challenges to the self-assurance of the West—"to the West's spirit, knowledge, and imperium."[13] In the United States, where oriental studies had begun to develop out of Biblical studies and Semitic philology, the new approach to oriental civilization was pioneered by the Egyptologist James Henry Breasted.[14] In 1919 Breasted founded the Oriental Institute of the University of Chicago, with funding from John Rockefeller, Jr. and the Rockefeller-funded General Education Board. Breasted's vision for the development of oriental studies in America was to transform it from a philological into a historical discipline "in which art, archaeology, political science, language, literature and sociology, in short all the categories of civilization shall be represented and correlated."[15]

The study of ancient "civilization" gave the field of oriental studies a broader base than its earlier formation in Bible studies. Yet the strength of the new Oriental civilization programs, typically associated with university museums, overseas archaeological missions, and the support of private benefactors, all focused on the ancient Near East, may have impeded the growth of another form of Near Eastern studies—the study of Islamic civilization. It is probably no accident that the first program to integrate the history and languages of the Islamic Near East in the United States was set up not at one of the universities with a broad commitment to the ancient Near East, such as Chicago, Columbia, Pennsylvania, or Yale, but at Princeton, where traditional Bible studies remained strong and comparative Semitics and archaeology were neglected. Princeton also had close personal connections to the Syrian Protestant College in Beirut, founded by American missionaries but by this point secularized and known as the American University of Beirut (AUB).[16] In 1927 Princeton established a Department of Oriental Languages and Literatures and brought the Lebanese historian Philip Hitti (1886–1979) from AUB as assistant professor of Semitics. "Unhampered by tradition," as he later wrote, Hitti turned the new department into the country's first program specializing in Arabic and Islamic studies. He also organized an interdepartmental Committee on Near Eastern Studies, which held three summer programs, in 1935, 1938, and 1941, sponsored by the Arabic-Islamic Committee of the American Council of Learned Societies. These offered courses on the languages, history, and culture of the Islamic Near East, intended for "historians, medievalists, Byzantinists, historians of fine arts, archaeology, and science, students of philosophy and religion and others who have become convinced of the necessity of acquiring some competence in the Arabic-Islamic phases of their respective disciplines."[17] After the wartime interruption, in 1947 the committee was institutionalized as the interdepartmental Program in Near Eastern Studies, the first U.S. area studies program devoted to region.[18]

These pre-war developments in the U.S., however, should not be separated from the more influential intellectual changes taking place in cities like Beirut itself, where Hitti taught from 1908, Cairo, Tangier, and Istanbul, and related developments in Europe. In Beirut, there was a great expansion of research at AUB on the contemporary region in this period.[19] In Tangier, the Mission Scientifique au Maroc was established by the French in 1904 and began publishing the *Revue du Monde Musulman* in 1906. In Cairo, the Socíeté d'Economie Politique was created in 1909, and began publishing research on contemporary Egypt in its review *L'Egypte Contemporaine;* and at same time the government set up a national statistics office and began to publish a statistical annual. Related developments occurred in Turkey, where the new republic established in 1923 began the publication of a statistical annual.[20]

In London, the Royal Institute of International Affairs in the 1930s commissioned a comprehensive survey of the Western impact upon the Arab world and Turkey since 1800. The authors drew up a plan for "an organic study of the life of the Moslem societies, and the force, ideals, and tendencies at work within them."[21] This plan of research and publication was a blueprint for the development of what would come to be called area studies. The overall project of "the tracing of social evolution and the bearing of this process upon present conditions"—or what would later be termed "modernization"—was divided horizontally into three time periods, reflecting the assumption that the region's history should be written in terms of its relation to the West: (i) a survey of the social institutions of Islamic society in the eighteenth century, "prior to the introduction of western influences;" (ii) an examination of the Western impact since 1800; and (iii) an investigation of present-day "conditions and forces in play."[22]

The research program further proposed twelve "vertical divisions" to break the field into manageable components, while stressing in the language of British social anthropology that "the interrelations of the various social functions" made rigid boundaries impossible. The vertical components were: the family, the village (including nomads), industry, commerce, the city, the army, government and administration, religion, education, law, slavery, and non-Muslim minorities.[23] The authors, H.A.R. Gibb and Harold Bowen, hoped eventually to produce a "synthetic study of the problems [of social evolution] as a whole, under such general heads as rationalization and the release of individuality," but pointed out that this would "occupy a whole staff of research workers for many years."[24] By 1939 they had managed to complete and send to press the first part of volume one on the eighteenth century. The outbreak of war, however, that supposed midwife of area studies, postponed its publication until 1950. The second part of volume one was delayed even further, until 1957, and the remainder of the project was abandoned.[25]

In 1950, the Royal Institute of International Affairs launched a successor project with the publication of *The Middle East: A Political and Economic Survey*. More importantly, however, Gibb and Bowen's program shaped the development of Middle Eastern studies in the U.S., including the work sponsored by the SSRC over two decades. In June 1942, Gibb traveled to the University of Chicago to speak at a conference on "The Near East: Problems and Prospects," attended by a mix of scholars of the ancient and modern Near East, foreign policy and state department officials, and representatives of corporate interests.[26] Ten years later, in October 1952, a series of papers were presented at a conference at Princeton University, "The Near East: Social Dynamics and the Cultural Setting," sponsored by the newly formed Committee on the Near and Middle East of the SSRC. The titles of the papers read like the table of contents of Gibb and Bowen's study: "the nomads," "the villager," "the industrial worker," "the bazaar merchant," "the entrepreneur class," "economic planners," "the army officer," "the clergy," "intellectuals in the modern development of the Islamic world," and "minorities in the political process."[27] The SSRC subsequently sponsored conferences and working groups on topics that began to fill in the Gibb and Bowen framework, including a meeting on Minorities in the Middle East and another (at Berkeley in 1966) on Middle Eastern Cities.[28]

Prewar proposals for an "organic" and "synthetic" study of the social evolution of the contemporary Middle East could draw upon a new generation of scholarship on the region. Besides the work conducted at research institutes in Cairo, Beirut, and other cities of the region mentioned above, a group of European sociologists and ethnographers was beginning to publish historical-ethnographic studies of the twentieth-century Arab world. These included Edmond Doutté (1867–1926), *Magie et Religion dans l'Afrique du Nord* (1908), Arnold van Gennep (1873–1957), *En Algerie* (1914), Robert Montagne (1893–1954), *La vie sociale et la vie politique du Berberes* (1931), Edward Westermark (1862–1939), *Ritual and Belief in Morocco* (1926), Winifred Blackman, *The Fellahin of Upper Egypt* (1927), Hilma Granqvist

(1890–1972), *Marriage Conditions in a Palestinian Village* (two volumes, 1931 and 1935), the early writings of Jacques Berque (1910–1995), and the work on the Sudan by the anthropologist Evans-Pritchard (1902–73), who taught at the Egyptian University in the 1920s.[29] In addition, by the end of the war a number of important economic and political-historical studies began to appear in Britain, mostly by scholars of Arab background, including Albert Hourani, George Antonius, and Charles Issawi.[30]

To this new body of literature, Orientalists such as Gibb and Bowen brought from Oriental Studies the idea that the Islamic world formed a cultural unity, based upon a common cultural core that only the Orientalist was equipped to decipher. As Gibb later argued in justifying the role of the Orientalist in area studies programs, his function "is to provide that core out of his knowledge and understanding of the invisibles . . . to explain the why, rather than the what and the how, and this precisely because he is or should be able to see the data not simply as isolated facts, explicable in and by themselves, but in the broad context and long perspective of cultural habit and tradition."[31] It is important to note that this scheme of "organic" knowledge of the Middle East as an interrelated whole did not seem, in the 1930s, to pose a problem of the relationship between area studies and the social science disciplines. The elaborate plan of vertical and horizontal divisions of the subject matter were based on a "natural principle" of demarcation according to occupational groups (the village, industry, commerce, the army, religion, and so on, all the way up to government and administration, conceived simply as another occupation). There was no separate analysis of "the state," nor of a distinct sphere called "the economy." Correspondingly, there was no theoretical or practical problem of how to relate this analysis to the distinct disciplinary domains of economics, political science, and sociology. At Oxford, where Gibb taught, these disciplines were not yet organized as separate faculties.

THE OTHER AREA STUDIES

When World War II shifted the center of gravity of academic research to the United States, two factors set back the development of Middle Eastern area studies. First, there was a rupture with the centers of research in the Arab world and the colonial ethnographers and other scholars who moved between Europe and the Middle East. The United States had no comparable scholarly base. Although wartime funds had supported crash programs in Middle Eastern languages at several U.S. universities, and individual scholars had been introduced to the Middle East through wartime service, in particular military or State Department intelligence work, it took two decades before Ford Foundation funding had produced a sizeable body of university specialists. In 1949, no American academic employed full time at any university could claim to be an expert in the economics, sociology or politics of the modern Middle East, according to an ACLS report, and only one American anthropologist was known to be conducting research on the area.[32] Historians were almost as scarce.[33]

Meanwhile, senior Orientalists had to be brought from Europe to lead the new Middle East programs and this too took time. Gibb moved from Oxford to head the Center for Middle Eastern Studies at Harvard in the mid 1950s; Gustav von Grunebaum, an earlier refugee from Vienna, moved from Chicago to head the center at UCLA; in 1956 Yale hired Franz Rosenthal, a German orientalist who had reached the U.S. in 1940; and in 1952 Berkeley appointed George Lenczowski, a French-trained Polish exile who had arrived in the U.S. in 1945.[34]

The second cause of delay was that, in contrast to the situation in prewar Europe, in the United States universities were already clearly divided into separate social science departments. The European practice of turning those trained in Oriental Studies into authorities on the modern period could not produce scholarship that qualified in the United States as social science.[35] Social scientists, on the other hand, had no training in Middle Eastern languages or history. The most influential work of social science on the region, Daniel Lerner's *The Passing of Traditional Society*, published a decade after the ACLS report in 1958, was produced by a scholar with no background in the study of the Middle East and no knowledge of its languages.[36]

However, while the division of the American academy into discrete professional disciplines impeded the study of the region, paradoxically it was also an important impetus to the development of the distinctively American phenomenon of area studies. This division of labor could trace its origins back as far as the turn of the century. But in the years either side of World War II it had taken on a new significance. In earlier decades what distinguished the disciplines was the different kinds of social questions they addressed. Economists were concerned with prices, markets, and business cycles; political scientists with public law, legislatures, and the behavior of parties and voters; and sociologists with the social problems arising from industrialization and the growth of cities. In a process beginning in the 1930s and completed by the 1950s, the social sciences transformed themselves into, as it were, a kind of area studies. Each invented an object that marked the exclusive territory of the discipline and defined its boundary with others.

The clearest example of this was provided by Economics, which from the late 1930s invented the term "the economy" as the object of its knowledge, a concept that was in general use only by the 1950s.[37] Political Science tried to do something similar by reworking the old idea of the state, but in the late 1940s and 1950s abandoned the state in favor of the more inclusive and scientistic idea of "the political system."[38] In Sociology there was a corresponding shift from the study of discrete social problems and processes to the analysis of society as a whole, or in the more elaborate Parsonian formulation, the social system. The change in Anthropology gathered momentum in same period, with Franz Boas, Ruth Benedict, Clyde Kluckhohn, A.L. Kroeber and others reorienting the discipline in the United States around a new definition of the term "culture," meaning the whole way of life of a particular country or people.[39] The word "area" was actually used at the time to refer to these newly mapped theoretical territories.[40]

These changes can be related to the professionalization of the social sciences in the middle third of the twentieth century, including the claims to scientific authority that could be built upon exclusive territorial control of new theoretical objects.[41] But they also registered and contributed to a broader political and intellectual change: what I would call the nationalization of social knowledge. Histories of nationalism focus on its origins in eighteenth and nineteenth-century Europe, and more recently on its colonial origins.[42] Yet it is easy to forget that the term "nationalism" came into common use only in the twentieth century, and that only in the interwar period did official and academic knowledge begin to picture the world as a series of nation states. With the growing strength of anti-imperialist movements in the colonial world, the collapsing of European empires, and the development by the United States of more effective forms of imperialism—in Central America and the Caribbean, the Pacific, and the Persian Gulf—based upon nominally sovereign local regimes, the globe came to be seen no longer as a network of empires but as a system of presumptively equivalent nation-states. Each geographical unit was imagined, in turn, to possess an economy, portrayed in terms of the novel statistical trope entitled national income; a self-contained political system or state; an homogenous body called society; and even a distinctive national culture. Each unit was also given a national history.

As professional, political, and academic knowledge came to see the world as a series of nation states, it also came to imagine it to consist of a series of discrete national economies, societies, cultures, and histories. The objects that now defined the intellectual territory of the social sciences had borders that coincided with those of the nation state. In the same decades as the world-encircling networks of commodities, wealth, and power came to be represented in the simplified form of a universal system of sovereign nation-states, the social science disciplines were reorganized around objects that in each case assumed the structure of the nation-state as their universal social template.

Thus the development of one form of area studies in the United States intersected with another. The attempt to construct "the Middle East" and other regions as distinct territorial objects defining a legitimate field of study crossed paths with the attempt to create "the economy," "the political system," "culture," and "society" as distinct social spaces, each taking the nation state as the its normal location and extension, and each defining the territory of a self-contained discipline.

The intersecting construction of two kinds of area study was the source of much of the importance attributed to area programs in the 1950s and 1960s. In the first place, the division of social analysis into the separate study of the economy, political system, culture and society, which seemed straightforward for the study of the United States and Europe, appeared premature for the study of the backward regions of the non-West. "Only a society that has already achieved a dynamic stability," wrote Halpern, "can afford to think of politics, economics, or culture as genuinely autonomous realms of existence and not merely convenient divisions for study. In a traditional society . . . or [one] that is entirely in flux, the connection between, say, politics and all other aspects of life is the heart of the issue." If the old tradition of Oriental Studies was no longer practical, "then the division of labor among disciplines nonetheless requires a sense of the whole—so that the common purpose of divided labor is not lost."[43] This sense of the whole was to be provided by a "new kind of Orientology," Halpern argued, in which area experts trained in the languages, history, and culture of the region would overcome the narrowness of their disciplinary focus.[44] Area studies was to compensate for the limitations of the new, professionalized social sciences.

Area studies had a second and even greater contribution to make to the development of the social sciences. Only through area studies could social science become universal. There were two ways, it was proposed, in which this contribution would be made. First, area studies would cleanse social theory of its provincialism. At a national conference on the study of world areas held in November 1947, Pendleton Herring of the Carnegie Corporation argued:

> Many specialists now interested in the study of areas have been trained in subject matter fields that are very much the product of our own Western culture. This holds particularly for economics, sociology, psychology and political science. The conceptual schemes upon which these disciplines are based are, in large measure, the product of Western thought and institutions . . . . Specialists whose training derives from this context are now attempting to apply their methods of analysis to cultures that are very different . . . . [I]f there be a provincialism within these disciplines, it will quickly be revealed when the expert applies his formulations to alien cultures."[45]

Area studies would serve as a testing ground for the universalization of the social sciences. Just as unusual data from other regions was incorporated into the natural sciences, area research was to be incorporated into the social sciences and even the humanities, "to bring comparative and concrete data to bear on generalization and theory."[46]

Second, with each social science devoted to its own area of social reality, area studies offered the means to overcome the new sense of professional isolation. For some scholars, area studies would provide the means for the social sciences to cross-fertilize one another, while retaining their territorial exclusivity as separate disciplines (something that they would risk losing if the same collaboration occurred in the study of American society). Others hoped to combine the insights of the different disciplines into what Talcott Parsons called a "total structure of scientific knowledge."[47] For these scholars, the area studies region could provide a definable whole in which the integration of the disciplines would take place. Area study was analogous to the study of medicine, Parsons suggested, the total human organism corresponding to the totality of human society. Just as the understanding of the practical problems of "the whole man" required collaboration among several sciences—"anatomy, physiology, biochemistry, bacteriology, and even psychology and some of the social sciences"—in the same way, the study of an area would provide "a concrete focus for the disciplines of the social sciences and related fields of the humanities and natural sciences."

Parsons described this integrated development of the disciplines borrowing the new language of the development of underdeveloped regions, including the same vocabulary of strategic importance. In two "comparatively new" disciplines, institutional sociology and social anthropology, the required "level of knowledge and competence is not as yet diffused, even within the professions themselves, to say nothing of diffusion to the proponents of the neighboring disciplines with which they must cooperate in area studies." Yet these newer fields provided a "fundamental bridge" between the "highly developed" disciplines of economics and political science on the one side and the developing field of psychology on the other. Sociology and anthropology were therefore "of particularly strategic importance to area studies" and it was necessary to "correct their uneven development." The geographical limits of an area would require specialists to pool their knowledge, forcing upon them the "teamwork" that would overcome this unevenness. By inducing the cooperation required for the integrated development of a total structure of knowledge, area studies "may have a profound effect on social science research."[48]

The development of area studies was not simply a reaction to the needs of the Cold War, but integral to the larger attempt to create a sovereign structure of universal knowledge—itself part of the project of a globalized American modernity to which the Cold War also belonged. It is in this larger context that I would like to place the present problem of area studies. The so-called crisis of area studies since the 1990s is better understood as a crisis in the ability of both kinds of territorial object—those of area studies and those of the social sciences—to delimit and legitimate a field of scholarship.

PROFESSIONALIZATION AND POLITICS

By 1967 a new generation of senior scholars had established Middle Eastern studies as an organized field of expertise. In December of that year the Middle East Studies Association, founded twelve months earlier by a group of fifty-one men and funded with a five-year grant of $56,000 from the Ford Foundation, held its first annual meeting in Chicago.[49] The initiative to establish MESA came from the Near and Middle Committee of the Social Science Research Council, also funded by the Ford Foundation. Morroe Berger, a Princeton sociologist and chair of the SSRC committee, became the association's first president. The MESA secretariat was housed at NYU, where NDEA funds had recently supported the creation of a Center for Near Eastern Studies. The NYU center joined eight others funded in 1959–61, at Harvard, Michigan, Princeton, John Hopkins, Portland State College, Texas, Utah, and UCLA, and three more established in the course of the 1960s, at Berkeley, Georgetown, and Pennsylvania.

Although many of these centers were still run by scholars trained in Oriental Studies, there was associated with them a growing number of senior social scientists, especially political scientists.[50] By 1967 there were tenured specialists in Middle Eastern politics at, among others, Harvard, Princeton, Michigan, UCLA, Northwestern, Chicago, Columbia, NYU, and Berkeley. (Thirty years later, there were tenured Middle East politics faculty only at the last three out of that list.) From the mid-1960s, this new generation of tenured, male social scientists began to take over the leadership of U.S. Middle Eastern studies.

If 1967 marked the full institutionalization of the Middle East field, it also marked the surfacing of new problems. In a report written in May 1967 and published in the second issue of the MESA Bulletin in November 1967, on the eve of MESA's inaugural annual meeting, Morroe Berger declared that the Middle East "has been receding in immediate political importance to the U.S. (and even in 'headline' or 'nuisance' value) relative to Africa, Latin America and the Far East."[51] As Edward Said has remarked, given the moment at which it was published, just after the June 1967 Arab-Israeli war, and even at which it was written, in the midst of the crisis leading up to the war, this was an extraordinary statement.[52] It seems to reflect something more than shortsightedness, something closer to a denial of the historical situation in which the field found itself, indicating perhaps the threat that this situation represented to the authority of the new area expertise.

As the MESA Board discussed in private, the June 1967 war had caused the cancellation of many research trips, the closing of U.S. embassies across the region, not to mention a shift in the course of the region's history. The MESA meetings held six months later did not discuss the event, however, and in fact the Board acted to prevent its discussion. A certain Mr. Shabatai proposed to present a paper on the history of the Arab-Israeli conflict, but the Board asked him "to withdraw his paper due to the sensitivity of his subject," and because, although a graduate student, he was affiliated with a foreign diplomatic service.[53] The incident was a symptom of the problems the field was beginning to face.

The authority of Middle Eastern studies was based upon its claim to a scientific status as a detached field of expertise. This claim did not require silence on political topics. Many of these experts wrote about contemporary issues, including those who supported the State of Israel, as a majority of the leading figures in the field did. What they could not easily allow was controversy among themselves, or the airing of "sensitive" issues that might produce such controversy. Controversy would perhaps reveal the precarious nature of their detachment. It would undermine the ability of scholars to speak with a single voice, from a singular position, as the authority of science and professional expertise required. It would challenge what Irene Gendzier and Vincente Rafael have in different ways described as the liberal, managerial style of knowing, with which area studies organized the problems and populations of the non-West and kept them at a safe remove.[54]

As a consequence, Middle Eastern studies tended to avoid the scholarly analysis of Israel and the issue of Palestinian rights. A review of the field in 1962 noted the relative absence of studies of Israel, while an influential *American Political Science Review* article of the same period laying out a framework for the study of the region deliberately excluded the state of Israel (and thus the Palestine question), as did Morroe Berger's *The Arab World Today* (1962).[55] At the November 1973 MESA annual meeting there was again no formal discussion of the Arab-Israeli war that had just ended.[56] In his MESA Presidential Address the following year, Leonard Binder of the University of

Chicago (an American who had fought in the Israeli army in the 1948–49 Palestine war while a student at Harvard and had begun learning Arabic when taken prisoner of war in Jordan) defended the absence of discussion of the Israeli-Palestinian conflict at the professional meetings. The silence was not because scholars had nothing to say, he explained, but was an issue of "what one may appropriately say in this context."[57]

The professionalization of Middle Eastern studies, confirmed by the founding of MESA in 1967, represented an attempt to define this "context" in which scholars could speak as scholars, and to establish what is was appropriate to say. Immediately before MESA's founding, the field's leading scholars had been embarrassed by an incident that raised questions about their academic detachment. In 1964, the journal *Middle Eastern Affairs*, launched in 1950, abruptly ceased publishing after it was discovered and publicized that it was subsidized by political sources.[58] The journal's editorial advisory board included senior Middle East scholars at Berkeley, Harvard, Yale, Columbia, and the Hebrew University of Jerusalem. Shortly afterwards, an organization called the American Association for Middle Eastern Studies, established in 1958 with an equally distinguished board of academic advisors, ceased its activities with the same abruptness, including the publication of the journal *Middle Eastern Studies* (1958–64), after it was accused of having undeclared connections with Zionist organizations.[59] AAMES published textbooks and ran summer courses to introduce college teachers to the Middle East. The courses were held in the region and divided into two parts, one in an Arab country, either Morocco or Egypt, and the other always in Israel.

The abrupt closure of these journals and associations raised the question of secret funding of Middle Eastern studies, including not only the possible role of Zionist organizations but also the part that may have been played by the United States Central Intelligence Agency.[60] Only recently has it been understood how widely the CIA influenced the production of academic and intellectual culture around the world in the second half of the twentieth century. The story of the Congress for Cultural Freedom, established by the CIA in Paris, is now well known, including its funding of the British magazine *Encounter*. The CIA's efforts extended well beyond this, to include the funding of art, music, academic and cultural congresses, books, translations, and a wide variety of journals willing to criticize Marxism or the Soviet

Union and to support, or at least remain silent on, American violence in Vietnam and other parts of the world.[61] Among the journals the agency funded overseas was an Arab counterpart to *Encounter* magazine, *al-Hiwar*, established in Beirut in the early 1960s under the editorship of a distinguished Palestinian writer, Tawfiq Sayyigh.[62] *Al-Hiwar* ceased publication in 1967 after the CIA funding of the Congress for Cultural Freedom was revealed.

No adequate research has yet been done on the extent of CIA involvement in Middle Eastern studies in the United States. A later episode involving Nadav Safran is the best known. Safran was Professor of Government at Harvard, where he taught for over thirty years. Like Binder, his counterpart at Chicago, he had served in the Israeli army in the 1948–49 Palestine war. In 1982 he received a grant of $107,430 from the CIA to carry out research on Saudi Arabia, the payment stipulating that he must keep the source of funds secret and clear the publication of his research with the agency. Although this restriction violated Harvard policy, the dean to whom he reported it raised no objection. Two years later he received a grant of $45,700 to organize a conference at Harvard on Islamic fundamentalism. News of the secret source of funds leaked out and on January 1, 1986, Safran was forced to resign as director of the Harvard Center for Middle Eastern Studies (but not as Professor of Government), not for accepting CIA funds but for failing to pay part of the grant as an overhead fee to the university.[63]

Many of the scholars who emerged as the field's first generation of social scientists around the mid-1960s had earlier connections with U.S. intelligence. William Zartman of N.Y.U. had served in naval intelligence in Morocco and developed close ties with the Moroccan armed forces. J. C. Hurewitz at Columbia, Manfred Halpern at Princeton, his colleague Morroe Berger, the Harvard anthropologist Carlton Coon, and a number of others had done intelligence research during the war or soon afterwards, some with the Office of Strategic Services (forerunner of the CIA), others at the State Department's Bureau of Research and Intelligence. None of them necessarily maintained their connections with U.S. intelligence after they became academics. Berger, however, the man who chaired the SSRC Near and Middle East Committee and became the founding President of the MESA, had also played a role in the creation of the National Defense

Education Act in 1958. As a student in New York in the late 1930s, Berger had been a member of the New York Trotskyist movement, with others like Irving Howe, Seymour Martin Lipset, and Gertrude Himmelfarb, many of whom became active anti-communists after the war and in several case moved far to the right.[64] Some of them, including the journalist Irving Kristol, the N.Y.U. philosopher Sidney Hook, and the editor of *Encounter*, Melvin Lasky, were later funded and supported by the C.I.A. Berger too had connections with the C.I.A. He was a member of the Congress for Cultural Freedom and was the scholar who recruited the editor for the Arab counterpart to *Encounter* magazine, *al-Hiwar*. The generous CIA money that he offered the prospective editor carried with it one stipulation: that the journal publish articles dealing with the position of Muslim communities in the Soviet Union.[65]

The founding of MESA so soon after the closure of the American Association for Middle Eastern Studies, and the overlap in the leadership of the two bodies, led some scholars to fear that MESA was simply a continuation of the earlier pro-Washington and pro-Israeli organization. It is not clear that there was any connection, but the suspicion persuaded a group of American scholars of Arab background to establish a rival professional organization. The 1967 war had shocked them into realizing that the scholars speaking about the Middle East in the United States, even the minority who seemed sympathetic to the Arab world, were not from the region and did not speak for the region. The Arab-American scholars began to challenge the style of academic detachment with which establishment scholars maintained both their status as experts and a silence about controversial issues, especially the Palestine question. In 1967–68 they set up the Association of Arab-American University Graduates (AAUG), which organized a series of annual conferences and publications under the leadership of Ibrahim Abu-Lughod.[66] For several years these were scheduled to conflict with the MESA meetings.

The AAUG began to contest not only the leadership of Middle Eastern studies, and its alleged professional detachment, but also its construction of the region of study. A decade later, Abu-Lughod together with Edward Said set up a research center under the auspices of the AAUG, the Institute of Arab Studies, which published the

journal *Arab Studies Quarterly* and supported research that defined the
Arab world, rather than the Middle East, as the region of study. Their
aim was challenge the premise of Middle Eastern Studies that "the
Middle East" was a single cultural region. They argued that this was a
colonial conception, which, by including Turkey and Iran with the
Arab countries, minimized the much stronger common culture of the
Arabic-speaking world. They also believed that expanding the region
to include the two non-Arab countries had made the anomalous
position of Israel, as a state established by Europeans in the midst of
the Arab world, less obvious.

THE CRISIS OF ORIENTALISM

These developments suggest the need to find an alternative way to
discuss the problems faced by area studies since the late 1960s and
early 1970s. The customary approach to the analysis of area studies
proceeds as a discussion of questions of theory. Questions about the
construction of the object of knowledge, or the relationship of U.S.
based scholars to the politics of the region, if they are discussed at all,
tend to be subsidiary to the story of the theoretical development of the
field. According to this story, the theory of modernization dominates
area studies scholarship until the late 1960s or early 1970s. It is then
challenged in the fields of history and political science by the theory of
dependency, which emerges in Latin American Studies and then is
imported into African, Middle Eastern, and other regions of area
studies. These fields attempt, with differing degrees of success, to catch
up with the theoretical advances of the Latin American field, which
itself moves on into criticisms of the dependency paradigm.

The history of Middle Eastern Studies suggests the possibility of
telling a different and more complex story, one whose narrative is not
organized in terms of the rise and decline of theories. There are several
features of the Middle East studies field that can complicate the story.
First, the Middle Eastern critique of modernization theory was first
written in the mid-1950s, more than a decade before the appearance of
dependency theory in Latin America, and indeed before the full
expression of modernization theory itself in works such as Walt
Rostow's *Stages of Economic Growth* (1960).[67] In 1957 a twenty-six year
old Egyptian defended a doctoral thesis in economics in Paris entitled

"On the Origins of Underdevelopment: Capitalist Accumulation on a World Scale." Borrowing the ideas of core and periphery from Raul Prebisch, Samir Amin gave them a new significance by arguing that the underdevelopment of the periphery is not a backward stage of development but an equally modern phenomenon of capitalist expansion and the constant "structural adjustment" (Amin's 1957 phrase) to which societies of the periphery are subjected. Capital accumulation is organized on a "world scale," he argued—two decades before Wallerstein's development of the theory of capitalism as a "world-system"—and it is on this scale that the problems of local societies should be studied.

Amin had been a student in Paris since 1947, part of a group of Arab, African, Vietnamese and other third-world students who published the journal *Étudiants anticolonialists* (1949–1953). He also contributed to the radical journal *Moyen Orient,* published in the same years under the editorship of the French Marxist Middle East scholar Maxime Rodinson. Following the completion of his thesis in 1957 Amin put the manuscript in a drawer and returned to Egypt, to engage in the post-Suez War political campaign for a more radical social transformation. In 1960 he was forced to leave Egypt, as the Nasser regime intensified its repression of the left. He spent his exile in West Africa and Paris, and in 1964 published a critique of Nasserist populism, *L'Egypte nasserienne,* under the pseudonym Hasan Riad.[68] Only in 1970, following the popularity of Latin American dependency theory, was he persuaded to publish his 1957 dissertation. The English translation, *Accumulation on a World Scale,* appeared in New York in 1974.[69]

This story begins to suggest the complexity of some of the factors that shape the "theory" that becomes, or does not become, American area studies. The encounter between the Arab world and the West created its own critique of the modernization paradigm, but under different conditions of migration and exile than those that shaped Latin American *dependencia.* The question of what Edward Said has referred to as "traveling theory"—the spatial displacements that can turn theory into critical consciousness—is an important part of the structuring of area studies. Exiled Arab intellectuals could not easily circulate from one capital of the region to another, as Latin American exiles did within their own region. In Paris they formed broader anticolonial coalitions, caught up in the 1950s struggles over Indochina and Algeria. In the urgency of such struggles, a thesis could spend a decade in a drawer.

Several other features of the Middle East studies field shaped its development in this period, yet are omitted from standard accounts written in terms of the rise and fall of theories. A second factor was the very success the field enjoyed in the U.S. academy in the 1950s and 1960s, compared to a relatively weak field like Latin American studies. The fact that eight or more of the dozen leading Political Science departments had a tenured Middle East specialist by the late 1960s may well have inhibited the development of rival paradigms. Perhaps the lower stature of Latin American scholarship gave more room for alternative views. For an established field like Middle Eastern studies, moreover, the failures of modernization by the late 1960s could be turned into another argument for the strengthening of area studies. Modernization, it was now claimed, was clearly so complex a process that its success or failure could not be the result of any one series of casual events, as scholars like Rostow had assumed. It must instead be the outcome of any one of a variety of possible combinations of a large number of factors. No single social science discipline, therefore, could provide an explanation. The problem of development could be resolved only in the interdisciplinary fields of area studies.[70]

A third factor follows from this. When dependency theory was taken up as a rival theoretical approach, it was by a cohort of junior scholars whose agenda was not simply the theoretical development of the field but the dismantling of its existing professional organization and the constructing of a new relationship between scholarship and the countries and peoples that it studied. In 1971 a group of young Middle East scholars and activists founded the Middle East Research and Information Project (MERIP), a collective that began publishing the periodical *MERIP Reports,* later renamed *Middle East Report.* At the 1977 MESA meeting members of the MERIP group and other progressives formed the Alternative Middle East Studies Seminar (AMESS) as a rival scholarly forum. MERIP and AMESS promoted political economy and dependency-related approaches to the region, the study of popular struggles and subaltern groups, a critique of the political oppression practiced by all regimes of the region and of the

corporate and government support for most of these regimes in the
United States, and the open discussion of the Israeli-Palestinian conflict
and the question of Palestinian national rights. In Europe in the same
period, the journal *Khamsin* began publishing the work of critical
Middle East scholars based mostly in Paris, Israel, and Turkey. A
group of more established scholars in Britain launched the short-lived
but influential *Review of Middle East Studies* (1975–76, with occasional
attempts at revival).[71]

Robert Vitalis, a later member of this loose network of critical
political economy scholars, argues that the belated incorporation of
dependency perspectives into Middle Eastern studies was shaped
more by the "metatheoretical" academic and intellectual commitments
of the period than by a concern for careful comparative historical
analysis. The resulting scholarship, he argues, misread the core
dependencia texts and was unfamiliar with the Latin American history
on which they were based. In the scholarship on Egypt, the country
most frequently analyzed, dependency was more a weapon in late
1970s debates about U.S. foreign policy and President Sadat's
abandoning of Nasser's statist populism and economic opening
towards the United States. Used in support of a general Third
Worldism that arose in response to the unrelenting first worldism of
establishment Middle East studies, the introduction of dependency
theory "foreclosed the possibility," Vitalis argues, of a more critical and
open-ended inquiry into social the organization and interests of
Egyptian capitalism.[72] If one accepts Vitalis's argument, then once
again it was not rival theories that drove the development of Middle
Eastern studies. Theory was a language used to authorize rival
strategies and commitments in the competing intellectual politics of
the field.[73]

The new Middle East studies scholarship included another element
that was to reshape the field. It criticized established scholarship for its
reliance on Oriental Studies and its incorporation of this work into the
study of the modern period. This critique built upon the earlier work of
Arab intellectuals published mostly in Paris, in particular Anouar
Abdel Malek's seminal essay "Orientalism in Crisis" and the essays of
Abdullah Laroui.[74] These works reflected the importance of Paris in the
intersection of different Arab exile and post-colonial itineraries. The
Algerian war of 1954–63 was an important context for the emergence of

post-colonial critiques. As Robert Young argues, the war was also a catalyst in the development of other critiques of modernity.[75] In the United States there was a related development beginning after the crisis of the 1967 war, as I mentioned, with the founding of the AAUG. Ibrahim Abu-Lughod also established a publishing house that began to publish the work of a new generation of Arab and Arab-American scholars and other like-minded critics, including the work of Edward Said, whose first writing on the U.S. and the Arab world appeared in response to the 1967 war[76] and whose critique of Orientalism was first articulated at the 1974 AAUG conference.[77] In London, the brief life of the *Review of Middle East Studies,* which emerged from the meetings of the Hull group, in which Talal Asad played a pivotal role, was devoted largely to essays critiquing the work of modern Orientalists such as Von Grunebaum, Bernard Lewis, Kedourie, and Gibb and Bowen. Asad himself had published an important collection of critical essays, *Anthropology and the Colonial Encounter* (1973).[78]

By that time, the link between Orientalism and area studies was already in question, even among its advocates. In 1974, the same year as Said's AAUG address, a short essay about Morocco, destined to be influential, rejected the theory of culture that had bought together Orientalists and social scientists.[79] In his MESA presidential address of that year, Leonard Binder, without mentioning Clifford Geertz by name, attacked the new view that "rejects anthropology's favored functionalism and argues that a culture is simply what it says it is."[80] Showing a new defensiveness, he praised the achievements of Orientalist scholarship but talked of the need to move beyond its limitations. And he put forward a new justification for area studies:

> In my own opinion area studies rest upon a single key idea and that is that the object of study, the thing we want to know, is the determining and organizing principle of the intellectual enterprise and not the method or discipline. Research methodology and disciplinary paradigms are not to determine what is selected for study, and they are not to limit observation. Area studies, from this perspective, holds that true knowledge is only possible of things that exist, while methods and theories are abstractions which order observations and other explanations according to non-empirical criteria . . . The question . . . is whether Middle Eastern events constitute a valid unity so that the consequence of their study could reasonably be called knowledge (4–5).[81]

The Middle East represents a field for the organization of scholarship simply because it is one of the "things that exist" and therefore an object of "true knowledge." There is no longer any grand theoretical scheme of total science that creates a reason for area studies. There is simply an empirical claim.

Three years later Said's *Orientalism* appeared, and repudiated this claim that the Middle East was simply an empirical fact. "But how does one know the 'things that exist,'" he asked after referring to Binder's address, and to what extent are they *"constituted* by the knower?"[82]

The publication of *Orientalism* put establishment Middle East studies on the defensive. It also opened the path to postcolonial theory, which offered the possibility of a form of area studies that did not treat the region as a "thing that exists" but explored in the representation of the non-West fundamental questions about Western ways of knowing and the project of a general social science. This possibility was most clearly developed in the field of South Asian studies.[83] Post-colonial theory engaged with the disciplines of history and anthropology (as well as literature), from which and into which its practitioners were drawn, but largely ignored the more nomothetic social sciences and the field of political economy they considered their own. In these disciplinary fields (political science, economics, parts of sociology) there was no corresponding preoccupation with the historical and social construction of the field of knowledge.

By 1978, then, the area studies field that had been professionally organized only a decade or so earlier was threatened on several sides. The assumption of a underlying and determining Middle Eastern cultural unity, the character of the Oriental Studies scholarship from which this assumption was drawn, the intellectual grounds that had enabled area studies to claim to unify the social sciences, the detached, managerial style of knowing to which the field laid claim, and its silences on the question of the Israeli-Palestinian conflict except where it could speak with an unchallenged expertise: all these features that had shaped Middle Eastern studies were now under interrogation. At the same time, the social sciences had begun to lose interest in area studies. They were developing new, non-territorial ways to affirm their credentials as scientific endeavors. They had lost the territorial ambition to become total sciences, by covering every part of social space—an ambition that had given area studies an integrating role. They now sought to establish their scientific status by their methodological rigor, a concern that would move them away from rather than towards the area studies programs.

THE CRISIS OF SOCIAL SCIENCE

The crisis of area studies at the close of the twentieth century was usually understood as the problem of how area fields were related to the academic disciplines. Typically, however, it was only one partner to this relationship that was considered the source of the trouble. Area studies scholars were told that their problems would be solved by getting back together with their disciplinary partners and accepting their authority. Reviews of the state of Middle Eastern studies, as of other regions, even those written by the more critical figures in the field, perhaps especially those, ended with appeals for area scholars to return to their disciplinary homes. The disciplines were more serious sites of scholarship, and most of them, it was said, "can claim to be more universal."[84] Yet it is in fact this claim to represent the universal that is in question in the authority of the disciplines. The future of area studies lies in their ability to disturb the disciplinary claim to universality and the particular place this assigns to areas.

The grounds on which the social science disciplines laid claim to their authority had changed from the situation fifty years ago when U.S. area studies first emerged.[85] Since the 1970s, the disciplines had gradually had to abandon the attempt to define themselves by asserting academic sovereignty over a particular area of social reality. Anthropologists had lost some time ago their confidence that cultures were something that could be located as distinct, coherent, total ways of life, handily coterminous with a particular nation state.[86] For political scientists, especially those outside the field of American politics, an effort was made in the 1970s and 1980s to reintroduce the idea of the state as the central object of the discipline. The attempt failed and no other object provided the discipline with a territorial focus.[87] Economists by the 1970s had abandoned their collective faith in Keynes, who had provided them with a common language for talking about "the economy." There was no subsequent agreement on whether the economy as a whole or individual rationality was the proper object of economic analysis and the economy itself became increasingly difficult to measure or demarcate.[88] Sociology had long ago accepted its status as a collection of subfields, many of which shared their territories with parts of other disciplines.

The inability of culture, the state, the economy, or society to survive as distinct territories of social scientific investigation—what one might call the deterritorialization of the disciplines—reflected another, related deterritorialization, that of contemporary global history. The confidence of the postwar period that cultures, economies, and social and political systems could each be the object of a separate social science represented an unexamined confidence in the total, self-enclosed, geographically fixed form of the nation-state as the assumed space of all social scientific inquiry. It was, after all, the nation-state that provided the whole of which economy, culture, state, and society were the components parts. Many, probably most, of the difficulties with the ideas of culture, society, state, and economy that emerged in the final decades of the century related to processes, identities, and forces that challenged or outreached the nation-state.

There was an irony here. Transnational forces and identities were said to be one of the major factors placing the future of area studies in question. A region such as the Middle East could no longer be assumed to define a legitimate field of study, it was argued, because so many of the forces of contemporary globalization transcended or cut at right angles to such a region. However, the same deterritorialization had, in a different way, undermined the ability of the social science disciplines to demarcate distinct territories for inquiry. Yet the Social Science Research Council did not call for the dismantling of the disciplines,[89] and very little effort was made to connect the future of area studies to the very real questions about the current crisis and future shape of the social sciences.

The response of the social sciences to this experience of deterritorialization was to rely increasingly on another means of defining their distinctiveness. They identified themselves by their method. For anthropologists and economists, the concepts of culture and economy had from the beginning come to correspond to distinctive methods of research—participant observation in one case, the mathematical representation of individual or collective equilibria in the other. In Economics, moreover, field research was left others: it was mostly conducted outside the academy, by statistical agencies of the state. Following deterritorialization, despite frequent disputes about how these methods should be carried out, and despite experiments with various alternatives at the margins, both fields maintained a consensus that participant observation and equilibrium analysis, respectively, whatever their difficulties, defined the essence of the discipline. Political science and sociology were less fortunate, unable to agree on a method, and increasingly divided by the effort of certain factions to identify the discipline in terms of one particular method.

The concurrent problems of area studies programs arose to a significant extent from this crisis in the social sciences. They arose particularly from the problems faced by Political Science. Although the course of every social science discipline affected what happened to area studies, anthropology and economics presented fewer problems. This was because in anthropology (as in history and literature) everyone was an area expert, while in economics no one was. So neither discipline typically presented its practitioners with the choice between being an area expert or a theorist. In economics you were always the latter (in different degrees of purity), in anthropology you aspired to be both. Sociology continued to be so focused on North America and Western Europe that it remained slightly removed from the debates over area studies, as least as regards a region as neglected as the Middle East. That left political science.

Political science was in an unusual position. A dominant coalition within the discipline sought the intellectual certainty and professional authority of a universal knowledge of politics. Within this coalition a powerful group, which began to control many of the leading departments, believed the formal methods of micro-economics provided the best or even the only means to this universal knowledge. Unlike economists, however, these political scientists could not rely upon the statistical agencies of the state (along with U.N. bodies and the international financial agencies) to carry out their field research for them. This was partly because such agencies concentrated on collecting economic rather than political facts, and partly because the extension of economic methods to the study of political questions very quickly began to involve those messy local details that economists liked to leave aside as so-called externalities. The result was that even the most (self-styled) theoretical of political scientists found it difficult to abandon the need for the kind of local political understanding traditionally supplied by area research. The project of a general social science still had a need for some kind of area studies.

These developments in political science had an implication for area studies. Foreign area studies would not be abandoned, it was said, but would be encouraged by and incorporated into political science. They would be incorporated, however, only as sources of the local and particular knowledge required for constructing the universal knowledge of the discipline. "We should engage more directly with this work [rational choice theory]," wrote David Laitin, "continually tantalizing theorists with uncomfortable data," and "us[ing] our area knowledge to discover interesting anomalies."[90] This procedure governed both the terms in which and the extent to which area studies was to be appropriated.

Two kinds of terminology became particularly common for establishing the particularity of foreign regions in relation to the generality of political science, the new language of "institutional outcomes" and the older one of "culture". The term "institutional outcome" refers to the assumption that some universal process of change governs the politics and history of non-Western regions, such as the process of development, democratization, globalization, or the introduction of free markets. The pure logic of these processes is locally inflected, however, by the existence of particular coalitions of interest groups, economic distortions, cultural factors, or other anomalies, which shape what is called the "institutional form" of the universal phenomenon.

The other term commonly used for expressing local difference was the old idea of culture. In fact "institutions" was in many uses simply an updated way of talking about cultures. The concept of an institution, understood as a set of rules or constraints that set limits to human action, had the advantage of appearing more compatible with the assumption that action itself was not a cultural process but the universal attempt to maximize individual utility. Both culture and institution, however, referred to those aspects of the social world that could not be explained as simply the actions of individuals maximizing their self-interest, and for this reason were often equivalent. "Cultures," Robert Bates explained, "are distinguished by their distinctive institutions."[91] In the later 1990s, the two terms were brought together under the name of "social capital," which rapidly became the catch-all word for every kind of cultural inheritance, social norm, and institutional practice that could not be reduced to expressions of individual self-interest.

The importance of terms like culture, institution, and social capital, was that by locating the sphere of the local, the particular, and the contingent, they referred to and guaranteed a separate sphere of the universal. This sometimes required political scientists to content themselves with a rather narrow understanding of terms such as culture. Bates, for example, refers to "the political significance of culture and the producers of culture: artists, priests and intellectuals."[92] Bates was no doubt aware that more than half a century earlier social theorists had broadened the concept of culture to refer not just to the "high culture" of religion, art, and literature but to encompass the whole way of life of a community, or the shared meanings out of which that life is formed. Even if the term was defined to exclude local, interpersonal forms of culture and restricted to the organized expression of ideas defining the public sphere of collective political life, or what was sometimes now termed "public culture," its range would include music, fashion, film, cuisine, advertising, sport, magazines, political debate, popular fiction, television, computer software, and the internet, among other things.[93] The "producers" of this public culture are diverse, and include some of the world's largest transnational corporations—whose prosperity has increasingly come to depend on the power to define, copyright, and manage the production of cultural forms. But political science tended to retain an older definition of culture, compatible with terms like "social capital," that predates the rise of its corporatized, twentieth-century forms. The reference to the producers of culture as "artists, priests, and poets" reflects this understanding. The older definition keeps culture as the residual and secondary phenomenon, distinct from the universal forms of economic or self-interested action, that the nomothetic methods of this form of political science require.

These considerations also governed the extent to which the study of non-Western regions could become incorporated into the discipline, and the circumstances under which this might occur. A review of work in Middle East political economy asked about "the mysterious alchemy through which world regions escape the confines of area studies and achieve legitimate status in general debates about development and underdevelopment."[94] The alchemy is less mysterious once one acknowledges the force of the term "general" in the question. World regions will be incorporated when, and, to the extent that, they can be made part of certain general narratives: a narrative about industrialization, about democratization, and so on. This is illustrated in the essay by Bates. The problem of studying world regions in political science is the problem of finding a "shared vision," he suggests, a consensus as to what constitutes meaningful research and normal science in the field. He argues that three potential research frameworks exist in the field: first (for studying middle income countries), democratic theory; second, the political economy of growth; and third, social theory, which examines "contemporary appeals to religion, ethnicity, and identity."[95] Bates is no doubt correct that only by fitting within such a consensus does area studies work get read by scholars of other regions. Each of these frameworks (even the third, as I discuss below) provides a way of incorporating the non-West into a universal story, whose narrative is always that of global history, which means the history of the West.

The consequence of this relationship between discipline and world region, then, is that the object of study remains defined and grasped only in terms of its relationship to the West, and only in terms of its place in a narrative defined in terms of the global history of the West.

THE MIDDLE EAST AND THE PROVINCIALIZING OF POLITICAL SCIENCE

It would not be possible within the space of this essay to give an adequate survey of the state of Middle Eastern Studies at the end of the twentieth century, or to do justice to the range of debates and research projects that animate the field or examine the place of these debates within larger intellectual discussions.[96] Since the relationship between area studies and disciplines is posed as a particular problem within political science, as I have just suggested, I will focus there, and in particular consider writings on political economy. Even within this narrower topic I do not aim to survey the state of the field. I will consider two or three examples, as illustrations of how the problem of discipline and area is resolved.

Modernization theory remains the dominant framework. The major synthetic study of the region's political economy, by Alan Richards and John Waterbury, states quite plainly the governing assumption that Europe provides the history against which all other histories will be measured, and other histories are to be understood as belated efforts to replicate, more or less successfully, the stages of Europe's history:

> Europe's structural transformation over a number of centuries from an agrarian to an industrial urban base has shaped our general understanding of the process [of development] but has not provided a model that will be faithfully replicated in developing countries. The latter may skip some stages by importing technology or telescope others. Developing countries will cope with population growth rates that Europe never confronted. So too, the process of class formation in the Middle East and elsewhere has varied considerably from that of Europe.[97]

The standard criticisms of this approach, from the perspective of capitalism as a structure of accumulation that was global from the beginning, have been written often enough and do not need repeating. I wish to simply make the following point. The authors claim that they are not taking the West as a model that can be faithfully replicated. Exactly so. They are taking it as a model that *cannot* be faithfully replicated. It is the failures, variations, skipped stages, and telescoped histories—all the forms of difference from the West, the "anomalies" to which David Laitin refers—that define the understanding of the region's history and politics. Historical itineraries, political forces, and cultural phenomenon will be included in the story principally in terms of how they cause the Middle East to fit or deviate from the narrative of the West's modernity. This is not simply a question of what is included or omitted. The story is a universal one of modernization, "a process that has a logic of its own" as Richards and Waterbury affirm.[98] This logic moves the narrative forward, representing the source of historical change and the motor of social transformations. The local variations, distortions, delays, and accelerations receive their meaning and relevance from this singular logic. They may divert or rearrange the movement of history, but are not themselves that universal movement. This is modernization theory without apologies. "One might object that all this is simply 'closet modernization theory,'{hrs}" Richards and Waterbury acknowledge, but the defensive tone is quickly abandoned. "If this be modernization theory, make the most of it!"[99]

Conventional modernization theory of this sort analyzes the political economy of the Middle East in terms of two simple, universal concepts: the state and the economy. In place of the complex workings of political power at different levels and in different social fields, it substitutes the narrow idea of the state and analyzes politics as the formulation and execution of a limited range of economic programs and reforms. The narrative assesses the success of these programs by describing changes in the size and structure of "the economy" as represented by conventional measures of GDP, sectoral balance, share of world trade, and so on.

A number of more critical works have explored some of the problems with this approach. Simon Bromley points out that the distinction between state and economy cannot be taken for granted in studying a region such as the Middle East. Following Karl Polanyi, he recalls that establishing this distinction was a central feature of the history of advanced capitalism in the West. The distinction removed the process of appropriating surplus value from the contested sphere of politics and increasingly confined it to the organization of economic life. Yet Bromley's critique turns out to have important limitations. Having reminded us that the separation of the economic and the political is not a universal phenomenon, Bromley assumes that the Middle East should nevertheless be understood in the same terms. The struggle to consolidate the separation of state and market "has been a large part of what the history of these societies has been about," he writes. It remains, however, "unfinished business." The positive step of provincializing categories that social science takes as universal (and as marking even the boundaries between the disciplines of universal social scientific knowledge) is undone by taking the formation of these social categories as the framework in which to understand the history of the non-west. This history then inevitably appears unfinished.[100]

Interpreting Middle Eastern histories as incomplete or even simply variant cases of universal processes can produce unusual readings of political developments. Kiren Chaudhry has been one of the most serious advocates of the need to reinsert the study of the Middle East into the general field of political economy, where it could become, she believes, "an important piece of the development puzzle."[101] In a well received study of state formation in Saudi Arabia and Yemen, she too follows Polanyi in understanding the creation of the national state as simultaneously the creation of a national economy, a process that matches "the broadest sequencing patterns of state-making in early modern Europe," with important local variations.[102] Yet to make the history of the Arabian peninsular fit the sequences of modern Europe requires a peculiar reading of that history. As in Europe, Chaudhry argues, state and national economy were built upon the development of taxation. To claim this, however, as Robert Vitalis points out, a variety of financial relationships specific to the history of Arabia—pilgrim revenues, British and U.S. subventions, extortions from merchants, advances on petroleum royalties—must be described as taxes.[103] And ARAMCO, the US oil consortium that created large parts of the Saudi state as extensions of its oil business, receives no more than a passing mention. The conclusion to Chaudhry's study acknowledges, realistically enough, that despite the aspiration to place the Middle East into a general narrative of modernization and development, no general statements about "the development puzzle" can be derived from her cases. Institutional outcomes, she admits, "can co-vary in highly irregular ways that cannot be captured in any formulaic fashion."[104] The foreign capital that transformed her two cases of state formation following the 1970s oil boom produced "both similarities and differences of institutional outcome." These outcomes "depend on a host of historically constituted relationships."[105]

Such examples could be multiplied. What they show is that, on present evidence, reinserting Middle East area studies into the generalizing languages of political economy does not produce any increase in a universal knowledge of politics. It may help undermine some of the unsupportable generalization of others, as Chaudhry shows convincingly in the case of the new institutional literature. But such general theories are usually adequately critiqued when they first appear.[106] The generalizations survive simply as unsupported "theories" to be endlessly refuted, long after they are dead, in area studies scholarship.

Writing about the politics of the Middle East as part of a general science of politics functions largely as a rhetorical device, providing linguistic markers of one's seriousness of purpose and scientific credentials. The phrasing of sentences and the titles of books constantly resituate the historical account as simply a specific instance of a set of vaguely specified universal phenomena. A particular case, it is said, "exposes the importance of domestic contingencies," while another shows that "[c]apitalists, disunited, can undo the efforts of nascent state builders," and so on.[107]

And there is, as I have been suggesting, a significant loss if one allows the authority of the social science disciplines to persuade us that the only worthwhile ways of engaging with the politics and history of other world regions is to the extent that they can be made to appear as particular instances of the universal stories told in and about the West. The language of political economy and the market now represent, as a contemporary form of modernization theory, the universal truth to which all local experiences must be related, and into whose language all local political expression must be translated. Chaudhry, for example, proposes as a model research project for further development of the field of Middle Eastern political economy a study of "ideational landscapes of economic deprivation."[108] Noting the great number of social movements across the region today involved in different forms of moral protest and struggles over political identity and community, she proposes a comparative study to examine, in these differences, the variety of ways in which "local economic and political interests are expressed in the language of religion and identity." She adds that "these different reactions promise insight into fundamental alterations in the relationship between economic and political organization, between government and citizens."[109] In other words, the diversity of languages in which communities articulate their political demands and identities, their visions and their apprehensions, are to be translated into the universal language of political economy. As Dipesh Chakrabarty points out in a different context, what this amounts to saying is that one has nothing to learn from what these subaltern groups are actually saying. The languages of political Islam, for example, can appear in Western scholarship only through a process of translation that enables them to speak in terms of the modernizing discourse of the West. There is no way around this problem of translation. But those anxious to contribute to the universal knowledge of the social sciences seldom seem to recognize it as a problem.[110]

The local forms of political organization and expression are understood as mere languages, meaning the cultural and "ideational" forms for expressing the more real interests that shape their world. The language into which these expressions are translated, political economy, is assumed by definition not to be an ideational form, not a cultural practice, but the transparent and universal terminology of economic reality. Thus, in discussing the economic crises in terms of which these cultural responses will be analyzed, Chaudhry notes that, "[t]hrough economic liberalization, domestic constituencies long protected from international prices experienced the *genuine* scarcities of their heretofore protected societies."[111] The prices of a protected national market are false, it is implied, those of the international market are genuine. Both markets, both sets of scarcities, however, are political arrangements, reflecting the enforcement of certain constructions and distributions of property, power, monopoly and social management. Both can exist only, if one wants to use the term, as ideational landscapes—that is, as arrangements formed in part out of understandings about property, wealth, prices, and so on. Political economy itself plays an important role in formulating and framing these understandings. Yet because the market, and especially the global market, is understood as a universal form, it cannot by definition be something "cultural," something locally made. The cultural refers to the particular and local, the province of area studies, not to the genuine and universal, the province of those other area programs, the social sciences.

The proposal that Middle Eastern area studies be strengthened by bringing them back under the authority and vision of the social sciences has been made at regular intervals. It reflects the larger desire that was expressed in the origins of area studies. During the consolidation of professional American social science between the 1930s to the 1950s, area studies programs were called into being to provide a supplement to social science, a supplement that would help make it whole. The ambition to create forms of social science whose knowledge expressed universal truths required the study of non-western regions, both to reveal any "provincialism within these disciplines," as Pendleton Herring argued in 1947, and to provide the physical "body" whose study could provide the living organism that would bring the separate disciplines together and overcome their new isolation. The professionalization of area studies was accomplished by the mid-1960s, yet from the same moment the impossibility of the project began to reveal itself. This impossibility, this resistance, did not appear so much at the level of what is called theory, although one can trace it at that level. It made itself felt in other ways, in careers, wars, organizations, problems over funding and so on. Scholars from the region of study, finding in their own lives the experience of being simultaneously scholars and objects of study, began to raise questions about the construction of the region as an object of study. Far more effectively than mere theory, these circulations of ideas, political forces, refugees, armies, and exiles began to dislocate the claim that area studies made to a disinterested, managerial expertise. More clearly, perhaps, than any other field, the crisis of area studies produced ways of grasping the conditions of possibility and the limits of Western social science.

Area studies has no compelling future as merely the servant of the American social sciences. In the 1990s, as we saw, area studies were called upon to "tantalize" the social sciences with uncomfortable data. To tantalize—to excite by offering something desirable, perhaps unobtainable—was the old role of the Orient in the Western imagination. Fifty years earlier, the disciplines hoped that areas studies would reveal the existence of provincialism in the social sciences, and enable them to overcome it. Area studies has taken up the theme of provincialism, but explored it in a different way. Chakrabarty has called for a writing of history that would "provincialize Europe," scholarship that re-writes the history of modernity as something contested and ambivalent, and make visible its repressions, marginalizations, and its necessary incompleteness. I have tried to suggest here a similar future for area studies: to provincialize the social sciences. Area studies offers a place from which to rewrite the history of the social sciences, and to examine how their categories are implicated in a certain history of Europe and, in the twentieth century, an unachieved American project of universal social science.

Timothy Mitchell is a Professor of Politics at New York University.

Notes

An earlier version of some sections of this essay also appear in "Deterritorialization and the Crisis of Social Science," in *Localizing Knowledge in a Globalizing World: Re-Casting the Area Studies Debate,* ed. Ali Mirsepassi, Amrita Basu, and Frederick Weaver (Syracuse University Press, 2003). Omnia Elshakry provided extensive assistance with the research for the paper. David Ludden, Robert Vitalis, and the late Ibrahim Abu-Lughod, gave advice. Alice Diaz, Michael DiNiscia, and Kristine McNeil also provided help. The author alone is responsible for the views expressed.

1. *Middle East Journal,* 1, no. 1 (Jan. 1947), 1–2.
2. Ibid., 2.
3. Ibid., 4.
4. James Bill, "The Study of Middle East Politics 1946–1996: A Stocktaking," *Middle East Journal* 50, no. 4 (Autumn 1996): 501–512.
5. Leonard Binder, "Area Studies: A Critical Reassessment," *The Study of the Middle East: Research and Scholarship in the Humanities and Social Sciences,* ed. Leonard Binder (New York: John Wiley and Sons, 1976), 1–28, at 16.
6. Manfred Halpern, "Middle Eastern Studies: A Review of the State of the Field with a Few Examples," *World Politics* 15 (October 1962): 108–122, at 117, 118.
7. The quotations in this paragraph are from Halpern, "Middle Eastern Studies," 121; Binder, "Area Studies," 19; Bill, "The Study of Middle East Politics," 501.
8. Stanley Heginbotham, "Rethinking International Scholarship: The Transition from the Cold War Era," *Items: Newsletter of the SSRC* 48, no. 2/3 (1994): 33–40. Critical studies of the Middle East have usually related its genesis to World War II and the Cold War. See Peter Johnson and Judith Tucker, "Middle East Studies Network in the United States," *MERIP Reports* 38 (1975): 3–20; Irene L. Gendzier, *Managing Political Change: Social Scientists and the Third World* (Boulder, Colo.: Westview Press, 1985); Lisa Hajjar and Steve Niva, "(re) Made in the USA: Middle East Studies in the Global Era," *Middle East Report* no. 205 (October/December 1997): 2–9.
9. Robert Hall, *Area Studies, with Special Reference to Their Implications for Research in the Social Sciences* (New York: Social Science Research Council, 1947); Vicente Rafael, "The Cultures of Area Studies in the United States," *Social Text* 41 (Winter 1994): 91–111. Rafael draws on Hall's influential report. On the prewar development of studies of the non-West see Frederick Cooper, "Modernizing Bureaucrats, Backward Africans, and the Development Concept," in *International Development and the Social Sciences: Essays on the History and Politics of Knowledge,* ed. Frederick Cooper and Randall Packard (Berkeley: University of California Press, 1997), 64–92.
10. Barbara Barksdale Clowse, *Brainpower for the Cold War: The Sputnik Crisis and National Defense Education Act of 1958* (Greenwood Press: Westport, Connecticut, 1981), 49. See also Rafael, "The Cultures of Area Studies.".
11. Clowse, *Brainpower for the Cold War,* 42–43.
12. Before the passing of the NDEA, Ford established the Foreign Area

Fellowships Program (1951) and a Division of International Training and Research (1952), with a mandate to establish university area studies centers. By the time it was terminated in 1966, the Division had awarded grants of $270 million to 34 universities. By comparison, cumulative NDEA funding of area studies centers from 1959 to 1987 amounted to only $167 million (of which 13.4 percent, or about $22 million, was allocated to Middle Eastern studies). Besides Middle East area studies centers, Ford also funded the establishing of the Center for Arabic Studies in Cairo (for language training), and the Middle East Technical University in Ankara (for training a regional managerial class), among other institutions. R. Bayly Winder, "Four Decades of Middle Eastern Study," *Middle East Journal* 41, no. 1 (1987): 40–63, at 54–55. The NDEA figures are calculated from table 4. They do not include amounts allocated for Foreign Language and Area Studies Fellowships.

13. Edward Said, *Orientalism* (New York: Pantheon, 1978), 248.

14. The emergence of ancient Near Eastern studies in the United States, in the period between the 1880s and 1930s, lies outside the scope of this essay. Bruce Kuklick traces how nineteenth-century German "higher criticism," which questioned the historical veracity of the Bible, prompted American biblical scholars, beginning at the University of Pennsylvania in the late 1880s, to mount the first scientific archaeological expeditions to Mesopotamia and the Nile Valley. These moved the focus of research away from ancient Palestine, and led to the creation of ancient Near Eastern studies outside the framework of Bible studies. *Puritans in Babylon: The Ancient Near East and American Intellectual Life, 1880–1930* (Princeton: Princeton University Press, 1996).

15. Robert McCaughey, *International Studies and Academic Enterprise* (New York: Columbia University Press, 1984), 101.

16. Winder, "Four Decades of Middle Eastern Study," 43–44.

17. Philip K. Hitti, "Arabic and Islamic Studies at Princeton University," *Muslim World* 31, no. 3 (1941): 292–4, quotations from 293 and 294.

18. James Kritzeck and R. Bayly Winder, "Philip K. Hitti," in *The World of Islam: Studies in Honour of Philip K. Hitti,* ed. James Kritzeck and R. Bayly Winder (London: Macmillan, 1960); Winder, "Four Decades of Middle Eastern Study," 41–43.

19. For example, see the bibliographies of literature dealing with the Mandate territories since 1919, published in the 1930s under the auspices of American University in Beirut (Social Science Series).

20. See also Dale F. Eickelman, *The Middle East and Central Asia: An Anthropological Approach,* 3rd ed. (Upper Saddle River, N.J.: Prentice Hall 1998), chap. 2.

21. Sir Hamilton Gibb and Harold Bowen, *Islamic Society and the West: A Study of the Impact of Western Civilization on Moslem Culture in the Near East,* issued under the auspices of the Royal Institute of International Affairs, vol. 1, part 1 (London: Oxford University Press, 1950); vol. 1, part 2 (London: Oxford University Press, 1957). See also H.A.R. Gibb, *Whither Islam?* (1932).

22. Gibb and Bowen, *Islamic Society and the West,* vol.1, part 1, 3.

23. Ibid., 4–14.

24. Ibid., 13–14.

25. Gibb and Bowen, *Islamic Society and the West*, vol.1, part 2.

26. *The Near East: Problems and Prospects*, Proceedings of the Eighteenth Institute of the Norman Wait Harris Memorial Foundation, University of Chicago, Chicago, Illinois, June 25–30 1942.

27. The program included four other topics: the Israeli farmer, the immigrant in Israel, the Palestine Arab refugee, and the crisis in the Near East, each reflecting the events of 1948–49. This willingness to include the study of Israel and the Palestine question as a normal part of an academic conference was soon to disappear, as I note below. The conference papers were published in Sidney N. Fisher, ed., *Social Forces in the Middle East* (Ithaca: Cornell University Press, 1955).

28. Morroe Berger "Middle Eastern and North Africa Studies: Development and Needs," *MESA Bulletin* vol. 1 no. 2, November 15 1967, 1–18, at 8; Elbridge Sibley, *Social Science Research Council: The First Fifty Years* (New York: Social Science Research Council, 1974). The papers of the 1966 SSRC conference were published in Ira Lapidus, ed., *Middle Eastern Cities: A Symposium on Ancient, Islamic, and Contemporary Middle Eastern Urbanism* (Berkeley: University of California Press, 1969); papers from another SSRC conference, in June 1967, were published in Michael A. Cook, ed., *Studies in the Economic History of the Middle East: From the Rise of Islam to the Present Day* (London and New York: Oxford University Press, 1970).

29. Edmond Doutté, *Magie et Religion dans l'Afrique du Nord* (Algiers: Jourdan, 1908); Arnold van Gennep, *En Algerie* (Paris: Mercure de France, 1914); Robert Montagne, *La vie sociale et la vie politique des Berberes* (1931); Edward Westermark, *Ritual and Belief in Morocco* (1926); Winifred Blackman, *The Fellahin of Upper Egypt: Their Religious, Social and Industrial Life To-day with Special Reference to Survivals from Ancient Times* (1927); Hilma Granqvist, *Marriage Conditions in a Palestinian Village* , 2 vols. (Helsinki: Finska vetenskaps-soceteten, 1931 and 1935); and Edward Evan Evans-Pritchard, *Witchcraft, Oracles, and Magic Among the Azande* (Oxford: The Clarendon Press, 1937), and *The Nuer, a Description of the Modes of Livelihood and Political Institutions of a Nilotic People* (Oxford: The Clarendon Press, 1940) (neither of which dealt with an Arabic-speaking community). Also important was the work of Hans Kohn on nationalism: *Geschichte der Nationalen Bewegung im Orient* (Berlin 1928), Eng. trans., *A History of Nationalism in the East* (New York, Harcourt, Brace and Co., 1929) and *Nationalismus und Imperialismus im Vorderen Orient* (Frankfurt 1931), Eng. trans., *Nationalism and Imperialism in the Hither East* (New York, Harcourt, Brace and Co., 1932). On the scholarship of this period, see Eickelman, *The Middle East and Central Asia*, chap. 2; Jean-Claude Vatin, ed., *Connaissances du Maghreb: Sciences Sociales et Colonisation* (Paris: Editions du CNRS, 1984); Talal Asad, ed., *Anthropology and The Colonial Encounter* (London: Ithaca Press, 1973); and three essays by Edmund Burke: "La mission scientifique au Maroc," in *Actes de Durham: Recherches recentes sur le Maroc moderne* (Rabat: Publication du

Bulletin Économique et Social du Maroc, 1979), 37–56, "The Sociology of Islam: The French Tradition," in *Islamic Studies: A Tradition and Its Problems*, ed. Malcolm H. Kerr (Malibu: Undena Publications, 1980), 73–88, and "The First Crisis of Orientalism, 1890–1914," in Vatin, *Connaissances*, 213–26.

30. A.H. Hourani, *Syria and Lebanon* (London 1946), George Antonius, *The Arab Awakening* (1946), Charles Issawi, *Egypt: An Economic and Social Analysis* (London: Oxford University Press, 1947), Majid Khadduri, *Independent Iraq, a Study in Iraqi Politics since 1932* (London: Oxford University Press, 1951), Afif Tannous, *The Arab Village Community in the Middle East* (Washington, D.C.: Smithsonian Institution, 1944), Alfred Bonné, *State and Economics in the Middle East: A Society in Transition* (London: Routledge and Kegan Paul, 1948), Bernard Augustus Keen, *The Agricultural Development of the Middle East* (London: H.M. Stationary Office, 1946).

31. H. A. R. Gibb, *Area Studies Reconsidered* (London: School of African and Oriental Studies, 1964), cited in Peter Johnson and Judith Tucker, "Middle East Studies Network in the United States," *MERIP Reports* no. 38 (1975): 3–20, at 7.

32. American Council of Learned Societies, *A Program for Near Eastern Studies in the United States* (Washington D.C. 1949), cited Winder, "Four Decades of Middle Eastern Study," 45. According to Winder, the anthropologist was probably Carlton Coon. Coon's writings included *Tribes of the Rif* (1931); *Southern Arabia: A Problem for the Future* (1944), *Caravan: The Story of the Middle East* (1951), and *The Impact of the West on Middle Eastern Social Institutions* (1952).

33. The only established historian in the U.S. who worked in any of the languages of the region was Philip Hitti at Princeton. Hamilton Gibb wrote in 1956 that "In England and France there are at most only three or four Orientalist scholars who are professional historians . . . In the United States it would be hard to find as many." H.A.R. Gibb, "Problems of Modern Middle Eastern History," in Middle East Institute, *Report on Current Research* (Washington D.C.: Middle East Institute, 1956), cited Halpern, "Middle Eastern Studies," 119.

34. Several other leading European-trained Oriental Studies scholars came to the U.S., including scholars of Islamic art (Richard Ettinghausen, Oleg Grabar), Islamic law (Joseph Schacht), and religion (Wilfred Cantwell Smith) and, in the mid 1970s, the historian Bernard Lewis. In the later 1980s and 1990s a second generation of senior European scholars moved to the U.S., almost entirely from Britain, including Talal Asad, Michael Cook, Patricia Crone, Michael Gilsenan, Roger Owen, and Peter Sluglett.

35. To give one example, Manfred Halpern described Bernard Lewis, *The Emergence of Modern Turkey* (1961) as "scholarly, brilliant, and written with style," but complained that "it lacks a systematic conceptual or theoretical framework." Halpern, "Middle Eastern Studies," 111.

36. Daniel Lerner, *The Passing of Traditional Society* (Glencoe, IL.: The Free Press, 1958).

37. Timothy P. Mitchell, "Fixing the Economy," *Cultural Studies*, vol. 12,

no.1 (1988): 82–101; and *Rule of Experts: Egypt, Techno-Politics, Modernity* (Berkeley: University of California Press, 2002).

38. Timothy P. Mitchell, "The Limits of the State," *American Political Science Review*, , vol. 85 (1991): 77–96; and "Society, Economy, and State Effect," in George Steinmetz, ed., *State/Culture: State Formation After the Cultural Turn* (Ithaca: Cornell University Press, 1999), 76–97.

39. The new concept of culture opened the way for post-war U.S. anthropology to study complex, literate societies, including those of the Middle East. Clifford Geertz, *After the Fact: Two Countries, Four Decades, One Anthropologist* (Cambridge: Harvard University Press, 1995), 43–44.

40. See the Harvard memorandum produced by Talcott Parsons, Clyde Kluckhohn, O. H. Taylor and others in the 1940s, "Towards a Common Language for the Areas of the Social Sciences," cited Clifford Geertz, "The Impact of the Concept of Culture on the Concept of Man," in *The Interpretation of Cultures* (New York: Basic Books, 1973), 41. See also Geertz, *After the Fact*, 99–109.

41. The professionalization of the social sciences during the interwar period and the rise of "scientism" is examined in Dorothy Ross, *The Origins of American Social Science* (Cambridge: Cambridge University Press, 1991).

42. For a discussion of the literature on nationalism, see my article, "The Stage of Modernity," in Timothy P. Mitchell, ed., *Questions of Modernity* (University of Minnesota Press, 2000), pp.1–34.

43. Halpern, "Middle Eastern Studies," 121.

44. Ibid., 111.

45. Pendleton Herring, quoted in Charles Wagley, *Area Research and Training: A Conference Report on the Study of World Areas*, SSRC Pamphlet No. 6 (New York: Social Science Research Council, June 1948), 6–7.

46. Wagley, *Area Research and Training*, 9.

47. Talcott Parsons, quoted in Wagley, *Area Research and Training*, 6.

48. Ibid., 5–6.

49. NYU, Hagop Kevorkian Center for Near Eastern Studies, "MESA" file. Vicente Rafael examines the gendered features of the construction of post-war area studies, "The Culture of Area Studies in the United States," 94–95.

50. Plans for attracting economists and sociologists into Middle East studies were much less successful. Of 81 faculty members teaching non-language courses on the Middle East at NDEA Centers in 1964–65, only four were in economics and three in sociology. Morroe Berger "Middle Eastern and North Africa Studies: Development and Needs," *MESA Bulletin*, 1, no.2 (November 15, 1967): 14.

51. Morroe Berger, "Middle Eastern and North African Studies," 16.

52. Said, *Orientalism*, 288–89.

53. Minutes of the Third Meeting of the Board of Directors, University of Chicago, December 9, 1967. Hagop Kevorkian Center, MESA file. At its fourth meeting, on March 18 1988, the Board amended these minutes to drop the reference to the sensitivity of the subject. Shabatai was an Israeli graduate

student, enrolled at the University of Chicago.

54. Gendzier, *Managing Political Change;* Rafael, "The Cultures of Area Studies," 92–98.

55. Halpern, "Middle Eastern Studies," 112–113; Leonard Binder, "Prolegomena to the Comparative Study of Middle East Governments," *American Political Science Review,* vol 51, no. 3 (Sep 1957): 651–668; Morroe Berger, *The Arab World Today* (Garden City, N.Y.: Doubleday, 1962).

56. Leonard Binder, "1974 Presidential Address," *MESA Bulletin* 9, no. 1 (Feb 1975): 10, discussing the previous year's meeting.

57. Ibid.

58. Winder, "Four Decades of Middle Eastern Study," 59–60. Winder does not mention which political sources subsidized the journal, but it was both pro-Washington and pro-Israel in its politics.

59. I. William Zartman, "History of MESA: The Middle East Studies Association of North America, Inc." Mimeo. Middle East Studies Association of North America, September 1970, p. 5. Later the same year, in October 1964, a journal of the same name was launched in London, under the editorship of Prof. Elie Kedourie of the London School of Economics.

60. On C.I.A. involvement in Middle Eastern studies see Mitchell, *Rule of Experts,* 148–52.

61. Frances Stonor Saunders, *The Cultural Cold War: The CIA and the World of Arts and Letters* (New York: New Press, 1999), originally published as *Who Paid the Piper: The CIA and the Cultural Cold War* (London: Granta Books, 1999).

62. Saunders, *The Cultural Cold War,* 334.

63. Winder, "Four Decades of Middle Eastern Study," 61–62.

64. Alan M. Wald, *The New York Intellectuals: The Rise and Decline of the Anti-Stalinist Left From the 1930s to the 1980s* (Chapel Hill: University of North Carolina Press, 1987), 311–21.

65. Personal communication from Ibrahim Abu-Lughod, August 3 2000. Morroe Berger had attempted to recruit Abu-Lughod to edit the magazine. Berger did not reveal the source of the funds, but the large amount of money on offer and the stipulation concerning the Soviet Union made Abu-Lughod suspicious. When the facts about their involvement with the CIA emerged in the late 1960s, many of the American intellectuals who received funds from the CIA claimed that they had not realized who was paying them. Saunders, *The Cultural Cold War,* using sources from within the CIA, raises powerful doubts about this claim.

66. See the booklet, *AAUG: The First Ten Years,* for a history of the group. My discussion of the AAUG also draws on a personal communication from Ibrahim Abu-Lughod, August 3, 2000.

67. Walt Whitman Rostow, *The Stages of Economic Growth: A Non-Communist Manifesto* (Cambridge: Cambridge University Press, 1960).

68. Samir Amin (pseudonym Hasan Riad), *L'Egypte nassérienne* (Paris: Editions de Minuit, 1964).

69. Samir Amin, *L'Accumulation à l'échelle mondiale,* Paris Anthropos, 1970,

Eng. trans. *Accumulation on a World Scale,* 2 vols. (New York: Monthly Review Press, 1974). My account is based on Amin's autobiographical account in *Re-Reading the Postwar Period: An Intellectual Itinerary,* trans. Michael Wolfers (New York: Monthly Review Press, 1994), chaps. 2 and 3.

70. Leonard Binder, "Area Studies: A Critical Reassessment," 13.

71. Lisa Hajjar and Steve Niva, "(re) Made in the USA: Middle East Studies in the Global Era," *Middle East Report* 205 (Oct—Dec 1997): 2–9.

72. Robert Vitalis, "The End of Third Worldism in Egyptian Studies," *Arab Studies Journal* 4, no.1 (Spring 1996): 13–32, at 26.

73. For a slightly different view of the period, see Hajjar and Niva, "(re) Made in the USA." Among the many important works that came out of the emphasis on political economy were: Roger Owen, *The Middle East in World Economy* (New York: Methuen, 1981); Joel Beinin and Zachary Lockman, *Workers on the Nile: Nationalism, Communism, Islam, and the Egyptian Working Class, 1882–1954* (Princeton: Princeton University Press, 1989) Huri Islamoglu-Inan, ed. *The Ottoman Empire and the World Economy* (Cambridge: Cambridge University Press, 1987); Peter Gran, *Islamic Roots of Capitalism* (Austin, Tex.: University of Texas Press, 1979); Irene Gendzier, *Managing Political Change: Social Scientists and the Third World* (Boulder, Co.: Westview, 1985); Caglar Keyder, *State and Class in Turkey* (London: Verso, 1987); Ervand Abrahamian, *Iran Between Two Revolutions* (Princeton: Princeton University Press, 1982); Fred Halliday, *Arabia Without Sultans* (Harmondsworth: Penguin, 1974) and *Iran: Dictatorship and Development* (Harmondsworth: Penguin, 1979). This period also saw the first serious attempts to introduce gender in the writing of Middle East history, such as Judith Tucker, *Women in Nineteenth-Century Egypt* (Cambridge: Cambridge University Press, 1985).

74. Anouar Abdel-Malek, "Orientalism in Crisis," *Diogenes* 44 (1959/1963), 103–140; Abdallah Laroui, *La crise des intellectuels arabes: traditionalisme ou historicisme?* (Paris: Maspero, 1974); Eng. translation, *The Crisis of the Arab Intellectual* (Berkeley and Los Angeles: University of California Press, 1976).

75. Young's overview of post-war theories of history overturns the standard historiographical interpretation of the emergence of post-structuralism: "If so-called 'so-called poststructuralism' is the product of a single historical moment, then that moment is probably not May 1968 but rather the Algerian War of independence—no doubt itself both a symptom and a product. In this respect it is significant that Sartre, Althusser, Derrida and Lyotard, among others [Cixous, Bourdieu, Fanon], were all either born in Algeria or personally involved with the events of the war." Robert Young, *White Mythologies: Writing, History, and the West* (New York: Routledge, 1991), 1.

76. Ibrahim Abu-Lughod, ed., The Arab-Israeli Confrontation of June 1967: An Arab Perspective (Evanston, Illinois.: Northwestern University Press, 1970); The Transformation of Palestine: Essays on the Origin and Development of the Arab-Israeli Conflict (Evanston, Illinois.: Northwestern University Press, 1971);

and Settler Regimes in Africa and the Arab World: The Illusion of Endurance (Wilmette, Illinois: Medina University Press International, 1974). Edward W. Said, "The Arab Portrayed," in The Arab-Israeli Confrontation, ed. Ibrahim Abu-Lughod.

77. Published in Naseer Aruri, ed., Middle East Crucible: Studies on the Arab-Israeli War of October 1973 (Wilmette, Ill.: Medina University Press International, 1975).

78. Talal Asad, ed., Anthropology and the Colonial Encounter (London: Ithaca Press, 1973).

79. Clifford Geertz, "Thick Description: Toward an Interpretive Theory of Culture," in The Interpretation of Cultures, 3–30. Already in Islam Observed (Chicago: University of Chicago Press, 1968), Geertz had criticized the Orientalists' view that there is a single cultural essence that shapes Islamic societies everywhere.

80. Binder, "1974 Presidential Address, Middle East Studies Association Annual Meeting," Middle East Studies Association Bulletin 9, no. 1 (1975): 1–11, at p. 4. Geertz's work helped lead to the emergence a decade later of cultural studies, which developed its own critique of area studies—and at the same time provided new themes for the organization of interdisciplinary programs and thus for means of escape from the narrow world of the social sciences, as area studies had provided a generation earlier.

81. Leonard Binder, "1974 Presidential Address.".

82. Said, Orientalism, 300, italics in original.

83. See the chapter by Nicholas Dirks in this volume.

84. Rashid Khalid, "Is There a Future for Middle East Studies?" MESA Bulletin, July 1995.

85. A related argument could be made about the discipline of history.

86. For recent discussions see Clifford Geertz, After The Fact, chap. 3; Arjun Appadurai, "Global Ethnoscapes: Notes and Queries for a Transnational Anthropology," in Modernity at Large (Minneapolis: University of Minnesota Press, 1996).

87. See Mitchell, "The Limits of the State.".

88. See Mitchell, "Fixing the Economy;" Robert Heilbroner and William Milberg, The Crisis of Vision in Modern Economic Thought (New York: Cambridge University Press, 1995), chaps. 4 and 5.

89. But see Immanuel Wallerstein et al., Open the Social Sciences (Stanford University Press, 1996).

90. David Laitin, "Letter from the Incoming President," APSA-CP (Newsletter of the Comparative Politics Section of the American Political Science Association) 4, no. 4 (1993): 3.

91. Robert Bates, "Letter from the President," APSA-CP (Newsletter of the APSA Comparative Politics Section) 7, no. 1 (1996): 1.

92. Robert H. Bates, "Letter from the President: Theory in Comparative Politics?", APSA-CP 8 no. 1 (1997): 1.

93. The study of these forms has developed, among other places, in the journal Public Culture.

94. "The Middle East and the Political Economy of Development," *Items* 48 nos 2/3, (1994): 41–49, at 42.

95. Bates, "Letter from the President: Theory in Comparative Politics? 1–2.

96. Two critical surveys by Lila Abu-Lughod provide a review of scholarship on the Middle East in anthropology and gender studies: "Anthropology's Orient: The Boundaries of Theory on the Arab World," (Get reference, 1990); and "Introduction," in *Remaking Women: Feminism and Modernity in the Middle East,* ed. Lila Abu-Lughod (Princeton: Princeton University Press, 1998).

97. Alan Richards and John Waterbury, *A Political Economy of the Middle East,* 2nd ed. (Boulder, Colo.: Westview Press, 1996), 37.

98. Ibid.

99. Richards and Waterbury, *A Political Economy of The Middle East,* 75.

100. Simon Bromley, *Rethinking Middle East Politics* (Austin, Tex.: University of Texas Press, 1994), 186.

101. Kiren Aziz Chaudhry, "The Middle East and the Political Economy of Development," *Items* vol. 48, nos 2/3 (1994): 41–49, at 49.

102. Kiren Aziz Chaudhry, *The Price of Wealth: Economics and Institutions in the Middle East* (Ithaca and London: Cornell University Press, 1997), 98.

103. Robert Vitalis, Review of Kiren Aziz Chaudhry, *The Price of Wealth, International Journal of Middle East Studies* 31 (1999): 659–61.

104. Chaudhry, *The Price of Wealth,* 314.

105. Ibid., 311, 314.

106. As Paul Cammack did with the new institutionalism, for example, in *Socialist Register* [get ref].

107. Chaudhry, *The Price of Wealth,* 310.

108. Chaudhry, "The Middle East and the Political Economy of Development," 45–48.

109. Ibid., 45, 46.

110. Dipesh Chakrabarty, "Minority Histories, Subaltern Pasts," *Perspectives,* November 1997, 37–43. See also Talal Asad, "The Limits of Religious Criticism in the Middle East: Notes on Islamic Public Argument," in *Genealogies of Religion: Discipline and Reasons of Power in Christianity and Islam* (Baltimore: The Johns Hopkins University Press, 1993).

111. Chaudhry, "The Middle East and the Political Economy of Development," 47, italics added.

Chapter 3

Area Studies in Search of Africa

Pearl T. Robinson

> The colonializing structure, even in its most extreme manifestations . . .
> might not be the only explanation for Africa's present-day marginality.
> Perhaps this marginality could, more essentially, be understood from
> the perspective of wider hypotheses about the classification of beings
> and societies.
>
> V.Y. Mudimbe, *The Invention of Africa*[1]

Whatever the field of inquiry, the best scholarship aims to change the way we think about its subject. Thus a comparative assessment of African Studies in the American academy must, in the final analysis, ask what kinds of new thinking have resulted from this enterprise. The Cold War rationale for area studies—with its geopolitical criteria for establishing priorities—gave us a world of regional hierarchies calibrated by relative power, levels of culture, and ideological cleavages. From the perspective of the area studies establishment, Africa's place at the bottom of those hierarchies was never in question. Yet the assumptions behind that marginality—and the contestations they engender—have combined to produce the rich/varied/tumultuous terrain that configures the current landscape of African Studies.

This is a complicated geography, fragmented into non-contiguous spatial arrangements. But it hasn't always been that way. Hence, to fully understand the intellectual history of African area studies, one must acknowledge the existence of, and tease out the relationships among, at least three spatially-differentiated spheres of endeavor: 1) the *World* of U.S. Research Universities—particularly the top research tier, which is the domain of the major Title VI African Studies Centers;[2] 2) the *World* of Diasporic PanAfricanist Scholars—a highly polyglot realm that includes the Historically Black Colleges and Universities (HBCUs), which were the first US institutions of higher learning to introduce African Studies into the curriculum; and 3) the *World* of

African Universities and Research Networks. Each of these *Worlds* has its own complex sociology of intellectual pace-setters, respected elders, epistemological debates, citation conventions, overlapping memberships, and identity politics configured around a mix of symbolic and substantive associations with the production and validation of knowledge about Africa. Research agendas differ. Moreover, funding sources have generally treated these spaces as separate and distinct.

It should come as no surprise to find that scholars working in these varied realms define the boundaries of "Africa" (i.e., the region of study) differently. Africanists trained at mainline universities in the US typically focus on Africa South of the Sahara. Diasporic PanAfricanist scholars engage with continental Africa and the African Diaspora, often taking as given a link between the two. Scholarly communities connected to African universities or research networks generally define Africa in continental terms. A notable exception was apartheid South Africa, which remained isolated from the major currents and communities of African scholars until the advent of majority rule in the early 1990s.

To be sure, these boundaries are constantly challenged and in flux. And sometimes the politics of boundaries spark hotly contentious debates. One such flare-up occurred at the University of Cape Town (UCT) in 1998, when the Social Sciences and Humanities Faculty decided to launch a new core course on "Africa" for the first year students. It fell to Mahmood Mamdani, a Ugandan national, to draw up the initial course outline. Mamdani had recently moved to South Africa to assume an appointment as the A.C. Jordan Professor of African Studies at UCT. Stunned when the Faculty rejected his course proposal and adopted instead an alternative syllabus prepared by a 3-person committee of longtime UCT academics, he went public with his critique. The Committee favored approaches and literature honed in the *World* of Western Research Universities. Mamdani accused his South African colleagues of failing to come to grips with the question of how Africa should be taught in a post-apartheid University. His retort was a discourse of spatial analysis: "(T)he syllabus reproduces the notion that Africa lies between the Sahara and Limpopo"[3] and "that this Africa has no intelligentsia worth reading."[4]He states further, "The idea that Africa is spatially synonymous with equatorial Africa, and socially with Bantu Africa, is an idea produced and spread in the context of colonialism and apartheid."[5]

Underlying this denunciation of UCT's curriculum reform project was a more fundamental critique of a set of hierarchical assumptions about race, historical agency, and human development.[6] Though Mamdani lost the skirmish, he gained a public airing for his larger point, and in so doing expanded the intellectual space for thinking more broadly about research agendas, pedagogy, and the legacy of apartheid in the South African academy. At the same time—thanks to the Internet—this debate traveled and was picked up by the African Studies community in the USA.

The contention that South African academics downplay the significance of scholarship by African intellectuals from equatorial Africa rests largely on an indictment of institutional racism.[7] However, explanations for the marginalization of Africanist scholars within the US academy are at once more subtle and more complex. Consider, for example, this personal revelation published by Harvard political economist Robert Bates in the Comparative Politics section newsletter of the American Political Science Association: "When I started out in political science in the late 1960s, comparative politics was marginal to the broader discipline. The sense of marginality was heightened by my location at Caltech, where the social sciences were marginal to the Institute; political science marginal within the social sciences; and the study of American politics king."[8] Africa's place at the bottom of that hierarchy goes without saying.

Bates' self-portrait of his early marginalization in academia is telling testimony of the difficulties faced by a theoretically-oriented Africanist determined to make his mark in the mainstream of political science. Over the years, he responded to this predicament by engaging the most "scientific" of the social science disciplines on their own terms: honing field-based techniques for a comparative political economy of rational choice, exploring interdisciplinarity by crafting analytical narratives, marshalling game-theoretic reasoning to solve behavioral puzzles, and eventually picking up the quantitative tools of formal modeling. Along the way, he served on the board of the US African Studies Association, co-edited a book on the contributions of African Studies to the disciplines, proclaimed the death of area studies, [9] promoted Africa as "the development challenge of our time," and eventually landed a chair as Eaton Professor of the Science of Government at Harvard University, where he is an active member of Harvard's Committee on African Studies and a Faculty Fellow at the Center for International Development. His book *Africa and the Disciplines*,[10] seeks to justify the place of African studies in the American university on the basis of contributions to theory and basic knowledge—thus moving away from the Cold War rationale and sidestepping alternative justifications grounded in multiculturalism.[11] Increasingly acerbic in his critique of the traditional area studies model, Bates has attempted to re-invent African studies in the image of a discipline-based American academy, and in so doing, to reposition himself—by virtue of theoretical and methodological contributions in the social sciences—from the margins to the center.

In fact, time and again we find that a creative response to a particular mindset about the place of Africa in a hierarchy of values becomes the driving force behind a move into new intellectual territory. Another powerful example of this triggering encounter is offered in the testimony of Nigerian-born social anthropologist Ife Amadiume:

> My initial reaction of anger and disbelief came when I was an undergraduate reading social anthropology in Britain in the second half of the 1970s. As the data were gathered selectively, and interpreted and applied according to the point of view and the politics of that period, which had to justify conquest and the subjection of indigenous people and their culture to foreign rule, the material produced was inevitably racist. . . . If non-Western cultures were described as primitive, barbaric, savage, etc., one can image how women in these cultures were presented. To early anthropologists, evolutionists that they were, 'primitive' women stood at the lowest end of the scale, described as no better than beasts and slaves, while the Victorian lady stood at the apex.[12]

Although this reference to "early anthropologists" occurs in a context that evokes the work of late-nineteenth century evolutionists,

Amadiume argued that old assumptions die hard. A revulsion to such representations planted the seeds for her own seminal work on sex and gender in an African society.

Amadiume took as a point of departure the construction of global feminism advanced by female academics and Western feminists of the 1960s and 1970s. What troubled her was the way some of the theorists and activists were appropriating and interpreting bits of data from Africa and elsewhere in the Third World in their writings about motherhood, marriage and the family. Particularly irksome was the universalizing assumption of women's social and cultural inferiority that, in her view, enabled white feminists to "fanaticize " a measure of superiority over African women.[13] As a corrective, Amadiume articulated the need for more empirically based social histories of the many thousands of societies worldwide that have never been studied by anthropologists.[14] Her own doctoral dissertation research on the Nnobi Igbo and subsequent book, *Male Daughters, Female Husbands,* were paradigm-making in this regard. Framed in terms of the new wave of women's studies that emphasized the social construction of gender, Amadiume's work took this form of analysis to a new level. Both the subject and method of her research brought to light data that reveal how the flexibility of Igbo gender construction affected women's access to economic resources and positions of power through the institutions of male daughters and female husbands. Indeed, only after British colonialism and the influences of Christianity introduced the more rigid gender ideology of the West did women in Nnobi society come to experience their maternal and domestic roles as constraining and unrewarding.

At the time, Amadiume's interpretation of her own research findings was at odds with the position of feminist theorists who hold that maternal and domestic roles account for the subordination of women worldwide.[15] Dismissive of this theory for its lack of a broadly based socio-cultural analysis, she insisted that the Nnobi data prove the contrary.[16] Denouncing the "racist" and "disrespectful trivialization" of feminist analysis grounded in categories and conceptual systems of a Western epistemological order, Amadiume rejected the logic that seeks to reposition Africa within this hierarchy.

Instead, she set out to generate a different type of knowledge about African women and societies. By so doing, she emerged as an important contributor to what Valentin Mudimbe calls "African discourses on otherness and ideologies of alterity."[17] Debates over whether female status is a cause or an effect of cultural values will no doubt continue. Meanwhile, Ife Amadiume has pioneered the production of a body of work that reaches beyond African studies and compels us all to rethink *feminism* as a cultural construct.

Mamdani, Bates, and Amadiume: their personal narratives illustrate how the field of African Studies is both constrained and propelled by discourses of knowledge and power on and about Africa. As scholars, each responded to Africa's marginality by confronting assumptions of hierarchy that make it acceptable to perceive this marginality as though it were common sense.[18] In *The Invention of Africa*, Mudimbe uses an approach guided by Foucaudian archeology to uncover what lies beneath the development of African Studies as a discipline. His analysis reveals the prevalence of hierarchy as an organizing principle and confirms the difficulty of transforming the types of knowledge produced about Africa.[19] Yet Diasporic pan-Africanist scholars—for reasons of their own history, location and social position—have often willingly embraced "rejected forms of wisdom" concerning Africa. And it was through their *World* that African Studies first entered the US academy.

The remainder of this chapter examines the development of African Studies in the USA, from its introduction in the historically Black colleges and universities (HBCUs) toward the end of the 19th century through its move into the academic mainstream. The study of Africa found an early home in the disciplines of Archeology and Anthropology. Later, helped by the interdisciplinary wedge of foundation- and government-supported area studies programs, teaching and research on Africa made inroads across the broader curriculum. As we shall see, the rationale for African Studies has shifted over time, while efforts to combat notions of hierarchy and the reality of marginalization have profoundly influenced its intellectual agenda.

AFRICAN STUDIES: THE EARLY YEARS

In 1873 William Tracy, a prominent member of the New York Colonization Society, wrote to William Dodge suggesting that either Lincoln Institute in Pennsylvania or Howard University in Washington, D.C. should establish a department of African Studies and recruit Edward Blyden from Liberia to teach Arabic language and African culture. Tracy and his friend Dodge, a white philanthropist and benefactor of black colleges, were dismayed that the African-American students at these institutions showed so little interest in Africa. They reckoned that courses on African civilizations and cultures would promote race pride and thus motivate some of these students to become missionaries in Africa, or to take up the work of African recolonization. [20]

The idea or recruiting Blyden was consistent with the mission of a select group of black colleges founded in the antebellum South to educate freed slaves. In contrast to the numerous schools and normal academies set up to provide basic literacy and teacher training, institutions such as Fisk, Howard, Lincoln, Wilberforce, Morehouse, Spelman, and Atlanta University offered their best students a classical education that, to paraphrase W.E.B. DuBois, sought "to furnish the black world with adequate standards of human culture and lofty ideals of life."[21] Blyden, a West Indian Black educated in England, was a professor in the College of Liberia and a Minister of the Ashum Presbyterian Church in Monrovia. Widely respected for his knowledge of Hebrew, Greek, Latin, French, German, Italian and Arabic, he was the author of several well-known works on Africa.[22] Though a frequent visitor to the United States and the recipient of several honorary degrees from U.S. institutions, he settled and remained permanently in Liberia and Sierra Leone. It was not until Leo Hansberry joined Howard University's History Department in 1922 that one saw the beginnings of a coherent approach toward a program in African Studies at an HBCU.

Hansberry arrived with an intellectual agenda. Troubled by the influence of social Darwinism, he sought to dispel derogatory myths and stereotypes about African culture and peoples by affirming the significance of African civilization. [23] Convinced that Howard had a special role to play in changing popular misconceptions, he urged the development of a program in African Studies on the grounds that it offered the University "the most promising and immediate opportunity to distinguish itself as a leader in the general cause of public enlightenment."[24] Despite some resistance, a series of courses on Negro Civilizations of Ancient Africa became part of an African Civilization Section in Howard's History Department.[25] Hansberry's lectures typically addressed aspects of state-building, nation-building, or statecraft and their applications.

When Ralph Bunche joined Howard's Political Science Department in 1928,[26] he brought an interest in Africa viewed through the then contemporary lenses of imperialism, colonialism, and proto-nationalist movements. His dissertation, defended in 1934, compared colonial rule in a League of Nations mandated area, French Togoland, with that in a French colony, Dahomey.[27] It was one of the earliest scholarly works on colonial administration.

Ralph Bunche was the first African-American to receive a Ph.D. in political science from Harvard University. Determined to establish his credentials as a modern social scientist, he used his dissertation as a platform to refute the myth of racial hierarchy as an explanation for imperialism. His research design combined comparative political analysis, economic determinism and hypothesis-testing to investigate whether the type of colonial administration made a difference in the life of the native. Fieldwork supported by a Rosenwald Fellowship enabled him to gather data on the internal dynamics of French colonial administration in the two settings. Finding little difference between the two, he then marshaled evidence to argue that French economic interests shaped colonialism in both Dahomey and Togo. For this ground-breaking study, Bunche won Harvard's Toppan Prize for the year's best dissertation in Political Science.

During the period between the two World Wars, Hansberry and Bunche, each in his own way, contributed to making Howard University a critical site for the study of Africa in the US. Hansberry's courses were popular with students. He organized symposia and lectured widely to audiences outside the University. Bunche was an active scholar, taught courses on imperialism and on colonialism in

Africa, and attracted international scholars to Howard for a conference he organized in 1936 on "The Crisis of Modern Imperialism in Africa and the Far East."[28] In 1934, when Hansberry and others formed the Ethiopian Research Council to mobilize American support for Ethiopia's efforts to resist the Italian invasion, Bunche served as the organization's advisor on international law.[29] Although the two men never collaborated to establish an interdisciplinary center for African Studies—indeed, they moved in different circles at Howard[30] – their pioneering efforts had ripple effects and connected with a scattering of developments at other institutions.

Lincoln University in Pennsylvania is a case in point. From its founding as the Ashum Institute in 1856, Lincoln had always educated significant numbers of African students.[31] Its educational program reflected the expectation that many graduates would "glorify God" through their work in Africa—as missionaries or otherwise. Nonetheless, the enrollment of Benjamin Nnamdi Azikiwe from Nigeria in 1929 and of Francis Kwame Nkrumah from the Gold Coast in 1935 infused new meaning into Lincoln's Africa mission. Azikiwe transferred to Lincoln from Howard, where he had studied African History with Hansberry and Political Science with Bunche.[32] He later played a role in recruiting Nkrumah to Lincoln. First as student leaders and then as Instructors, both these future heads of state sought to equip themselves, and the general student body, with knowledge that would hasten the liberation of Africa.[33] They found inspiration in their studies of political philosophy, anthropology, race relations and imperialism. And they drew elements from Africa's rich cultural endowments to fashion the fundamentals of a new African nationalism. While a student, Azikiwe lobbied successfully for the introduction of a course on Negro History at Lincoln. Serving briefly as an Instructor after graduating, he taught the course himself—using an approach that connected the past with the present by juxtaposing the history and cultures of Africa with the struggles of New World Blacks.[34]

By the early 1930s, material on both early Africa and colonial Africa began to make its way into the liberal arts curriculum at leading Black colleges. For instance, a two-semester Negro History offering at

Spelman College for women surveyed Ancient Africa, the slave trade and US slavery, the Civil War, Reconstruction, the partitioning of Africa, Haiti and Cuba, and "the Negro in America today."[35] W.E.B. DuBois introduced a course on Ancient Africa at Atlanta University in 1936. Then the publication in 1939 of his book *Black Folk: Then and Now*, written expressly for use in schools, combined in one comprehensive volume a history of the African past with contemporary debates on the slave trade, emancipation, the political control of Africa, and the future of world democracy.[36] DuBois' stated objective was to correct the belief that "the Negro has no history."[37] When the book appeared, it was widely reviewed and its reception generally sympathetic—with at least one commentator noting its "success in demolishing concepts of racial inferiority."[38] The intersection of race and history so prevalent in DuBois' *Black Folk* was a harbinger of contentious debates that would latter clutter the intellectual landscape of African Area Studies. For in the U.S., the power to define and interpret knowledge about Africa has been inextricably linked with American history, race relations and the precarious status of the African-American.

For decades, the treatment of African history at the HBCs typically sought to promote race pride and combat race prejudice by recovering the glories of Africa's past. Then in 1930 the anthropologist Melville Herskovits turned this approach on its head by proposing to treat the New World as an historical laboratory to study the presence of Africanisms and their functions.[39] Rejecting the conventional wisdom that American Blacks had lost all vestiges of their African cultural heritage, he mapped out a multi-faceted research agenda for studying the conditions under which African culture "has maintained itself under stress and strain."[40]. Years later he explained the importance of establishing the existence of African survivals in the New World as follows:

> To give the Negro an appreciation of his past is to endow him with the confidence in his own position in this country and in the world, . . . which he can best attain when he has available a foundation of scientific fact concerning the ancestral cultures of Africa and the survivals of Africanisms in the New World. . . .[W]hen such a body of fact, solidly grounded, is established . . . [and] this information diffused

over the population as a whole, [it] will influence opinion in general concerning Negro abilities and potentialities, and thus contribute to a lessening of interracial tensions.[41]

By declaring the systematic study of Africans in the New World "a matter of utmost scientific importance," Herskovits held out the promise of contributing answers to "some of the basic questions that confront the study of man."[42] This boldly ambitious research agenda helped secure a place for Africanist anthropologists squarely in the academic mainstream and ultimately gained recognition for its author as the preeminent American scholar of Africa. At the same time, it set forth criteria for establishing a scholarly hierarchy around issues of credibility and scientific authority. Understanding how these issues played out at Howard University can shed light on the complex power/knowledge dynamics that accompanied the development of African Area Studies in the U.S.

In 1925 the young Herskovits went to Howard as a lecturer in Anthropology. A recent Columbia University Ph.D. and student of Franz Boas, he was at the time a National Research Council Fellow in Biological Sciences working on the problem of variability under Black-White racial mixing. At Howard, he found Leo Hansberry preparing to launch courses on ancient African civilizations, and the philosopher and cultural critic Alain Locke advancing his concept of "The New Negro." Locke, a Harvard-trained Ph.D. and the first black Rhodes Scholar, considered the Harlem Renaissance of the 1920s the flowering of a New Negro Movement based on a growing race consciousness, self-confidence and sophistication among urban Blacks. He attributed these traits to the development of an independent black cultural tradition that blended "a deep-seated aesthetic endowment" from the ancestral African past with the folk traditions of American Blacks, then "blossomed in strange new forms."[43]

Herskovits initially dismissed this claim of cultural uniqueness, preferring instead to emphasize "the Negro's Americanism." In an essay on black urban culture included in Locke's edited volume *The New Negro: An Interpretation*, he reported having found in Harlem "not a trace of Africa."[44] However after moving to Northwestern University in 1927, Herskovits reversed himself on the matter of African survivals—reporting that various research findings from his fieldwork in Dutch Guyana, Haiti and Trinidad "repeatedly forced revision of prevailing hypotheses."[45] He would henceforth become a lifelong student of African cultural retentions in the New World.

What distinguished the work of Herskovits and his associates from that of other earlier proponents of African cultural survivals was a solid grounding in a research program designed to gather evidence, generate theories, and test hypotheses.[46] Alain Locke also encouraged scientific approaches to the study of Black people. Though a humanist, he saw in science an antidote for the stereotype of the Old Negro—a figure whom, in Locke's view, the American mind seemed always to consider "from the distorted perspective of a social problem." [47] However as the discourse of positivism swept the U.S. academy, broad generalizations, reliance on secondary sources, and interpretive analyses were no match for purportedly *objective* observations based on primary source data gathered in the field. And in this context, an eminent philosopher such as Locke was marked by his *subjective* motivation as a "race" man. Hence his scholarship could be dismissed—rightly or wrongly—as polemical, exaggerated, or merely interpretative commentary.

Hansberry's situation was more fragile. He never earned a doctorate,[48] lacked the requisite political support at Howard, was unable to get to Africa for fieldwork until 1953,[49] and had to self-finance most of his instructional projects. In 1932, the same year he received an MA from Harvard, Hansberry sought advice on whether, as a black American, he might have difficulty joining a British archeological expedition to Egypt. A letter from Dows Dunham of Boston's Museum of Fine Arts confirmed his apprehension:[50]

> To be perfectly frank with you, if I were in charge of such an expedition, I should hesitate long before taking an American Negro on my staff. . .. I should fear that the mere fact of your being a member of the staff would seriously affect the prestige of the other members and the respect which the native employees would have for them.[51]

Dunham's response conveyed the increasingly prevalent view in American Africanist circles that racially mediated hierarchies affected access to data and determined success in the field. Ironically, Hansberry was caught in a conundrum that used subjective criteria such a motivational bias and racialized authority structures to determine who was suitable for training and who could be trusted to carry out objective fieldwork in Africa.

By the 1940s, historically black colleges were no longer the pacesetters of Africa-related curriculum development in American higher education. Specialists on Africa remained few, but they began to surface at major research universities. Anthropology and archeology more than any other disciplines took center stage as the legitimizers of knowledge about Africa. And Herskovits, recognized for his expertise on both Continental and New World Blacks, became a gatekeeper for research and training opportunities in African-American as well as African Studies. Not until the publication in 1939 of E. Franklin Frazier's *The Negro Family in the United States* did Herskovits face a significant challenge to the scholarly merits of his work on African survivals. That challenge was launched from Howard University.

Franklin Frazier arrived at Howard in 1934 as Professor and Chair of the Sociology Department. Trained at the University of Chicago where he received his Ph.D. in 1931, he put great store in the discipline and skills of sociological research. His abiding concern with the progress, organization, and functions of the black American family was wedded to an insistence that behaviors could be understood only in terms of the social conditions that shaped them. And in this regard he was among the most strident critics of the notion of African survivals. Frazier effectively rekindled the debate over African cultural survivals in the New World—this time taking Herskovits to task for a lack of scientific rigor.

Rejecting as fatally flawed the attempts to build theory on inferences drawn from "scraps of memories" and "fragments of stories concerning Africa," Frazier argued instead that the conditions of life in the United States destroyed the significance of the slaves' African heritage.[52] This position was by no means without controversy, for it stood to undermine all who would use Africa to counter the myth that American Blacks have neither a past nor a history. But Frazier found explanations of behavior that rely on race and African culture problematic. According to Charles Henry, an astute analyst of African-American political culture, "Frazier denie[d] the possibility of African survivals in order to refute the biological claims that Black deviance from [the] middle-class family norm [was] due to the less-evolved status of the Black race."[53] This prospect led him to refute the evidence of Africanisms among U.S. Blacks, and to develop an alternative theory to explain why and how the conditions of plantation slavery in the American South caused subsequent generations to lose all meaningful connection to their African cultural heritage. In response, Herskovits spent the next 30 years sharpening his conceptual apparatus, honing more sophisticated theoretical arguments, and developing the first consistent applications of the ethnohistorical method—as he sought to validate the thesis of African cultural survivals.

What is striking—and peculiarly American—about this early period of African Studies in the U.S. was the synergism generated by the movement of ideas and individuals between the historically Black colleges and the mainstream research universities. Major scholars in both *Worlds* took notice of each other's work, engaged each other in debates, and generally functioned as part of a connected—albeit compartmentalized—epistemic community. Trans-disciplinary exchanges were the rule. Moreover, the legacy of slavery and the meanings of history served to bridge African and African-American Studies—and at times facilitated cross-fertilization that was paradigm-making.

What cannot be denied—and this too is peculiarly American—is the enormous resource gulf and racial divide that precipitated the development of distinct *Worlds* of African Studies within the U.S. academy. Through the early 1930s, an African-American scholar could only expect to get funding from three sources: the Rosenwald Foundation, the General Education Fund, and Phelps-Stokes.[54] In the Preface to *Black Folk*, DuBois apologized for producing a book that "is not a work of exact scholarship" but, rather, "as good as I am able to command with the time and money at my disposal."[55] Bunche, who did his dissertation fieldwork with a Rosenwald Fellowship, was more fortunate. He received a grant from the Social Science Research Council (SSRC) in 1936 to study the effects of colonial rule and Western culture on Africans. What's more, the SSRC took the unusual step of making a two-year award, stipulating that he acquire the anthropological training deemed necessary to successfully undertake research on acculturation.[56] And Bunche remained the only African-American funded by a private foundation to make a research trip to Africa until the 1950s. As for Hansberry, it was 1953 when he received a Fulbright Fellowship that finally got him to Egypt, Ethiopia and Sudan for field research.

Given the circumstances, it is indeed remarkable that serious academics were able to engage in productive, creative, and even contentious dialogue across this chasm. Whether at an HBC or a major research university, scholars in the field of African Studies worked against the backdrop of a broader set of assumptions about human development, cultural hierarchies and social marginality. Some did more than their share to contribute to the proliferation of marginalizing discourses through the production of knowledge about Africa. But the best of the lot were concerned to change the way people think about Africa.

INSTITUTIONALIZING BASIC RESEARCH

In 1995 the Ford Foundation engaged Jane Guyer to prepare a report on African Studies in the United States. Guyer, who had recently moved to Northwestern as director of the Program of African Studies and professor of anthropology, was keen to establish that scholarly interest in Africa significantly pre-dates the Cold War phase of area studies. To this end, she picked up the story in the 1930s, when Africa gained currency as a laboratory for investigators interested in human behavior and cultural factors. Using a periodization structured around a distinction between theoretically-driven basic research and more practically-oriented policy research, she chronicled the entrance of African Studies into the mainstream academy.

Guyer's account explains how two sets of forces converged to prepare the ground for constituting Africa as an academic field. These included scientific concerns derived from classic history, basic studies in linguistics, social theory and evolutionary theory together with late colonialism's interest in modernization. For some two decades, scholars working in anthropology, archeology, paleontology and linguistics were able to have considerable influence on research agendas in their respective disciplines.[57] Initially few in number, they began building an interdisciplinary canon of African Studies. During this period Africa found itself at the vortex of disciplinary conventions based on distinctions between the study of Western and non-Western societies, tribal peoples and high civilizations, and cultures deemed agents of history versus those construed as ahistorical or frozen in the past.[58] To be sure, many of the perspectives advanced by those pioneering Africanists have now succumbed to the scrutiny of contemporary intellectual challenges. [59] Nevertheless, Guyer does well to remind us of a moment when mutually intelligible discourses emerged around a shared interest in the diversity of human societies and their dynamics of change.[60]

Over time, the institutional landscape of African Studies evolved from clusters of individual professors with a scholarly interest in Africa to the proliferation of formally organized programs devoted to the study of Africa.[61] For instance, Hansberry's courses on Negro Civilizations of Ancient Africa were housed within Howard's History Department and emphasized the connections between Ancient Africa and equatorial Africa.[62] When Herskovits moved to Northwestern in 1927, he introduced the first African Program offered as part of a liberal arts curriculum in an American university. In this setting the boundary was Africa South of the Sahara and the scope primarily anthropological. Yet from the beginning, Northwestern devoted considerable resources to developing a comprehensive library of Africana—a repository that today is unparalleled as a resource for scholars working in wide-ranging disciplines.

World War II marks a watershed in the expansion of African studies into the American academic mainstream. The shifting currents became noticeable as early as 1941, when the University of Pennsylvania set up a Committee on African Studies (CAS) with a mandate to focus on modern Africa. Conyers Read, a professor of history, had left Penn to go to work for the new Office of the Coordinator of Information (COI) in the Library of Congress.[63] The COI was soon transformed into the Office of Special Services (OSS), and

Read headed the British Empire Section of its Research and Analysis Branch. Efforts to recruit staff made him keenly aware of the paucity of scholars knowledgeable about emerging developments across the African continent. The CAS sought ways to address this situation.

The group at Penn was an interdisciplinary Committee drawn from the departments of political science, economics, linguistics, geography, earth sciences and botany. This mix of disciplines signaled a different scholarly orientation toward Africa—one that no longer privileged the history of ancient civilizations or the anthropology of small-scale societies. Its members fashioned a graduate curriculum that combined courses on contemporary African issues with instruction in African languages—Swahili for East Africa and Fanti for West Africa. Kwame Nkrumah, then a graduate student at Penn, helped mobilize support for the establishment of an Institute of African Cultures and Languages.[64] As one of a new generation of ardent African nationalists, he seized the opportunity to associate with an initiative that would bring Africa out of the shadows and into the academic mainstream. But more than anything else, geopolitical concerns, stoked by the war effort, gave rise to Penn's foray into African Area Studies.

Meanwhile, Read recruited Howard University's Ralph Bunche to fill the position of Africa specialist in the Office of the COI. Bunche's multidisciplinary, graduate level training in political science and anthropology; dissertation and post-doctoral fieldwork in Africa; and a vast interracial network of personal contacts in Africa, Europe and the Us made him—ironically—the only American scholar of Africa deemed fully prepared to meet the academic requirements of this sensitive national security assignment.[65] When the OSS was up and running, Bunche joined a team that included two historians, two economists, a China expert, a Russia expert, a South America specialist, and an expert on Germany.[66] Their mission: "to provide the President and key military officials with the information necessary to fight the war."[67]

Within months Bunche morphed from an outspoken critic of New Deal policies into a dispassionate foreign policy insider. His new intelligence duties were extensive: He gathered information about African colonial policies and problems; race relations in British Africa;

events in French, Portuguese and Spanish Africa; and the situation in Liberia. He prepared documents and country guides, including maps, for American troops who would be deployed in South Africa, North Africa and West Africa. He offered advice on how to handle the impact of US racial attitudes on the war effort. And he counseled the need for Americans to understand African points of view—particularly African nationalism and African attitudes toward the war.[68] Ultimately, the substantive and operational concerns of the researchers who staffed the OSS influenced the profile of what was to become the wartime foreign area specialist. And in many respects, Bunche set the standard. After a year on the job he won high praise from Read as "the ablest man in his field in America" and was the only staffer in the British Empire Section to receive an A-1 performance rating."[69]

When the SSRC's Committee on World Regions issued a report in 1943 calling for a new strategic approach to area studies training, its recommendations reflected thinking that had been honed in the heat of battle. Anticipating US responsibilities in the post-war world, the Committee pressed the case for training "thousands of Americans" who would combine professional and technical competence with "knowledge of the languages, economies, politics, history, geography, peoples, customs, and religions of foreign countries." Japan, China, and Latin America were identified as priority regions. More to the point, the need for social scientists grounded in the different regions of the world was equated to the requirements for "military and naval officers familiar with ... actual and potential combat zones."[70] Following this rationale, it seemed only logical that the onset of the Cold War in 1945 should affect an abrupt shift in area priorities to the Soviet Union and China.[71]

But another debate was stirring within the SSRC. Initially keen to embrace geopolitical considerations in its advocacy of area studies, the Council began to refine its position. A new advisory committee on World Area Research, chaired by Robert Hall, expressed concern with a wartime model of area studies that stressed "content without scientific principles." There was a sense that the SSRC should not be in the business of promoting educational programs that veer from the objectives of a liberal arts education, or neglect training for basic research. As a corrective, the Hall committee called for a national program of area studies that would eventually work toward complete world coverage and be undertaken by "first-class centers of study."[72] Given the impossibility of doing everything at once, the Committee proposed a phase-in using global power relations and notions of cultural hierarchy as ordering principles. The following recommendations from its 1947 report anticipate how fine lines of distinctions might be drawn.

> The relative power of an area is one important consideration. Does the area in question generate an excess of power; . . . or does it simply submit to the power exerted from other areas? Another consideration lies in the level of culture existing in an area. Presumably we have more to gain from the study of China or India than we have from, say, the Congo Basin or New Guinea."[73]

Social Darwinism buttressed by the principles of *real politique* accentuated the marginalization of Africa. Nevertheless, the proposition held that serious scholars of the Congo along with many other regions of the globe could be found to advance the development of a universal social science.[74] The assumption that sub-Saharan Africa held little attraction for American academics in fields other than anthropology simply meant that the critical social science disciplines would have to actively recruit students to work on contemporary African issues. For the necessary resources, private philanthropy stepped into the breach.

Grant programs of the Carnegie Corporation and the Rockefeller Foundation have actively fostered international studies in U.S. higher education since the 1930s. Though Africa was never a major target of these early initiatives, Herskovits and his Africanists colleagues at Northwestern received funding from Carnegie in 1948 to start a Program on African Studies (PAS) and to build up graduate offerings in economics, geography, history and political science. That same year the SSRC launched its first program of area research training fellowships—again with funding from Carnegie. But it was the Foreign Area Fellowship Program (FAFP), launched by the Ford Foundation in 1952, that marked the beginning of a coherent strategy to support individuals as well as institutions committed to specializing in the contemporary cultures of major foreign areas.[75] The basic architecture comprised four pillars: fellowships for research and training, area studies centers, professional associations for the area studies communities, and area studies committees appointed jointly by the SSRC and the American Council of Learned Societies (ACLS).[76]

Africa as an area field became established and spread into major research universities as part of this comprehensive strategy. In line with the Hall Report's recommendation that these new programs should be undertaken by "first class centers of study," Harvard University was approached—but declined to host a major African Area Studies center. So in 1953 Ford funded the start-up of a totally new graduate level African Studies Program at Boston University and also awarded modest support to Howard University to establish an M.A. degree program in African Studies.[77] Howard, an HBCU, was not considered a major research university, but its track record and longstanding involvement with the study of Africa could not be denied. Nevertheless, the prevailing view of influential scholars such as Herskovits, as well as decision-makers at key funding agencies held that African Americans could not be relied upon to produce scientifically objective research on Africa. Two years later Northwestern's PAS received an institutional strengthening grant. Then in 1957 a group of 36 American Africanists representing a variety of disciplines met in New York City to discuss formation of a professional association. They founded the African Studies Association (ASA) as a national membership organization. Melville Herskovits was elected its first president. At this point, three of the four pillars were in place.

While these developments in African Studies and other area studies fields were consequential, advocates of international studies considered the job to be done immense and the overall funding level grossly inadequate.[78] The SSRC began casting about for a way to secure federal funding without government control. Ironically, the Soviet Union obliged. The launch of Sputnik on October 4, 1957 created a national security crisis with implications for American higher education. Congress responded by passing the 1958 National Defense Education Act (NDEA). Under Title VI of the NDEA, area studies centers around the country receive grants for core support to programs, student fellowships, library resources, and language faculty (many of the instructors of African languages have been non tenure-track). The grants are subject to competitive renewal every three years and have resulted in the designation, at various times, of more than twenty U.S. universities as National Resource Centers for Africa.

Appointment in 1960 of a Joint Committee on African Studies (JCAS) by the SSRC and the ACLS marked the coming of age of the African area field. Other joint committees had already been set up for the Slavic area (1948), Asia (1949), the Near and Middle East (1951), China (1959), and Latin America (1959).[79] Initially these groups of scholars administered grant-in-aid programs for their respective regions. Later they assumed responsibility for research planning as well. Within a short period of time the JCAS was functioning to broaden and alter the orientation of what began as a Cold War area studies agenda.

At the same time another, more troubling development was underway. As African Area Studies moved more solidly into the academic mainstream, the historically Black colleges and universities were increasingly marginalized—if not excluded—from the enterprise. Each piece of the architecture (FAFP, Title VI Centers, the ASA, and the JCAS) carried resource endowments that were largely denied to these earliest advocates of African Studies. Training and research fellowships for dissertations as well as faculty post-docs almost always went to candidates from major research universities. When the first Title VI Centers for Africa were designated, Howard University was passed over. Moreover, the founders of the ASA set up a two-tiered membership structure in which voting membership was limited to a Roster of Fellows who had to apply for admission on the basis of past academic achievement and experience in the Africa field. Taken on their own, these various measures were consistent with the goal of establishing the area fields at "first class centers of study." However, they also served to de-link the new Africa field from its historical roots in the United States, and to constitute African area studies as a *World* unto itself.

ESTABLISHING RESEARCH AGENDAS

Once the architecture was in place, the best scholarship succeeded in changing the way we think about Africa. The initial mission seemed simple: to fill in the map with knowledge. Yet unlike specialists of many other world regions, Africanists must frequently confront the marginality of their region in the realm of ideas. This intellectual challenge has generated a remarkably steady stream of works that raise epistemological questions about the nature and grounds of knowledge. It has pushed researchers to invest in methodological approaches and to devise logical constructs, analytical categories, theoretical arguments and discursive modes that enable them to more accurately explain and interpret African realities. These strategies have affected research agendas in myriad and profound ways—offering up theoretical insights and practical understandings with implications that carry far beyond African studies.

Projects sponsored by the area research training fellowships during the 1950s concentrated on fundamentals and were designed in large part to enable American researchers to familiarize themselves with contemporary issues in late colonial Africa. Some of the topics investigated were similar to those tackled by Ralph Bunche when he was an active scholar: colonial administration, acculturation, emerging leaders, and developments in South Africa. Others were more immediately current: political development, urbanization, and political institutional transfer. A concerted effort was made to shift the gaze of the anthropologists away from the traditions of tribal societies and onto the new dynamics of socio-cultural change. More political scientists were attracted into the field.

Modernization theory was the dominant paradigm in the 1950s and early 1960s, and African societies were prime candidates for its application. But the task for empirical research was to explain the mechanism of change, and on this score the data from Africa were decidedly mixed. The excitement associated with the appearance of David Apter's *The Gold Coast in Transition* (1955) was due at least in part to the sense that Apter told a story of *Africa rising:* "This book, a case study of political institutional transfer, . . . deal[s] . . . with the Gold Coast, an area marked by singular success in the transformation from a tribal dependency to a parliamentary democracy, a success which has aroused major interest throughout the world."[80] Apter believed that this transition of the Gold Coast colony into Independent Ghana under the charismatic leadership of Kwame Nkrumah would cause the world to look at Africa differently. In many respects he was right—though not in the ways anticipated. Even so, it was not long before the proliferation of fieldwork on modernization would produce its own critics.

Table 1. Area Research Training Fellowships for Africa, 1950–1960

1950-51	Dissertation (TB)	Anthropology	Northwestern	Gold Coast	Culture of the Fanti
	Dissertation	Anthropology	Northwestern	Nigeria	Acculturation of the Ibbibio
	Dissertation	Anthropology	Northwestern	Nigeria	Role of Women in Ibo Culture
	Dissertation	Anthropology	Northwestern	Nigeria	Impact of Colonialism on the Ibo
	Dissertation	Anthropology	Columbia	West Africa	Emergence of the Urban African
1951-52	Dissertation	Political Science	Princeton	Gold Coast	Political Institutional Transfer
1952-53	Dissertation	Anthropology	Yale	Sierra Leone	A Stratified Negro Community
	Dissertation	Political Science	Northwestern	Br E Africa	Direct and Indirect Rule
1953-54	Post-doc	Anthropology	Columbia	Nigeria	Language and acculturation
1954-55	Post-doc	Political Science	Smith	In the US	S. Af party system and race relations
1955-56	Dissertation	Political Science	Syracuse	In the US	Native participation in African govt
1956-57	Missing data				
1957-58	Post-doc	Political Science	McGill	In England	Br Colonial Policy in Uganda
	Dissertation	Political Science	Princeton	Nigeria	Political Development in N. Nigeria

Table 1. Area Research Training Fellowships, 1950–1960 (cont.)

	Post-doc	History	UCLA	S. Africa	Missionary influence in S. Africa
	Dissertation	Geography	U of Chicago	Uganda	Cultural differences in habitats
1958-59	Post-doc	Anthropology	Atlanta U	Nigeria	Law & Legal Thinking in Nigeria

Sylvester Whitaker, Jr. began his studies of political change in Northern Nigeria with a 1957–58 area research training fellowship. The eventual publication of *The Politics of Tradition: Continuity and Change in Northern Nigeria, 1946–1966* (1970) helped to explode a host of purported certainties about the modernization process. With an ironic twist, his argument acknowledged the hierarchical premise of political modernization, then proceeded to attack the unilinear assumptions of a model that sees conflict between modernity and tradition as inevitable:

> . .[T]he principal objection to the prevailing notion of modernization is that it unsoundly rests on a strictly a priori assumption that for all societies there is only one direction of significant change, culminating in the essentials of modern Western society. This conceptual attachment to a unilinear model of change . . . places the societies that one is most familiar with or admiring of at the top of a descending scale of human virtue.[81]

Whitaker's book contributed much to our understanding of the role of tradition in contemporary politics in general and to Nigerian politics in particular. It also marked the ascendance of a revisionist critique of modernization theory, which in turn gave way to a wave of new theoretical and methodological departures coming from both the humanities and the social sciences.

This rupture in the basic program of African Area Studies dates from 1968 and will be discussed in greater detail below. It came in the wake of a rush of unsettling developments—including the 1965 overthrow of Ghana's Kwame Nkrumah; a 1966 *coup* in Nigeria that escalated into the Biafran secession and a 3-year civil war; prolonged drought and famine in the Sahel (1968–72); and a troubling secular decline in food production.

In the midst of this spreading turmoil, behavioral responses of elites and ordinary Africans alike were multifaceted and often strategic. Individually and collectively, they developed survival mechanisms, tailored and husbanded resources, selectively innovated and repudiated, manipulated the urban environment, reinterpreted old understandings, developed new solidarities, and equivocated.[82] Post-colonial Africa posed numerous puzzles that could not be adequately addressed within the modernization framework. Henceforth, no single paradigm would be able to dominate the field or control the research agenda in its hegemonic embrace.[83] With a push from the Joint Committee on African Studies (JCAS), pluralization of the research agenda became the new mantra. In the process, a gap opened and began to widen between African Area Studies and the national security agenda of Cold War area studies.

COLD WAR AFRICAN STUDIES

The conventional view that African Area Studies developed largely free from the influence of Cold War concerns is only partially accurate. It is based on the assumption that no vital US interests were at play in the region.[84] However in matters of policy, where you stand depends on where you sit. By 1962 the State Department's *Guidelines for Policy and Operations* in Africa had concluded that Africa was "probably the greatest open field of maneuver in the world-wide competition between the [Sino-Soviet] Bloc and the non-Communist world."[85] Moreover, the treatment of America's African descended population was considered a serious liability in the context of East-West competition—particularly in light of the Soviet Bloc's anti-colonialist and anti-imperialist reputation.[86]

A close reading of the security issues delineated in the 1962 Africa *Guidelines* suggests the outlines of a research agenda for Cold War African Studies. Its major strategic objective was "denial to the Sino-Soviet Bloc of military bases and, to the maximum extent practicable, of military influence in any African country."[87] North Africa and the Horn of Africa were singled out for their strategic location and importance in securing NATO's southern flank. Nigeria was identified as a moderate "bellwether" country with potential for exerting positive influence on the African continent. Tanganyika, Ivory Coast, Sudan and Senegal seemed capable of being included in this category. Among the subjects highlighted as essential to the long-term success of US Africa policy were information about leadership dynamics; trade union movements; trends in education, social and economic development; factors affecting the shape of political institutions; and African perceptions of race relations.

In short, Cold War exigencies created a demand for knowledgeable and sophisticated American analysts capable of projecting the US position on world issues in terms consistent with local African attitudes and preoccupations.[88] Hence, national security served as a rationale for the generous funding that paved the way for African Area Studies into the academic mainstream. That the Cold War never became a dominant motif is due in large part to bottom-up agendas articulated in the various *Worlds* of African Studies ... and to the dialectics of change.[89]

PROLIFERATING RESEARCH AGENDAS

A review of the African area research supported by the SSRC beginning in the 1950s reveals the imprint of a Cold War agenda. Discernible in the early years, it receded with the proliferation of new thematic, theoretical and methodological frameworks. By 1953 a shift from the hegemony of Anthropology to a flux in the disciplinary mix from year to year was evident. Overall, during the 1950s, at least 10 FAFP research awards for Africa went to anthropologists. However available data show that between 1953 and 1960, only 4 of these fellowships went to anthropologists, while 5 went to political scientists, one 1 to a geographer, and one to a historian. (see Table 1).[90] But it was the establishment of the Joint Committee on African studies (JCAS) in 1960 that placed a multidisciplinary group of Africanist scholars in a position to allocate resources in ways that would broaden and reconfigure the general orientation of the field. The Committee's writ was Africa South of the Sahara. Its geopolitical boundaries made no allowance for Africa's diaspora. Through its dual role as a research planning vehicle and a selection committee for dissertation and post-doctoral grants, the JCAS began to override the Cold War agenda with scholarly and practical concerns that ranged widely across the social sciences and humanities.

The 1960s

The Committee launched its research planning activities by convening small interdisciplinary conferences and workshops. These initial meetings were largely strategic mapping exercises—pulling together the current state of knowledge and research activity in a given area. The themes were an eclectic mix: urbanization in Africa, the role of the traditional artist in contemporary African societies, competing demands for labor in traditional African societies, African architecture, African intellectual reactions to Western culture, and sub-national politics. Results were published in edited books, special issues of journals, and as review articles with the expressed intention of directing attention of researchers to these areas.

Consistent with the SSRC's general orientation to establish area studies at "first class centers of study," members of the Africa Committee were drawn from top research universities. For the first decade and a half, at least 50% of those appointed were based at institutions designated NDEA Title VI African Studies Centers. Unwittingly, the combination of this location bias, the convention of separating Egypt from sub-Saharan Africa, and the delinking of the African area field from its diaspora distanced critical constituencies of African-American scholars and students from the African Studies mainstream. It was not until 1969, after Black Power advocates disrupted the annual meeting of the African Studies Association (ASA) in Montreal, that the JCAS re-examined its position on the issue of boundaries and considered broadening the scope of its work to include Africa in the New World. But after exploratory talks, little changed. The Committee members opted to continue limiting their focus to continental Africa below the Sahara. But they also successfully lobbied the SSRC to create a new Committee on African American Societies and Cultures. Though this proved to be a short-term venture, from 1968 to 1972 a separate SSRC committee with its own budget, staff, and

research planning activities represented the *World* of Diaspora Pan-
Africanist scholars.

The 1970s

The events at the ASA meeting in Montreal left their mark on
programmatic agendas in African Studies for the next decade and
beyond. Diaspora Blacks accused white scholars of controlling access
to knowledge about their African homeland. Progressives faulted the
ASA for its policy of political neutrality. Together, critics accused the
African Studies establishment of cozying up to colonial governments,
remaining silent about the injustices of apartheid, and condoning a
whole host of abuses that weighed heavily against the welfare of
Africans. Donor agencies were taken to task for financing such
developments. Reactions were many and varied. Two new
organizations were born: the African Heritage Studies Association
(AHSA) and the Association of Concerned Africa Scholars (ACAS).[91]
The ASA opened up its membership, made room in its annual
meetings for panels organized by the ACAS, and created a new journal
to accommodate scholarly debates on politically charged issues.[92]

In this climate, The Ford Foundation was compelled to take another
look at both the impact and the outcomes of its training support for
Africanists through the FAFP and found an unanticipated trend. The
number of African-American recipients of these SSRC administered
fellowships—though never high—had suffered a secular decline.
Because the opportunity to do fieldwork is critical to a successful
scholarly career in African Studies, this development gave weight to
the contention that the *World* of African Area Studies supported the
access of white scholars—to the detriment of Blacks. To address this
situation, Ford established the Middle East and Africa Field Research
Program (MEAFP) for Afro-Americans. Although the MEAFP was
phased out after eight years, it has proved the single most effective
vehicle devised to date to encourage talented African-Americans to
pursue careers as scholars of Africa.[93]

The reaction of the Joint Committee to the criticisms hurled at
Montreal was deliberate and multifaceted, but side-stepped the issue
of African-American exclusion. Rethinking its purpose, the JCAS opted

to diversify its membership *internationally,* initiate a new *domestic* program of regional research seminars, and change the eligibility requirements for dissertation fellowships to allow support for non-U.S. citizens. In this politically charged atmosphere, critical policy areas became the hook for efforts by U.S.-based Africanists to engage scholars in Africa. This new focus was at least in part donor-driven, as significant levels of funding became available for projects designed to address issues affecting African development. The JCAS launched new research planning activities—identifying the crisis in African agriculture, problems of health and disease, and the breakdown in local-level governance and service delivery as subjects that could benefit from the interdisciplinary approaches of areas studies specialists. Special SSRC grant programs of post-docs, dissertation fellowships and conferences sought to interest more scholars in the North in studying these problems.[94]

By the early 1970s it was no longer tenable for strategic actors in African Area Studies to ignore the region's looming crisis in higher education. Politicization of the universities, the erosion of academic freedom, the drying up of financial resources, and the early phase of the brain drain were all taking a toll.[95] With a push from the Ford Foundation, the JCAS turned its attention to the research needs of African scholars and what might be done to help meet those needs. For the first time, the Committee reached out and established formal ties with the *World* of African universities and research institutions, welcoming B. J. Dudley from the University of Ibadan (Nigeria) and [Σϑκϑνϑ]Mody Cissoko from the University of Dakar (Senegal) in 1973. These new JCAS members facilitated the launch of SSRC training institutes in Africa that provided instruction in the use of quantitative methods and computer applications in the social sciences. The first of these institutes was held at the University of Ibadan during the summer of 1976, and it set the model of including graduate students from U.S. universities doing fieldwork in the region.

A proliferation of research, policy and training agendas further relaxed the grip of the Cold War on African Area Studies. By the late 1970s the development crisis loomed so large that *it* had become the focal point of uneasy tension between theoretically-driven and pragmatically-oriented researchers.[96] As funding for development institutes and applied departments expanded, resources available for basic research became increasingly scarce. Some critics of this trend linked government funding for policy relevant research with Cold War clientage and support for dictators. But for the pragmatists, US-AID supported initiatives such as the Sahel Development Program created new opportunities for people with degrees in African Studies at a time when the area studies bubble of academic jobs had burst.

Meanwhile the publication in 1974 of two prize-winning books by prominent scholars of Africa underscored the start of a new round of challenges to the disciplines and their conventions for studying social change. One, Immanual Wallerstein's *The Modern World System: Capitalist Agriculture and the Origins of the European World Economy in the Sixteenth Century*, was awarded the American Sociological Association's Sorokin prize in 1975. The other, Elliott Skinner's *African Urban Life: The Transformation of Ouagadougou*, was co-winner that same year of the African Studies Association's Herskovits prize. Both are mature works by senior scholars who first went to Africa in the 1950s and later rose to prominence in their respective disciplines.

Skinner, an anthropologist, broke new ground with his study of urbanization in Ouagadougou by connecting the daily lives and outlooks of ordinary Africans with the larger, global socioeconomic trends shaping the modern world. Writing in the *Preface* to *African Urban Life,* he took his discipline to task for undervaluing the multidimensionality of the African subject. The message was clear and to the point:

> This book appears at a time when the ethics of individual anthropologists are being severely questioned, and when the relevance of our discipline to the modern world is seriously challenged. . . . Third World peoples . . . can now insist that anthropologists view them in all their humanity and deal with all their problems rather than highlight only some aspects of their societies and cultures. Moreover, these people reject the notion that it took the West to make them conscious of themselves. To the contrary, they are now reasserting their humanity after being considered objects by the West.[97]

Wallerstein, a sociologist, zeroed in on two problematic aspects of disciplinary distinctions: the unit of analysis and the parcelization of knowledge. The book's overarching thesis grew out of his own intellectual trajectory as a regional specialist. As Wallerstein explains, having first gone to Africa to study the process of decolonization, he became deeply interested in the fate of these new states *after* independence. Analytic questions turned his attention to the broader category of "states in the period after formal independence but before they had achieved something that might be termed national integration."[98] The logic of this line of inquiry then led him to examine early modern Europe and the process of modernization. He eventually resolved that Africa's story was embedded in the larger story of social change and the world as a social system. Hence the *Epilogue* to *The Modern World System* calls for an end to artificial divisions of knowledge: "When one studies a social system, the classical lines of division within social science are meaningless. . . . They make certain limited sense if the focus of one's study is organizations. They make none at all if the focus is the social system. I am not calling for a multidisciplinary approach to the study of social systems, but for a unidisciplinary approach."[99]

Wallerstein and Skinner, each in his own way, drew attention to the need for more critical reflection about the relationship between area studies and the disciplines. Ironically, these clarion calls came at about the same time that institutional support for area studies had leveled off, and disciplinary forces were becoming more aggressive in the competition for faculty positions and tenure.

By 1977 the JCAS had dropped the expectation that its grant recipients would necessarily do fieldwork and began welcoming proposals for comparative theoretical research in nonfield settings. This move reflected the changing demands for career advancement faced by the younger cohort of Africanist scholars at major research universities. Indeed, regional specialists faced a double bind: an increasingly tight job market, plus the control of most academic positions by disciplinary departments rather than area studies centers. And in the departments, theory was king. Beyond the pressure to publish, involvement in theoretically oriented work was weighted more heavily in the criteria for tenure and promotion. As Guyer acknowledged in her assessment of African Area Studies, this turn of events had positive as well as negative consequences: "[T]he return to the library did allow us to concentrate on the big picture, the long term and the essential conceptual and analytical issues. . . . The unforeseen result . . . was the decreasing regular involvement of the theoretical wing in day-to-day Africa, and a certain myopia about the current state of Africa on the part of some in the academy."[100] In short, theorizing the study of Africa took on a life of its own.

The 1980s

The 1980s saw the launch of a particularly successful attempt to create a new canon—one characterized by theoretical paradigms that cross disciplinary boundaries, attention to constellations of issues germane to the Africa region, and a rethinking of conceptual tools and methods. Between 1981 and 1994, this thrust was shaped and advanced in a series of 21 research overview papers commissioned by the JCAS and published in the *African Studies Review*. These "state of the art " reviews initially stressed strategically chosen themes (e.g., the household and gender analysis, Africa's agrarian crisis, health and healing, political economy and the state). However their most enduring legacy has been the impact of the ten or so papers commissioned with the specific intent of raising the profile of the Humanities in African Studies. For more than a decade, review articles on philosophy and social thought, literature and oral traditions, the visual and popular arts, history and social processes, religious movements, and performance studies served as prime sites for debates and paradigmatic shifts in African Area Studies.[101]

This was, as well, a period when American universities reaped enormous benefits from Africa's brain drain. Perhaps the single most influential scholar to emerge from an extraordinarily gifted talent pool was Valentin Mudimbe—philosopher *cum* cultural critic. Mudimbe left Lovanium University in Zaire for Haverford College in New England before moving to Duke University as R.F. DeVarney Professor of Romance Studies, professor of comparative literature, and professor of cultural anthropology. Recruited to the JCAS in 1981, he was asked to write an overview paper surveying African philosophy. The resulting essay, "African Gnosis: Philosophy and the Order of Knowledge," is breathtaking in its range.[102] An expanded version of this overview paper was published as *The Invention of Africa: Gnosis, Philosophy and the Order of Knowledge*, a book that immediately catapulted its author into the ranks of America's most distinguished paradigm-setting Africanists. A co-winner of the 1989 Herskovits prize, Mudimbe's *Invention* combines a sophisticated perspective on traditional African thought with a Foucaultian analysis of power, knowledge and discourse, to construct an argument about epistemological shifts in the study of Africa as a scientific discipline "from the perspective of wider (Darwinian) hypotheses about the classification of beings and societies."[103]

Thus a number of developments converged during the 1980s to elevate the prominence of theory in the works of Africanists operating in the academic mainstream. Moreover, as the growing ranks of postmodernist and postcolonial researchers moved into area studies across the board, a shared discourse of theoretical understandings facilitated trans-regional dialogues and meta analyses—though sometimes at the expense of close attention to facts on the ground. On the upside, this infusion of new conceptual frameworks heightened the visibility of a few of the more theoretically inclined African scholars (e.g., Mudimbe, Achilles Mbembe, Paulin Hountondji, and Kwame Anthony Appiah),[104] and facilitated their incorporation into the American academy as world class intellectuals.[105] On the downside, the tilt toward higher-level abstractions accentuated longstanding cleavages between theoretically focused and empirically oriented scholars.

Some critics have derided this trend as the privileging of knowledge distanced from the daily lives and struggles of African people.[106] That debate is ongoing. Even so, for nearly two decade the intellectual center of gravity for African Area Studies was defined by the cross-disciplinary, Humanities centered canon forged in the 1980s. Almost immediately, the influence of the research overview papers could be seen in the works of Herskovits Prize laureates writing about religion: James Fernandez, *Bwiti: An Ethnography of the Religious Imagination in Africa* (1982) and J.D.Y. Peel, *Religious Encounters and the Making of the Yoruba* (2001); philosophy and social thought: Paulin Hountondji, *African Philosophy: Myth and Reality* (1983), T.O. Beidelman, *Moral Imagination in Kaguru Modes of Thought* (1986), Mudimbe, *The Invention of Africa* (1988), Kwame Anthony Appiah, :*In*

My Father's House: Africa in the Philosophy of Culture (1992); visual and popular arts: Johanes Fabian, *Power and Performance: Ethnographic Explorations through Proverbial Wisdom and Theatre in Shaba, Zaire (1990),* Susan Mullin Vogel, *Baule African Art, Western Eyes* (1997), Karin Barber, *The Generation of Plays: Yoruba Popular Life in Theater;* and history and social processes: John Iliffe, *The African Poor: A History* (1987), Jonathan Glassman, *Feasts and Riot: Revelry, Rebellions and Popular Consciousness on the Swahili Coast, 1856–1888* (1995) Keletso Atkins, *The Moon is Dead! Give Us Our Money! The Cultural Origins of an African Work Ethic, Natal, South Africa, 1843–1900* (1993), Nancy Rose Hunt, *A Colonial Lexicon: Of Birth Ritual, Medicalization, and Mobility in the Congo* (1999), and Diana Wylie, *Starving on a Full Stomach: Hunger and the Triumph of Cultural Racism in Modern South Africa* (2002). (See Table 2 at end of chapter.)

Table 3. Melville J. Herskovits Award Winners, 1965–2002

1965	Ruth Schacter Morganthau, *Political Parties in French-Speaking West Africa* (Oxford University Press)
1966	Leo Kuper, *An African Bourgeoisie* (Yale University Press)
1967	Jan Vansina, *Kingdoms of the Savanna* (University of Wisconsin Press)
1968	Herbert Weiss, *Political Protest in the Congo* (Princeton University Press)
1969	Paul and Laura Bohannan, *Tiv Economy* (Northwestern University Press)
1970	Stanlake Samkange, *Origins of Rhodesia* (Praeger Publishers)
1971	René Lemarchand, *Rwanda and Burundi* (Praeger Publishers)
1972	Francis Deng, *Tradition and Modernization* (Yale University Press)
1973	Allen F. Isaacman, *Mozambique: The Africanization of a European Institution: The Zambezi Prazos, 1750-1920* (University of Wisconsin Press)
1974	John N. Paden, *Religion and Political Culture in Kano* (University of California Press)
1975	Lansine Kaba, *Wahhabiya: Islamic Reform and Politics in French West Africa* (Northwestern University Press)
	Elliott P. Skinner, *African Urban Life: The Transformation of Ouagadougou* (Princeton University Press)
1976	Ivor Wilks, *Asante in the Nineteenth Century* (Cambridge University Press)
1977	M. Crawford Young, *The Politics of Cultural Pluralism* (University of Wisconsin Press)
1978	William Y. Adams, *Nubia: Corridor of Africa* (Princeton University Press)
1979	Hoyt Alverson, *Mind in the Heart of Darkness: Value and Self-Identity Among the Tswana of Southern Africa* (Yale University Press)
1980	Ronald B. Lee, *The !Kung San* (Cambridge University Press)
	Margaret Strobel, *Muslim Women in Mombasa, 1890-1975* (Yale University Press)
1981	Gavin Kitching, *Class and Economic Change in Kenya: The Making of an African Petite Bourgeoisie, 1905-1970* (Yale University Press)

Table 3, cont.: Melville J. Herskovits Award Winners, cont.

	Gwyn Prins, *The Hidden Hippopotamus: Reappraisal in African History: The Early Colonial Experience in Western Zambia* (Cambridge University Press)
1982	Frederick Cooper, *From Slaves to Squatters: Plantation Labor and Agriculture in Zanzibar and Coastal Kenya, 1890-1925* (Yale University Press)
	Sylvia Scribner and Michael Cole, *The Psychology of Literacy* (Harvard University Press)
1983	James W. Fernandez, *Bwiti: An Ethnography of the Religious Imagination of Africa* (Princeton University Press)
1984	Paulin Hountondji, *African Philosophy: Myth and Reality* (Indiana University Press)
	J.D.Y. Peel, *Ijeshas and Nigerians: The Incorporation of a Yoruba Kingdom* (Cambridge University Press)
1985	Claire Robertson, *Sharing the Same Bowl? A Socioeconomic History of Women and Class in Accra, Ghana* (Indiana University Press)
1986	Sara Berry, *Fathers Work for Their Sons: Accumulation, Mobility, and Class Formation in an Extended Yoruba Community* (University of California Press)
1987	Paul M. Lubeck, *Islam and Urban Labor in Northern Nigeria: The Making of a Muslim Working Class* (Cambridge University Press)
	T.O. Beidelman, *Moral Imagination in Kaguru Modes of Thought* (Indiana University Press)
1988	John Iliffe, *The African Poor: A History* (Cambridge University Press)
1989	Joseph C. Miller, *Way of Death: Merchant Capitalism and the Angolan Slave Trade, 1730-1830* (University of Wisconsin Press)
	V.Y. Mudimbe, *The Invention of Africa: Gnosis, Philosophy and the Order of Knowledge* (Indiana University Press)
1990	Edwin Wilmsen, *Land Filled with Flies: A Political Economy of the Kalahari* (University of Chicago Press)
1991	Johanes Fabian, *Power and Performance: Ethnographic Explorations through Proverbial Wisdom and Theater in Shaba, Zaire* (University of Wisconsin Press)
	Luise White, *The Comforts of Home: Prostitution in Colonial Nairobi* (University of Chicago Press)
1992	Myron Echenberg, *Colonial Conscripts: The Tirailleurs Senegalais in French West Africa, 1857-1960* (Heinemann Educational Books)
1993	Kwame Anthony Appiah, *In My Father's House: Africa in the Philosophy of Culture* (Oxford University Press)
1994	Keletso E. Atkins, *The Moon is Dead! Give Us Our Money! The Cultural Origins of an African Work Ethic, Natal, South Africa, 1843-1900* (Heinemann)
1995	Henrietta L. Moore and Megan Vaughn, *Cutting Down Trees: Gender, Nutrition, and Agricultural Change in the Northern Province of Zambia, 1890-900* (Heinemann, James Curry, University of Zambia)
1996	Jonathan Glassman, *Feasts and Riot: Revelry, Rebellion, and Popular Consciousness on the Swahili Coast, 1856-1888* (Heinemann)
1997	Mahmood Mamdani, *Citizens and Subjects: Contemporary Africa and the Legacy of Late Colonialism* (Princeton University Press)
	Charles Van Onselen, *The Seed Is Mine* (Hill & Wang)
1998	Susan Mullin Vogel, *Baule African Art, Western Eyes* (Yale University Press)
1999	Peter Uvin, *Aiding Violence: The Development Enterprise in Rwanda* (Kumarian Press)
2000	Nancy Rose Hunt, *A Colonial Lexicon: Of Birth Ritual, Medicalization, and Mobility in the Congo* (Duke University Press)

Table 3, cont.: Melville J. Herskovits Award Winners, cont.

2001	Karin Barber, *The Generation of Plays: Yoruba Popular Life in Theater* (Indiana University Press)
	J.D.Y. Peel, *Religious Encounters and the Making of the Yoruba* (Indiana University Press)
2002	Judith Carney, *Black Rice* (Harvard University Press)
	Diana Wylie, *Starving on a Full Stomach: Hunger and the Triumph of Cultural Racism in Modern South Africa* (University Press of Virginia)

The 1990s

The end of the Cold War and the concomitant failure of regional specialists to predict the demise of the Soviet Union ultimately called into question the geopolitical rationale that had carried the area studies enterprise for some 40 years. One of the unanticipated consequences of this crisis of legitimacy was the opening up of intellectual space along myriad new fronts. This was certainly the case for African Area Studies.

Africanists interested in conflict and its resolution began migrating to the field of security studies—bringing with them rich lodes of theoretical and empirical analyses on topics ranging from ethnic conflict to state collapse. Crawford Young's 1976 book, *The Politics of Cultural Pluralism,* together with I. William Zartman's 1995 volume *Collapsed States,* became essential reading for anyone seeking to understand post-Cold War developments in East and Central Europe.[107] Shifting currents in the academy also created space for strong theorists to make more visible the contributions of Africa research to major developments in the core disciplines. Take, for example, economist Paul Collier's chapter in the 1993 Bates, Mudimbe and Jean O'Barr volume, *Africa and the Disciplines.* Sounding like a salesman making a pitch to bottom-line university administrators, Collier describes advances that place African research at the forefront of several major developments in his field:

> Africa is a gold mine to economics because its economic history has been so extreme: booms, busts, famines, migrations. Because there are so many African countries, often following radically different economic policies, Africa offers a diversity ideally suited to the comparative approach, which is the economist's best substitute for the controlled

experiment. Until recently this potential has not been realized. . . . However, the situation is rapidly changing.[108]

The contrast between Collier's emphasis on disciplinary contributions and the rationales for area studies articulated during the Cold War signals the beginning of a new era.

Along with disciplinary knowledge, gender analysis gained a steadier foothold in African Area Studies during the 1990s. To be sure, Africanists in the *World* of research universities have always heralded at least a few scholars who placed women at the center of their work. At least four of the 45 winners of the Herskovits Prize between 1960 and 2000 adopted women or gender as an explicit focus: Margaret Strobel's *Muslim Women in Mombasa, 1980–1995*, Claire Robertson's *Sharing the Same Bowl*; Luise White's *The Comforts of Home: Prostitution in Colonial Nairobi*, and *Cutting Down Trees: Gender, Nutrition and Agricultural Change in the Northern Province of Zambia, 1890–1990* by Henrietta L. Moore and Megan Vaughn.[109] In recent years, epistemological contributions honed in the field of women's studies have posed increasingly strident challenges to the gender-neutral paradigms that have guided the study of Africa.

Feminist research methods and objectives are concerned with giving voice to the women studied. The researcher generally prefers an ethnographic approach, seeks to be more egalitarian and collaborative, and strives to both hear and amplify what is being said. The devices of feminist scholarship have come to include life histories, testimonies, multiple authorships, and oral histories. Anthropologist Gwendolyn Mikell, writing in the Introduction to her 1997 edited volume *African Feminism: The Politics of Survival*, explains that the new feminist scholarship is committed to revealing how African women "think of themselves" as they grapple with "affirm(ing) their own identities while transforming societal notions of gender and familial roles."[110]

A more recent development to emerge from this reflective methodology accords high value to the practice of reciprocity—played out in terms of accountability to people interviewed and greater respect for research subjects. Political scientist Aili Tripp has gone so far as to urge feminist scholars to re-think the hierarchies of power that structure their relations with the women they study by incorporating these women into the process of *theorizing*. Relating a personal epiphany while doing fieldwork on women's politics in Uganda, Tripp recalls: ". . . I found, as one who is deeply interested in women's agency, that I needed to pay attention to how women analyzed their own circumstances. . . . I had to find ways of engaging in mutual learning and dialogue and take people seriously at a conceptual level, not simply as a source of data."[111]

Although Tripp has consistently engaged the work of African feminist scholars and seeks their feedback on an ongoing basis, she found that "theorizing at the grassroots" provided a unique opportunity to create new knowledge together with the women she was studying. The book that resulted from this research—*Women and Politics in Uganda*—won the American Political Science Association's 2001 Victoria Schuck Award for the best book published on women and politics. Gender analysis and disciplinary knowledge come together in this penetrating study about how women's political activity can be embedded in multipurpose organizations.

Many more voices from the slow but steady stream of African émigré scholars who arrived during the 1990s are now also being heard above the din. Mamdani moved to Columbia University in the city of New York. Amadiume took up a position at Dartmouth College in Hanover, New Hampshire. The Malawian historian, essayist and novelist Paul Tiyambe Zeleza has emerged as a particularly active presence. He left a position in Canada to become Professor of History and Director of the Title VI African Studies Centre at the University of Illinois, Champaign-Urbana. Zeleza's *A Modern Economic History of Africa, Volume I,* won the 1994 Noma Award for Publishing in Africa. The jury citation praised the book for "its bold and convincing challenge to hitherto accepted orthodoxies, terminologies, and interpretations, about the nature and development of African societies and economies."[112] A few years later he published *Manufacturing African Studies and Crises,* a provocative and at times irreverent collections of essays that examine African studies and those who study it.

Through empirical research and critical essays, *Manufacturing African Studies* makes visible the separateness of the *Worlds* of African studies, and the power hierarchies that structure their different realities. Analyzing the contents of five leading English-language African studies journals between 1982 and 1992,[113] Zeleza concludes that Africanist publishing is largely a preserve of white male scholars, while research by African scholars rarely appears in Western academic media.[114] He attributes these imbalances to structures of power that are articulated with spatial, gender, racial and ethnic hierarchies. Moreover, he insists that the only solution to the intellectual marginalization of Africa in the production of knowledge about Africa lies in Africans developing and sustaining their own publishing channels.[115]

BRINGING THE DIASPORA BACK IN

Security studies, gender studies, and a greater emphasis on disciplinary knowledge—these are three of the hallmarks of post-Cold War African Area Studies. When the SSRC phased out the JCAS in 1996, an Africa Regional Advisory Panel (RAP) was established in its place. The RAP facilitates dialogue and the development of shared research themes among U.S.—based Africanists and networks of African scholars located on the Continent. This new direction reflects the SSRC's efforts to become more truly international in its client base. Still, the burning question at the start of this new millennium is whether the study of Africa as a scientific discipline will continue to be fragmented into different, separate *Worlds.*

On balance, it is clear that the Joint Committee on African Studies succeeded in its mission of giving intellectual coherence to Africa as a field of study. By promoting interdisciplinary graduate training, encouraging the study of African languages and literature, overseeing fellowship programs for graduate and post-doctoral fieldwork, and giving its imprimatur to context-sensitive research, the Committee did a great deal to channel Africa into the U.S. academic mainstream.

Yet the JCAS was also constrained by the networks of its members. The Committee did well to recruit scholars from Europe, Africa and a more diverse cross-section of North American universities and research institutes. These additions facilitated connections with a larger universe of regional specialists and intellectual currents. Regrettably, my own tenure as the only African-American to chair the

JCAS (1991–93) occurred during the Committee's final years, and hence was essentially a holding operation. But more importantly, the outreach efforts never extended to Historically Black Colleges and Universities in the U.S. And as greater numbers of black faculty and students were recruited by majority white universities, it became easier for the institutional pillars of the African Area Studies establishment to justify their exclusion of the HBCUs from African Studies networks.[116] A list of the institutional affiliations of JCAS members from 1960 through its phase-out in 1996 is telling. As Table 4 (see end of article) indicates, not a single scholar based at an HBCU ever served on the Committee.[117]

One can always identify the occasional individual whose networks straddle two or more *Worlds* of African studies. Therefore the issue of absence/exclusion is posed here in institutional terms in order to shed light on the assumptions and exclusionary consequences of practices involved in bounding the academic mainstream. Because of the strategic role played by the SSRC in the development of area studies as far back as the 1940s, the universities represented on its various Joint Committees map the ecology of each region's academic high ground. The absence of HBCUs from the Council's African Area Studies landscape became part of a process that transformed what were once permeable lines of differentiation into walls of separation. Opportunities for the kinds of formative interactions that the young Herskovits had with senior scholars at Howard in the 1920s and 1930s were indeed rare by the 1980s. Missed opportunities in the wake of this disconnect remain a matter for speculation. Yet ironically, the consequences of separate development may have been more liberating than deleterious for the field of African Diaspora Studies.

When Historian Joseph E. Harris convened the First African Diaspora Studies Institute (FADSI) at Howard University in 1979, the JCAS was preparing to launch its research overview papers. Postmodernism and a new post-colonial paradigm were beginning to drive much of the theoretically oriented work in the humanities. And rational choice theory had found an opening through the social sciences in Africa. However Harris' project was more empirically grounded. Participants in the FADSI were invited to consider the meanings, relevance and location of boundaries as diasporas impinge on the economies, politics, and social relations of both homeland and the host country or area.[118] Papers presented at that inaugural session were published in 1982 in *Global Dimensions of the African Diaspora,* edited by Harris.[119] This seminal volume—with case studies from Europe, Asia, Africa and the Americas—laid the groundwork for a reevaluation of the dispersion of Africans across the globe. Its co-authors treat these diasporas as dynamic and push us to think about Africa and its population movements in relational terms. The Second African Studies Diaspora Institute (SADSI) met in Kenya in 1981 with a mostly African audience. What SADSI did was to reach out and link that way of thinking about Africa's population movements—i.e., in dynamic, relational terms—to continental African scholars.[120]

Situating FADSI's genesis squarely in the *World* of Diasporic PanAfricanist scholars, Harris explains the intellectual roots of African diaspora studies as follows:

> African-American social scientists and humanists have had at the core of their research on Africa and blacks generally . . . the motivation to change the way of thinking about both. That motivation linked the black or African world to the struggle for human rights. Thus most university educate African-American scholars have employed research concepts and methodologies to discover and present "the facts" . . . [in order] to educate and thus bring about change through another way of understanding. This commitment expressed itself in pan-African approaches to the study of Africa and led to the evolution of the diaspora concept. . . . Hansberry, Rayford Logan, Bunche and others conveyed this in their teaching and research at Howard University.[121]

Two years after the publication of *Global Dimensions,* sociologist Ruth Simms Hamilton and historian Leslie Rout, Jr. co-founded the African Diaspora Research Program (ADRP) at Michigan State University. This project enlarged the purview of Africa diaspora studies with a model that incorporates in-depth comparative historical analysis into a conceptualization of the African diaspora as a global social formation. Four intersecting components frame the ADRP's approach to the analysis of global identity formation: (1) geosocial mobility and displacement, (2) Africa-diaspora-homeland connections,

3) relations of dominance and subordination, and 4) cultural production and endurance.[122]. This formulation marked a major departure from the longstanding legacy of Herskovits' research program on African retentions in the New World, and his emphasis on links to West Africa.[123] The former orientation had relied heavily on work in cultural anthropology, history, and the visual and performing arts. By fostering researcher on modes of dispersion other than slavery, and by emphasizing the global sociological dynamics of the African diaspora, the ADRP spurred interest in contemporary economic, social and political realities. What's more, institutionalized African Diaspora Studies took root at Michigan State alongside one of the original Title VI African Studies Center—creating opportunities for synergism.[124]

Harris and Simms Hamilton are major figures in the *World* of Diasporic PanAfricanist scholars. Both attended HBCUs: Harris, a product of Howard, studied with Hansberry; Simms went to Taladega College, where there was no focus on Africa.[125] Both found their way to Northwestern as doctoral students in the early 1960s: Harris went there to specialize in African History, Simms Hamilton's initial interest was mainstream Sociology. Exposure to the *World* of African Area Studies at Northwestern led her to enroll in African Studies courses, including language study, and to eventually do dissertation fieldwork on urban sociology in Ghana. Harris broke new ground in 1971 with the publication of *The African Presence in Asia*,[126] an examination of the East African slave trade to Asia. He then broadened his research agenda to include two-way migration patterns—particularly emphasizing the trajectories of voluntary population movement by African origin peoples around the globe. Simms Hamilton's foray into African Studies from a disciplinary base anticipated developments that would be promoted as "new" in the 1990s.[127] Her role as Director of the ADRP, has involved overseeing a program that trains scholars in African Diaspora Studies, promotes scholarship on the African diaspora, and facilitates curriculum enrichment. The ADRP publishes *Connexões*, a newsletter that is distributed to more than 50 countries in Europe, Africa, Asia and the Middle East.

The launch of the Howard Institute, of Michigan State's ADRP, as well as the publication of Yale art historian Robert Farris Thompson's

Flash of the Spirit (1983) were part of the same critical moment. [128] These projects—grounded in the study of Africa—sowed the seeds for a renaissance in African Diaspora Studies. With frames of analysis that elicit thick description in tandem with comparative and interpretive work, each in its own way operates on assumption that linkages tying the diaspora to Africa must be articulated and are not inevitable.[129] Farris Thompson's pioneering text—which documents the richness of detail and moral wisdom of Yoruba, Bakongo, Fon, Mende and Ejagham art and philosophy, and examines their fusion with other elements overseas—pointed the way for diaspora studies to look more closely at ethnicity and cultural identities *within* Africa.[130]

Today, the networks of scholars growing out of these stirrings in African Diaspora Studies generally differ in several important ways from those fostered by the traditional African Area Studies model: The HBCUs are recognized as major sites of activity, scholars of Africa North as well as South of the Sahara are part of the mix, and pride of place is given to specialists in local/global linkages—regardless of whether they are trained as Africanists. Take, for example, Ronald Walters, a leading specialist in African-American Politics who served as Head of Howard University's Political Science Department for more than a decade before moving to the University of Maryland in the 1990s. Walters followed Farris Thompson as Chair of the SSRC's short-lived Committee on African American Societies and Cultures—the post-Montreal Committee that was phased out in 1972. His *PanAfricanism in the African Diaspora* (1993) is framed around a central question: *What forces drive people of African descent to continue identifying with the source of their origin?*[131] In this work, the *linkages* between Africa and its diasporas—real and imaginary—are the unit of analysis. Surveying the politics of cultural mobilization in the U.S., the Caribbean, and Britain, Walters weaves together many local stories of African legacies and their reinvention in the cause of political empowerment and community development. This is clearly not a book that would fit the rubric of African Area Studies. Nor was it meant to be.

However, a millennial year article by Harvard historian Emmanuel Akyeampong written to mark the hundredth anniversary of the Royal

African Society, declares that it is time to "rethink the boundaries of African Studies as well as the definition of who is an African."[132] Arguing that the late 20th century has given rise to "a unique African who straddles continents, worlds and cultures" he characterizes today's world of globalized capital and culture as terrain where Africa and its diaspora "exist in a closer physical union than in any previous period."[133]

Following this logic, the metamorphosis of identity has emerged as a prominent theme in diaspora studies in general, and African Diaspora Studies in particular.[134] Indeed, some of the most inspired scholarship in the field examines processes of identity transformation over time. Michael Gomez's *Changing Our Country Marks: The Transformation of African Identities in the Colonial and Antebellum South* (1998) is an extraordinary achievement in this regard. Gomez, an anthropologist with strong interdisciplinary training—especially in history—has mined the wealth of data now available thanks largely to some 70 years of African Area Studies scholarship to produce a work that emphasizes the crucial role played by slaves' African background in the determination of African-American identity. Consider his sources: secondary literature on North American slavery and the transatlantic slave trade, anthropological theory on the acculturative process, historical and anthropological studies on West and Central Africa, and a corpus of primary materials consisting of runaway slave advertisements from southern newspapers.[135] The result is an historical account of the ethnogenesis of African-American identity in Charleston, South Carolina that is impressive in its breadth eclectic in its methodological sophistication.

Revisiting the Herskovits/Frazier debate and the methodologies that informed their divergent positions, Gomez builds on, and discards, aspects of both. Acknowledged is the enduring contribution made by Herskovits' use of the comparative analytical approach to New World slave societies as he sought to validate the thesis of African cultural survivals. But Gomez rejects Herskovits' conclusion that in the few cases where Africanisms persisted in the U.S., they were "almost never directly referable to a specific tribe or definite areas."[136] Gomez then embraces Frazier's view that the debate should turn on an analysis of the organization and functions of the black family in America and the social conditions that shaped them. But he dismisses Frazier's conclusion that the conditions of life in the U.S. destroyed the significance of the slaves' African heritage.

In the end, facets of conceptual and methodological approaches pioneered by both Herskovits and Frazier made it possible to recover the cultural, political, and social background of regions in Africa directly affected by the slave trade, and to show how a distinct African American cultural identity emerged through a process of forging family life under the difficult conditions of slavery. Gomez's treatment of ethnicity—based on scholarship that was not available to Herskovits or Frazier—provides traction for explaining the resilience of African cultures in the New World. His development of a methodology for examining continuity through the lens of ethnicity is a major contribution to research on cultural survivals—a topic that has found new audiences through the resurgence of diaspora studies.

It is well to remember that Melville Herskovits devoted a lifelong research program to African cultural survivals in the New World—in short, African Diaspora Studies. However the area studies model that emerged in the aftermath of World War II moved the diaspora from the center to the periphery of the new African Studies canon. Ironically, even the African Studies Association took the position that books about Africa's diasporas would not be eligible for its prestigious Herskovits Prize. This paradox was finally put to rest with the selection of Judith Carney's *Black Rice*[137] as a co-winner of the 2002 Herskovits Prize. Carney, a geographer, treats rice production in West Africa as an indigenous knowledge system that was transferred to different parts of the Americas. Detailing how African slaves from the rice cultivating regions of Senegambia used their knowledge to develop productive systems of rice cultivation in several different environments, she offers "an analysis of technology transfer that recognizes the central and innovative role of African slaves." *Black Rice* is a model diaspora history that links what Africans did to what African-Americans did. It is a powerful book.

Bringing the diaspora(s) back in is opening up the study of Africa in exciting new ways. It is giving rise to a host of new sites of intellectual activity in which scholars are variously theorizing African diasporas; collaborating around major research agendas; doing all manner of innovative, interdisciplinary, comparative research; reading each others' work; engaging each other in debates; and either envisaging, launching or strengthening research institutes. Beyond Europe, the New World, and Asia, contemporary studies of African diasporas stretch into Indian Ocean societies, the Islamic world, and virtual spaces.[138] For example, the Afro-diasporic historian Robin D.J. Kelley has teamed up with historian Tiffany Ruby Patterson in a highly ambitious project that treats the African diaspora as a unit of analysis in a larger process of migrations in world history.[139] Their goal: to move beyond narratives of displacement and launch a research agenda for the new millennium, conceptualized in terms of Black globality and its connections to other forms of internationalism.[140] In a paper presented at the 1999 annual meeting of the ASA, Kelley and Patterson mapped out a conceptual framework that emphasizes

1. the historical construction of the African diaspora;
2. the development of a diasporic identity and its social, cultural, and political manifestations;
3. the contributions of black migrant/colonial intellectuals to rethinking the modern West;
4. and the continual reinvention of Africa and the diaspora through cultural work, migrations, transformations in communications, as well as the globalization of capital. [141]

To this list I would add a fifth—introspective—connection to globality: the construction (by Africans) of imaginary "spaces" associated with areas outside of Africa that become part of extraverted strategies for personal mobility and betterment.

This last category evokes the notion of virtual diasporas—i.e., spaces where one can access personalized channels within global markets, or be "wired" into Western culture without permanently leaving the homeland. It directs attention to a particular kind of response to economic globalization and cultural marginalization—one that is anchored in the realm of the imagination yet extends into the socio-cultural and economic empowerment strategies of daily life. These virtual diasporas are rendered palpably real in work such as economic historian Yvette Djachechi Monga's article, "Dollars and

Lipstick: The United States through the Eyes of African Women."[142] Here, she details the ways in which the varying strata of Cameroonian women in her research are able to "redefine or symbolically reinvent their lives" by appropriating certain signs of American culture.[143] Strategies run the gamut from investing in the future by arranging to give birth in the United States to children who will become American citizens, to buying made-in-America beauty products through reliable trading networks that can authenticate the source. According to Djachechi Monga, the United States becomes a "vessel" into which these women "pour their dreams."[144]

*

At the dawn of a new millennium we find that widening networks of diaspora scholars are straddling the various *Worlds* of African Studies, making connections across continents or across racial divides. Michael Gomez is one of many examples: An African-American Africanist who studied with Joseph Harris at Howard,[145] he held positions at historically black Spelman College and the University of Georgia at Athens before to moving to New York University, where he joined a stellar group of African diaspora scholars that includes the Africanist historian Fredrick Cooper[146] and Afro-diasporic historian Robin D.J. Kelley. At an institutional level, there are stirrings that hold the promise of breathing new life into the 1981 SADSI initiative, which earlier resulted in the introduction of a scattering of courses on the African Diaspora at the Universities of Zambia, Zimbabwe and Malawi. In an essay entitled "Imagining PanAfricanism in the 21st Century," Zeleza proposes the establishment of African Diaspora Studies centers at African universities. Such centers would further alter the conventional boundaries of African Studies as scholars in Africa undertake research and teaching about Africans and people of African descent who straddle continents, worlds and cultures. These centers might also serve as bridges for linking African scholars and black scholars in the diaspora in a common intellectual project. Zeleza promotes such collaboration as a way to begin redressing the hegemony of white male scholars in the production of Africanist knowledge.[147]

As new directions in diaspora research further problematize our conventional notions about geographic boundaries and point to the effects of globalization processes on all facets of life, the institutional landscape of African studies in the U.S. is changing as well. Hence we are witnessing the launch of 21st century research centers related to Africa yet different from the Title VI centers in their various missions and geographical reach. For instance, the University of Maryland's Driskell Center for the Study of the African Diaspora, established in 2001, is committed to scholarly endeavors that promote "a full understanding of African and African-American life." To this end it will encourage research that is inter- and multi-disciplinary, and that bridges the humanities, performing and visual arts, and social sciences. The start up of UCLA's Globalization Research Center-Africa (GRCA) in 2002 signals yet another departure from the conventional area studies model. GRACA will foster research on the impact of global forces on African societies, on the influence of African societies on globalization processes, and on cross-national and cross-cultural comparisons of global processes as they relate to Africa. The founding directors of both these centers—Eileen Julien at Maryland and Edmond Keller at UCLA—are African Area Studies specialists whose long records of scholarship and intellectual activism straddle three *Worlds* of African Studies.[148] Zeleza, who is involving Champaign-Urbana's African Studies Center in the project of institutional transformation at universities in Africa, advocates the development of PanAfricanist networks that "consciously cross the various boundaries of scholarly production and communication" to engage burning issues related to Africa wherever they are raised. [149]

Thus we have come full circle. Research agendas that highlight the contributions of black migrants and colonial intellectuals to the making of the modern West, or that explore the ways in which African societies influence globalization processes, are framing alternatives to the assumption of Africa's marginality. Diaspora studies and research on globalization are bringing to light new understandings of present-day Africa. And some of the work being done in these fields is contributing to epistemological shifts in the study of Africa as a scientific discipline. In spite of these trends, however, who validates knowledge about Africa remains a point of contention.[150]

Whether African diaspora(s) studies or studies of globalization will emerge as sites for connecting the various *Worlds* of African studies remains an open question. Whatever the case, the best scholarship on Africa will continue to emerge from context sensitive research rooted in the specificities of the region's diverse and varied cultural, political, socioeconomic, and gender realities. The era of Cold War area studies has ended. But the contributions of research in Africa to the disciplines and to more practically-driven policy issues are ongoing. Meanwhile, explaining and framing alternatives to Africa's present-day marginality remains a fundamental mission of African studies.

Pearl T. Robinson is an Assistant Professor of Political Science at Tufts University.

Notes

1. V.Y. Mudimbe, *The Invention of Africa: Gnosis, Philosophy, and the Order of Knowledge* (Bloomington and Indianapolis: Indiana University Press, 1988), p. 6.

2. Title VI of the National Defense and Education Act established area studies centers with funding from the US Department of Education.

3. Mahmood Mamdani, "Statement to the Faculty of Social Science and Humanities, 13 March 1998," p. 14, in Mahmood Mamdani, Martin Hall, Nadia Hartman and Johann Graff, *Teaching Africa: The Curriculum Debate at UCT* (Cape Town: University of Cape Town, Center for African Studies, 1998).

4. Mamdani, "Is African Studies to be Turned into a New Home for Bantu Education at UCT?" Seminar on the Africa Core of the Foundation Course for the Faculty of Social Sciences and Humanities, in Mamdani *et al, Teaching Africa*, p. 46.

5. Mamdani, "Statement to the Faculty," p. 14.

6. Mamdan's proposal would have structured the curriculum in terms of key [dataqtes]. He argued that the course developed by his UCT colleagues implied that Africa had no social history before the presence of the White man on the continent, revealed an ignorance of scholarly debates in the equatorial African academy, and used a textbook informed by debates in the North American academy. These points were addressed and refuted by UCT Professors Martin Hall and Johann Graaff, who accused Mamdani of putting too much emphasis on the political agenda in the production of knowledge at the expense of empirical evidence in reconstructing the African past. They argued that "very few students come to university with an empirical basis for

understanding their common humanity, or with a sense of history through the full range of time and space." See Martin Hall, "Teaching Africa at the post-Apartheid University of Cape Town: a response," in *Teaching Africa*, p. 27; and Johann Graaf, "Pandering to Pedagogy or consumed by content: Brief thoughts on Mahmood Mamdani's 'Teaching Africa at the post-apartheid University of Cape Town,'" pp. 51–56.

7. Institutional racism, as distinct from individual racism, lays the blame on processes, legacies, and patterns that flow from established conventions and may operate at a subconscious level.

8. Robert H. Bates, "Letter from the President: Area Studies and the Discipline," *APSA-CP Newsletter*, Vol. 7, No. 1 (Winter 1996), pp. 1–2.

9. Specifically, Bates wrote that ". . .within the academy, the consensus has formed that area studies has failed to generate scientific knowledge." See Bates, "Letter from the President," p. 1.

10. Robert Bates, V.Y. Mudimbe, and Jean O'Barr, eds., *Africa and the Disciplines: The Contributions of Research in Africa to the Social Sciences and Humanities* (Chicago: University of Chicago Press, 1993).

11. Matt O'Keefe, "Emerging Africa: Coming to terms with an overlooked continent," *Harvard Magazine* (March—April1999), Vol. 101, No. 4, p. 62.

12. Ife Amadiume, *Male daughters, female Husbands: Gender and Sex in an African Society* (London and New Jersey: Zed Books, 1987), pp. 2.

13. Amadiume, *Male Daughters*, Preface, pp. 1–10.

14. Citing Maurice Godelier in 1987, Amadiume reports that there could be as many as 10,000 societies, of which anthropologists had studied between 700 and 800.

15. Regarding feminist scholars who support the theory that maternal and domestic roles account for the universal subordination of women, Amadiume references M.Z. Rosaldo, "Women, Culture and Society: a Theoretical Overview," P.R. Sanday, "Female Status in the Public Domain," N. Chodorow, "Family Structure and Feminine Personality," and S. B. Ortner, "Is Female to Male as Nature is to Culture?" all in M.Z. Rosaldo and L. Lamphere, eds., *Women, Culture and Society* (Palo Alto: Stanford University Press, 1974) .

16. Amadiume, *Male Daughters*, Conclusion, p. 191.

17. Mudimbe, *The Invention of Africa*, p. xi).

18. See the discussion of hegemony in Quintin Hoare and Geoffrey Nowell Smith, ed. and trans., *Selections from the Prison Notebooks of Antonio Gramsci* (New York: International Publishers, 1971).

19. Mudimbe, *The Invention of Africa*, pp. x–xi).

20. Horace Mann Bond, *Education for Freedom: A History of Lincoln University, Pennsylvania* (Lincoln University, PA: Lincoln University, 1976), pp. 494–5.

21. W.E. Burghardt Dubois, "Of the Training of Black Men," *The Atlantic*

Monthly 90 , No. DXXXIX (September 1902): 292. See also, Joe M. Richardson, *A History of Fisk University, 1865–1964*, (Tuscaloosa: University of Alabama Press, 1980).

22. Edward Blyden, *Liberia's Offering* (New York: J. A. Gary, 1862), *Liberia: Past, Present and Future* (Washington City: McGill & Witherow printers, 1869); *The Negro in Ancient History* (Washington City: McGill & Witherow printers, 1869); *Christianity, Islam and the Negro Race* (London: W. B. Whittingham & Co, 1888); and *Africa and Africans* (London: C.M. Phillips, 1903).

23. Joseph E. Harris, "Profile of a Pioneer Africanist," in Harris, ed., *Pillars in Ethiopian History: The William Leo Hansberry African History Notebook*, Volume I (Washington, D.C.: Howard University, 1974), pp. 4–18.

24. Leo Hansberry cited by Harris, ed., *Pillars of Ethiopian History*, pp. 9–10.

25. Three offerings formed the core: Negro Peoples in the Culture and Civilizations of Prehistoric and Proto-Historic Times, Ancient Civilizations of Ethiopia, and The Civilization of West Africa in Medieval and Early Modern Times.

26. Ralph Bunche taught at Howard University from 1928—1941. He joined the faculty. in 1928 upon receiving his MA from Harvard and established Howard's Political Science Department. He completed his Ph.D. in 1934.

27. In Benjamin Rivlin, ed., *Ralph Bunche: The Man and His Times* (New York and London: Homes & Meier, 1990), the following chapters are especially instructive on Bunche's career as an Africanist scholar: Nathan Irvin Huggins, "Ralph Bunche the Africanist pp. 69–82; Lawrence S. Finkelstein, "Bunche and the Colonial World: From Trusteeship to Decolonization," pp. 110–113; Charles P. Henry, "Civil Rights and National Security: The case of Ralph Bunche," pp. 51–53; and Martin Kilson, "Ralph Bunche's Analytical Perspective on African Development," pp. 83–95.

28. Charles P. Henry, *Ralph Bunche: Model Negro or American Other?* (New York and London: New York University Press, 1999).

29. Harris, *Pillars of Ethiopian History*, p. 24.

30. In the 1930s, Bunche was part of a remarkable groups of black scholars at Howard known as the Young Turks: Alaine Locke, E. Franklin Frazier, Sterling Brown, Abram Harris, Charles Houston and William Hastie. These were men of exceptional intellect and academic credentials who, except for racism, would have had appointments at major research universities. Prolific scholars and leftists, they were the epitome of DuBois' "talented tenth."

31. Lincoln's founding mission included the training of Africans and African-Americans who would become part of the governing elite in the new Republic of Liberia and work with the Presbytery of West Africa. The first African student enrolled in Lincoln in 1857; he came from Liberia. In its first hundred years, Lincoln graduated 159 African students. They came from Liberia (39), South Africa (22), Nigeria (58), Sierra Leone (18), the Gold Coast (14), Kenya (3), and one each from Ethiopia, French Cameroun, Gabon, South West Africa, and Uganda.

32. Explaining why he moved from Howard to Lincoln, Azikiwe recounts that in contrast to Howard, Lincoln had a reputation for training people who would "minister to the needs of Africa" by involving themselves with operations on the ground. Bond, *Education for Freedom*, pp. 499–50.

33. Kwame Nkrumah became Prime Minister and then President of Ghana, which gained its independence in 1957. In 1960, when Nigeria attained independence, Nnamdi Azikiwe became its first President.

34. The Negro in History: This course ... considers, first, the anthropological and ethnological background of the Negro; second, the part played by the Negroid races in Egypt, Nubia, Ethiopia, India, and Arabia; third, the role of the Negro in medieval times in Songhai, Ghuna, Melle, etc.; and fourth, the contemporary Negro in Africa, the West Indies, Latin America, and the United States. Instructor, Mr. Azikiwe. *Lincoln University Herald*, 1933–34, p. 46.

35. This course was cross-listed and open to the men of neighboring Morehouse College, *Annual Catalogue 1933–34*, pp. 81–82.

36. W.E.B. DuBois, *Black Folk Then and Now: An Essay in the History and Sociology of the Negro Race* (New York: Henry Holt and Company, 1939). Prior to the publication of *Black Folk*, the basic text was Carter G. Woodson, *The African Background Outlines or Handbook for the Study of the Negro* (Washington, D.C.: The Association for the Study of Negro Life and History, 1936).

37. DuBois, *Black Folk: Then and Now*, Preface to the 1975 edition (Millwood, NY: Kraus-Thomson Organization Ltd.), p. vii. DuBois wrote the manuscript while a Professor of Sociology at Atlanta University, an HBC specializing in graduate studies.

38. Edward A. McDowell, Jr., cited by Herbert Aptheker, "Introduction," to DuBois, *Black Folk: Then and Now*, 1975 edition, p. 14.

39. Melville J. Herskovits, "The Negro in the New World: The Statement of a Problem," *American Anthropologist* New Series, Vol. 32, No. 1 (January—March 1930): 45–155.

40. Herskovits, "The Negro in the New World," p. 150.

41. Herskovits, *The Myth of the Negro Past* (Boston: Beacon Press, 1958), p. 32.

42. Herskovits, "The Negro in the New World," p. 150.

43. Alain Locke, "The Legacy of the Ancestral Arts," in Alain Locke, ed., *The New Negro: An Interpretation* (New York: Albert and Charles Boni, 1925), p. 254.

44. Herskovits, "Americanism," in Alaine Locke, ed., *The New Negro*, p359. See also, M. J. Herskovits, "Acculturation and the American Negro," *Southwestern Political and Social Science Quarterly.* 8 (1927), 211–225.

45. Herskovits details how he came to reverse his position on the significance of African retentions in *The Myth*, pp. 6–7 and Chapter I, footnote 10, pp. 300–301.

46. Herskovits, "The Negro in the New World," pp. 145–156.

47. Alaine Lock, "The New Negro," pp. 3–4.

48. Hansberry received a BA degree from Harvard in 1921 and a Harvard MA in 1932.

49. In 1953 he became a Fulbright Research Scholar and spent a year doing fieldwork in Egypt, Sudan and Ethiopia.

50. Dunham had been a trusted advisor to Hansberry since his undergraduate days at Harvard. He sought advice about whether being black might disqualify him from joining an expedition to Egypt being planned by the English Egyptologist F.L. Griffeth. See Harris, *Pillars*, p. 12–14.

51. Dows Dunham, quoted in Harris, "Pioneer Africanist," p. 13.

52. Edward Franklin Frazier, *The Negro Family in the United States* (Chicago: University of Chicago Press, 1939)

53. Charles Henry, *Bunche*, p. 60.

54. Huggins, "Bunche the Africanist," in Rivilin, *Ralph Bunche*, p. 72.

55. Dubois, *Black Folk*, Millwood edition, p. vii.

56. Following a program worked out with the SSRC, Bunche traveled to Northwestern to study with Herskovits, to the London School of Economics to study with Bronislaw Malinowski, and to Capetown University to study with Isaac Shapera. See Henry, *Ralph Bunche*, p. 75.

57. Jane I. Guyer, *African Studies in the United States: A Perspective* (Atlanta: African Studies Association Press, 1996).

58. In the traditional division of labor, anthropology focused on "primitive peoples," while Oriental studies were the domain of non-Western "high civilizations." Traditional ethnography sought to reconstitute or preserve knowledge of pristine cultures, and critics of Orientalism point to a presumption that non-Western civilizations are incapable of autonomous modernization. See Immanuel Wallerstein, "The Unintended Consequences of Cold War Area Studies," in Noam Chomsky, *et al*, *Cold War and the University: Toward an Intellectual History of the Postwar Years* (New York: New Press, 1997), pp. 198–199.

59. Mudimbe, *Invention of Africa*. For another powerful critique, see Edward Said, *Orientalism* (New York: Vintage Books, 1979).

60. Guyer, *African Studies*, p. 5

61. Much of the discussion of the institutional expansion of African Studies programs in the U.S. is based on Adelaide Cromwell Hill, "African Studies Programs in The United States," in Vernon McKay, ed., *Africa in the United States* (new York: Macfadden-Bartell Corp., Student Edition, 1967, p. 65–88.

62. Harris, *Pillars of Ethiopian History*, Ch. 1—Profile of a Pioneer Africanist, pp. 3–30.

63. The OCI later became the Office of Strategic Services (OSS), which was the precursor to the CIA.

64. Bond, *Education for Freedom*, p. 507.

65. For an in-depth view of Bunche's extensive South Africa contacts, see *An African-American in South Africa: the travel notes of Ralph J. Bunche, 28 September 1937 — 1 January 1938*, ed. By Robert Edjar (Athens: Ohio University

Press, 1992). Bunche published four scholarly articles on colonial Africa and nationalist responses: "French Educational Policy in Togo and Dahomey," *Journal of Negro Education* 3/1 (January 1934); "French and British Imperialism in West Africa," *Journal of Negro History* 21/1 (January 1936); "The Land Equation in Kenya Colony," *Journal of Negro History* (24/1 (January 1939); and "The Irua Ceremony Among the Kikuyu of Kiamba District, Kenya," *Journal of Negro History* 26/1 (January1941).

66. Economists Charles Hitch and Emile Dupres, Russian expert Gerald Robinson, China expert Burton Faho, historians Conyers Read and Hajo Halborn, South American agent Maurice Halperin, and German expert Herbert Marcuse.

67. Henry, *Ralph Bunche,* p. 124.

68. Henry, *Ralph Bunche,* p. 126.

69. Conyers Read to William Langer, October 29, 1942, Bunche Papers, cited in Henry, *Ralph Bunche,* p.127.

70. SSRC, Committee on World Regions, *World Regions in the Social Sciences; Report of a Committee of the Social Science Research Council* (New York: Social Science Research Council, 143), pp. 1–2, cited in Immanuel Wallerstein, "The Unintended Consequences of Cold War Area Studies," p. 195.

71. Among the early advocates of the Cold War shift in regional priorities was Harvard University's Committee on Educational Policy. See *Report of the Subcommittee on Language and International Affairs,* Faculty of Arts and Sciences, November 12, 1945, cited in Wallerstein, "Unintended Consequences," pp. 201–202.

72. Robert B. Hall, *Area Studies: With Special Reference to Their Implications for Research in the Social Sciences* (New York: Social Science Research Council, 19467), pp. 17–18, cited by Wallerstein, "Unintended Consequences," pp. 199–200.

73. Hall, *Area Studies,* pp. 82–83, quoted in Wallerstein, "Unintended Consequences," pp. 203–204.

74. Charles Wagley, *Area Research and Training: A Conference Report on the Study of World Areas,* No. 6 (New York: SSRC, June 1948), cited in Wallerstein, "Unintended Consequences," p. 205.

75. The FAFP was created to support American graduate students and to facilitate doctoral and post-doctoral field research opportunities.

76. Elbridge Silbey, *Social Science Research Council: The First Fifty Years,* pp.98–99.

77. William O. Brown, a sociologist and specialist on African affairs at the US State Department, became the first Director of the new Boston University program. E. Franklin Frazier was named Director of the Program at Howard. From 1953 to the early 1970s, BU received nearly $1.2 million from the Ford Foundation for its African Studies Program. By contrast, Howard University received a total of $70,000 from 1954 to 1962.

78. Wendall Clark Bennett, *Area Studies in American Universities* (New York: Social Science Research Council, 1951).

79. Joint committees for Japan (1967), Korea (1967) and Eastern Europe (1971) were established after the Joint Committee on African Studies.

80. David E. Apter, "Preface," Northwestern University 1955, in *Ghana in Transition* (New York: Atheneum, 1963), p. iii.

81. C. S. Whitaker, Jr., *The Politics of Tradition: Continuity and Change in Northern Nigeria 1946–1966* (Princeton: Princeton University Press, 1970), p. 3.

82. C. S. Whitaker, Jr., "Foreword," in Pearl T. Robinson and Elliott P Skinner, eds., *Transformation and Resiliency in Africa* (Washington, D.C.: Howard University Press, 1983), p. ix.

83. Although the rational choice modelers predict victory, the paradigm has generated a host of critics. See Bates' challenge in the *APSA-CP Newsletter,* as well as Jon Elster, "Rational Choice History: A Case of Excessive Ambition," *APSR* (September 2000), and Robert H. Bates, "The Analytic Narrative Project," *APSR* (September 2000).

84. Guyer, *African Studies in the United States,* p. 5. See also, Immanuel Wallerstein, "The Unintended Consequences of Cold War Area Studies."

85. Department of State, *Guidelines for Policy and Operations, Africa,* March 1962, Secret, declassified 5/7/76, p, 1.

86. Department of State, *Guidelines 1962,* p. 5

87. Department of State, *Guidelines 1962,* p. 21.

88. Department of State, *Guidelines 1962,* p. 35.

89. Wallerstein, "Unintended Consequences."

90. Data on all SSRC International Doctoral Research Fellowships (not just those for study in Africa) from 1965 to 2000 (N = 540) show substantial fluctuations in the disciplinary mix, with economics and political science receiving smaller percentages of the awards today than they did in the 1960s; anthropology and economics in 1965 received roughly equal shares, while two decades later anthropology's proportion had increased substantially, while that of economics had declined. It appears that shares awarded to anthropology and history were inversely related, which may be a result of shifts in review committee composition. See Angelique Hjaugerud and Wendy Cadge, "Forging Links Between Disciplines and Area Studies," in the SSRC's *Items & Issues,* vol. 2, no. 1–2, summer 2001, figure 1 on p. 9.

91. The African Heritage Studies Association is an autonomous association catering to people of African descent. The Association of Concerned Africa Scholars functions as an activist caucus within the ASA.

92. *Issue: A Journal of Opinion* began publication in 1971.

93. I was one of a critical mass of African-American scholars who benefited from an MEAFP awards. Several from my cohort have provided extraordinary service to the field of African Studies as well as to their respective disciplines. Three have served as Directors of African Studies Centers (Edmond Keller at

UCLA, Sheila Walker at the University of Texas -Austin; and Gwendolyn Mikell at Georgetown). Two are past presidents of the ASA (Keller and Mikell). Mikell is also the Senior Fellow for Africa at the Council on Foreign Relations and was the founding president of the Association of African Anthropologists. Keller is the founding director of UCLA's Globalization Research Center-Africa. Ernest J. Wilson III is Director of the Center for International Development and Conflict Management at the University of Maryland and a past director of the University of Michigan's Center for Research on Economic Development.

94. SSRC annual reports for the 1970s.

95. Peter Ekeh, "Colonialism and the Two Publics in Africa: A Theoretical Statement," *Comparative Studies in Society and History* 17 (1975); 91–112, and Mamadou Diouf and Mahmood Mamdani , eds., *Academic Freedom in Africa*. (Dakar: CODESRIA, 1994).

96. Guyer, *African Studies in the United States*, pp. 6–7.

97. Elliott P. Skinner, *African Urban Life: The Transformation of Ouagadougou* (Princeton: Princeton University Press, 1974), p. vii.

98. Immanual Wallerstein, *The Modern World System: Capitalist Agriculture and the Origins of the European World Economy in the Sixteenth Century* (New York: Academic Press, 1974).

99. Wallerstein, *Modern World System*, p. 11.

100. Guyer, *African Studies in the United States*, p. 7.

101. An energetic advocate of the Humanities thrust was JCAS member Ivan Karp, curator of African ethnology at the Smithsonian, who, together with Charles Bird, convinced Indiana University Press to launch a new series on African Systems of Thought.

102. V.Y. Mudimbe, "African Gnosis: Philosophy and the Order of Knowledge," *African Studies Review* 23(2/3), June/September, 1986, pp. 149–233.

103. See introductory quote at the start of this article.

104. See, for example, Kwame Anthony Appiah, "The Postcolonial and The Postmodern," in *In My Father's House: Africa in the Philosophy of Culture* (New York and Oxford: Oxford University Press, 1992), Ch. 5, pp. 137–157; and Achilles Mbembe, "Provisional Notes on the Postcolony," *Africa* 62, 1 (1992): 3–7; Paulin Hountoundji, *African Philosophy: Myth and Reality* (Bloomington: Indiana University Press, 1983) and Appiah's *In My Father's House* won the ASA's Herskovits Prize in 1984 and 1993, respectively.

105. In this regard, the contrast with the 1970s, when the Joint Committee's relationship to African scholars was framed in terms of a rescue operation, is most striking.

106. See, for example, Mahmood Mamdani, "A Glimpse at African Studies, Made in USA," *CODESRIA Bulletin* (Number 2, 1990): 7–10; and Oyekan

Owomoyela, "With Friends Like These...A Critique of Pervasive Anti-Africanisms in Current African Studies Epistemology and Methodology," *African Studies Review* 37/3 (December 1994): 77–101.

107. M. Crawford Young, *The Politics of Cultural Pluralism* (Madison: University of Wisconsin Press, 197x and I. William Zartman, ed., *Collapsed States: The Disintegration and Restoration of Legitimate Authority* (Boulder and London: Lynne Rienner Publishers, 1995).

108. Paul Collier, "Africa and the Study of Economics," Ch. 2 in Bates et al, *Africa and the Disciplines*, p. 58.

109. Margaret Strobel, *Muslim Women in Mombasa, 1890–1975* (New Haven: Yale University Press, 1979); Claire C. Robertson, *Sharing the same bowl? A socioeconomic history of women and class in Accra, Ghana* (Bloomington: Indiana University Press, 1984); Luise White, *The Comforts of Home: Prostitution in Colonial Nairobi* (Chicago: University of Chicago Press, 1990); and Henrietta L. Moore and Megan Vaughn, *Cutting Down Trees: Gender, Nutrition, and Agricultural Change in the Northern Province of Zambia, 1890–1990* (Portsmouth, N.H.: Heinemann, London: James Currey, Lusaka: University of Zambia, 1994).

110. Gwendolyn Mikell, ed., *African Feminism: The Politics of Survival in Sub-Saharan Africa,* (Philadelphia: University of Pennsylvania Press, 1997), Introduction, p. 1.

111. Aili Mari Tripp, *Women and Politics in Uganda* (Oxford: James Currey, Kampala: Fountain Publishers and Madison: University of Wisconsin Press, 2000), p. xxiii.

112. Tiyambe Zeleza, *A Modern Economic History of Africa, Volume 1: The Nineteenth Century* (Dakar: CODESRIA, 1993).

113. The journals are *The Journal of Modern African Studies, African Studies Review, Research in African Literatures, Canadian Journal of African Studies,* and *Journal of African History.*

114. Paul Tiyambe Zeleza, *Manufacturing African Studies and Crises,* Ch. 4., "Trends and Inequalities in the Production of Africanist Knowledge," p. 61.

115. Zeleza has managed to negotiate these power hierarchies in his own professional life by tacking back-and-forth between Africa, the Caribbean, Canada and the US, and by refusing to publish his scholarly work in Western outlets.

116. I thank Joseph Harris for insisting on the importance of this development. (Personal communication with the author, 10 July 2002.)

117. The records show several instances of individuals at HBCUs being brought in to serve on various screening panels or fellowship selection committees.

118. Joseph E. Harris, "The dynamics of the global African diaspora," in Alusine Jalloh and Stephen E. Maizlish, eds., *The African Diaspora* (Arlington, TX: Texas A & M University Press, 1996), p. 7.

119. Joseph E. Harris, ed., *Global Dimensions of the African Diaspora* (Washington, D.C.: Howard University Press, 1982).

120. One result was the establishment of courses on the African diaspora at the Universities of Zambia, Zimbabwe and Malawi. Joseph Harris, personal communication with author, 10 July 2002.

121. Joseph E. Harris, personal communication, 10 July 2002.

122. Ruth Simms Hamilton, ed., *Routes of Passage: Rethinking the African Diaspora,* "(Michigan State University Press, forthcoming); and Simms Hamilton, "Toward a Conceptualization of Modern Diasporas: Exploring Contours of African Diaspora Social Identity Formation," in H. Eric Schockman, Eui-Young Yu, and Kay Songs, eds., *Contemporary Diasporas: A Focus on Asian Pacifics,* University of Southern California, The Center for Multiethnic and Transnational Studies Occasional Paper Series (Monograph Paper No. 3, Vol. II, 1997)..

123. Melville J. Herskovits, "The Significance of West Africa for Negro Research," *Journal of Negro History* 21/1 (January 1936): 15–30..

124. The African Diaspora Research Project, *A Report on Progress, 1986–1993.*

125. Joseph Harris attended Howard University, where he was a student of Leo Hansberry. Ruth Hamilton is a graduate of Talladega College in Talladega, Alabama.

126. Joseph E. Harris, *The African Presence in Asia: Consequences of the East African slave trade* (Evanston, IL: Northwestern University Press, 1971).

127. The International Predissertation Fellowship Program (IPFP) was an effort to forge stronger links between disciplines and area studies for students pursuing field research in "developing" nations. With funding from The Ford Foundation, the SSRC awarded nearly 350 training fellowships to students from 23 eligible U.S. universities between [19891]—2000. The program also sponsored workshops and conferences. See "Haugerud and Cadge, "Forging Links Between Disciplines and Area Studies," pp. 8–10.

128. Robert Farris Thompson, *Flash of the Spirit: African and Afro-American Art and Philosophy* (New York: Vintage Books, 1983).

129. Tiffany Ruby Patterson and Robin D.G. Kelley, "Unfinished Migrations: Reflections on the African Diaspora and the Making of the Modern World," *African Studies Review,* 43, no. 1 (April 2000), 20.

130. Patterson and Kelley, "Unfinished Migrations," p. 16.

131. Ronald Walters, *PanAfricanism in the African Diaspora: An Analysis of Modern AfroCentric Movements* (Detroit: Wayne State University Press, 1993).

132. Emmanuel Akyeampong, "Africans in the Diaspora: The Diaspora and Africa," *African Affairs,* 99 (2000), p. 213.

133. Akyeampong, "Africans in the Diaspora," p. 188.

134. Patterson and Kelley, "Unfinished Migrations," pp. 19–24.

135. Announcements of runaway slaves frequently assigned ethnic identities. Gomez was able to roughly match overall patterns of slave

importation with references to specific individuals and communities. Michael Gomez, *Exchanging our Country Marks: The transformation of African identities in the colonial and antebellum South* (Chapel Hill: University of North Carolina Press, 1998).

136. Herskovits, cited in Gomez, *Country Marks*, Ch. 1.

137. Judith Carney, *Black Rice*, (Cambridge: Harvard University Press, 2001).

138. Edward Alpers, "The African diaspora in the Northwest Indian Ocean: reconsideration of an old problem, new directions for research," *Comparative Studies in South Asia, Africa and the Middle East*, 17, no. 2 (1997), 61–80. Patterson and Kelley, "Unfinished Migrations," pp. 13–14.

139. Anthropologist Johnetta Cole, an African-American Africanist, was president of Spelman College when Gomez and Patterson were recruited to the faculty.

140. Their frameworks for understanding black internationalism in the modern world are 1) the trans-Atlantic system, 2) Diaspora, 3) international socialism, 4) women's peace and freedom, 5) anticolonialism, 6) Third World solidarity, and 7) Islam.

141. Patterson and Kelley, "Unfinished Migrations," p. 13.

142. Yvette Djachechi Monga, "Dollars and Lipstick: The United States through the Eyes of African Women," *Africa* 70, no.2 (2000), 192–208.

143. Djachechi Monga, "Dollars and Lipstick," p. 201.

144. Djachechi Monga, "Dollars and Lipstick," p. 193.

145. For a discussion of Afro-American Africanists, see Robinson and Elliott P. Skinner, eds., *Transformation and Resiliency in Africa.*

146. Fredrick Cooper authored the first JCAS African Research Overview paper on the theme "Africa and the World Economy," *African Studies Review* 24 no. 2/3 (June/September 1981), 1–86.

147. Zeleza, "Imagining PanAfricanism for the 21st Century," in *Manufacturing African Studies and Crises*, p. 518.

148. Eileen Julien, a specialist in Comparative Literature, has served as president of the African Language and Literature Association, and as Director of the Darkar-based West African Research Consortium. Edmond Political Scientist Edmond Keller is a past president of the African Studies Association and served for a decade as Director of UCLA's Title VI African Studies Center. Both are African-Americans.

149. Zeleza, "Imagining PanAfricanism for the 21st Century," p. 518.

150. Zeleza, "Trends and Inequalities in the Production of Africanist Knowledge.

Table 2. Africa Research Overview Papers, 1981–1994

Author	Institution	Title	Reference
Frederick Cooper.	University of Michigan, Ann Arbor	"Africa and the World Economy"	*African Studies Review*, 24(2/3) June/Sept 1981, pp. 1–86
Jane Guyer	Harvard University	"Household and Community in African Studies,"	*African Studies Review*, 24(2/3) 1981, pp. 87–137
John Lonsdale,	Trinity College, University of Cambridge	"States and Social Processes in Africa: A Historiographical Survey,"	*African Studies Review*, 24(2/3), 1981, pp. 139–225
Wyatt MacGaffey	Haverford College	"African Ideology and Belief: A Survey,"	*African Studies Review*, 24, (2/3) 1981, pp. 227–274
Paul M. Richards	University College, London	"Ecological Change and the Politics of African Land Use"	*African Studies Review*, 26(2), June 1983, pp. 1–72
Bill Freund	University of Cape Town	"Labor and Labor History in Africa: A Review of the Literature"	*African Studies Review*, 27(2), June 1984, pp. 41–58
Sara S. Berry	Boston University	"The Food Crisis and Agrarian Change in Africa: A Review Essay."	*African Studies Review*, 27(2) 1984, pp. 59–112
Harold Scheub	University of Wisconsin	"A Review of African Oral Traditions and Literature"	*African Studies Review*, 28(2/3) June/Sept 1985, pp. 1–72
Steven Feierman	University of Wisconsin	"The Social Origins of Health and Healing in Africa"	*African Studies Review*, 28(2/3) 1985, pp. 73–148
V.Y. Mudimbe	Haverford College	"African Gnosis: Philosophy and the Order of Knowledge"	*African Studies Review*, 28(2/3) 1985, pp. 149–233
Terence O. Ranger	University of Manchester	"Religious Movements and Politics in Sub-Saharan Africa"	*African Studies Review*, 29(2) June 1986, pp. 1–69
Paul Riesman	Carleton College	"The Person and the Life–Cycle in African Social Life and Thought"	*African Studies Review*, 29(2) 1986, pp. 70–138
Karin Barber	University of Birmingham	"The Popular Arts in Africa"	*African Studies Review*, 30(3) Sept 1987, pp. 1–78
Paula Ben–Amos	Indiana University	"African Visual Arts From A Social Perspective"	*African Studies Review*, 32(2) Sept 1989, pp. 1–55

Table 2. Africa Research Overview Papers, 1981–1994 (page 2)

Author	Institution	Title	Reference
Karin Barber	University of Birmingham	"The Popular Arts in Africa"	*African Studies Review*, 30(3) Sept 1987, pp. 1–78
Monni Adams	The Peabody Museum, Harvard University	"African Visual Arts from an Art Historical Perspective"	*African Studies Review*, 32(2) 1989, pp. 56–103
Bogumil Jewsiewicki	Laval University (Quebec)	"African Historical Studies, Academic Knowledge as 'Usable Past', and Radical Scholarship"	*African Studies Review*, 32(3) Dec. 1989, pp. 1–76
Lynne Krieger Mytelka	Carleton University (Ottawa)	"The Unfulfilled Promise of African Industrialization"	*African Studies Review*, 32(3) Dec. 1989, pp. 77–137
Allen Isaacman	University of Minnesota	"Peasants and Rural Social Protest"	*African Studies Review*, 33(2) Sept. 1990, pp. 121–203
Akin Mabogunje	Pi Associates, Ibadan	"Urban Planning and the Post–Colonial State in Africa."	*African Studies Review*, 33(2) 1990, pp. 121–203
Catherine Coquery Vodrovitch	University of Paris VII	"The Urbanization Process in Africa (From the Origins to the Beginning of Independence)"	*African Studies Review*, 34(1) April 1991, pp. 1–98
Margaret Thompson Drewal	Northwestern University	"The State of Research on Performance in Africa"	*African Studies Review*, 34(3) Dec. 1991, pp. 1–64
Robin Luckham	University of Sussex	"The Military, Militarization and Democratization in Africa: A Survey of Literature and Issues"	*African Studies Review*, 72(2) Sept. 1994, pp. 13–75

Table 4. Institutional Affiliations of Members of the JCAS, 1960-1996

Year	U.S. Universities with Title VI African Studies Centers	Historically Black Colleges & Universities	Other U. S. Universities	African Universities & Research Centers	European, Canadian, and Mexican Universities	Other Research Centers
1960-61	Columbia, Northwestern, UCLA		Brandeis, Johns Hopkins, Stanford			
1961-62	Columbia, Northwestern, UCLA		Same as previous year			
1962-63	Columbia, Indiana, UCLA		Stanford, UMichigan, Yale			
1963-64	Columbia, Indiana, UCLA, UWisconsin		Stanford, UMichigan			
1964-65	Same as prev. yr.		Same as previous yr.			
1965-66	Same as prev. yr.		Same as previous yr.			
1966-67	Same as prev. yr.		Stanford, Berkeley, U Maryland, Yale			
1968-69	Columbia, Indiana, UPenn, UWisconsin		Same as previous yr.			
1969-70	Columbia, Indiana, UWisconsin		Same as previous year.			
1970-71	Indiana, UPenn, UWisconsin		Stanford, SUNY Albany, UC Berkeley, U Maryland, Yale			
1971-72	UPenn, UWisconsin, Yale		SUNY Albany, Swarthmore, Berkeley, U Maryland,			
1972-73	Indiana, Northwestern, UPenn, Uwisconsin, Yale		Swarthmore, Berkeley, UChicago,			
1973-74	Indiana, UCLA		Dartmouth, SUNY Purchase, Berkeley, UChicago	U of Ibadan, U of Dakar		

Table 4. Institutional Affiliations of Members of the JCAS, 1960-1996 (page 2)

Year	U.S. Universities with Title VI African Studies Centers	Historically Black Colleges & Universities	Other U.S. Universities	African Universities & Research Centers	European, Canadian, and Mexican Universities	Other Research Centers
1974-75	Columbia, Indiana, UCLA		Dartmouth, SUNY Purchase, U Chicago	UNairobi, UIbadan, UDakar		
1975-76	Same as prev. yr.		Princeton, SUNY Purchase, U Chicago	UIbadan, UDakar		
1976-77	Boston U, Columbia, UCLA, UPenn, Uwisconsin		Princeton, Uchicago	CODESRIA, Uibadan		
1977-78	Columbia, UKansas, UPenn, UWisconsin		UC Santa Cruz, Wellesley	CODESRIA UDar es Salaam	Oxford University	
1978-79	Same as prev. yr.		Santa Cruz, UMinnesota, Wellesley	CODESRIA	Same as prev. yr.	
1967-68	Same as prev. yr.		Same as previous yr.			
1979-80	Columbia, UKansas, Upenn		Same as previous year.	CODESRIA Unairobi	Same as prev. yr.	
1980-81	Ukansas,		Santa Cruz, Uminnesota	CODESRIA, UNigeria, Nsukka, Unairobi	Same as prev. yr.	
1981-82	UKansas, Uwisconsin, UCBerkeley		Harvard, Haverford, UC San Diego, Uminmesota	CODESRIA Unairobi		
1982-83	Uwisconsin, UCBerkeley		Same as previous year.	Same as prev. yr.		

Table 4. Institutional Affiliations of Members of the JCAS, 1960-1996 (page 3)

Year	U.S. Universities with Title VI African Studies Centers	Historically Black Colleges & Universities	Other U. S. Universities	African Universities & Research Centers	European, Canadian, and Mexican Universities	Other Research Centers
1983-84	Same as prev. yr.		Same as previous year.	Addis Ababa U, Zimbabwe Inst. of Dev. Studies	El Colegio de Mexico	
1984-85	Uwisconsin, UCBerkeley. Yale		Carleton, Harvard, Haverford, UC San Diego, UMinnesota,	Same as prev. yr.	UParis VII	The Smithsonian Institution
1985-86	Same as prev. yr.		Carleton, Harvard, Haverford, , UMichigan, UMinnesota, USC	Addis Ababa U	UParis VII	Smithsonian
1986-87	Boston University, UCBerkeley		Tufts, UMinnesota, URochester, USC	Addis Ababa U, National Museum of Mali	School of Oriental & African Studies, UParis VII	Smithsonian, Woodrow Wilson Int'l Center
1987-88	Same as prev. yr.		Carleton, Cornell , Tufts, UMichigan, URochester, USC	West African Museums Project, Dakar	SOAS, University of Toronto	Smithsonian, Woodrow Wilson Center
1988-89	Same as prev. yr.		Cornell, Tufts, UChicago, UColorado, UMichigan, Urochester	Same as prev. yr.		Brookings Inst., Smithsonian
1989-90	Same as prev. yr.		Cornell, Johns Hopkins, Tufts, UChicago, UColorado, UMichigan, URochester	Same as prev. yr.		Brookings Inst.

Table 4. Institutional Affiliations of Members of the JCAS, 1960-1996 (page 4)

Year	U.S. Universities with Title VI African Studies Centers	Historically Black Colleges & Universities	Other U. S. Universities	African Universities & Research Centers	European, Canadian, and Mexican Universities	Other Research Centers
1990-91	Indiana University		Duke, Johns Hopkins, Tufts, UChicago, UColorado, UMichigan, UNC Chapel Hill, URochester	CODESRIA, WAMP	Queen's U Ontario, University College	Brookings Inst., Smithsonian
1991-92	Same as prev. yr.		Harvard U, Johns Hopkins SUNY Binghamton, Tufts, UColorado, UMichigan, UNC-CH	CODESRIA	Same as prev. yr.	
1992-93	Same as prev. yr.		Harvard, Johns Hopkins SUNY Binghamton, Tufts, UColorado UNC Chapel Hill	Same as prev. yr.	U Laval, Quebec Wageningen Agr U, The Netherlands	Centre for the Study of African Economies (Oxford)
1993-94	Same as prev. yr.		Harvard, Southern Methodist U, Tufts, UKentucky, UNC Chapel Hill	Same as prev. yr.	Same as prev. yr.	
1994-95	Same as prev. yr.		Same as previous year.	Same as prev. yr.	Same as prev. yr.	
1995-96	Same as prev. yr.		Same as previous year.	Same as prev. yr.	Same as prev. yr.	

Chapter 4

Japanese Studies
The Intangible Act of Translation

Alan Tansman

If Area Studies can be understood as an enterprise seeking to know, analyze, and interpret foreign cultures through a multi-disciplinary lens, translation may be the act par excellence of area studies. As the translator of Japanese literature Edwin McClellan wrote in 1969, translation is an implicit act of criticism:

> ... to translate a novel in such a way that the mood, the style, and even the intellectual content of the original are transferred into a totally different language is, because of the very intimacy of the process, the purest form of literary interpretation there is. The better the translator, the more alternatives he is aware of when he is trying to translate some particular passage. Presumably it is in this act of choosing from many alternatives that his critical faculty is involved. Of course, his choice is to a great extent determined by intangibles; and it is perhaps because his critical intelligence is applied to the evaluation of intangibles that the need for it in a translator is not readily recognized by those scholars who are engaged in the examination of more tangible problems.[1]

Beneath the Area Studies umbrella, scholars of the most "tangible" and those of the most "intangible" subjects have had little to say to one another. Scholars working specifically in Japanese studies are no exception. An analyst of postwar voting patterns and an interpreter of postwar poetry will find little common ground outside their shared experiences as learners of the Japanese language. Such benign indifference among scholars is, in itself, not a particularly troubling characteristic of Japanese Studies.

Rather, a push-and-pull between what McClellan calls "tangibles" and "intangibles" has been both a fracturing and an energizing force. It has pitted scholars who claim a disinterested attitude toward their material against scholars who reject such a stance as naive and disingenuous. This dynamic has also been played out in tensions between loyalty to a traditional academic discipline and loyalty to a geographically and linguistically defined "area" of study. It has led to polemics over the relative importance of theoretical models drawn from outside the "area" and archival work drawn from within it. Such tensions, while seeming to constitute a threat to the continued viability of Japanese Studies, are arguably the greatest source of its vitality and potential.

It is in the field of literary study that these tensions may be most threatening and most productive. I will make the polemical claim in this essay that the vitality and potential of Japanese Studies, and by implication of Area Studies, might be seen most pointedly in the case of the literary scholar, who presents an exemplary picture of the difficulties, challenges, and excitements of Japan Area Studies work. Though both the literary scholar and the social scientist engage in acts of translation[2], at the very heart of the literary scholar's work—and of Japanese Studies—is the careful reading of the Japanese language itself. By "reading," I mean more than making one's way through the language; I mean a disciplinary skill that involves a close consideration of the texture, contexts, and ramifications of language.) The "intangible" work of the translator of that language will come to represent the quintessence of the work of the Japan Studies scholar.

Japanese Studies is the offspring of two contradictory impulses. On the one hand, it has been explicitly motivated by the desire for engagement with the world; on the other, it has yearned for scholarly seclusion. Masao Miyoshi, a scholar of Victorian literature turned scholar of modern Japanese literature, has narrated the story of American Japanology with sensitivity toward its political valences:

> The lineage of the Japanologists in America began with the religious and industrial missionaries who went to the Far East to civilize and democratize the barbarians. Then the imperial evangelists of civilization took over the role of teachers and advisors on their return home around the turn of the century. Their godsons, who had been dormant for a while, were mobilized into a cadre of interpreters and administrators during the Second World War and the postwar years. A noticeable advance in Japanology was made by this generation of Occupation-trained specialists, and their impact on scholarship remains both powerful and definitive. Because of the historical circumstances of mission and conquest, this genealogy has no shortage of those uncritical (or even unaware) of their own ethnocentric and hegemonic impulses.[3]

Miyoshi highlights the transformative impulse (what he might more sharply call the missionary impulse) of Japanese studies. Indeed, if Japanese Studies begins with Jesuits learning about Japan in order to transform Japanese, it has more recently been practiced by Americans attempting to transform America through what they have learned about Japan.

Japanese studies came relatively late to the United States, with pre-World War II scholars like Asakawa Kan'ichi at Yale, Hugh Borton and Ryûichi Tsunoda at Columbia, and Edwin Reischauer at Harvard. By the 1930's, substantial Japanese language collections had been established in the Library of Congress, Columbia, Harvard, and Berkeley; by 1935 twenty-five schools offered classes in Japanese studies, though only eight offered courses in language study. But it was the second generation of scholars that most reasonably might be called the founding generation of American Japanese Studies. These scholars, including Marius Jansen, Donald Keene, Edward Seidensticker, and Howard Hibbett, were trained in the language to deal with the "enemy," and many were, as Miyoshi points out, missionary children.

Thus, Japanese studies in the United States is largely a postwar phenomenon. Before the war, the field was dominated by part-time practitioners and amateurs offering only the bare beginnings of training. By 1950 it was being taught at Columbia, Berkeley, Michigan, Washington, Yale, and Harvard. In 1970, there were 597 academic specialists working on Japan; this had tripled by 1984, and almost tripled again by 1989.[4]

Although born of missionary impulses and fueled by confrontation with an enemy in war, the reaction of the immediate successors of the postwar founding generation was, according to one argument, a turning away from those impulses. Patricia Steinhoff, author of the massive 1993 Japan Foundation study of Japanese studies, argues that the next generation of Japanese studies scholars, while still somewhat linked to the context of war and the American occupation of Japan, were barely affected by politics and power relations. Indeed, she argues that their work grew and thrived precisely because of its purported irrelevancy: "I think the majority of my generation who entered Japanese Studies in the 1960s and early 1970s were, like me, attracted by the intriguing puzzles of Japan's difference and the sheer intellectual challenge of cracking the *kanji* code, rather than by the promise of financial support. . . . " Such scholars, argues Steinhoff, were attracted to Japanese studies because of " . . . the prospect of a quiet academic life pursuing our endless fascination with Japan." Theirs was a wholly private endeavor: "In effect, the second generation of postwar Japan specialists entered the field for private and personal intellectual reasons, fully aware of the obscurity of the field."[5]

It would be hard to argue that the work of this generation of scholars was not affected by politics. What Steinhoff seems to be getting at is that at the very least they felt themselves to be apolitical. For Steinhoff, the nature of postwar Japanese studies stems from its minuscule size and general irrelevance not only to politics but to American academic life, along with the decision of the first postwar generation to integrate Japan specialists into academic disciplines rather than place them solely in language and culture programs. (Steinhoff's analysis implies that this decisive factor may have prevented the isolation of Japanese Studies.) In part, the decision reflected budgetary concerns, but had the salutary effect of creating Japan specialists trained in broad theoretical and methodological principles, and compelled to apply those principles to Japan: "In general, those disciplines whose internal intellectual organization and dominant theoretical orientations included some geographic or cultural division were more hospitable to the incursion of area specialists . . . "[6]

Despite their distribution across departments, scholars working on Japan developed a second tier of affiliation with other Japan specialists (which may have both attenuated and enriched the effect of their disciplinary allegiances), creating what might be termed an area-studies affiliation. Had these early specialists been clustered in Japanese language and culture departments, their intellectual orientations would probably have been different; had they been more densely collected in distinct, insular disciplines, their concerns would have been more exclusively cohesive with those of each discipline.[7] But as things turned out, with a foot in each camp, they developed their work along interdisciplinary lines and so, one might add, created the beginnings of what might be thought of as a cultural-studies approach, without cultural studies' political imperatives.[8] This development depended on Japan specialists not being completely isolated from one another, or from their non-Japanologist disciplinary peers. No better testimony could be offered against the establishment of false dichotomies between disciplinary and area studies work, or what has been more tendentiously discussed as the split between "theory" and "archive". In fact, the very image of a scholar—a scholar of Japanese literature, for sure, but also of other fields as well—working *either* with theory *or* the archive is a figment of a tendentious imagination. I hardly know a scholar who does not read both and try to incorporate each into her work. This is, I would add, a happy development.

The experience of one of the fathers of Japanese Studies is instructive for understanding the early configuration of intellectual affiliations and its nascent tensions. Robert Smith, perhaps the dean of Japan anthropologists, was the youngest member of the postwar founding generation of Japanese Studies. As a graduate student in the late 1940's and early 1950's at Cornell University, he cut his teeth on the community-study approach to anthropology and the culture-and-personality studies commissioned by the Defense Department. As Cornell had no Japanese Studies Program at the time, he worked in applied anthropology, in the Cornell University Studies in Culture and Applied Science. The work of Ruth Benedict, commissioned by the Defense Department, had created the methodological foundations for anthropological work on Japan. Benedict worked through what was called "the study of culture at a distance," an idea instituted in the early 1940s when the Office of Wartime Information established centers for national culture studies. She ran the Institute for Intercultural Studies at Columbia University with a staff including Margaret Mead and Catherine Bateson (it was dissolved in 1947). Such centers studied "enemy" countries inaccessible to field work. To Smith, Benedict's *The Chrysanthemum and the Sword* was "the last great prewar work on Japan by an American, and although it was addressed to a general audience rather than to specialist scholars, there is a sense in which all of us have been writing footnotes to it ever since it appeared in 1946. . . . for whatever one's orientation toward it, her book undeniably set the terms of the discourse on Japan for more than a generation."[9] Though I will later argue for the centrality of language skills in Japanese studies, it should be noted here that this book, important to Japanese and American scholars alike, did not rely on expertise in Japanese.

Smith's generation of the progenitors of Japanese Studies was later taken to task for claiming to do "disinterested" scholarship and for disavowing the influence of their own emergence as scholars in a politicized context, the very context that produced such "engaged" scholarship as Benedict's. Roger Bowen has argued that the work of the postwar generation of scholars trained in military language schools was not "neutral." Larger social concerns were not irrelevant to them: "Arguably, this new breed of Japanologists studied aspects of Japanese society, history, and politics that did not conflict either with their politically conservative beliefs, nurtured by the emerging Cold War, or with the Occupation's attempt at politically engineering a democratic Japan remolded in America's image of itself."[10] These scholars suspended criticism of Japan and saw it as "a homogeneous, nonsectarian, and economically unified Japan . . . at peace with itself". Such a view allowed this generation of scholars to be proud of their accomplishments: "Japan's former occupiers-turned-Japanologists could look with pride and satisfaction on the salutary effects of American-sponsored land reform, educational reform, and the like. . . . " Such scholars were perhaps blinded to a more complex Japanese past: "In this context, thoughts about a Japan with a possible revolutionary past, not to mention an oppressive and even violent present, were seemingly beyond serious consideration by conservative Japanologists during much of the postwar era."[11]

The self-proclaimed objective scholarship discussed by Bowen had, he argues, its own politics, helping to mold an image of Japan that had direct or indirect repurcussions on American policy. The Japan specialist's development of a picture of Japan as a younger brother to be nurtured in the American image was encouraged by, and helped shape, a series of six conferences between 1965 and 1969 on the "modernization" of Japan, funded by the Ford Foundation and conceived and developed by the Committee on Modern Japan. Each conference culminated in a book; the resulting series now stands as a landmark in postwar social science and international studies and was to determine the direction of Japanese studies for years to come.[12] Indeed, in 1998 Helen Hardacre argued that "no over-arching, unifying perspective" had yet replaced the modernization framework as a means of conceptualizing the study of Japan.[13]

Later projects funded by the Social Science Research Council through the Ford Foundation, however, examined Japan's more troubled past and thus went far to break the mold the earlier volumes had helped to cast. The SSRC funded conferences on urbanization, business history, health and medicine, infant psychology, and family and life-course, resulting in such volumes as *Japan in Crisis, Conflict in Modern Japanese History, Postmodernism and Japan,* and *Uncommon Democracies,* all essential for bringing into Japanese studies questions of imperialism, colonialism, and post-colonialism.

Never fully replaced, the canon of Japanology created by the modernization project has been harshly criticized, by, among others, H.D. Harootunian. Like Bowen, Harootunian has cautioned against naively accepting the assumption that the first generation of postwar scholars consisted of "disinterested" scholars, and has reminded us of their presumptions and illusions of value neutrality. The dismissal of conflict models of Japanese history for the "modernization" theories, which depicted a Japan successfully transforming itself according to United States standards and theories of development, can, according to Harootunian, be held responsible for the diminishing of the reputation of Canadian marxist scholar E.H. Norman. Harootunian sees the first generation of postwar scholars as implicated in "..the relationship between American missionary experience, now inscribed in Japanese studies in the United States, and the promotion of a self-righteous prescriptive disguised as a "description" of Japan's "modernization" that resembles a Calvinist mind-set that earlier presumed to "bring enlightenment to a backward country."[14] Harootunian implies here, not that these scholars were untheoretical, but that they hid their theoretical concerns in a language of empirical description. In 1970, Japanese anthropologist Sofue Takao concurred with such critiques of modernization theorists when he argued that American social scientists had a tendency to see deviations from the American standard as a deviation from the norm.[15]

The passion evident in Robert Smith's response to attacks like Harootunian's is a measure of the depth of fissures in the field, fissures that continue to haunt it. To Smith, Harootunian's charges are a " ... remarkably uninsightful, dismissive characterization of both the individuals and their work. . . . " They are "charges that cannot go unanswered because they combine bad history with patricidal impulses." To the charge that roots in military training schools and missionary impulses must be taken into account when understanding his generation, Smith responds: "To anyone who has the faintest notion of how people were recruited into the military language programs during the war—and who these "former American military officers" are in real life—the characterization of them and their values is as hilariously wrong as it is irritatingly smug . . . the denunciation of former teachers as "thugs" and "sons of missionaries" has no proper place in academic discourse, but I suspect both commentators are simply outriders for a larger force of revisionists about to appear on the scene."[16]

Too often, the fissure here has been cast as that between "theory" and "description," between those who work empirically with the archive and those who reach beyond it analytically. The Japanese historian Stephen Vlastos articulates this schism in stark terms. He argues that there has been an isolation of Japanese Studies from other areas of scholarly pursuit, and that this isolation has been the direct result of a distance from politics and a resistance to theory: "Compared with colleagues in more crowded and politically contentious fields, Japan specialists have enjoyed considerable latitude professionally and intellectually. . . . The irrelevance of Japan Studies to American academia, I believe, is partly self-imposed: the consequence of indifference if not hostility toward theory."[17]

Vlastos may be exaggerating this dichotomy. The tension might be better understood as that between proclaimed and implicit theory, between theory that announces itself and theory that remains unstated. The "irrelevance" associated with stances characterized by implicit theory has been linked by Masao Miyoshi to the problem of ethnic representation, particularly to the absence of Japanese-American scholars in the field: "Such an absence is cognate with the scarcity of oppositional readings of Japanese literature that might have provided a dialectic context for criticism. Area specialists in the Japan field are likely to be inbred and ghettoized, conversing only on rare occasions with scholars in other areas and disciplines."[18]

I would not suggest that the dichotomy described by Vlastos, which mirrors the tensions between disciplinary and area studies affiliations, is wholly absent. In particular, it indicates a sharp point of tension in the study of Japanese literature. The critique against traditional archival scholarship has been strongly presented in political terms by Richard Okada, a scholar of classical Japanese literature:

As we know, the American academic study of Japanese literature, especially pre-modern literature, constituted no self-aware or definable "discipline," but—behind a mask of rigorous linguistic training, which was in most cases no more than an alibi for translation—it did rely on the de-politicized,   positivistic inside-outside textual dichotomies of the New Criticism and the old historicism—otherwise known as translation and introduction and/or commentary. Being housed safely within "area studies," literature professors were sheltered from their colleagues in English or other literature departments and left pretty much to their own devices.[19]

There may be less to this critique than Okada's charged tone allows. As Andrew Gordon has trenchantly shown, the fundamental position of area-based research on Japan has always linked theory and archive, or discipline and area. That natural meshing of theory and archive, first conceived by historian John W. Hall in 1966, was echoed in SSRC language in 1996. While the former was a call to "reunite area studies" with "methodological and theoretical advances in the social sciences," the latter urged scholars to "integrate discipline-based scholarship" with the "often unique perspectives provided by local—or area-based—knowledge."[20]

Japanese Studies has been criticized for merely providing case studies against which to test theories, rather than producing theoretical breakthroughs. As a consequence, workers in this field have been seen as the "fetchers" of data, to use Andrew Gordon's term. Gordon convincingly argues that instead of rebutting this criticism one should question the premise that "something called 'scientific knowledge,'{hrs}" or theory, or social sciences, or the disciplines, stands outside and above area knowledge."[21] The difficulty of answering the criticism of insufficient theory "lies in the treachery of the question, the way it dichotomizes scientific knowledge and area study to the disadvantage of area. One response must be to argue vigorously against the terms of the question, asserting that the processes of theorizing and studying areas are integrated ones . . . "[22] Gordon would argue that "knowledge in the social sciences and humanities is in some fundamental ways not about universal political or social behavior. It is about the particular."[23] In the best work, the pursuits of fetching and analyzing are indivisible. Moreover, he argues, even the most empirical of Japanese studies should be taken seriously because they have produced pictures worth having, even by those outside the field. As examples, Gordon cites Thomas C. Smith's work on the agrarian origins of modern Japan, Tak Fujitani's Foucauldian study on the symbolic production of monarchy, and Anne Allison's studies of Japanese comics and sexuality. The question of whether Japanese studies has produced a model from the ground up is an unreasonable one to Gordon. Studies of Japan have, however, produced alternate theoretical models, and here Gordon cites Chalmers Johnson's work on the late developmental state, and Doi Takeo's study of Japanese relationship patterns, *The Structure of Dependence*.

Like Gordon, Martin Colcutt sees the tension between Japanological and disciplinary pulls as pragmatically productive, and raises the vital question of the nature of student training:

> That tension is going to continue. But for those of us working in the field and for our graduate students, a good grounding and disciplinary relationship is vital. It is out of the disciplinary context that many of the theoretical and methodological questions will come which we can use to inform our own research and put to Japanese colleagues for them to consider.[24]

This happy conclusion, however, is not shared by all, as Okada's critique cited above indicates. Though he certainly underestimates the complexity of literary translation and the intellectual sophistication of its practitioners, in whose hands it could be an act of criticism based on (perhaps unstated) theoretical assumptions, Okada rightly points to the cloister in which an earlier generation of scholars of Japanese literature worked, and in which many scholars today feel frustrated. Most Japanologists surveyed in 1993 by the Japan Foundation considered Japanese studies weaker as an intellectual endeavor than the disciplines. This sense was strongest among social scientists, two thirds of whom thought so.[25] Perhaps one indication of the social sciences' relatively low opinion of Japanese Studies as an area of endeavor distinct from a disciplinary affiliation can be inferred from the responses of Japanologists to the question of the disposition of replacements of Japanologist faculty lines. The great majority of

Japanologists in language and literature departments—73%—said they would replace a Japan specialist with the same; this dropped to 53% for history and 33% for the social sciences. Conversely, the numbers go up in a similar proportion for those who said they would not replace a Japan specialist with the same.[26] While this does not necessarily imply a higher regard for Japanese studies by humanists working with Japan, it indicates at the very least that they find specialists in Japan more indispensable to their fields.

Of course, the relative regard given Japan specialists can also be connected to the nature of materials in each discipline. Japanologists perceive the importance of language skills differently depending on their objects of study. A scholar of literature has no choice but to work with original language materials; a scholar of politics might rely less so on them. In the humanities, 78% use Japanese as the primary language of research; in the social sciences, 58%.[27] Yet it may also be possible to conclude that the attitude toward one's object of study, and the very formation of that object of study, are shaped by the levels of competence in Japanese. A political scientist may be able to "get away" with fewer language skills than a literary scholar, and, having "gotten away," can construct a field where those skills are less called for. He or she will thus naturally turn more toward his disciplinary colleagues, with whom he shares a language of theory. In practical terms, political scientists may have been quick to develop a common language across geographic areas than have literary scholars across language groups. In part, this may be attributed to the relative amount of time needed to master theory as opposed to the archive. A scholar of Japanese literature, who can simply not "get away" with not working in the language, has less time to spend on theory, and may tend to become more closely connected to other scholars of Japanese literature and to other scholars of Japan than to disciplinary colleagues in, say, Euro-American literature. This tendency toward linguistic isolation is excacerbated by a particular configuration of institutional affiliation. Virtually all Japanologists, except literary scholars, are formally housed with discipline-based departments, or at least are affiliated with them. Scholars of Japanese literature are rarely affiliated with, let alone placed within, comparative literature or literature programs. This is a situation not unlike that of Greek and Latin, but the level of anxiety about ghettoization seems a relatively recent thing.

Social scientists, conversely, seem naturally drawn toward disciplinary affiliations, where less developed language skills can be compensated by use of English-language materials.[28] By the same token, lack of sufficient language skills may induce scholars to move from area into discipline. Carried to an extreme, this can result in the dismissal of the importance of language skills and the belittlement of scholarship that speaks in less theoretically weighted language—what amounts to a social scientific dismissal of area expertise. The ironic but happy result of this, however, may be the opening of area studies further into the disciplines.[29]

*

Situated at the farthest reach from non-language based scholarship on Japan is the study of literature. Hermetically sealed within Area Studies, linguistically and institutionally separated from the disciplines, the study of Japanese literature provides an example of Area Studies work par excellence.

Perhaps it is not too prosaic to suggest that the tension between theory and archive in Japanese Studies can be linked to the practical exigencies of mastering the archive. Here, study of literature may present the most extreme case, for it is arguably the subject requiring the most reading of original-language materials. For the scholar of Japanese literature, even the best intentions and the most conscientious research habits are undermined by the sheer volume of Japanese-language material needed to be mastered in the thorough investigation of a Japanese literary topic, particularly if it is to be treated in an area-studies fashion, from a cross-disciplinary and multi-geographical standpoint. To write on Natsume Sọseki (1869–1914), the emblematic Japanese novelist of the crisis of modernity, and, perhaps, the most studied modern Japanese writer, one would, in good conscience, read all, or certainly most of his own writing, totaling over thirty closely-packed volumes. In addition, one would need to familiarize oneself with the bulk of secondary literature about him, in English and Japanese, numbering in the hundreds of books and articles, as well as the theoretical and contextual material, in both English and Japanese, needed to make an argument of interest to peers in the American academy.

Some of these tasks seem reasonable. Reading everything that has been written on Sọseki in English, for example, would be simple; even reading enough theoretical and contextual material to formulate an approach to the material and articulate it with some degree of naturalness would be no great chore, although it would require reading as well in the Chinese literary and philosophical classics (in which Sōseki was raised) and gaining some understanding of Confucianism and Buddhism, the history of English literature, and the work of the Pre-Raphaelites (important influences on Sōseki). But reading in Japanese literature itself during Sōseki's time and before, as it developed from pre-modern prose to modern, would occupy many years, and reading everything by Sōseki in the time allotted a dissertation would be impossible (certainly a student of Dickens would be expected to read most of what he wrote); the thirty-odd volumes of his works would occupy one for years. Finally, the mere thought of reading everything about Sōseki written in Japanese would certainly lead one to a more lucrative and practical profession. Writing about Sōseki would require discussing passages of his writing, and each time one did so would be no mere matter of copying from book to computer and analyzing. One must translate first, a seemingly brief detour that can occupy one for hours or days.

Now, nobody who has written about Sōseki has done all this—nor should anyone be expected to. All scholarship requires carving out a manageable corpus from a morass of material. Japanese literary scholarship is no different. The difficulty here is not merely due to the massive amount of information available on virtually any scholarly topic; nor simply to the practical difficulties of working with Japanese materials. It is certainly not due to problems of access to the archive. Indeed, one (mixed) blessing of the field is the enormously easy access to a treasure of well-kept and carefully catalogued and stored materials, to which United States scholars have easy access. All Japanologists stand on the shoulders of an extraordinary tradition of scholarship written in Japanese in all disciplines and virtually all topics. If anything, scholars in the United States have a burden of influence so great it threatens hopes for originality.

Yet, with all these treasures open to us, we face the hard truth (and the almost dirty-little-secret) that few students enter a Ph. D. program in Japanese literature having read even a single novel in Japanese. While a third-year college class in Spanish might require the reading of a novel or a few short stories per week, a comparable class in Japanese, taught by the best possible teacher in the best possible program to the best possible student, would allow perhaps that much per term. Entering graduate school, an American student of Japanese literature has read less in her field in the original language than a student of English has read in high school. Such a situation leads to another dirty-little-secret of Japanese literature graduate training, pointedly remarked upon by Edwin McClellan a number of years ago, but still relevant today, despite increased numbers of students college with high-school Japanese or bilingual backgrounds. It is still common for graduate students to rely on translations for access to literature that is not of immediate concern to them. One is consistently being surprised by how little some graduate students in Japanese have actually read in the original language. Presumably, when these become teachers, they must still depend nearly as much on translations for their own general knowledge of the field.[30]

Of course no individual is to blame for this situation. The United States Foreign Language Institute places Japanese in the group (including Arabic, Chinese, and Korean) of the most difficult languages for English speakers to learn, requiring 1,320 hours of instruction in an intensive program in order to bring students to the same level of proficiency reached after only 480 hours of instruction in a language in category 1, which includes French and Spanish. According to the doyen of Japanese-language studies, Eleanor Harz Jorden, Japanese language-learning difficulty even transcends the others in its category if both the spoken and written languages are included.[31]

Masao Miyoshi, among many others, cautions against the mystification of this difficulty, through which, he argues, "a sort of proprietorship is maintained by some Japanologists, who impress outsiders with the difficulty of the Japanese language and the exceptionality of Japanese culture."[32] But the experience of those who have both learned the language as non-natives and taught and translated it seems more instructive. In the words of Van Gessel, "My own experience of studying the language, combined with a seventeen-year career spent trying to teach it in the classroom, leaves me persuaded that Japanese has earned its reputation for difficulty."[33] To become able to read a fairly easy Japanese novel with naturalness, that is, not as a language chore, takes perhaps eight to ten years. After the standard six years of graduate training, the typical student of modern Japanese literature has read (in the most rigorously archive-based programs), say, 75 novels in Japanese, and a small amount of criticism—less than an educated American has read before entering college.[34]

Such a language-learning scenario might leave even the most serious scholar in despair, especially when confronted with the enormously erudite works preceding her on almost any writer. To counter this despair, scholars have developed strategies of containment: translation and commentary studies, an enterprise undertaken by the first generation of literature scholars through the 1960s, but now a way of ensuring, at many institutions, termination in the tenure year; the single-author study, which at least limits the purview, though this has been increasingly denigrated for narrowness of scope; and finally, the increasingly prestigious and common theoretical approaches to a topic, which can compensate for thin archival reading with theoretical acumen; or the cultural-studies approach, which can reduce the amount of original-language material used. The potential problems inherent in the cultural studies approach are arguably the most daunting. A dissertation on the literature written under the American Occupation would require the reading and absorbing, in Japanese, of hundreds of novels, short stories, and essays, just to get the foundation built; and then analysis of law, politics, and material culture. A cultural studies dissertation on the literature of Japanese colonization would require mastery of both literature and politics, as well as the tools of more than one methodology.

It is certainly laudable that scholars have increasingly been attempting to leave what has been called the ghettoized world of Japanese literary studies, and that their interests have led them to intellectual affiliations not easily made within Japanese Studies (affiliations already present in an earlier generation, as Steinhoff describes). A scholar interested in the resonance between Japanese fascism and aesthetics, for example, might have more to learn from Italian, French, and German scholars and sources than from scholars of classical Japanese poetry, economics, or political science. Writing about Japanese modernism might lead one just as naturally to European sources as to Japanese or Asian—and much the same could be said for work on sexuality, colonialism and post-colonialism, and popular culture, to name a few topics of recent interest to Japan humanities scholars.

Work on Japan that reaches beyond the confines of Japan, and literary work that goes beyond literature, are potentially important and exciting; such work shows off the benefits of a flexible Area Studies orientation. Yet it should be kept in mind that it risks a thinning of the archive for a thickening of theory. Art historian John Rosenfield describes this danger well, reminding us that for scholars of Japan the pull between archive and theory is linked with that between Japan and the West:

> . . . if we lose ourselves in theoretical concerns and ignore the positivist, empirical basis of Japanese studies, we run the risk of repeating one of the most flagrant crimes of Orientalism: applying Western standards and principles of analysis without a deep understanding of the Eastern subject. Moreover, if we lose ourselves in the dense thickets of theory, we run the danger of "substituting poetics for poetry," of ignoring the expressive properties of works of art—the vital expression, the felt excitement—that should serve as the prime focus of our efforts. When we lose sight of that, we surrender the most powerful resource of our profession.[35]

To put this differently, one has only so many hours in the day, and so many years to ensure job security. To do work such as I have described above requires great pruning. For better or worse, much of this pruning has been of the archive, if for no other reason than the lateness of mastery of the language, and the slowness of reading that continues to accompany most non-Japanese scholars of Japan throughout their careers. These scholars' desires to be on a par with and able to speak to colleagues working in French, Spanish, German, and comparative literatures, and also with those in anthropology and history, make the drudgery of the archive an unappealing venture. The disciplinary or theoretical emphasis also poses the threat of discouraging students from the laborious philological work needed to study subjects such as, for example, Japanese classical literature and Buddhism.

The dilemma of the Japan scholar (especially of literature) wishing to do rigorously theoretical and concretely grounded work directly reflects the tension between area studies and discipline. The most sophisticated theoretical work, even that which does grapple seriously with a wealth of Japanese material, has often been sharply criticized for language errors upon which conceptual arguments are built; work that completely eschews theory has been criticized for being hermetic, not serious, and retrograde.

No easy solution can be offered to this problem. It might be suggested, however, that one cannot work with theory unless one has mastered the archive. Or, at the very least, that the balance of power between the two need be tilted toward the archival material; one must fetch before analyzing. The scholar of literature who does not base her work on the archive risks turning herself into a mere amateur historian, anthropologist, philosopher, or literary theorist. One cannot but ponder the advisability of guiding dissertations that leave young scholars swimming in a sea of theoretical formulations without the ballast of the archive—though no doubt buoyed up. Yet what point would there be in leaving that young scholar cemented in the concrete archival foundation with no means of going beyond it? One might suggest, at the very least, that while theory can be learned throughout one's career, the foundation of the archive is built early on, or, perhaps, not at all. Of course, an early dismissal of theory can leave a student unable to conceptualize her materials so as to communicate with scholars outside her field.

Scholarly rigor may be threatened by the contrary pulls of theory and archive, and the multiplicity of intellectual affiliations of young scholars reveals a question that strikes at the very heart of Japan Area Studies configurations. Is modern Japanese literature (or history, economics, political science) more productively understood alongside other modern literatures, or against other disciplines studying Japan and China? Why is Japan studied as part of the geographical unit of Asia? For convenience? University libraries have provided different answers (inadvertently, perhaps). At Yale, Japanese literature is shelved with its literary cohorts across the world; at Harvard and Columbia, with East Asian Studies.

East Asian programs function as administrative units, but colleagues in them are as likely to discuss office space and enrollments as they are ideas. Scholars of East Asian literatures are often linked through the mission of teaching the most difficult languages to Americans. But the association fostered by language teaching has not been all to the good. Seen by their colleagues as performing a service to the field, providing tools for later "intellectual" work, they are cordoned off from the disciplines. Often, literary scholars are in the anomalous situation of being hired to teach, in addition to their specialty, language, a professional expertise in which most have not been trained and which they are not inclined to use. Indeed, this is a misuse of their skills, but more importantly, such hiring practices diminish the seriousness of language teaching as an art and profession, and have baleful effects on the work conditions—job security, teaching loads, and salaries—of teachers exclusively trained in language pedagogy.

Furthermore, as most language teachers are women, it seems plausible to suggest here a connection between the feminization of this work and its inadequate conditions. The closer a literary scholar's connection to the work of language, the lower her status can fall. In no other discipline is a scholar expected to be teaching in what is not her discipline. (The Asianist historian asked to teach world history will still be working in her discipline.) Moreover, language teaching is time-consuming and labor intensive. One might thus speculate that it reduces the literary scholar's research output and stature, and, ultimately, the progress of the field itself.

*

The burden of language mastery in the study of Japanese literature and the diminishing status of all language-related work may be responsible for the separation of Japanese literature from other areas of Japanese studies and for the larger difficulty of linking the humanities and the social sciences more closely. Nevertheless, Richard Lambert applauds the potential in the marriage of the humanities and the social sciences, whose tie "presents an unusual opportunity for intellectual cross-fertilization through dialogue with scholars in disciplines with which they normally have little contact." Yet, according to Lambert, the enduring relative prestige of hard numbers still stymies this potentially fruitful combination. Most social sciences in area studies are of the "soft" kind, their research related to humanities-oriented topics. "The pervasive humanities aspect of much of area studies," Lambert continues,

> is immensely enriching. However, for many social scientists not engaged in area studies, particularly those at the "hard" end of the spectrum, the close ties of area studies with the humanities reinforces

their perception that area studies is not a scientific activity. From the perspective of the "hard" social scientist, the humanities are nondisciplinary. The fact that humanistic disciplines have their own distinctive conceptual and methodological framework does not alter their judgment since these disciplines do not follow the social science paradigm. To the extent that social science research in area studies leans toward the humanities, it is likewise considered nondisciplinary.[36]

Despite the centrality of the humanities, and of language study, to Japan Area Studies, then, social sciences continue to define the terms of debate.[37] Even arguments for Area Studies that endorse the centrality of language learning and cultural mastery and reject the "scientific" claims of rational choice theory have seemed to capitulate to the terms of the opposition. "Soft" humanists yield to the terms of "hard" social scientists. As Jacob Heilbrun writes:

> What is ironic is that those new internationalists who oppose the political scientists' economism often share their disregard for detailed, humanistic knowledge. In a sense, by latching onto globalism, area studies has unwittingly surrendered new territory to the rational choice theorists. For, despite the paeans to diversity and difference among the new area studies savants, they, too, assume that all cultures can be comprehended with a few globally valid formula . . . [38]

Against the prestige of hard numbers it is difficult to argue the value of intangibles. Yet the humanities must explain without embarrassment that much of its endeavor involves the intuitive reading of aesthetic materials—that it relies on a personal sensibility born of deep and hard reading of aesthetic material. This way of scholarship has tended to result in a diminishing of the humanities in the area studies enterprise. It might be argued, however, that confronting the problems facing the humanities, particularly the study of literature, is necessary for the continued viability of Japanese studies. The challenges facing scholars of Japanese literature can be seen as a concentrated and extreme version of those facing all Japanologists.

In so far as issues of globalization are intrinsically no more important than issues of identity, and in so far as the humanities identifies language as a pointer of identity, the study of language and the humanities should be as central to the intellectual enterprise of Area Studies as are the social sciences. The persistent focus on a perceived contradiction between the humanities and social sciences (some times more real than others) impedes the realization of one of Area Studies' defining ideals: to be an interdisciplinary and cross-cultural field that allows a disciplinary freedom not easily found within traditional discipline-based departments, and a geographic freedom not found in traditional single-area based departments. Some feel that the contradiction has been resolved, but in a far-from-equitable way; the political scientist Chalmers Johnson has bemoaned that "what is new today is that the competition between theory and area studies has come to an end—with the virtual defeat of the latter," a view perhaps colored by a social science prism.[39] From another angle, Area Studies seems far from dead. Area Studies—as institutional affiliation or scholarly attitude—can smooth the way for a literary scholar of Japan interested in art, architecture, and history, in Japan, and perhaps in China and Korea. For enrichment in other areas, however, she will still need walk down the hall to speak to her colleagues in German and French.

For scholars of Japanese literature, the social science perspective has not been productive. They are institutionally segregated from social scientists and historians, the former often housed in language and literature programs, the latter in institutes or centers. In Japanese Studies, scholars and students of literature seem more inclined to pay attention to their Asian Studies social science colleagues than vice versa; and are themselves often viewed as belle-lettrists or service teachers of language skills, no doubt in part because they are generally housed with (or double as) language teachers. Seeing colleagues in Japanese literature as no more than language teachers whose work could not possibly be relevant to that of other scholars diminishes scholarly possibilites for cross-fertilization. This is especially striking—and dispiriting, one should add—considering that texts usually associated with the humanities, and particularly literature, have become the center of the most fruitful converging of disciplines in the study of an "area," that is, of cultural studies.

If the humanities, and literature in particular, have long been the uneasy handmaidens of the social sciences within Area Studies, the advent of cultural studies has provided an interesting response to geopolitical complexity and variety outside Area Studies. Blurring disciplinary boundaries, cultural studies is commonsensically described by Michael Holquist as "a way of grouping the increasing number of works that bring together insights formerly apportioned among the social and human sciences."[40] Within the rubric of cultural studies, the books that had always been important to literary scholars become equally important to art historians, anthropologists, and historians. They are books with a literary core, and the language of these non-literary scholars is often peppered with the language of literary scholarship. Benedict Anderson's *Imagined Communities*, for example, argues that nations are held together by the power of narratives, that a community must create a narrative about itself that is not an actual past but a more compelling teleological tale, in Holquist's words.[41] The philology of Erich Auerbach and Walter Benjamin have provided literary models for questioning assumptions about time and space in communities. In both, "literary texts are the most intense and comprehensive expressions of the cosmologies of the cultures in which they are enshrined.[42] In the work of Hayden White and Donna Haraway, history and anthropology are seen as shaped by tropes and narratives. Literature-centered scholars can see this as asserting the literariness of nonliterary phenomena, and extending the relevance of literature as "master in a house of cultural discourse." Cultural critics can see this as decentering the centrality of literature.

Literary texts have thus become indispensable to the study of society, and the lynch-pins for interdisciplinary work that touches on "real" life: as in the work, for example, on trauma and the Holocaust by historians, psychiatrists, and literary scholars. Scholars of Japanese literature, then, need not rely on the social sciences to be engaged—if they so desire—in the "real world." Through the analysis of language, they can confront questions of power, as the scholar of American literature, Richard Poirier, has argued. Literature, writes Poirier, "is not in itself an effective political form of action . . . At best, it can help us deal more critically and effectively than we otherwise might with rhetorics outside literature, as a regular game of neighborhood softball might have the unintended effect of preparing someone to cope a little better with the rigors of the workplace.[43]

Cultural studies, which examines questions of identity, gender, and politics and culture, represents both a way out and an enriching of the old Area Studies model. In cultural studies, disciplinary and theoretical boundaries are crossed through the use of psychoanalysis, anthropology, history, linguistics, sociology, and political science; scholars are linked through a broad range of intellectual figures across disciplines.

Much of the recent interdisciplinary Japan scholarship, including anthropologist Jennifer Robertson's work on theater and imperialism, literary scholar John Treat and anthropologist Brian Moeran's edited volumes on popular culture, and historian John Dower's book on race propaganda in The Pacific War, *War Without Mercy,* has grown from this soil. *Japan in the World,* edited by Masao Miyoshi and H.D. Harootunian's in 1991, was a landmark in Japan scholarship that cuts across disciplinary and geographical boundaries. The volume set out, in literary scholar Edward Fowler's words, to "remove Japan from the cultural and geopolitical vacuum in which it paradoxically finds itself . . . "[44] Arguing that the familiar binarism of the Cold War cannot explain how states relate to one another, the book includes contributions by Perry Anderson on comparisons to Germany, Eqbal Ahmed on U.S.-Japan relations and racism, Arif Dirlik on Sino-Japanese relations, a conversation between Japanese novelist Oe Kenzaburo and British novelist Kazuo Ishiguro, Frederic Jameson on Natsume Sōseki and Rob Wilson on Korea and Japan, among others. Another example of such multi-dimensional work that involves both Japanese and Americans is the joint research project of Rikkyo University and the University of Chicago in 1988 called "The Intellectual History of Postwar Japan," which resulted in 1990 in the publication of the Daedelus special issue, *Showa: The Japan of Hirohito,* and its Japanese translation, *Nichibei no Shōwa.*[45]

These are positive developments and need not be feared, and which one hopes will not be forestalled merely through unfamiliarity, impatience, crankiness, or simple dismissal. But there are downsides as well. Art historian John Rosenfield speaks eloquently of the generational fissure the new scholarly languages create: "Graduate students today tend to dismiss the paragons of traditional scholarship" in favor of French theorists. For Rosenfield, postmodern critics' "baffling, obscurantist language" has proved frustrating. Rosenfield recognizes that these ideas have permeated academia today, and that a new generation of cultural studies scholars is emerging. With an intellectual generosity that should set an example, he "does not join those who dismiss it as trendy nonsense (or worse)" but sees it as "the product of serious thought by serious people," and potentially "a tonic that clarifies and renovates obsolete ways of thinking—when correctly applied."[46]

Energizing this generational split is the desire among some for scholarship that seems relevant to questions of power. The desire for "relevance," both outside the academy to the sphere of politics and within the academy to the world of theory, has fueled interesting work. Yet it is worth being aware that this may also be threatening the possibility of academic work that seems less concerned with the worlds of politics and power and with self-conscious theorizing. The fetishization of perceived relevance may be particularly damaging to the close study of an obscure writer, the careful examination of a literary imagination, the laborious working-through of a difficult textual problem—in short, areas of intellectual endeavor which the academy can—and should—protect from becoming antiquated and institutionally precluded tasks by the pressures of the marketplace or the rise and fall of popular trends. Like other scholars of literature, scholars of Japanese literature have drawn more and more on theories from non-literary thinkers, and have applied themselves to non-literary texts with increasing frequency. This has the potential to produce vital work but also to diminish the prestige, or relevance, of literature, and literary study. What one would like to see appear amidst the "thickets of theory" is what Jennifer Robertson calls a "reality check" of reading. If the dearth of citations of Japanese-language materials is dismaying in anthropology, it is perhaps more so in literary scholarship. Robertson writes:

> If there is one gatekeeping concept that is unequivocally appropriate for Japan scholars to employ it ought to be "bibliophilia": the long cultural history of literacy and enormity and diversity of textual production in Japan are reasons compelling enough to demand (greater) attention to bibliography.[47]

Of all fields within Japanese Studies, none has become more fractured by the clash between claims for theoretical and archival work than Japanese literature. This is somewhat peculiar, considering that a good many scholars occupy a middle ground, finding compromises between mastering primary sources and thinking through them with the tools of hard-learned theory. The vehemence of the discussion stems, one would suggest, not from calls for theoretical work, which all scholars engage in either explicitly or implicitly. The passion stems from an association made between theory and political advocacy on the one hand, and between lack of theory and scholarly disinterest on the other. In the case of Japanese literary studies, one senses an inverse relationship

between the felt irrelevance of literature to society and the need to treat literature as a tool of power. What better way to hide its origins as belle-lettres than in a call-to-arms?

Masao Miyoshi and Harry Harootunian's trechant argument against any naiive self-proclamation of "irrelevance" is pertinent here. They remind us that no scholarship has been completely innocent in its motives or effects. Their argument also, however, reveals the pitfalls of demanding of the humanities a this-worldly orientation.

> Japanologists have mobilized their expertise to differentiate Japan from the hegemonic West: this cannot be described in any other term but ethnocentrism. . . . Other experts employ their   knowledge   to represent Japan as a model of rational efficiency, management, and order. This group has seen in such contemporary Japanese achievements an exemplar for a failing American economic social order. . . . .An earlier appreciation of Japanese literature and arts has visibly declined in recent years and has been replaced by a preoccupation with political economy. . . . Assuming the existence of genuine interest in Japanese history, literature, and culture among the college-age generation today, we see too few places where such curiosity can be satisfied, given the current agenda dominating Japanology.[48]

A welcome warning against the baleful effects of prescriptive scholarship, the statement implicitly worries about the fate of scholarship and teaching that does not take on the real world. This can only be good for the humanities—and for the freedom of intellectual work. Yet, as literary scholar Edward Fowler argues, the argument seems targeted solely against "engaged" scholarship when it is "within the paradigm of American global supremacy." What of the viability of "unengaged" scholarship? Fowler asks an important question of Harootunian:

> Is this what ultimately distinguishes (intellectual) historians and other humanists from social scientists, one wonders: the urge by those in the one field merely to reflect on the human condition versus the urge by

those in the other to mold it according to their vision?[49]

The reliance upon social scientific parameters to frame this argument, purportedly made in support of the humanities, paradoxically reveals the utter absence of any consideration of "unengaged scholarship" as a legitimate practice.[50]

The pressures to be relevant have been most dire for that branch of literary scholarship that seems most untheoretical and least engaged with politics and power: the work of translation. To become a translator is a perilous choice for scholars seeking tenure and promotion. Though demeaned institutionally for intellectual irrelevance (for "fetching" rather than theorizing), and incorrectly assumed to be disconnected from the "real world," translation has, like other forms of interpretation, been a shaper of intellectual fields, while being shaped by larger social forces.[51]

The act of translation, to return to the opening of this essay, is the work of cross-cultural analysis and interpretation. It requires getting under the skin of another culture and communicating its thought and beauty in a new idiom. It calls on great stores of learning but requires an evaluation of intangibles, through intangible variables like instinct and sensibility and taste. When enacted between literary languages as separated by history and culture as are Japanese and English, translation seems well near impossible:

> When the languages are so very different, when the cultural contexts also are very different, and, finally, when literary standards are really much further apart than we sometimes like to admit, perhaps the translator must have the kind of freedom of expression which, though purporting to be translation, amounts in fact to explanation.[52]

Styles of translation change in keeping with changes in this-worldly conditions. Thirty years ago a bow might have been translated as a handshake, closeness to the Japanese sacrificed to accessibility to the English-language reader. Increased familiarity with things Japanese might now allow, in Edward Fowler's words, for "a more rigorous linguistic account of what is actually going on in the Japanese—even at the expense of "'readability'." It may now be time, he argues, to let the "foreignness seep into the text" and to "come to grips with what is different."[53] This does not mean belittling the achievements of past translations. Rather, we might recognize the brilliance of Arthur Waley's 1926 translation of the eleventh-century *Tale of Genji* "without entertaining thoughts of mimicking his habit of making it seem sometimes as if his Heian ladies wear farthingales and live at Hampton Court." We might "set our sights as readers a notch higher."[54]

That higher notch would be where Japanese Studies is grounded in politics, not in the narrow sense of tendentious arguments, but in its self-awareness as an epistemological arrangement of disciplines and geographic areas responding to a complex world and its cultures, both high and low. In an atmosphere of intellectual honesty, all Area Studies work would be conceived as acts of translation, in which scholars would grapple with foreign materials in their own terms and strive to render clearer what seemed opaque. They would link their analyses to larger intellectual problems through a language of theory that did not swallow up the original object. They might even arrive at original theoretical insights. Their "grappling" with foreign textual and lived experience would be accomplished through the same tools used in the work of translation: the deep and wide, but careful and close reading of the archive. These translators' sensibilities and analytical skills would be honed by expansive reading across disciplines and in a range of theory, and guided by rigorous disciplinary training in the tools of interpretation. They would possess the flexibility to recognize the value of humility before an awesome undertaking, and the place in their work of other intangibles like intuition and talent. Japan Area Studies would no longer call a Japanese kimono a farthingale, but it would understand why, even now, no better word might be found.

Alan Tansman is a Professor in East Asian Languages and Cultures at the University of California, Berkeley.

Notes

1. "Translation from Japanese: A Symposium," *Yearbook of Comparative and General Literature,* number 14, 1965, p. 54.

2. My thanks to an anonymous reader of this essay for reminding me of this, and for making other valuable suggestions.

3. Masao Miyoshi, "Against the Native Grain: The Japanese Novel and the "Postmodern" West" in *Off Center: Power and Culture Relations Between Japan and the United States* (Cambridge: Harvard University Press, 1991), p. 67. The

study of Japan by non-Japanese goes back almost two millennia and, through its first centuries, was developed by those interested in conquest or conversion. The first known written record about Japan by an outsider dates to a Chinese text dating from the year 54. In the thirteenth century Marco Polo "introduced Japan" to Europe, and in the sixteenth century Jesuit missionaries produced the first studies of the people and their language. From the first, translation in its multiple forms was to become a primary tool in the process of cross-cultural communication. The first translation of Japanese words into Western languages appears in a 1593 Latin text discussing the conjugation of verbs in Latin, Japanese and Portuguese, published by Emmannuelis Alvari e Societate Jesu, and in the same year Father Luis Frois wrote a history of Japan; a Japanese-Latin dictionary was published in 1595; in 1603 the first dictionary of Japanese in a modern Western language (Portuguese) was published, and Father Rodriguez wrote the first grammar in 1604. The first writing about Japan in English was a history of Japan written by the German doctor Engelbert Kaempfer, published in 1727, and then translated into Dutch, French, and German. Peter the Great, with the guidance of a shipwrecked Japanese, initiated the study of Japan in Russia with the opening of a Japanese language school in St. Petersburg in 1737. The first translation into English was Ernest Satow's, of an 1865 "Diary of a Member of the Japanese Embassy to Europe in 1862–63 (literally, "A Confused Account of a Trip to Europe Like a Fly on a Horsetail"). In 1882 Basil Hall Chamberlain published his translation of the ancient chronicle *Kojiki*. William Aston translated the ancient chronicle *Nihongi* in 1886 and the thirteenth-century Buddhist prose-poem *Hojoki* in 1893. The first chair of Japanese studies was inaugurated in 1909 at the University of Hamburg, and the School of Oriental and African Studies in England began teaching the language in 1917. The earliest British Japanologists, including Rutherford Alcock, Ernest Satow, William Aston, and Basil Hall Chamberlain, served as diplomats in Japan. Chamberlain also became Professor of Japanese Language at Tokyo Imperial University in 1886. Aston's grammar appeared between 1871 and 1873, and his history of Japanese literature, still in print today, in 1899. And in 1904 the first translation of a modern novel appeared in English. Little of this early work on Japan was free of institutional interests; as university professors, Chamberlain and Ernest Fenellosa were employees of the Japanese government. See Yasuko Makino and Masaei Saito, "National Approaches: Parallel Developments or Schools of Great Masters—some remarks on the history of Japanese Studies in Europe," in *A Student Guide to Japanese Sources in the Humanities,* Center for Japanese Studies, The University of Michigan, 1994, p. 61; Hide Ikehara Inada, *Bibliography of Translations from the Japanese into Western languages from the 16th century to 1912* (Tokyo: Sophia University Press, 1971); and Edward Fowler, "Rendering Words, Traversing Cultures: On the Art and Politics of Translating Modern Japanese Fiction," *Journal of Japanese Studies,* volume 18, number 1, 1992, pp. 1–44.

4. From 1,535 to approximately 4000 in 1989. See Patricia Steinhoff, *Japanese Studies in the United States: The 1990s* (Ann Arbor: The Association of Asian Studies, 1996), p. 6.

5. Patricia Steinhoff, "Japanese Studies in the United States: The Loss of Irrelevance" in *The Postwar Development of Japanese Studies in the United States—A Historical review and Prospects for the Future* (Tokyo: International House of Japan, 1993), p. 24.

6. Steinhoff, p. 28.

7. Steinhoff, p. 28.

8. Certain fields of study, like religion, have been interdisciplinary by nature, without such institutional causes. See Helen Hardacre, "The Postwar Development of Studies of Japanese Religions," in *The Postwar Developments of Japanese Studies in Japanese Religions,* edited by Helen Hardacre (Brill: Leiden, 1998), p. 219.

9. David W. Plath and Robert J. Smith, "How "American" are Studies of Modern Japan done in the United States?" in Harumi Befu and Josef Kreiner, eds., *Otherness of Japan: Historical and Cultural Influences on Japanese Studies in Ten Countries,* (Munchen: Iudicium-Verl., 1992), p. 206. After 1947 national character studies turned to the Soviet Union and China, but from 1946 on, the mantle of studies on Japan was carried by former members of the Civil Information and Education Section of the American occupation, like Herbert Passim, who undertook the first field studies since that done by John Embree. The opening of the University of Michigan research center at Okayama University in 1950 went hand in hand with the scholarly eschewal of national character studies, replaced now by more microscopic, community studies by scholars who had studied language at army language schools. From 1960, on rural lifestyles studies decreased among American scholars, and new categories, such as the environment, urban planning, work, suicide, etc. came to the fore. See Takao Sofue, "An Historical Review of Japanese Studies by American Anthropologists: The Japanese Viewpoint," pp. 232, 238.

10. Roger Bowen, "Japanology and Ideology: A Review Article," in *Comparative Studies in Society and History* 31 number 1, 1989, p. 185.

11. Bowen, p. 186. It should be noted that although this stance of lofty disengagement persisted throughout the 1960s and 1970s, it was decidedly not true of sinologists, who did not hesitate to express their political convictions far more than Japanologists, in journals like the *Bulletin of Concerned Asian Scholars.*

12. The inaugural conference was sponsored by the University of Michigan and held in Hakone, Japan. The six books produced by the endeavor are: *Changing Attitudes Toward Modernization,* ed., Marius Jansen; *The State and Economic Enterprise in Japan,* ed., William Lockwood; *Aspects of Social Change in Modern Japan,* ed., Ronald Dore; *Political Developments in Modern Japan,* ed., Robert Ward; *Dilemmas of Growth in Prewar Japan,* ed., James Morley; *Tradition and Modernization in Japanese Culture,* ed., Donald Shiveley.

13. Hardacre, p. xiii.

14. Harry D. Harootunian, "E.H. Norman: His Life and Scholarship, ed. Roger Bowen", *Journal of Asian Studies,* no. 4, 1988, p. 878.

15. Sofue, p. 238.

16. Plath and Smith, p. 217.

17. Stephen Vlastos, "Panel Discussion," in *Japanese Studies in the United States: The Loss of Irrelevance*, p. 47.

18. Miyoshi, p. 167. Sylvia Yanagisako also raises the question of the relationship of Asian-Americans to Asian Studies: "The unspoken Gentlemen's Agreement of mutual exclusion between Asian Studies and Asian-American Studies betrays their mutual commitment to a structuralist-functionalist theory of personality, culture, and society. This holistic vision of cultural and social integration justifies the boundary between Asian Studies and Asian-American Studies, treating it as a natural geographic feature in a topography of academic spaces." See "Asian Exclusion Acts," p. 6.

19. Richard Okada, "Disciplines, Areas, and Premodern Japanese Literature," p. 6.

20. Andrew Gordon, "Taking Japanese Studies Seriously: Draft for the 25th Anniversary Project of the Reischauer Institute of Japanese Studies, "p. 5.

21. Gordon, p. 6.

22. Gordon, p. 27.

23. Gordon, p. 23.

24. Martin Colcutt, "Panel Discussion," p. 44.

25. Steinhoff, *The 1990s*, p. 118.

26. Steinhoff, p. 242.

27. Steinhoff, p. 147.

28. Steinhoff, p. 160.

29. The American Japanologist perception of the need for language skills has continued to grow in all areas: in 1993 57% thought it indispensable to understand Japanese (52% to speak, and 67% to read); 10% thought it not necessary at all. One should hardly be surprised at the high correlation between ability and perceived utility.(ibid.,87) Even given these differences among fields, there has been an overall weakening of affiliation studies among Japanologists within Japanese studies. In 1984, 30% of scholars submitted for publication work solely on Japanese studies; by 1995 this had shrunk to 16%. Japanologists' choices of affiliation have also shifted. Between 1984 and 1995, the percentage of Japan scholars who turned to a Japan specialist in their own discipline for critique of their work had risen from 57% to 70%; the percentage of those who turned to a non-Japan specialist in their own discipline rose from 21% to 43%; of those who turned to a specialist in other disciplines from 10% to 22%; and of those who turned to a non-Japan specialist in other disciplines from 2% to 12%. Not surprisingly, humanists are more likely than social scientists to seek out Japan specialists in their own discipline. More than half of social scientists turn to non-Japan specialists in their own disciplines, while under 40% of humanists do so. This might imply that the continued viability of area studies depends on the centrality of the humanities. Steinhoff, *The 1990s*, pp. 87, 156–59.

30. Edwin McClellan, "The Study of Japanese Literature in the Unites

States," p. 72.

31. Van Gessel, "Teaching "The Devil's Own Tongue": The Challenges of Offering Japanese in a College Environment," *ADFL Bulletin* volume 28, number 2, 1997, p.7.

32. Miyoshi, p. 11.

33. Gessel, p. 9.

34. Despite these difficulties, or perhaps in ignorance of them, Japanese language enrollments have increased dramatically since 1960, when according to MLA figures 1,746 students were enrolled nationwide. This number increased seven-fold by 1980, to 11,506; and then truly boomed in the next six years, almost doubling to 23, in 1986, then doubling again by 1990, to 45,717. In these four years, Japanese had grown by 95%, while Russian had grown by 30% and Spanish by 29%. No doubt these figures represent the impact of Japan's economy, along with media images of a rising Japan that presented trade barriers and possibly jobs for language speakers. Steinhoff, *The 1990s*, p. 9.

35. John M. Rosenfield, "Japanese Art Studies in America in 1945," in Hardacre, p. 189.

36. "Blurring the Disciplinary Boundaries: Area Studies in the United States," in *American Behavioral Scientist* volume 33, number 6, 1990, p. 731.

37. The disciplines chosen by doctoral students do not accord with this hegemony. In 1995, political science accounted for 14%, and comprised the biggest single discipline, but the combination of humanities or humanities-inflected disciplines accounted for a far greater number: history 13%, literature 11%, anthropology 10%, linguistics 9%, art history 5%, religion and philosophy 5%, sociology 4%, education 3%, performance 3%. (Economics accounted for 3%.) Steinhoff, *The 1990s*, p. 38. From 1970 to 1993 the number of students declined by one-third to 16.3%; language and literature remained steady at 22%; economics increased slightly from 4 to 6%, and art history from 5 to 6%; anthropology dropped from 10 to 6%, political science from 10 to 8%. Seen in larger clusters, the humanities (history, art history, philosophy, religion and literature) in 1995 accounted for 38%; social sciences (anthropology, economics, political science, sociology), 31%, language and literature, 6%, the arts (performing and practicing) 3%, interdisciplinary studies, women's studies, urban studies, and Asian studies 5%. Steinhoff, pp. 28–29.

38. "The News Everywhere: Does Global Thinking Threaten Local Knowledge? The Social Science Research Council Debates the Future of Area Studies," *Lingua Franca*, May/June 1996, pp. 55–56.

39. *The National Interest*, 1994, p. 13.

40. "A New Tour of Babel: Recent Trends Linking Comparative Literature Departments, Foreign Language Departments, and Area Studies Programs," *ADFL Bulletin*, fall, 1995, p. 108.

41. Holquist, p. 111.

42. Holquist, p. 112.

43. Richard Poirier, *The Renewal of Literature, Emersonian Reflections* (New

York: Random House, 1987), p. 48.

44. Edward Fowler, "Reflections on Hegemony, Japanology, and Oppositional Criticism," *Journal of Japanese Studies,* volume 22, number 2, 1996, p. 401.

45. Such examples are rare, however. English-language scholarship on Japan has not had a significant impact in Japan. Most is produced for Japan specialists outside Japan, and requires citation of sources in both languages. stein. Citation indexes reveal that American Japan specialists are still fairly invisible, bypassed by American scholars for native Japanese scholars in Japan. While this can be taken as a sign of internationalization of American research, it reveals a resistance to homegrown specialists. Indeed, three quarters of the scholarship on Japan by Americans is not by specialists: one quarter is by American social scientists working in collaboration with Japanese; and one half by non-specialists alone, relying on English-language sources. Steinhoff, *The 1990s,* p. 33.

A survey sponsored by the Japan Foundation in 1993 speaks to the question of scholarly relations between Japanese and Americans. Less than 5% of American scholars of Japan know no Japanese scholars; less than one quarter know less than five, and over one-third more than 10. American scholars sought out these relationships to keep abreast of scholarship, maintain access to research facilities, have their work critiqued; many also indicate they share a common culture of research activity, teaching, and mentoring of graduate students. Steinhoff, p. 110.

Though the influence of English-language Japan scholarship on Japanese scholars has not been great in terms of amount of work translated into Japanese (only 29% of Japan specialists have publications translated into Japanese; 24% have written in Japanese) a number of books have been quite influential in Japan. For example, E.H. Norman's *Japan's Emergence of a Modern State* (1940) was translated in 1947. It appealed to broad range of Japanese scholars—reaching both the Marxists, whose reemergence was sparked by the postwar rebirth of social sciences, and the non-Marxists, who were attracted Norman's liberal humanism. Japanese anthropologist Sofue Takao points to Ruth Benedict's The *Chrysanthemum and the Sword* (1946), which was translated in 1948 and became a best seller in Japan in 1949, and John Embree's 1939 *Suye Mura,* 1939, as a source of new research methodology in rural sociology. The translator of the book wrote in 1987: "To me, Embree's book was a kind of mystery for a long time . . . John Embree did not speak any Japanese, and yet he was able to write such a wonderful book, which became one of the most important classics in the study of the Japanese rural village." Sofue, p. 232.

46. "When misapplied," he continues, "it can be harmful, even lethal, and the proper dosage is not easy to discern." See John Rosenfield, "Japanese Art Studies in America Since 1945," in Hardacre, p. 168. The dismissal of new styles of theorizing can be seen throughout the volume. Historian Harold Bolitho quips that "it is obvious that, notwithstanding all the posturing, when

the principles are translated into practice the postmodernist bite proves considerably less painful than its bark." Important to Bolitho is the question, "What were the Japanese people of the time really like?" and though this is certainly worth asking, it is certainly not all there is to ask, and need not yield the conclusion that scholars struggling with new ideas are merely pouring old wine into new bottles: "In Japan, at least, the wave of the future does not seem to have overtaken the past." One wonders why, to Bolitho, heavy citation of Japanese scholarship is necessarily better than heavy citation of Western, and why the latter need be dismissed for that reason. Harold Bolitho, "Tokugawa Japan: The Return of the Other? " in Hardacre, pp. 106–110.

47. Jennifer Robertson, "When and Where Japan Enters: American Anthropology Since 1945," in Hardacre, p. 307.

48. *Japan in the World*, ed. Masao Miyoshi and H.D. Harootunian, (Durham: Duke University Press, 1993), p. 69.

49. Fowler, "Reflections on Hegemony," p. 408.

50. Japanese studies, like other area studies, was born in the political press of the Cold War. According to Bruce Cummings, "to be in "Korean studies" or "Chinese studies" was daily to experience the tensions that afflicted Korea and China during the long period of the cold war." "Boundary Displacement: Area Studies and International Studies after the Cold War,"

51. The translation of modern Japanese literature is primarily a postwar phenomenon. The first postwar translations of modern Japanese literature, published primarily by Knopf, were, in Edward Fowler's view, chosen for their evocations of exotic Japaneseness and their thematizing of a search for the past. Japan had been an enemy and was now an ally, alluring to Western readers for its sensuality and beauty. This, Fowler argues, set a "very broad consensus" on translatable literary values: the elusive, misty, delicate and taciturn. These novels include Kawabata Yasunari's *Snow Country* in 1956, Ooka Shohei's *Fires on the Plain* in 1957, Mishima Yukio's *The Sound of the Waves* in 1954, *The Temple of the Golden Pavilion* in 1957, *Confessions of a Mask* in 1958, Natsume Soseki's *Kokoro* in 1957, Dazai Osamu's *Setting Sun* in 1956. The extent to which Japanese have presented these very same values to the world should not be overlooked; and in recent years the norm has been translations of edgier, more fractured and disturbing novels speaking from Japan as a modern nation with modern woes to other sufferers of modernity; or translations born of a playful post-modern sensibility; or of popular genres like detective fiction and comics.

While the early translators from Japanese made their sporadic contributions, translations into Japanese were made in the hundreds and thousands. The trade imbalance in translation continues into the 1990s: of the almost 50,000 titles translated world-wide per year, 2,011 out of 2,754 translated into Japanese are from English; while only 54 titles of 1,086 translated from Japanese are into English. Edward Fowler, "Rendering Words, Traversing Cultures: On the Art and Politics of Translating Modern Japanese Fiction," *Journal of Japanese Studies*, volume 18, number 1, 1992, pp. 1–44.

52. McClellan, "Translation,"p. 57.

53. Fowler, "On Naturalizing and Making Strange: Japanese Literature in Translation," *Journal of Japanese Studies,* volume 16, number 1, Winter, 1990, p. 131.

54. Fowler, p. 132.

Chapter 5

Soviet and Post-Soviet Area Studies

Victoria E. Bonnell and George W. Breslauer

This paper was originally prepared for the Revitalizing Area Studies Conference, April 24–26, 1998. Soon afterward, the paper was made available as a Berkeley Program in Soviet and Post-Soviet Studies working paper and sent out to many colleagues. We received comments and suggestions from Mark Beissinger, Robert Conquest, Archie Brown, Gregory Grossman, David Hooson, Robert Huber, Charles Jelavich, Bruce Parrott, Nicholas Riasanovsky, T.H. Rigby, Thomas Remington, Gil Rozman, Peter Rutland, Michael Urban, and Reginald Zelnik. In early 2000 we completed a second set of revisions on the paper. Three external reviews of the second version of the paper reached us in October 2002. Two of these reviews were anonymous and a third came from James R. Millar. In response to these comments and suggestions and in anticipation of the publication of this volume, we prepared a third updated version of the paper which was completed in November 2002. Our thanks to all who have given us feedback on various drafts. We are grateful to David Engerman for his assistance in the preparation of the original version of the paper.

INTRODUCTION

The remarkable feature of Soviet area studies is that, as a field of scholarly inquiry, it disappeared in December 1991, along with the Soviet Union as a national entity. Many geographical areas in the world have undergone significant geopolitical changes since the Second World War, but the dissolution of a major subject area—one of the largest in the world—is unprecedented. Beginning in 1992, specialists on the Soviet Union—"Sovietologists"—were called upon to reorient themselves to the fifteen successor states that had been carved out of the former Soviet Union. Whereas one powerful nation-state was the unit for analysis before 1992, now specialists studied such diverse countries as Lithuania, Ukraine, Georgia, Kazakhstan, Tadzhikistan, or, in many cases, Russia.

The change in geographical boundaries coincided with a fundamental reconfiguration of the questions and topics addressed by specialists. As Edward W. Walker put it in 1993: "No longer challenged to explain order, stability, institutionalization, or the functioning of the 'Soviet system,' we find ourselves confronted by dysfunction, fundamental and disjunctive institutional change, rapid attitudinal and behavioral adjustments to an ever-changing structure of opportunities, anti-regime mass mobilization, ethnic violence, and the driving force of intense nationalism."[1] With the breakup of the Soviet Union, a new field emerged: post-Soviet studies or, to put it another way, FSU (former Soviet Union) studies.

This essay traces the origins and development of Soviet area studies from their inception in the early 1940s to the present. In the first part, we examine the institutional framework and the funding sources for Soviet and post-Soviet area studies. The second part concentrates on the connection between area studies and the disciplines. Next, we consider intellectual trends and map the major changes that have taken place in the conceptualization of Soviet area studies from the Second World War to the collapse of the USSR. In the final section, we provide an overview of the formation of post-Soviet area studies.

The focus of our inquiry is Soviet and post-Soviet area studies *in the United States*. A large Sovietological community developed in the United Kingdom; important, but smaller communities emerged in Canada, Australia, France, West Germany, Sweden, Italy, Israel, and elsewhere. For the sake of manageability, however, and given the purposes of the project of which this essay is a part, we will confine our attention to the United States, which has produced a large proportion of the Western specialists and publications dealing with the Soviet Union.

INSTITUTIONAL INFRASTRUCTURE AND FUNDING

It is often said that Soviet area studies are an offspring of the Cold War, a circumstance that has indelibly marked the field institutionally and intellectually.[2] There can be no doubt that the Cold War provided an enormous stimulus for the expansion of American Sovietology and its elaboration as a field of research and teaching within the university.

Nevertheless, it is well to remember that the phenomenon of area studies generally, and Soviet area studies in particular, actually originated during World War II, before arctic breezes separated the wartime allies.

In fact, much of what subsequently constituted "Soviet area studies" in American universities was originally conceived in 1943, prior to the Cold War era.[3] The USSR Division of the Office of Strategic Services, which in 1943 was directed by the historian Geroid Robinson and had sixty social scientists, "constituted a research agenda that would literally define the field of postwar Sovietology."[4] The wartime roots of the postwar Soviet area studies centers can be found in the general approach of key figures in the USSR Division who advocated "integrated, multidisciplinary coverage of one country" while maintaining a grounding in a traditional discipline.[5] This conception of area studies also gained early support from other influential sources. In 1943, the Committee of World Regions of the Social Science Research Council (SSRC) recommended a similar approach to the study of "foreign regions," as did the Committee on Area Studies at Columbia University.[6] A sixteen-week Russian area program organized at Cornell University in 1943 and 1944, with funding from the Rockefeller Foundation, put into practice the multidisciplinary conception of area studies.[7]

With the establishment of the Russian Institute at Columbia University in 1946, Soviet area studies moved permanently into a university setting. The Russian Institute was only the first of a series of multidisciplinary centers that provided broad "integrated" area training for scholars rooted in a particular discipline.[8] The centers, which usually issued either a certificate or an M.A. degree for graduate students, prepared specialists for teaching and scholarly research, government service and research, or the professions (journalism, business and law, and administration).[9]

The Columbia program, and others established soon afterward at Harvard University (1948), the University of California at Berkeley (1948)[10], and elsewhere, typically had "few resources in teaching and scholarship, and almost no tradition, on which to build."[11] Over the next decade, however, area centers grew rapidly, with the addition of new faculty and substantial graduate student enrollments.[12] By the end of the 1950s, thirteen major American universities (University of

California at Berkeley, Columbia University, Fordham University, Harvard University, Indiana University, University of Illinois, University of Michigan, University of Minnesota, University of Notre Dame, Syracuse University, University of Washington, Wayne State University, University of Wisconsin, Yale University[13]) operated centers, institutes, committees, programs or boards with a focus on Russia, Slavic Studies, the Soviet Union, Soviet Policy, and in some cases, Eastern Europe as well. Notwithstanding the many variations in title, virtually all of them focussed primarily on Russia and were dominated by Russianists. The multi-ethnic composition of the Soviet Union was noted but seldom studied in depth. [14]

Although area centers continued to expand throughout the 1950s, they remained subject to a variety of circumstances and pressures—domestic and foreign—that both encouraged and inhibited their progress.[15] The need to "know your enemy" was counterbalanced by a suspicion of everything connected to the Soviet Union, sometimes extending to individuals and institutions devoted to research on that country. In retrospect, it is clear that the large and flourishing centers and institutes of the 1950s would not have been possible without cooperation among three important groups: university administrations, philanthropic foundations, and the US government. In some public universities, the state legislature was also a factor.[16]

University administrations varied greatly in their reception of Soviet area studies, but without their support and the allocation of resources, no program could succeed.[17] Major foundations provided considerable incentives to cooperate. In 1946 Columbia's Russian Institute drew much of its initial funding from the Rockefeller Foundation, as did UC Berkeley's Institute of Slavic Studies two years later.[18] Foundations sometimes took the initiative in identifying universities that provided suitable sites for future area studies centers. For example, in 1947 Carnegie Corporation Vice President, John W. Gardner, considered Harvard, Columbia and Stanford as possible sites for a Russian studies center. The Carnegie Corporation subsequently decided to fund the Harvard Russian Research Center, which opened formally in February 1948.[19]

Foundations supported Soviet area studies in other ways as well. In

1952, the Ford Foundation launched the Foreign Area Fellowship Training Program designed to fund graduate training, research, and travel in all "non-Western areas."[20] This program, which continued until 1972, provided substantial support for students and scholars in the Russian field.[21] The overall commitment of the Ford Foundation to area studies can be gauged from its expenditure of $270 million between 1951 and 1966 for the International Training and Research Program, designed to promote "multidisciplinary research and training in the humanities and social sciences focused on particular regions of the world."[22]

Foundations also supported important scholarly organizations, such as the Joint Committee on Slavic Studies, established in 1947.[23] Appointed by the American Council of Learned Societies (it was an enlargement of the ACLS Committee on Slavic Studies) and the SSRC, the Joint Committee provided general guidelines and fellowships for Soviet area studies.[24] The Joint Committee was also a prime mover in setting up a scholarly exchange with the Soviet Union. This effort, designed to alleviate some of the problems faced by scholars operating in a data-poor environment, came to fruition in 1958 with the signing of the first US-Soviet exchange agreement, to be administered by the Inter-University Committee on Travel Grants (IUCTG), which was superceded in 1968 by a new entity, the International Research and Exchanges Board (IREX)."[25]

The IUCTG and IREX exemplify the cooperative relationship that developed among scholarly associations, foundations and the U.S. government in the field of Soviet area studies. IREX, for example, was established by the ACLS and SSRC; one half of its funds came from foundations, while the other half came from the government-sponsored National Endowment for the Humanities and the U.S. International Communication Agency.[26]

In the 1940s and 1950s, the U.S. government played an active and critical role in supporting and encouraging the development of Soviet area studies. Many specialists of the immediate post-World War II era had served in government during the war[27] and were well disposed to cooperate with government agencies, both before and after the onset of the Cold War. Although the full story of federal government involvement has yet to be told, the newly established Soviet area studies institutes and centers often had ties of one sort or another with

government agencies and branches of the military services. The best
known example is the collaboration between the US Air Force and
Harvard's Russian Research Center to carry out the Refugee Interview
Project. Beginning in 1948, the Air Force contracted with the Russian
Research Center to fund a large-scale project involving Soviet refugees.
It aimed at constructing a "working model" of Soviet society and
delineating a social-psychological profile of its citizens in the event of
atom bomb operations against the USSR. The project, which continued
until 1954, generated four books and thirty-five articles.[28]

Cooperation between area centers and the U.S. government took
other forms as well. Between 1946 and 1951, for example, Columbia's
Russian Institute invited twenty members of the Department of State's
Foreign Service to participate in the Institute in order "to improve their
knowledge and understanding and at the same time add another
dimension to the student body by attending the Institute."[29] With the
onset of the Cold War, the Soviet Union acquired new and urgent
importance for national security. A 1991 SSRC report described the
situation[30]:

> The ideological conflicts of the Cold War became an important motive
> force driving American Soviet studies. Government agencies became an
> important employer for Soviet studies specialists. At the same time,
> many of the specialists on the Soviet Union initially available to
> American universities were refugees from the Soviet Union and Eastern
> Europe. Not surprisingly, the combination of these forces rapidly
> enlarged the field but heavily skewed the intellectual agenda toward
> policy studies. Because on-the-ground access was limited, close links
> developed between many American scholars of the region and the
> American intelligence agencies that were in a position to generate
> useful information on the Soviet Union.

Access to information about the Soviet Union was indeed one of the
major problems facing American specialists. To improve this situation,
the U.S. government negotiated the first US-Soviet scholarly exchange
in 1958, and subsequently helped to fund the program in conjunction
with private foundations. After the launching of the first Sputnik in
October 1957, the Eisenhower administration persuaded Congress to
pass the National Defense Education Act (NDEA) in 1958. In

accordance with Title VI of NDEA, substantial support was channeled to area studies centers and individuals willing to study languages and areas considered critical to national security.[31] The scope and impact of this funding was considerable. Although the initial appropriation to Title VI was less than $500,000, it had expanded to $14 million in 1966.[32]

By the end of the 1950s, an institutional infrastructure for Soviet area studies had become established in the United States. The major pillars of this large and expanding edifice consisted of university-based area studies centers, the Joint Committee on Slavic Studies, and the American Association for the Advancement of Slavic Studies (AAASS, established in 1948). They were supported financially by university administrations, large foundations, and the U.S. government. They were bolstered intellectually by specialized journals such as *Slavic Review* (a quarterly journal, with various titles, published by the AAASS), *The Russian Review* (a quarterly journal dating from 1941), *Problems of Communism* (a USIA publication dating from 1952), *Soviet Studies* and *Survey* (quarterlies published in Great Britain). They were assisted in their knowledge-production by research and daily reports of the Munich-based Radio Liberty, and aided by important translation services: *Current Digest of the Soviet Press* (founded in 1948 at Ohio State University); *Foreign Broadcast Information Service — Daily Report, Soviet Union;* and the *Joint Publications Research Service* (both produced by the US Government).

The 1960s marked a transitional decade for Soviet area studies, when turbulent domestic events (including the rise of popular movements among African-Americans, students, and women) combined with the Vietnam War to shift national priorities and intellectual agendas. As a consequence of these developments, foundations and government agencies began to turn "from international and foreign area studies to domestic problems."[33] In the course of the 1970s, funding for area studies generally and Soviet area studies in particular underwent a sharp decline. One telling indicator is the Ford Foundation, which had been a major source of funding. Its allocation for Soviet area studies dropped from $47 million in 1966 to slightly more than $2 million in 1979.[34]

There were, however, some countervailing forces in the 1970s. The American Council of Teachers of Russia (ACTR) was founded in 1974 as a professional association among university and secondary teaching of Slavic languages to promote research and training. Two years later, ACTR began to conduct academic exchanges, a program that was considerably expanded with the creation of the American Council for Collaboration in Education and Language Study (ACCELS) in 1987.

In December 1974, the Kennan Institute for Advanced Russian Studies, a division of the Woodrow Wilson International Center for Scholars, was established with support from both the US Government and grants and gifts from foundations, corporations, and individuals.[35] The Institute was intended to "bring scholars. . .into closer contact with interested persons from government, industry, and the press."[36] Three years later, a new funding agency was created by the US government: the National Council for Soviet and East European Research. Initially supported by the Department of Defense and the Department of State and subsequently assisted by the Arms Control and Disarmament Agency as well, but administered by an independent Board of Trustees composed entirely of academics from leading US universities, the National Council was designed to bring "the independent research efforts of qualified academic specialists to bear in broad areas of interest identified by the participating Government agencies."[37] In 1983, Title VIII ("The Soviet and East European Research and Training Act") was promulgated by the United States Congress and came to provide annual infusions of national resources for a variety of exchange, research, and teaching institutions.

Spurred by the collapse of détente in the late-1970s, and by the renewed militancy in U.S.-Soviet relations during the first Reagan administration, large foundations turned their attention once again to Soviet studies. The Rockefeller Foundation gave million-dollar awards each to Columbia, Berkeley-Stanford, and UCLA-Rand to build innovative programs of research, training, and public education in Soviet foreign policy. The Carnegie Corporation and the MacArthur Foundation awarded large institutional grants to scholars and graduate students within leading Soviet area centers, and more broadly within leading universities, to generate area and non-area knowledge pertinent to our understanding of the requisites of international security. As most of these grants went to the social sciences, the Mellon Foundation decided to right the imbalance by issuing large block grants to a number of leading Soviet area centers for funding of history and the humanities But by the early 1990s, a series of trends converged from several directions to place great stress once again on the fiscal solvency of post-Soviet (FSU) studies. Many of the foundation grants were nonrenewable, or went through limited numbers of renewals. More consequentially, the major foundations began to redirect a significant proportion of funds previously allocated to US institutions of higher education into the regions themselves, helping scholars and institutions within the FSU to develop expertise, organization, and community. At the same time, the trend in the social sciences toward cross-regional research and globalization themes led to a further redirection of foundation funds away from post-Soviet area studies *per se,* with the exception of US scholars working in collaboration with FSU counterparts.

Organizational changes with financial consequences accompanied these trends. The Social Science Research Council and the American Council of Learned Societies eliminated their "Joint Committees" on the Soviet Union and on East Europe, though SSRC continues to support area studies in other ways. A major exception to these generalizations has been the truly huge sums expended by the National Science Foundation and The Carnegie Corporation of New York on scholarly surveys of mass and elite opinion in the FSU, which has developed into a veritable cottage industry within post-Soviet studies.

With the introduction of Gorbachev's reforms and the gradual opening up of Soviet society, a variety of new institutions and organizations began to provide American scholars with opportunities for research in the Soviet Union. Although IREX continued to serve as a major government-funded institutional focus for the exchange of scholars between the U.S. and U.S.S.R (and later, with the Soviet successor states), it was now supplemented by university-to-university exchanges and more importantly, by the American Council for Collaboration in Education and Language Study (ACCELS). Since 1998, under the new rubric of American Councils for International Education, ACCELS has become a leading organization in the administration of government-funded exchange programs with Russia and Eurasia. In 1997 the Ford Foundation allocated four million dollars for the World Wide Fund for Area Studies, in an effort to encourage US institutions of higher education to develop new conceptions of area studies that could withstand the assaults on area studies implicit in the cross-regional and globalization tendencies within the social sciences. In addition, Ford allocated another four million dollars to "strengthen key organizations and scholarly associations working in area studies." Of this, two million has been awarded to the SSRC for international programs administered jointly with the ACLS.[38]Meanwhile, the federal government began to reexamine the affordability of continuing contributions to Soviet/post-Soviet studies, given the disappearance of the "enemy" that needed to be "known," and given the fiscal crisis of U.S. government inherited from the Reagan years. This posed an imminent and major threat to both Title VI (Department of Education) and Title VIII. Title VI funding declined in real dollars, but continued to provide the base institutional funding of more than a dozen centers.[39] Title VIII also survived despite substantial cuts, and provided support for many organizations including IREX, the Kennan Institute, the National Council for Eurasian and East European Research,[40] and many others. A new source of government funding was made available in 1991 through the National Security Education Act. Supported by the Department of Defense and the Central Intelligence Agency, the National Security Education Program (NSEP) is designed to "support graduate training of area studies specialists and study abroad for undergraduate students."[41]

All these sources of financial stringency were compounded by the fiscal crisis experienced by U.S. universities in the 1990s. Fewer positions were being refilled after retirements, deaths, and separations than had been the case in previous decades. Some departments that formerly had substantial faculty now found themselves facing a situation of diminishing resources. [no new paragraph here] In view of these converging fiscal pressures during the 1990s, the leading centers of research and training in post-Soviet studies turned to private-sector fundraising as insurance against losses of their base funding. The goal—at Harvard, Columbia, Michigan, Stanford, Berkeley, and others—has been to build an endowment large enough to ensure that the center continues to flourish in perpetuity. To be sure, scholars at these centers continue to raise funds from foundations and other sources in support of their individual and collaborative research projects. But the basic infrastructural needs of the centers, still funded by Title VI, and the need to support graduate students at public universities, was increasingly held hostage to the success of efforts to raise endowments.

In the aftermath of the events of September11, 2001, the funding situation and institutional context for post-Soviet studies changed once again. A growing awareness and fear of global terrorism, in combination with the realization that Soviet successor states have strategic importance for the U.S., precipitated dramatic reordering of priorities in funding by the federal government, foundations, and universities. Allocations for Title VI National Resource Centers and FLAS fellowships were steeply increased in 2002, testimony to the renewed and heightened concern with this part of the world.

The formal organization of Soviet studies in the United States has remained relatively intact since the collapse of communism.. As before, post-Soviet studies is marked by about fifteen major centers and institutes in leading universities, funded by the Department of Education. Among these, the most prominent centers, as before, are (in alphabetical order) Berkeley, Columbia, Harvard, Illinois, Indiana, Michigan, Stanford, UCLA, the University of Washington and Wisconsin. Some changes have occurred in the names attached to these centers. In a number of cases, "Eurasia" has been added to signify coverage of all the Soviet successor states.[42]

With the disintegration of the Soviet bloc and the USSR, and the end of the Cold War, pressures immediately arose for a redefinition of "area" and a reshuffling of academic jurisdictions. In some universities, this has resulted in pressures for a formal separation of East European studies from FSU studies, and the inclusion of the former within centers or institutes devoted to the study of "Europe." In some universities, FSU studies and centers have been incorporated into European studies institutes. Similarly, Middle Eastern studies centers have looked to expand their purview into former Soviet Central Asia, though we are not aware of major universities at which such a formal transfer has taken place. Most frequently, we have seen the emergence of new programs, freestanding or within Europe or FSU centers, for research and instruction on Central Asia, the Caucasus, or the Baltic states. The human capital to staff such programs is currently spread very thin, a situation that will almost certainly improve in the aftermath of September 11, 2001 as the strategically located states of the South Caucasus (Armenia, Azerbaijan, and Georgia) and Central Asia (Kazakhstan, Kyrgyzstan, Uzbekistan, Tajikistan, and Turkmenistan) attract the attention of scholars and funding agencies.

AREA STUDIES AND THE DISCIPLINES

From its inception in the second half of the 1940s, Soviet studies as a field of inquiry encompassed many disciplines, subject areas, and varieties of scholarship. Many of the scholars who led the way in creating Soviet area studies centers specialized in history, anthropology, sociology, economics, and psychology.[43] Over time, however, political scientists became more and more central to Soviet area studies and the other social sciences—especially sociology and anthropology—receded in importance.

In 1959, there were about thirty sociologists with professional training in Russian studies.[44] Ten or twenty years later, the number had dwindled to far fewer. If we look at the disciplinary distribution of the Ford Foundation's Foreign Area Fellowships between 1952 and 1972, we will see why. Ford made a total of 469 awards to graduate students in the Soviet and East European fields during these two decades. Historians received by far the largest number of awards (178 or 38% of the total); political scientists received the second largest number (112 or 24%) followed by language and literature (49 or 8%) and economics (48 or 8%). History and literature—disciplines relatively remote from the Cold War—together received 46% of the funding from this important source. Throughout this entire period, only six sociologists and two anthropologists were awarded fellowships.[45]

The trends in disciplinary specialization coincided with intellectual and practical developments in the field. A combination of circumstances—including the obstacles to primary research and an aversion to Soviet cultural products—drew historians and specialists in Russian literature to the period before 1917. Since field research in the Soviet Union was extremely limited for American scholars (even after the creation of an exchange program with the Soviet Union in 1958), anthropologists, sociologists, and psychologists – who had played such a leading role in Harvard's Refugee Interview Project—turned their attention elsewhere once that unique source of data had been exhausted. By the 1960s, research on the Soviet Union was mainly carried on by three groups: literary scholars studying "the thaw" in Russian culture after Stalin's death, and political scientists and economists attempting to make sense of the post-Stalin era. The latter groups of "Sovietologists" faced formidable research obstacles and were prone, for either ideological or practical reasons, to place "heavy emphasis. . .on events and personalities in Moscow, on 'Kremlinology'—psyching-out the conflicts and motivations of the top political and military leadership."[46] Some political scientists undertook broad-ranging research on Soviet history as well as contemporary developments.[47]

In the 1970s, a new source of data became available with the emigration to the West of hundreds of thousands of Soviet Jews (and some Soviet Germans). Several major projects were created to take advantage of this new research opportunity. The United States government allocated about ten million dollars to interdisciplinary teams of scholars to conduct mass surveys, with a sample of 3000 respondents and intensive interviews with scores of specialists among the émigrés. The Soviet Interview Project drew in political scientists, economists, and a few sociologists, and made important contributions to understanding how Soviet society had changed between the 1930s and the 1970s. It resulted in dozens of articles published in area and disciplinary journals, as well as several book-length volumes.[48] The Berkeley-Duke Project on the Second Economy of the USSR was created in 1977 by Gregory Grossman and Vladimir Treml. The samples for both the questionnaires and the intensive interviews were of a magnitude comparable to the Soviet Interview Project and the project yielded numerous occasional papers, chapters and articles. Among other accomplishments, the Berkeley-Duke Project highlighted the important role of the Soviet "second economy."

Since the collapse of the Soviet Union, significant changes have taken place in the disciplinary distribution of area specialists generally and within particular disciplines. For the first time since the 1940s and 1950s, growing numbers of sociologists and anthropologists—at both the faculty and graduate student levels—have embarked on research in the field of Russian, Soviet, and post-Soviet studies. Some are established scholars who have been drawn to the region by the remarkable changes taking place there; others are young scholars and graduate students who have recently entered the field. These disciplines have witnessed a small but significant influx of students eager to take advantage of the new opportunities for ethnographic, field, survey, and other types of research in these newly independent states of the FSU.[49]

The demise of the Soviet Union has also led, paradoxically, to the legitimation of Soviet history as a subfield within history departments. Before that time, highly restricted access to archival sources kept historians focused mainly on the Civil War period and the 1920s. While Russian archives are not completely open even today, enough has changed to allow for meaningful archival research on virtually the entirety of Soviet social, economic, and political history. New works of scholarship are appearing that draw upon Soviet sources formerly unavailable to scholars.

Even post-World War II diplomatic history has benefited from the availability of new sources. The Woodrow Wilson Center for Scholars, in Washington, DC houses the "Cold War International History Project," which has helped to induce further declassification of both Soviet and non-Soviet diplomatic documents from the first decades of the Cold War.[50] Brown and Harvard Universities have organized conferences of former Soviet and US high officials, which have greatly deepened our understanding of the Cuban Missile Crisis, the rise and decline of détente in the 1970s, and the winding down of the Cold War during the Gorbachev era.[51] The National Security Archive in Washington, DC, has accomplished a great deal in declassifying both Soviet and US documents from recent decades of Cold War history.[52] These and other projects have fostered major advances in our understanding of the factors that led the Cold War to last as long as it did. As a result of informational *glasnost'* now enjoyed by those conducting research on all aspects of Soviet history, history departments are slowly but steadily seeking to hire historians of the Soviet period.

The locus of research on post-Soviet economics has shifted as a result of the collapse of the USSR and the efforts to build market economies where once command economies were the rule. The World Bank, OECD, EBRD, and other international organizations have hired, full-time or part-time, numerous academic specialists (or economics PhDs) on Soviet and East European economies, who conduct research on the transformations of these economies and publish the results in outlets of those organizations. Some of the best work on these economic transitions, therefore, first appears not in area or disciplinary journals, but rather in periodicals, ephemera, and working papers of the international organizations themselves. Moreover, the resistance of economics departments to hiring area specialists, in light of their preference for hiring individuals noted principally for their contributions to econometrics, game theory, and formal modeling, has led a good number of area economists to work for international organizations and the United States Government by default.[53] A decline in undergraduate and graduate student enrollments in courses on Russian language, politics, and history took place on many campuses during the 1990s. The reasons for this decline are mysterious, but we can speculate. Historically, enrollments have surged during crucial turning points: at the height of the Cold War in the late 1950s and early 1960s; after the invasion of Afghanistan and the collapse of the limited détente of the 1970s; and during the excitement of the Gorbachev era. After the collapse of communism, however, Russia's loss of status as the "other superpower," and her lack of luster as a place in which to invest one's scholarly dreams and personal fortunes, led students to drift more toward other areas, such as East Asia.[54]

Declining enrollments, together with changing intellectual fashions and shifts in funding priorities, have combined to modify the distribution of faculty in some departments. Few history departments have maintained three positions to cover Medieval Russian, Imperial Russian, and Soviet history; most have been able to fill only one or two of the three. For more than a decade, many of the leading economics departments have not been hiring faculty in applied economics such as area studies and economic history. Senior scholars in Russian economic studies have retired or are approaching retirement and are unlikely to be replaced. Young economists are working outside academia, with a few notable exceptions. Area specialists have struggled to resist adverse trends in political science departments which often seek the best "comparativist," regardless of geographic specialization

Slavic languages and literatures departments have also seen their faculty strength threatened, as enrollment in Russian language courses, the mainstay for most departments, declined during the 1990s. Departments responded in three ways. First, they broadened the scope of their language courses to include texts from the more specialized fields, like business, law, and politics. Second, they incorporated a range of courses that, on the one hand, bring their literature and culture coverage to the late Soviet and post-Soviet periods and, on the other, include popular culture, especially, film. Finally, they have expanded geographical coverage. Even before the collapse of communism, Slavic departments offered instruction in the languages and literatures of other Slavic countries in East Europe (e.g., Poland, Czechoslovakia, Yugoslavia) or republics within the Soviet Union (e.g., Ukraine) and occasionally even non-Slavic East European languages and literatures (e.g., Hungary and Romania). Over the past decade, some Slavic departments have offered on an occasional basis the languages and literatures of some of the non-Slavic Soviet successor states (e.g., Armenia, Georgia, Azerbaijan, Latvia, Lithuania, Uzbekistan, Kazakhstan) and non-Russian speaking areas of the Russian Federation (e.g., Chechnya and Ingushetia).[55]

An exception to these general trends can be found in sociology and anthropology departments. Here there were relatively very few faculty specializing in the study of the Soviet Union before the 1990s. The collapse of communism removed the obstacles to field research that had earlier discouraged scholars in these disciplines from studying the region.. Over the past decade, major sociology and anthropology departments have sought to attract faculty whose research explores the unprecedented transformations unfolding in this part of the world and the theoretical and comparative implications of these developments. Some of these are younger scholars who did their graduate work during perestroika or the 1990s; others are scholars who have shifted the focus of their research to study late Soviet and post-Soviet society.[56]

There are indications on some campuses of renewed interest in the successor states of the former Soviet Union. Since the late 1990s, undergraduate and graduate enrollments at some institutions have been gradually increasing in courses relating to the region of the former Soviet Union.[57] This trend has accelerated in the aftermath of the events of September 11, 2001, which stimulated interest in national security issues and the threat of global terrorism. In this new environment, it is possible that we will see further shifts in research agendas and geographical focus, with more emphasis on non-Slavic countries and groups in the region and attention to themes that are shaped by a post-9/11 rather than a post-Soviet perspective.

INTELLECTUAL TRENDS

Soviet area studies have, over the decades, made significant contributions to our understanding and conceptualization of Soviet-type societies. The most well known and most controversial concept generated during the early years of Soviet area studies was that of "totalitarianism." Originally used in Italy in the 1920s, the term was put forward in the 1950s to illuminate the common, essential features of the Stalinist and fascist systems.[58] With the changes in state-society relations following "de-Stalinization" precipitated by Nikita Khrushchev's speech to the Twentieth Party Congress of the CPSU in 1956, Western scholars began to debate the usefulness of the term and its continued applicability to Soviet-type systems.[59]

The totalitarian model was both influential and widely applied in the U.S., particularly by political scientists writing in the 1950s and early 1960s. But the model was not applied with either consistency or uniformity, in part because of definitional confusion. Some scholars used the term to mean "the total state," one that monopolizes the polity, society, and economy. Others used the term to mean a total state marked by terroristic despotism a la Hitler and Stalin. The result of this confusion was that a good deal of scholarly energy was wasted in terminological disputes and evasions when post-Stalin changes maintained the total state but eliminated the terroristic despotism.. But already in the first half of the 1950s, some scholars avoided these debates by thinking of the Soviet experience more broadly. They conceptualized Soviet rule as a distinct form of dictatorship that coincided with a particular stage in the process of modernization. Several versions of this "developmental" approach entered into the general discourse of Soviet area studies. Proponents of this approach proceeded from contrasting theoretical positions but reached the general conclusion that the Soviet system would eventually be subject to change as modernization proceeded.[60]

Following the de-Stalinization campaign of the late 1950s and early 1960s, debates between totalitarian and developmental approaches centered on analyses of the extent to which the system was adapting to changing societal and environmental conditions. The focus tended to be on changes in elite composition and regime policies, and only secondarily on broader social groups. The research obstacles facing Sovietologists partly account for the focus on elites; at least information was available concerning official pronouncements, the public conduct of elites, policy changes, and the backgrounds of elites. By contrast, almost nothing was known about non-elite groups in society, especially life outside the capital cities (Moscow and St. Petersburg) where research by American scholars was generally obstructed or forbidden by the Soviet authorities. Given this situation, Harvard's Refugee Interview Project provided a unique and valuable source of information on the lives and perceptions of ordinary people, albeit one that applied to the society of the early 1940s, when these refugees were displaced westward.[61]

Research agendas and orientations began to shift during the 1960s and early 1970s. Among political scientists, two major points of view emerged concerning the trajectory of the Soviet system: rationalization and degeneration.[62] Both approaches moved beyond the totalitarian model, often drawing upon Max Weber for inspiration. There was renewed interest in theories that drew upon the approach, with an emphasis now on the transformative impact of technocratic rationalization. The degeneration argument took several forms but one of the most influential versions applied the concept of "neo-traditionalism" to Soviet-type regimes and political culture.[63] Derivative of these general approaches were studies of bureaucratic politics, trends in interest articulation, leadership, and policy-making that illuminated either the rationalizing or the degenerative components of the political process. A large body of literature also developed, based on the works of dissidents, which identified key ideological and social cleavages that later became extremely important when the society liberalized. Though impeded by both Soviet censorship, in the first case, and skepticism among many Western readers about the credibility of literature produced by dissidents, in the second, these studies produced some innovative and insightful evidence and interpretation of Soviet politics and society. They also produced spirited debates about which prism for interpreting Soviet reality was likely to prove the more useful.[64]

Soviet foreign policy studies were also marked by debates over the sources and evolution of Soviet international behavior. Numerous volumes of revisionist literature on the origins of the Cold War argued that Stalinist foreign policy was driven largely by defensive concerns, which was a minority position in the Sovietological literature of the 1950s and 1960s. Post-Stalin changes in Soviet foreign policy yielded heightened ambiguity and consequent debate about the interpretation of Soviet actions on the international scene. At least three paradigms emerged (some would say five) that ran the gamut from viewing Soviet foreign policy as a product, at one extreme, of a systemic need for expansion that could only be countered through credible, military deterrence to a view of the phenomenon, at the other extreme, as defensive, driven by fear, and capable of being altered through reassurance.[65]

Studies of the Soviet economy followed a path somewhat analogous to that traversed by political science. Gregory Grossman's conceptualization of the Soviet economy as a "command economy" in 1963 formalized what had been the dominant perspective to that point.[66] At the same time, seminal work by Joseph Berliner, within the context of the Harvard Interview Project, revealed the nature of informal relations within the Soviet factory and the interaction between the formal and informal dimensions of the command economy.[67] Expansion of the informal sector in the decades following the death of Stalin led Grossman eventually to formalize its depiction as a "second economy" that had grown up within, and in response to the dysfunctions of, the command economy.[68] In the meantime, Abram Bergson's monumental study of Soviet national income put the field's quantitative studies on a firm empirical footing,[69] while de-Stalinization led to the publication of annual Soviet statistical handbooks beginning in 1957 and to census data later. This changed the way economists worked, for now they could construct econometric models and conduct comparative economic studies. Discussion of the possibilities for successful reform of the Soviet command economy began seriously among Western economists during the Khrushchev years and intensified following the "Kosygin reforms" of 1965. Western, East European, and Soviet economists debated the possibility of combining plan and market, and the discussion grew especially intense with the introduction of major economic reforms under Gorbachev. Oskar Lange's model of market socialism represented the main theoretical model for those who argued that central planning and markets could be combined successfully. But by the end of the Gorbachev era, most Western economic specialists had concluded that the combination was unlikely to succeed.[70]

Novel approaches and subject matter also made an appearance in historical research of the 1960s and 1970s dealing with intellectual history, the history of state institutions and government policies, and particularly, labor and society. Inspired by Leopold Haimson's 1964–1965 articles on urban Russia between 1905 and 1917[71] and Edward Thompson's monumental study, *The Making of the English Working Class* (1966), historians of Russia began to turn their attention for the first time to empirical research on lower class groups and popular movements that brought the Bolsheviks to power. This research, which drew on Soviet archival and other primary sources and was strongly influenced by Western European studies in the fields of labor and social history, aimed at providing an account of the Russian revolutions "from below." The trend toward history "from below" also stimulated research on related topics, such as peasants and women. These studies became possible because scholars could take advantage of the IUCTG and IREX programs and spend up to nine months conducting research in Soviet libraries and archives, in a few cases including those in provincial cities.

By the 1980s, historians turned their attention to the social history of the Soviet period, most notably the Civil War, the New Economic Policy, and the First Five-Year Plans.[72] Following the examples set by Moshe Lewin, and a few others , social historians found ingenious means of gaining access to selected primary sources in order to shed new light on some of the most compelling and complex issues in Soviet history. The overriding question in historical studies—why did the Soviet experiment lead to the Gulag?—was hotly debated by historians who focused on a variety of explanations, variously emphasizing ideology and culture, leadership, national character, and according to a new "revisionist" approach, pressure from lower levels of Soviet society.[73]

The initiation of Gorbachev's reforms allowed scholars to observe a real-world test of the reformability of the Soviet political and economic systems, behavioral dispositions of the Soviet population, and the transformability of Soviet foreign policies. Much debate, among members of the policy community and academics alike, concerned the extent to which Gorbachev's unfolding policies and rhetoric indicated his sincerity about overhauling the Soviet system ("is he for real?") and his capacity to do so ("if he is for real, can he get away with it?"). As Gorbachev's reforms, and foreign policy changes, became increasingly far-reaching, scholarship concentrated more on the causes and consequences of the changes: the implications of each for our thinking about the nature of the prior system ("where did Gorbachev come from?"), its reformability ("can there be a 'third way' between statist socialism and market democracy"?), and the potential assertiveness of the Soviet population. Not surprisingly, those most skeptical about the reformability of the system tended to be those who embraced some variant of totalitarian imagery of the old system, while those most optimistic tended to embrace some variant of a developmental paradigm.[74]

The substantive intellectual agenda of Soviet studies did not deepen very greatly during the Gorbachev era. To be sure, the excitement generated by Gorbachev's increasingly radical changes enriched the field with a multiplicity of novel observations of policy changes and societal reactions; students of the Brezhnev era were being rewarded for their patience with levels of excitement equaled only by the tedium of the previous twenty years. But debates still concerned the implications of current events for our thinking about totalitarian versus modernization images of the old political-social-economic system, and for our thinking about the viability of a democratic or market socialism. Comparative referents employed to think about the nature and prospects of the system did not extend much beyond that. There was some effort to import concepts and propositions from the literature on "transitions from authoritarianism," but these had not developed very far before the Soviet system collapsed and a new intellectual agenda emerged.

What most changed in Soviet studies during the Gorbachev era was the methodological repertoire of the field. *Glasnost'* increasingly diminished the level of data poverty that had hobbled the field since its inception. From a trickle in 1986, *glasnost'* opened a floodgate by 1989–90; censorship declined dramatically; increasingly sensitive archives were opened both to Soviet and non-Soviet scholars; exposes about the past and the present gushed forth; both scholarly and cultural creativity were allowed increasingly to express themselves. This had profound implications for Soviet specialists in all disciplines. Political scientists could reevaluate Soviet political history based on memoirs, archives, and interviews. Sociologists and anthropologists could suddenly go beyond printed sources to study Soviet society itself through direct, ethnographic observation, participant observation, mass and elite surveys, and related tools of scholarly investigation in "open" societies. Economists were now able more systematically to compare their previous statistical aggregations with a much-widened base of statistics and anecdotes about Soviet economic realities.

Anthropologists, like sociologists, were no longer treated largely as *personae non gratae* by Soviet officials. Students of Soviet nationalities suddenly were able to examine ethnicity in Soviet society and to do so in the republics of the USSR; previously, this had been one of the most heavily censored, off-limits realms of inquiry, though a number of impressive, empirical works on aspects of nationality problems had been produced nonetheless. Students of Russian and Soviet history more generally were now able to reevaluate all the major issues that had animated debates among historians of the tsarist and Soviet eras, based on exciting new flows of information from previously closed or restricted archives. Students of Soviet literature enjoyed benefits similar to those of the historians, including newly opened archives, published memoirs, and oral histories. Moreover, taking advantage of the "new historicism" in literary studies, with its emphasis on historical and especially cultural contextualization of literary texts, some specialists in Soviet (and Russian) literature began to focus on hitherto neglected topics in Soviet culture.

Specialists on geography of the USSR have also been affected by the new trends. The collapse of both communism and the USSR has turned the spotlight on the regional dimension of Eurasia—both the newly independent states themselves and the variegated regions within Russia and other former republics. Those regions turn out to have deep meaning for their inhabitants, both as historical points of reference and as cultural communities. Despoliation of the natural environment has contributed to inflaming nationalist sentiments, and has galvanized regional as well as ethnic identities. There is an increasing call, therefore, for a geographical approach that combines cultures, environments, and regional identities.[75]

In addition to new sources of information, scholarship in all disciplines benefited from newfound opportunities for collaboration with Soviet colleagues. After an initial period of caution and disorientation, Soviet scholars became increasingly emboldened to speak their minds (and to disagree both with each other and with official policy) at international conferences, to use their contacts to wedge open new archives, to expand the limits of permissible inquiry, and to arrange for genuinely collaborative research projects with foreign colleagues. Increasingly, Western scholarly journals published articles authored or co-authored by Soviet scholars, though the decimation of some Soviet social science disciplines by the old regime, and the heavy politicization of Soviet life, encouraged a polemical or publicistic style that frustrated many a Western co-author and journal editor.[76]

While the Gorbachev era opened huge vistas for overcoming the data poverty of the field, scholarship was still confined by its single-country focus (which limited inter-country comparisons that might have tested causal propositions) and by uncertainty about the appropriate comparative referents for thinking about the type of transition under way in the USSR. These confining conditions were to change profoundly as a result of the collapse of the USSR.

POST-SOVIET AREA STUDIES

With the demise of the communist system came the discrediting of conventional narratives (both Western and Soviet) about the fate of Russia and the Soviet Union in the twentieth century. The era of communist domination had concluded, abruptly and unexpectedly, and now the "story" of Soviet rule had not just a beginning and a middle but also, miraculously, an end! The end of the Soviet era required not just an explanation for the concluding years and months of the regime that had once seemed so stable to so many observers. It also required a reconceptualization of the entire seventy-four years of Soviet power. As Allan Wildman put in 1996: "The abrupt collapse of the Soviet Union has deflated our shopworn scenarios that turned on 1917 and Stalinism, and the present challenge is to devise new ways of representing the past, discovering new trajectories around which to weave a story."[77]

Western scholars since 1991 have gradually but steadily begun to register this need to reconceptualize the entire project of comprehending the Soviet era. This has taken a variety of forms, including the study of hitherto neglected cultural dimensions; identities, traditions and collective behavior of national and ethnic minorities and political and other outcasts in the Soviet Union; themes such as space, time, trust, folklore, and collectivism; and practices such as funerals, shamanism, black markets, sexuality, and civic activism.[78] Much of this new and original research draws upon the theories and methods associated with the "cultural turn" that has been so influential in historical studies more generally since the late 1970s. Practitioners of these approaches can be found in a wide range of disciplines, encompassing both the social sciences and the humanities.

After 1991, fifteen independent countries came into existence where before only one had stood. All of them shared cultural and other legacies of having been a part of the USSR; all of them suffered the severe disorganization and disorientation attendant upon the collapse of the old system; and all of them were seeking to find their way in an era of "postcommunism." But what their separate existences made possible was the emergence within political science, economics, and sociology of a genuine subfield of inquiry that might be called "comparative postcommunism."

Given the similarities of their recent legacies and current circumstances, but given the numerous differences among them in precommunist heritage, ethnic composition, resource endowments, location, and mode of transition from communism,[79] these fifteen states provided the ideal laboratory for structured, focused comparisons of their trajectories of postcommunist development.[80] Moreover, regional and ethnic differentiation *within* many of these newly independent states led to a burst of inter*regional* comparisons, within and across these states, that enrich the comparative exercise by allowing for still greater variations along both dependent and independent variables.[81] More broadly, but not within the purview of this essay, the field of postcommunism cast its comparative net even more widely, encompassing the countries of the former Soviet bloc in Eastern Europe, as well as the former Yugoslavia and Albania, which had similar legacies of communism and faced similar challenges of postcommunism.

Collapse of the USSR led to a proliferation of analogues with which to conceptualize the nature of postcommunism. The totalitarianism versus modernization debate about the nature of the old system was echoed in debates over how to conceptualize the "Leninist legacy" that constrains or shapes the scope and nature of the transition.[82] But beyond that, scholars were struck by the diverse challenges facing these countries, and the implications of those challenges for how we think about the nature of this transition. The challenges have included: (1) how to build a viable state on the ruins of the previous state; (2) how to construct a viable "nation" (a sense of "we-feeling" and common identification) among the peoples of these new states; (3) how to deal with forces pushing for democratization of the state; (4) how to stabilize, marketize, privatize, and demilitarize the economy; (5) how to integrate the economy into the global capitalist economy; and (6) how to define one's identity, interests, and role in the international political order.

In terms of the sheer volume of scholarship, a glance at the tables of contents and titles of "books received" in area and disciplinary journals would show that many published works in the 1990s focused on the ways these countries were dealing with the challenges of democratizing their polities, marketizing their economies, and integrating into the international economic and political orders. Moreover, the bulk of primary-source scholarship dealt with Russia, a reflection of the linguistic competence of most Western specialists on the region.. To be sure, significant work was published on matters of state-building and nation-building, demilitarization, and the transformation of foreign relations. But the concern with constructing a marketized, liberal democracy that is integrated into global capitalism captured a great deal of scholarly attention.

The proliferation of periodicals, journals, and information sources illustrates the new directions in scholarship. Some preexisting journals broadened their focus and in some instances, also changed their title to reflect the shift in orientation.[83] New publications appeared that were devoted in whole or in part to tracking the transition experience in the FSU and Eastern Europe: *Demokratizatsiya; East European Constitutional Review; Transitions* (Open Media Research Institute); *Transition* (The World Bank), *Communist Economies and Economic Transformation; Russian Economic Trends;* to mention but a few. A major cross-regional journal appeared in 1990, *Journal of Democracy*, which regularly devoted a portion of its coverage to democratization processes in Eastern Europe and the FSU. Internet sources of information also proliferated, with daily compilations of information and interpretation reaching our computer screens, in some cases free-of-charge, with such frequency and volume that no scholar could possibly keep up with the flood.[84] New newspapers, magazines, journals, and internet-based information outlets have also proliferated *within* the FSU. Western libraries can barely afford to maintain subscriptions to all the important new sources, forcing scholars to make hard choices about recommended subscriptions.

The proliferation of new topics has also led to a much broader integration of post-Soviet, Western scholarship into the dominant theoretical concerns of the social science disciplines. A significantly larger proportion of articles in *disciplinary* journals is now devoted to analysis and conceptualization of changes in the postcommunist area. Similarly, in area journals, the theoretical repertoire of publications has vastly expanded. Footnotes now proliferate that cite theories of state-building, nation-building, democratization, marketization ("transition economics"), and the transformation of international systems. While the dominant analogies used initially to capture these processes were those of "transitions to democracy" and "early capitalism," those comparative referents were rapidly supplemented by analogies with early-European state-building and nation-building projects; "transition to feudalism"; Third World stagnation or "dependency"; the transformation of earlier international systems; and the collapse of earlier imperial systems.[85] With respect to all these theoretical concerns, scholars have sought either to use theory to help illuminate postcommunist processes of change or to enrich theory by demonstrating how distinctive features of postcommunism create unprecedented "solutions" to familiar challenges.[86]

Collaboration with post-Soviet scholars in the study of these phenomena has expanded significantly beyond the levels achieved in the Gorbachev era, as has the frequency of publication in Western journals by scholars from the FSU. Post-Soviet scholars have advantages that few Western scholars can match: native linguistic skills; a "feel" for the situation on the ground————a sensitivity to unique cultural meanings and privileged access to sources. Their Western collaborators have the education in social science theories and methodologies, as well as experience in writing to Western journals' epistemological, ontological, and discursive standards, that most post-Soviet scholars sorely lack. We are currently witnessing a growing trend that combines the best of each of these: scholarship produced by talented Soviet colleagues who have been educated in, and received PhDs from, Western universities.[87]

The proliferation of theoretical interests has also led a considerable number of Western theorists, who had not previously worked on the region, to devote themselves to the study of the postcommunist world. Some of them lack the linguistic skills and collaborate with post-Soviet scholars to compensate for that drawback.[88] Others have gone so far as to learn new languages and immerse themselves in on-site, ethnographic fieldwork.[89] In either case, their inquiries are informed by in-depth familiarity with analogous phenomena elsewhere. The purposes of their studies are varied. Some are driven by prescriptive concerns: to suggest strategies by which post-Soviet decisionmakers might attain positive goals (economic stability and growth; marketization and privatization; democratization; stable federalism; etc.) or avoid negative ones (ethnic conflict; political and social instability; poverty, ill health, and environmental disaster, etc.). Others are driven by predictive concerns: to foretell the prospect that post-Soviet countries will attain these goods or avoid these negative outcomes. Still others are most concerned with theory-development: use of the postcommunist laboratory as a means of identifying novel solutions to familiar problems (e.g. new approaches to nation-building, constitutionalism, multilateral organization) or of enriching our understanding of the explanatory power of varied causal factors (culture, ethnicity, class, gender, region, institutions, economics, leadership, etc.) at the micro, meso, or macro levels.

Much of the research on the Soviet system before *perestroika* focused on "regime studies" (among political scientists and political sociologists),[90] on aggregate economic trends (among economists), and on social stratification (among the few sociologists). These narrow agendas, and their focus largely on "macro-level" phenomena, were necessitated by Soviet censorship. A good number of political scientists had worked on Soviet local government, but their studies did not benefit from candid interviews or access to information about the most important issues (such as the size and sources of local-governmental budgets). This too has changed in the post-Soviet era. Research is now taking place on the full range of micro-level phenomena, under constraints that mirror only those found in the study of any region.[91] The bulk of research falls under the analytical categories delineated above (democratization, marketization, nation-building, etc.). But what is noteworthy about those categories is that they are amenable to study at any level of analysis (micro, meso (i.e. institutional), and macro), depending on the formulation of the research question. This facilitates comparisons between phenomena and trends in the postcommunist area and those in other regions of the world, an intellectual trend that has also burgeoned during the past decade.[92]

There was always a cross-national component to the study of the Soviet Union. The totalitarian model grew out of observation of the similarities between Hitler's Germany and Stalin's Russia, and the dissimilarities between either of these and traditional, "authoritarian" dictatorships. The developmental approach to Stalinism treated the Soviet regime as a type of modernizing dictatorship that sought to break out of the constraints on economic and political transformations found in most Third World countries.[93] In accordance with this general type of approach, the *post-Stalinist* USSR was viewed as a product of the Stalinist developmental experience: a society that had achieved certain features of "modernity" and "industrialism" analogous to those in Western Europe and North America, which raised pressures on the regime to adapt its political-organizational and administrative formats accordingly.

Political scientists who embraced these ways of thinking about the USSR sometimes sought to test convergence theory, albeit in a very specific and novel form: that "they" will converge in "our" direction.[94] Totalitarian theorists emphasized the unique features of the Soviet political system, and its inability to tolerate, much less sponsor, such convergence. Those who embraced some variants of the developmental model tended, by contrast, to emphasize growing societal and economic pressures for adaptation to the alleged "imperatives" of legitimacy and efficiency in the post-totalitarian phase of Soviet history.

Convergence theory lost its luster as it became evident during the 1970s that, whatever the adaptations the Soviet regime was willing to countenance, these did not include liberal democracy or a privatized economy. But the postcommunist era has revived interest in convergence theory. Advocacy of market democracy, and the faith that it can be made to succeed in the post-communist world, represents a revival of that variant of convergence theory that was most popular in mainstream US scholarship in the 1950s: that "they" will converge in "our" direction. But whereas in the 1950s the scholarship on the theory was not driven by prescriptive concerns, that is no longer the case, as the former Soviet Union is now much more open to specific Western pressures or demands ("conditionality") for the adoption and implementation of certain types of policies.

The current prescriptive trend in scholarship ("as long as they listen to us, they will become more like us") has been reinforced by trends within the theoretical development of the social sciences. Area studies have come under attack by social scientists who argue that intellectual progress can best be achieved either through cross-regional comparisons or through the application to specific areas of theories based on universal assumptions about human nature ("rational choice theory") or about the homogenizing impact of the international system ("globalization theory"). Cross-regional comparisons are said to foster intellectual progress by de-ghettoizing area studies. The effect has been the production of some very good scholarship comparing analogous processes in Latin America, Africa, West Europe, East Asia, etc.[95] But too little attention has been paid to determining the relative payoff of such a research strategy, compared to the payoffs from exploiting more fully the newfound opportunities for intra-regional comparison.[96]

Other trends are still more threatening to area studies, as they posit its growing irrelevance. Many theories of "globalization" predict the homogenization of most socio-economic orders and the standardization of policy options in the face of imperatives dictated by the capitalist international economy and the global revolution in information-processing. Those that fail to adapt to these pressures will simply lose their capacity to provide for their populations, and will become the losers in the international system. Hence, over time, they or their political successors will learn the Darwinian lesson and accommodate to reality. To embrace this theory is to relegate scholarship on specific areas to the study of whether or not given countries' elites have as yet learned the appropriate lesson.

Similarly, rational choice theory, in one or the other of its numerous variants, is making a bid for hegemony within political science, just as it has long since dominated the discipline of economics. What the theory assumes is that, in crucial respects, all people are alike; once we specify that commonality, it argues, we gain considerable power to predict certain kinds of political behavior regardless of cultural, ethnic, class, or gender differences.

A variant of rational choice theory that has made the greatest inroads in post-Soviet studies is so-called "rational-choice institutionalism." According to this theory, if institutions are designed properly, human beings will ultimately adapt their behaviors to the patterns being rewarded by the incentive structure built into those institutions, even if attitudinal and cultural change lags behind behavioral change. The Darwinian process of natural selection, as in the case of globalization theory, treats these transformations as lengthy processes, not "single-play games"; but the assumption is that people will eventually adapt to the new incentive structure or suffer the obvious consequences. Hence, area specialists need only document this process of either adaptation or deselection.

One attraction of both globalization and rational choice theories is that the outcome of current processes is treated as both knowable and desirable, if institutions are designed properly. Hence, predictive and prescriptive concerns are merged. Moreover, no near-term time frame is offered for testing whether the assumptions underlying the theories proved to be untenable. Hence, the faith that the theory is tenable is difficult to undermine; in the case of entirely open-ended time frames for prediction, it is, in fact, impossible to falsify either the predictive or the explanatory claims.

The recent hegemony within comparative politics and international relations theory of the subfield of political economy has reinforced the attractions of globalization and rational choice theories. Political economy examines the interaction between governments and economies, and should not be confused with classical political economy, whether Marxist or otherwise, which remains influential within sociology and anthropology. Its analyses are more amenable to "systematic" analysis because of the ease with which economic flows can be quantified. As in economics, so increasingly within political economy, non-quantifiable studies are dismissed as "soft." Formal modeling of expected relationships, while not required in order to make one's point, is increasingly valued as a sign of rigorous, systematic, and cumulative scholarship.

These tendencies will probably never come to achieve the dominance within political science and sociology that they have achieved in economics. Since the "currencies" of politics and social life –power and status—are not as easily quantified as money, quantification will reach natural limits. Since most of comparative analysis in international studies focuses on fluid, often turbulent, situations in which people have great difficulty knowing precisely where their interests lie, the assumptions underlying rational choice theory, and the formal modeling that often accompanies it, will be so at odds with the facts of situations as to lose credibility as a universal explanatory device. Since comparative analysis should be interested primarily in documenting and explaining *differences* among states, nations, societies, cultures, regions, and classes, the field is not likely to succumb to the hegemony of theories based on simplifying assumptions about human rationality. Moreover, and perhaps most powerfully, the events of September 11, 2001 have undercut optimism about both the inexorable march of globalization and the "rationality" of human nature. They have revealed the dark side of both phenomena as well as the urgency of understanding the negative side effects, and potentially apocalyptic consequences, of formulating policies based on those assumptions. And yet, given the disciplines' pretensions to being social "sciences," and given the large numbers of students being trained in the economics of social and political exchange relationships, the challenge to area studies within the social sciences will be a continuing one.

From a methodological standpoint, that challenge is often expressed in bogus terms as a choice between descriptive work (by area specialists) and theoretical insights (of the theorists).[97] While there was something to this distinction in the divisions within scholarship of the 1930s through the 1950s, there has been no substance to the distinction for at least 25–30 years. Whether they were political scientists, sociologists, or economists, Soviet area specialists came to be trained in theories, and comparative referents, thought to be relevant to their interests within the area. Modernization theory (at the macro level) and interest group theory (at the micro or meso levels), for example, were at the basis of the challenge to the exceptionalism of totalitarian theory. Today, the vast majority of those who produce serious scholarship on the postcommunist world relate their studies to relevant bodies of theory; often, they seek to revise the received theoretical wisdom.

Intellectually, what is at stake in the misguided debate over theory versus area studies is the types of theories we seek to construct. Does intellectual progress result from a search for grand theories that apply across regions and cultures? Or does it result from a search for contextually specific theories that apply across a specifiable domain of cases? As the reader will have guessed, we favor the second approach, although we believe that the level of contextual specificity will vary, depending on the issues and contexts in question. Hence, we endorse the tendency that is currently dominant within postcommunist studies: to study middle-range processes in postcommunist systems, informed by an understanding of the existing literature on analogous processes outside the postcommunist area.[98]

Hopefully, the acrimonious debate about "area studies" versus "theory" will subside and give rise to a more balanced appreciation of the real question: how to combine the two. For example, processes of globalization are fully evident in the post-Soviet region, as are a diversity of responses to them. The role of contextual knowledge in the examination of the impact of global pressures should be to focus on how the global and the local interact, and what that teaches us more generally about the varying impacts of globalizing pressures. Similarly, empirically-grounded analyses of strategic interaction among actors within our area can enrich our understanding of the conditions under which the assumptions about human rationality built into the theory are, and are not, likely to be reflected in the behavior of actors in this region.[99]

The push for overgeneralization in the self-proclaimed social *sciences* is counterbalanced to some extent by the opposite tendency within anthropology, portions of sociology, much of the humanities, and even an occasional political scientist. Here, largely inspired by the works of Geertz, Foucault, and Bourdieu, the trend has been toward close study and interpretation of the particularities of situations at the micro or local level.[100] Similarly, in studies of post-communist nation-building, particularizing inspiration derives from seminal theoretical work by Eric Hobsbawm ("the invention of tradition") and Benedict Anderson ("imagined communities").[101] The postcommunist context is fertile ground for such studies, both because of scholars' new-found access to the grassroots and because the institutional turbulence and the popular search for new meanings taking place in those countries invites non-structural analyses that seek to explore the emerging shape of things in their own terms. Hence, whereas middle-range theory-building in the social *sciences* looks at processes of institution-building, state-building, nation-building, the construction of a market economy, and the like, the particularizing trend resists such a degree of aggregation or teleology. Instead, in ways that echo Weber's concern for "meanings," practitioners of the new cultural history seek to deconstruct the ways in which individuals and collectivities within postcommunist countries understand themselves and their contexts.

At present, contextually-specific structural analysis remains dominant within post-Soviet studies in political science and sociology, universal deductive theory is dominant within post-Soviet studies in economics, and post-modernist particularizing approaches are dominant within post-Soviet studies in anthropology and much of the humanities. In all disciplines, though to varying degrees, these are contested hegemonies. As noted, globalization and rational choice theory challenge the prevailing hegemony within political science. The new subfield of "transition economics" is challenging universalizing tendencies in the wake of disappointing results of "shock therapy" in Russia and elsewhere. Traditional ethnographic work, with an explanatory focus and a commitment to replicability and falsifiability, challenges post-modernist approaches within anthropological studies of postcommunism. And, in the humanities, textual analysis and deconstruction are challenged by those who prefer to treat literature as a body of evidence about real-world conditions in society (as a "window on society and culture"). The latter approach qualifies its practitioners more as empirical sociologists or arms-length ethnographers than as literary theorists. We believe that the uniqueness and complexity of postcommunist phenomena cannot adequately be analyzed through a single intellectual framework or disciplinary perspective. The distinctive features of the political, social, economic, cultural, and international landscape of the former Soviet Union require the creative application of diverse theories and methodologies drawn from several disciplines and traditions, including some (such as sociology and anthropology) that have hitherto received relatively little attention from Western specialists on the region. Scholarship will be impoverished by the imposition of orthodoxies within the individual disciplines or by rigid adherence to disciplinary boundaries. When studying world-historical changes of such magnitude, novelty, and diversity, we must beware of premature intellectual closure, be it theoretical or methodological. A healthy eclecticism should reign.

In sum, the dramatic changes in the Soviet Union and the world during the past decade have vastly broadened and transformed the intellectual enterprise of post-Soviet studies. New issues dominate the agenda, and new methods of inquiry have become available. What has changed most has been the end of censorship and the flood of new archival and other evidence, which have allowed for exciting new studies that bear on continuing efforts to weigh the relative strengths of arguments on each side of age-old questions.

Victoria E. Bonnell is a Professor of Sociology at UC Berkeley and Chair of the Center for Slavic and Eastern European Studies. George

Breslauer is a Professor of Political Science at UC Berkeley (Area: Soviet and Post-Soviet Studies).

Notes

1. Edward W. Walker, "Sovietology and Perestroika: A Post-Mortem" in Susan Solomon, ed., *Beyond Sovietology: Essays in Politics and History* (Armonk, N.Y, 1993), p. 227.

2. An influential version of the argument can be found in Stephen F. Cohen, *Rethinking the Soviet Experience: Politics and History Since 1917* (New York and Oxford, 1985), pp. 8–19.

3. The study of Russia and Eastern Europe was first undertaken at Oberlin College in 1945. Robert F. Byrnes, "USA: Work at the Universities," in Walter Z. Laqueur and Leopold Labedz, eds., *The State of Soviet Studies* (Cambridge, Mass., 1965), p. 25. For a discussion of early developments in U.S. Russian studies, see David Charles Engerman, "America, Russia, and the Romance of Economic Development," Ph.D. dissertation, UC Berkeley, 1998.

4. Barry M. Katz, Foreign Intelligence: Research and Analysis in the Office of Strategic Services 1942–1945 (Cambridge, Mass., 1989), p. 137.

5. Ibid., p. 160. As Geroid T. Robinson put it in his application to the Rockefeller Foundation in 1945 on behalf of Columbia's Russian Institute: "war time experience in training Americans to meet the needs of government, the armed forces, and business has indicated the great value of the regional approach." Quoted in Robert F. Byrnes, *A History of Russian and East European Studies in the United States* (Lanham, New York, London, 1994), p. 207.

6. Immanuel Wallerstein, "The Unintended Consequences of Cold War Area Studies," in *The Cold War and the University: Toward an Intellectual History of the Postwar Years* (New York, 1998), p. 195–197. Both these reports placed priority on the study of Latin America, China and Japan. By the end of 1945, priorities had shifted to the Soviet Union and China. Ibid., p. 201.

7. Byrnes, *A History of Russian and East European Studies in the United States*, p. 213. The program was designated as "Intensive Study of Contemporary Russia Civilization" and participants wrote a series of articles on the USSR for the *Encyclopedia Americana*, reprinted together in a book, *USSR: A Concise Handbook*, ed. Ernest J. Simmons (Ithaca, NY, 1947). Contributors included: Frederick J. Schuman, Sir Bernard Pares, John Hazard, and Lazar Volin.

8. In 1946, the World Areas Research Committee of the SSRC defined the criteria for a graduate program in area studies: "five disciplines or more, working closely together, intensive language training, substantial library resources, administrative recognition of the program within the system of instruction." Harold H. Fisher, *American Research on Russia* (Bloomington, 1959), p. 9.

9. Clarence A. Manning, *A History of Slavic Studies in the United States* (Milwaukee, 1957), p.76. See Cyril E. Black and John M. Thompson, eds.,

American Teaching About Russia (Bloomington, 1959), p. 65, for data on the placement of Russian area students, 1946–1956. One third went into academia; nearly two-fifths went into government service and research. According to Robert F. Byrnes, "as early as October 1952, fifty-five alumni of the [Columbia] program were in government service, thirteen were engaged in government-sponsored research, and forty-six were teaching in colleges and universities." Byrnes, *A History of Russian and East European Studies,* p. 215.

10. The UC Berkeley Institute for Slavic Studies established in 1948 under the direction of historian Robert J. Kerner was renamed and reconstituted in 1956 as the Center for Slavic Studies (subsequently renamed the Center for Slavic and East European Studies). Whereas the Institute granted degrees (B.A., M.A., Ph.D.), the Center was constituted as a research unit. Nicholas Riasanovsky, "University of California, Berkeley," Paper delivered to the American Association for the Advancement of Slavic Studies, Annual Meeting, November 14, 1996; Gregory Grossman, personal communication, April 21, 1998..

11. Black and Thompson, eds., *American Teaching About Russia,* p 52; Fisher, *American Research in Russia,* pp. 24–25.

12. Columbia's Russian Institute alone educated about 235 graduate students; Harvard's Russian Research Center prepared about 100 students with M.A. degrees in regional studies. Ibid., p. 53.

13. Black and Thompson, eds., *American Teaching about Russia,* p. 56.

14. A 1991 report by the Review Committee on Soviet Studies of the American Council of Learned Societies and the Social Science Research Council noted: "Traditional Soviet studies in the West has failed to capture the regional and ethnic wealth of the country. . . .." Reasons included the focus of political scientists on "where the power is, i.e., at the center" and the obstacles to field research. "Beyond Soviet Studies," The Review Committee on Soviet Studies [Blair Ruble, Carol Avins, Nina Garsoian, Abbott Gleason, Robert Huber, David Szanton, and Myron Weiner], November 1991, p. 5.

15. These included the House Un-American Activities Committee, the Korean War, Khrushchev's secret speech in 1956, the launching of Sputnik.

16. At Indiana University, for example, the state legislature was induced to support a Soviet/East Europe program after it was revealed that the state had a substantial ethnic population with roots in the region. Bonnell's interview with Professor Charles Jelavich at UC Berkeley, February 2, 1998.

17. Ibid.

18. Manning, *A History of Slavic Studies,* p. 76; Byrnes, *A History of Russian and East European Studies in the United States,* p. 206; Nicholas Riasanovsky notes that the Berkeley Institute was established with the aid of a $100,000 Rockefeller Foundation grant in addition to state support. Riasanovsky, "University of California, Berkeley," p. 5.

19. Charles Thomas O'Connell, "Social Structure and Sciences: Soviet Studies at Harvard," UCLA (Department of Sociology) Doctoral Dissertation,

1990, especially, pp. 141,170–171.

20. Byrnes, A History of Russian and East European Studies, p. 205.

21. Black and Thompson, eds., American Teaching about Russia, p. 67. See below for further discussion of this program.

22. "Crossing Borders: Revitalizing Area Studies," Ford Foundation, 1997, p. 1.

23. The Ford Foundation made grants to the SSRC totaling $87.7 million between 1950 and 1996, primarily to support area studies. Ibid., p. 2

24. Fisher, American Research on Russia, p. 9. The Joint Committee on Slavic Studies was replaced in 1968 by the Joint Committee on Slavic and East European Studies. In 1971 a Joint Committee on East European Studies was formed that operated separately from the Joint Committee on Soviet Studies.

25. Ibid., p. 10. Gregory Grossman observes that "IREX was not just a 'renaming' of IUCTG but a transformation, in terms of both formal structure and procedures." Personal communication, April 21, 1998.

26. "Federally-Financed Research and Communication on Soviet Affairs: Capabilities and Needs," U.S. General Accounting Office, July 2, 1980, pp. 23–24.

27. For example, Abram Bergson, Geroid T. Robinson, Alex Inkeles, Sidney Harcave, and Barrington Moore, Jr. had worked in the OSS; Alexander Dallin worked in Army Intelligence; Clyde Kluckhohn was involved in the U.S. Strategic Bombing Survey; John Hazard was in the U.S.S.R. Division of the Foreign Economic Administration; Robert F. Byrnes joined the Foreign Economic Administration and then the special Branch of Military Intelligence; Robert Tucker worked at the American Embassy in Moscow. Byrnes, A History of Russian and East European Studies, pp. 210; 247; O'Connell, "Social Structure and Sciences," p. 407. In addition, some future specialists obtained Russian language and area training in the Foreign Area and Language Curricula of the Army Specialized Training Program (for enlisted personnel) and the Civil Affairs Training Schools (for officers). Wallerstein, "The Unintended Consequences of Cold War Area Studies," p. 199.

28. O'Connell, "Social Structure and Sciences," p. 332, 353, 385, 429–430. The project subsequently employed six dozen people in data collection and was headed by Raymond Bauer (field director) and Eugenia Hanfman (deputy director). Interviews were completed in 1951; data processing took place between 1951 and 1954. According to O'Connell, the Air Force reviewed the manuscript version of How the Soviet System Works: Cultural, Psychological and Social Themes (Cambridge, 1959) by Raymond A. Bauer, Alex Inkeles, and Clyde Kluckhohn, and removed reference to the Air Force as a source or partner in the project. Ibid., pp. 444–446. O'Connell's count of four books generated by the project may be understated, depending on the definition of "generation." We can think of at least five such books.

29. Byrnes, A History of Russian and East European Studies, p. 209. Byrnes notes that Geroid T. Robinson, the first director of the Russian Institute between 1946 and 1951, was "resolutely dispassionate" and "avoided

government service and political programs" after 1945. Ibid., 215.

30. "Beyond Soviet Studies," p. 7

31. Wallerstein, "The Unintended Consequences of Cold War Area Studies," p. 209; John Richards, "In Defense of Area Studies," Occasional Paper no. 95–01. Global Forum Series, Center for International Studies, Duke University, January 1995, pp. 3–4. Under the Title VI program, the U.S. Office of Education has funded university centers "for the study of critical areas and their languages." Ten to twelve National Resource Centers have been funded for each world region.

32. "Crossing Borders: Revitalizing Area Studies," p. 2. In 1961, the Fulbright Hays Fellowship was established and eventually came to include the countries of Eastern Europe and the Soviet Union.

33. Stephen F. Cohen, *Rethinking the Soviet Experience: Politics and History Since 1917* (New York and Oxford, 1985), pp. 3–4.

34. Ibid., p. 4.

35. The Kennan Institute was established by Ambassador George F. Kennan, in collaboration with James Billington, Director of the Wilson Center, and the historian S. Frederick Starr. It was named in honor of George Kennan, "The Elder," an explorer of Russia and Siberia in the nineteenth century.

36. "Federally-Financed Research," p. 24.

37. Ibid., pp. 10, 25.

38. "The Shifting Emphasis at Ford: A Sampling of $50-million in New Grants," *The Chronicle of Philanthropy*, May 1, 1997, p. 12. Apart from funds for SSRC and ACLS international programs, Ford allocated $95,000 for a project at the University of California at Berkeley for a workshop, conference, and volume on "Rethinking Area Studies."

39. It is worth noting that according to a recent study by the Ford Foundation, the Fulbright-Hays programs have declined 58% in purchasing power from the mid-1960s to 1995. By 1996, they had declined by 70%. Miriam A. Kazanjian, "Funding Trends for Selected Federal Programs Supporting Study and Research on World Wars Other Than the U.S.", 1996, cited in "Crossing Borders," p. 6 n. 2.

40. The National Council for Soviet and East European Research was renamed after the collapse of communism.

41. Richards, "In Defense of Area Studies," p. 14. The NSEP program is administered by the Department of Defense and supervised by a Presidential Board which includes the Secretary of Defense and the Director of the CIA. The program has drawn criticism from some area studies scholars seeking to avoid any linkage between scholars and the CIA.

42. In August 2000, the U.C. Berkeley Center for Slavic and East European Studies (founded in 1957) was reconstituted the Institute of Slavic, East European, and Eurasian Studies (ISEEES). In July 2002, Harvard's Kathryn W.

and Shelby Cullom Davis Center for Russian Studies became the Davis Center for Russian and Eurasian Studies. Soon afterward, Stanford's Center for Russian and East European Studies was renamed the Center for Russian, East European and Eurasian Studies.

43. Geroid T. Robinson, founder and first director of Columbia's Russian Institute, was an historian; Harvard's Russian Research Center's first executive committee included the sociologists Talcott Parsons and Alex Inkeles, and anthropologist Clyde Kluckhohn (also Director of the Russian Research Center); the "Field Director" of the Harvard Refugee Interview Project, Raymond Bauer, was a psychology professor. Berkeley's Slavic Institute was founded by historian Robert J. Kerner.

44. Fisher, *American Research in Russia*, p. 77.

45. Table 1: Distribution of Fellowships by Disciplines and Geographic Area of Interest—1952–1972, *Directory: Foreign Areas Fellows 1952–1972* (Joint Committee on the Foreign Area Fellowship Program of the ACLS and SSRC, 1973).

46. "Beyond Soviet Studies," p. 8.

47. Cohen, *Rethinking the Soviet Experience*, makes this point, p. 5. Merle Fainsod's historical research exemplifies this phenomenon. See, especially, *How Russia Is Ruled* (Cambridge, 1953, 1963, 1965) and *Smolensk Under Soviet Rule* (Cambridge, 1958).

48. See, in particular, James Millar, ed., *Politics, Work, and Daily life in the USSR: A Survey of Former Soviet Citizens* (New York, 1987), Donna Bahry, "Society Transformed?: Rethinking the Social Roots of Perestroika," *Slavic Review* 52, 3, Fall 1993, pp. 512–554;Paul Gregory, *Restructuring the Soviet Economic Bureaucracy* (New York, 1990).

49. Peter Rutland, who served on IREX's FSU Selection Committee from 1996–1998, reports in a personal communication that many good applications were received from the discipline of anthropology.

50. See the Project's irregularly published *Bulletin* and *Working Papers Series*, which compile translations of recently declassified documents on specific episodes in the history of the Cold War, and analyses of the value-added of those documents; they are distributed free of charge.

51. Several volumes on the Cuban Missile Crisis, based on these conferences, have been published under the editorship of James Blight, including James G. Blight and David A. Welch, *On the Brink: Americans and Soviets Reexamine the Cuban Missile Crisis*, 2nd ed., New York, 1990; and James G. Blight and David A. Welch, Intelligence and the Cuban Missile Crisis, London, UK, 1998.

52. For an overview of what they have accomplished on this score, consult their website at http://www.seas.gwu.edu/nsarchive.

53. On the condition of "comparative economics" within economics departments today, see Peter Rutland, "Comparative Economics and the Study of Russia's Regions," paper prepared for the international symposium, "Regions: A Prism to View the Slavic-Eurasian World," Sapporo, Japan, July

22–24 1998. Rutland reports in a personal communication that only one application was received by the IREX FSU Selection Committee from 1996–1998 from economists in those three years.

54. It is noteworthy that the decline in Russian studies coincides with a more general decline in the enrollments in Western European studies in some disciplines, such as history.

55. For example, the Department of Slavic Languages and Literature at the University of Indiana at Bloomington offered a summer workshop in 2000 that included undergraduate and graduate instruction in the following languages on a varying basis: Polish, Czech, Slovak, Hungarian, Slovene, Serbian and Croatian, Romanian, Bulgarian, Georgian, Uzbek, Azeri, Turkmen, Kyrgyz, Kazak, Estonian, Latvian, Lithuanian, Chechen. The UC Berkeley Department of Slavic Languages and Literatures in academic year 2002–2003 offers instruction in Bulgarian, Czech, Hungarian, Polish, Russian, Serbian/Croatian (S/C), Georgian, Armenian, and Uzbek and supervised tutorials in Chechen-Ingush, Latvian, and Lithuanian.

56. It is noteworthy that a sociologist who has devoted himself for many years to research on Hungary and Russia, Michael Burawoy, was elected president of the American Sociological Association in 2002.

57. At U.C. Berkeley, for example, graduate and undergraduate enrollment in courses pertaining to East Europe and the territory of the former Soviet Union doubled between academic years 1998–1999 and 2001–2002. Institute of Slavic, East European, and Eurasian Studies, National Resource Center Title VI Proposal, November 2002, p. 11 and Appendix B.

58. The seminal volumes were Carl J. Friedrich, ed., *Totalitarianism* (Cambridge, 1954) and Carl J. Friedrich and Zbigniew Brzezinski, *Totalitarian Dictatorship and Autocracy* (Cambridge, 1956). The term "totalitario" is attributed to Benito Mussolini., who applied it to the Italian fascist state.

59. For two notable examples, see Cohen, *Rethinking the Soviet Experience* and Martin Malia ("Z"), "To the Stalin Mausoleum," *Daedalus*, 119, 2:95–344, Spring, 1990. A review of these controversies and an alternative approach is put forth in George Breslauer, "In Defense of Sovietology," *Post-Soviet Affairs*, 1992, 8, 3:197–238. See also the recent book on the subject by Abbott Gleason, *Totalitarianism: The Inner History of the Cold War* (New York, 1995). The concept of totalitarianism has come to occupy a central place in the discourse of Russian scholars and publicists in Russia and Eastern Europe in the 1980s and 1990s.

60. For a Marxist variant of this kind of argument by a non-U.S. scholar, see Isaac Deutscher, *Russia: What Next?* (New York, 1953). A Weberian approach can be found in Barrington Moore, Jr., *Terror and Progress—USSR* (Cambridge, 1954).

61. See, especially, Alex Inkeles, *The Soviet Citizen* (Cambridge, MA, 1959). On the late 1940s and early 1950s, see Vera Dunham's superb use of literature

to decipher attitudinal changes evident in Soviet society, *In Stalin's Time: Middleclass Values in Soviet Fiction* (Cambridge, England, 1976).

62. For a discussion of these issues, see Breslauer, "In Defense of Sovietology," pp. 222–227.

63. Ken Jowitt's influential articles (beginning in 1974) on this theme appear in *New World Disorder: The Leninist Extinction* (Berkeley, 1992).

64. For a still-useful British survey of trends in Western studies of Soviet politics at the time, see A.H. (Archie) Brown, *Soviet Politics and Political Science* (London, 1974).

65. For an overview and categorization of diverse perspectives in the 1940s, 1950s, and 1960s, see William Welch, *American Images of Soviet Foreign Policy: An Inquiry into Recent Appraisals from the Academic Community* (New Haven, 1970).

66. Gregory Grosssman, "Notes for a Theory of the Command Economy," *Soviet Studies*, vol. XV, no. 2 (October 1963).

67. Joseph S. Berliner, *Factory and Manager in the USSR* (Cambridge, MA, 1957).

68. Gregory Grossman, "The 'Second Economy' of the USSR," *Problems of Communism*, vol. XXVI, no. 5 (September-October 1977), pp. 25–40.

69. Abram Bergson, *The Real National Income of Soviet Russia Since 1928* (Cambridge, MA, 1961).

70. We are grateful to James Millar for insights in the previous two paragraphs.

71. Leopold Haimson, "The Problem of Social Stability in Urban Russia, 1905–1917," *Slavic Review*, part 1, vol. 23, no. 4 (December 1964), pp. 619–642; part 2, vol. 24, no. 1 (March 1965), pp. 1–22.

72. A major stimulus for these efforts came from the Seminar in Twentieth-Century Russian and Soviet Social History, organized by Moshe Lewin and Alfred Rieber of the University of Pennsylvania. The seminar met for the first time in 1980. Subsequent meetings focussed on the Russian and Soviet peasantry (1982), the Imperial and Soviet bureaucracy (1983), the social history of Soviet Russia during the Civil War (1984), the New Economic Policy (1986), Soviet industrialization (1988). Work presented at these seminars was subsequently published in several edited volumes.

73. See, for example, J. Arch Getty, Origins of the Great Purges : the Soviet Communist Party Reconsidered, 1933–1938 (New York, 1985); Lynn Viola, The Best Sons of the Fatherland : Workers in the Vanguard of Soviet Collectivization (New York, 1987).

74. It is worth recording here that *Marxist analyses* encompassed a wide band of theorists about the USSR. Trotskyist analyses treated the system as bureaucratic-statist; their perspectives most closely resembled those of the non-Marxist totalitarian theorists. "Democratic socialists" among Marxists, at the other extreme, held out hope for the evolution of the system toward a socialist (not "social") democracy. These analysts more closely resembled the non-Marxist "modernization" theorists. What is most striking about American

Sovietology was how little attention it paid to Marxist literature on the USSR, except to dismiss it in passing (e.g., "in contrast to Marxism, the economic base did not determine the political superstructure"). The best Marxist analyses of the USSR tended to be concentrated in non-mainstream or sectarian journals (e.g. *Telos, The Socialist Review*). Occasionally they would appear in the British mainstream journal, *Soviet Studies*. For a heated critique of American Sovietology's alleged methodological, theoretical, and political biases, see Michael Cox, ed., *Re-Thinking the Soviet Collapse* (London, 1998), *passim.*, which includes several post-mortems on Western Sovietology by prominent Marxist specialists on the USSR.

75. David Hooson, "Ex-Soviet Identities and the Return of Geography," in David Hooson, ed., *Geography and National Identity* (Oxford, 1994).

76. Few Soviet social scientists shared the methodological standards of data-collection, analysis, and reportage of results that were dominant within US social sciences.

77. "Who Writes Our Scripts?" *The Russian Review*, vol. 55, no. 2 (April 1996), p. v.

78. Most of these topics were among those funded by SSRC Fellowships and Grants 1991–1996.

79. The Central Asian states, Moldova, and Belarus had not experienced the rise of large national liberation movements" in the late-1980s.

80. For a most recent example, see Joel S. Hellman, "Winners Take All: The Politics of Partial Reform in Postcommunist Transitions," *World Politics*, 50, 2, January 1998, pp. 203–234; for an earlier, book-length study, see Jane I. Dawson, *Eco-Nationalism: Anti-Nuclear Activism and National Identity in Russia, Lithuania, and Ukraine* (Durham, NC, 1996). For looser comparisons of trajectories among FSU countries, see the ten-volume series, *The International Politics of Eurasia*, edited by Karen Dawisha and Bruce Parrott (Armonk, NY, 1994–1998); also, Ian Bremmer and Ray Taras, *New States, New Politics: Building the Post-Soviet Nations* (New York, 1997), and Timothy J. Colton and Robert C. Tucker, *Patterns in Post-Soviet Leadership* (Boulder, CO, 1995).

81. For example, M. Steven Fish, *Democracy from Scratch* (Princeton,, 1995); Kathryn Stoner-Weiss, *Local Heroes* (Princeton, 1997); Daniel Treisman, *After the Deluge: Regional Crises and Political Consolidation in Russia* (Ann Arbor, MI, 1999); Mark R. Beissinger, *Nationalist Mobilization and the Collapse of the Soviet State* (Cambridge, UK and New York, 2002).

82. Ken Jowitt, *New World Disorder: The Leninist Extinction* (Berkeley, CA, 1992); Beverly Crawford and Arend Lijphart, eds., *Liberalization and Leninist Legacies* (Berkeley, CA, 1997).

83. Thus, Soviet Studies became Europe-Asia Studies; Problems of Communism became Problems of Post-Communism; Studies in Comparative Communism became Communist and Post-Communist Studies; Soviet Economy became Post-Soviet Affairs; Soviet Geography became Post-Soviet

Geography and Economics. Journals such as Slavic Review, The Russian Review, and Nationalities Papers retained their former title but participated, to varying extents, in scholarly discussions and debates inspired by postcommunism.

84. For example, Johnson's Russia List, Jamestown Prism, Jamestown Monitor, Radio Liberty (RL) Daily Reports, to note but a few.

85. From the latter perspective, Russia was the "core" of an "empire" that included an "inner" and an "outer" periphery: the fourteen other republics of the USSR, and the Eastern European members of the Warsaw Pact, respectively. For excellent work in this genre, see Karen Dawisha and Bruce Parrott, *The End of Empire? The Transformation of the USSR in Comparative Perspective* (Armonk, NY, 1997). On the "transition to feudalism," see Katherine Verdery, *What was Socialism and What Comes Next?* (Princeton, 1996).

86. For exemplars of how specialists on post-communism can improve received social theories, see Gerard Roland, *Transition and Economics: Politics, Markets, and Firms* (Cambridge, MA, 2000); Richard D. Anderson, M. Steven Fish, Philip Roeder, and Stephen Hanson, *Postcommunism and the Theory of Democracy* (Princeton, 2001); Michael McFaul, *Russia's Unfinished Revolution: Political Change from Gorbachev to* Yeltsin (Ithaca, NY, 2001); Thomas F. Remington, *The Russian Parliament: Institutional Evolution in a Transitional Regime, 1989-1999* (New Haven, CT, 2001); Pauline Jones Luong, *Institutional Change and Political Continuity in Post-Soviet Central Asia* (Cambridge, UK and New York, 2002); Rawi Abdelal, *National Purpose in the World Economy: Post-Soviet States in Comparative Perspective* (Ithaca, NY, 2001).

87. For example, Oleg Kharkhordin, The Collective and the Individual in Russia: A Study of Practices (Berkeley and Los Angeles, 1999); Vadim Volkov, Violent Entrepreneurs: The Use of Force in the Making of Russian Capitalism (Ithaca, 2002).

88. For example, Mikhail Myagkov, Peter Ordeshook, and Alexander Sobyanin, "The Russian Electorate, 1991–1996," *Post-Soviet Affairs*, 13, 2, April-June 1997, pp. 134–166.

89. For example, David Laitin, *Identity in Formation: The Russian-Speaking Populations in the Near Abroad* (Ithaca, NY, 1998); Michael Burawoy and Pavel Krotov, "The Soviet Transition from Socialism to Capitalism: Worker Control and Economic Bargaining in the Wood Industry." *American Sociological Review* 57(1): 16–38 (1992); "The Rise of Merchant Capital: Monopoly, Barter, and Enterprise Politics in the Vorkuta Coal Industry." *Harriman Institute Forum*, Vol.6, no.4. (1992);—Michael Burawory, Pavel Krotov, and Tatyana Lytkina, "Domestic Involution: How Women Organize Survival in a North Russian City," in Victoria E. Bonnell and George W. Breslauer, eds., *Russia in the New Century: Stability or Disorder?* (Boulder, CO, 2000).

90. See Cohen, *Rethinking the Soviet Experience*, ch. 1 on "regime studies."

91. For example, repressive dictatorships, including those in the postcommunist world (Turkmenistan, Uzbekistan, Belarus),tend to exclude scholars investigating regime-compromising subjects.

92. For example, in March 1999, the University of Wisconsin hosted a major conference, "Beyond State Crisis?: The Quest for the Efficacious State in Africa and Eurasia." Organized by (Africanist) Crawford Young and (FSU specialist) Mark Beissinger, the conference probed analogous dimensions of the political crises that have enveloped Africa and Eurasia in the wake of the collapse of communism in Eurasia and a deepening crisis of the state in Africa. A stimulating volume emerged from this conference: Mark R. Beissinger and Crawford Young, eds., *Beyond State Crisis?: Postcolonial Africa and post-Soviet Eurasia in Comparative Perspective* (Washington, DC, 2002).

93. See, for example, Charles Wilber, *The Soviet Model and Underdeveloped Countries* (Chapel Hill, NC, 1969); Chalmers Johnson, ed., *Change in Communist Systems* (Stanford, 1970); Kenneth T. Jowitt, *Revolutionary Breakthroughs and National Development: The Case of Rumania* (Berkeley, 1971).

94. For a useful survey of the many variants of convergence theory in the literature of the 1950s and 1960s, see Alfred G. Meyer, "Theories of Convergence," in Chalmers Johnson, ed. *Change in Communist Systems* (Stanford, , 1970); by contrast, among economists ideas also circulated of a mutual convergence between the US and Soviet economies. Jan Tinbergen's view of convergence as an "optimal regime" was the most widely accepted. We are grateful to James Millar for drawing this to our attention.

95. See, for example, Victoria E. Bonnell and Thomas B. Gold, eds., *The New Entrepreneurs of Europe and Asia : Patterns of Business Development in Russia, Eastern Europe, and China* (Armonk, N.Y., 2002).

96. See the running debate over appropriate comparative referents in the pages of *Slavic Review:* Philippe C. Schmitter and Terry Lynn Karl, "The Conceptual Travails of Transitologists and Consolidologists: How Far to the East Should They Attempt to Go?" *Slavic Review,* 53, 1, Spring 1994, pp. 173–185; Valerie Bunce, "Should Transitologists Be Grounded?" *Slavic Review,* 54, 1, Spring 1995, pp. 111–127; Terry Lynn Karl and Philippe C. Schmitter, "From an Iron Curtain to a Paper Curtain: Grounding Transitologists or Students of Postcommunism?" *Slavic Review,* 54, 4, Winter 1995, pp. 965–978; Valerie Bunce, "Paper Curtains and Paper Tigers," *Ibid.,* pp. 979–988. The tenor of this debate (and others going on in the field over methodological, epistemological, and theoretical issues) reveals that one does not need Cold War passions to generate emotional defenses of intellectual positions on this area.

97. See the tendentious caricatures of area studies, and the self-serving definitions of "theory," in debates published in selected issues of *APSA-CP: Newsletter of the APSA Organized Section in Comparative Politics,* volumes 5–7, 1993–1996; see the same tendency among some scholars quoted in Christopher Shea, "New Faces and New Methodologies Invigorate Russian Studies," *The Chronicle of Higher Education,* February 20, 1998, pp. A16-A18.

98. This is not a blanket rejection of rational-choice theory, only a call for putting its utility into perspective. For example, the widespread tendency toward "nomenklatura privatization" in the FSU is explicable without reference to ideology, identity, or culture: a ruling elite saw clearly that its political and economic survival were at stake, and saw equally clearly that a path existed through which it could exploit its political position to gain material security and riches in the emerging system. Many other situations in the fluid, post-communist environment, however, do not so uniformly threaten physical, political, and material security, and do not so clearly present "outs" for those so threatened. To explain choices under those circumstances requires a more subtle intellectual apparatus.

99. For examples of the application of rational choice theory in the FSU, see Timothy Frye, *Brokers and Bureaucrats: Building Market Institutions in Russia* (Ann Arbor, MI, 2000); Andrei Shleifer and Daniel Treisman, *Without a Map: Political Tactics and Economic Reform in Russia* (Cambridge, MA, 2000); Steven Solnick, *Stealing the State: Control and Collapse in Soviet Institutions* (Cambridge, MA, 1998); Laitin, *Identity in Formation*. For a rebuttal of its use in determining economic strategies of transition, see Lawrence R. Klein and Marshall Pomer, eds., *The New Russia: Transition Gone Awry* (Stanford, CA, 2001).

100. See, for example, Kharkhordin, The Collective and the Individual in Russia: A Study of Practices ; Michael Burawoy and Kathrine Verdery, eds., Uncertain Transition: Ethnographies of Change in the Postsocialist World (Lanham, 1999); Caroline Humphrey, The Unmaking of Soviet Life : Everyday Economies After Socialism (Ithaca: 2002); Ruth Mandel and Caroline Humphrey, eds., Markets and Moralities : Ethnographies of Postsocialism (Oxford ; New York, 2002).

101. For one of many examples, see Kathleen Smith, *Mythmaking in the New Russia* (Ithaca, NY, 2002).

Chapter 6

Eastern Europe or Central Europe?
Exploring a Distinct Regional Identity

Ellen Comisso and Brad Gutierrez

Perhaps even more than area studies in other regions of the world, East European studies in the United States developed as an artifact of the Cold War. As an object of study, the area was, in effect, the poor cousin of Soviet/Slavic studies, emerging as a distinct field just as detente was getting under way.[1] Thus, despite the very different prewar traditions and concerns of the two areas, postwar East European and Soviet studies developed in tandem with each other in the United States, sharing both funding sources and institutional bases. If 1991 saw the "disappearance" of Soviet area studies, the fall of the Berlin Wall in 1989 had analogous consequences for East European studies, and major questions were raised as to what the boundaries of a region called "Eastern Europe" were and indeed, whether it existed at all.

Local colleagues, some at home and some residing abroad, led the charge here, arguing that the postwar definition of Eastern Europe was little more than an intellectual legitimation of the Yalta agreements.[2] The movement to recast the region as "Central Europe" took on major proportions in the 1980s; while the view of what Central Europe included varied according to the particular intellectual espousing it, there was broad agreement as to what Central Europe was not—namely, the Soviet Union and Russia.

From the perspective of a field which, in the United States, had always recognized—and even had a vested interest in recognizing—a distinction between Eastern Europe and the Soviet Union, it might well be argued that simply changing an adjective makes little difference. Yet it is worth beginning an analysis of contemporary area studies with the debate on Central Europe, since that discussion often seems to imply a different boundary to the area as well as a novel set of features that would link its parts together, issues any overview of regional studies must confront. I shall try to show here that the fact that such a debate exists at all is itself a sign of a distinct regional identity, that the "Central Europe" appellation is no less (and no more) a political construct than the former "East European" title was, and that the factors that defined Eastern Europe as a distinct region in the postwar period continue to define Central East Europe today.

Once establishing the contours of a distinct regional identity, I review the field's evolution prior to the Great Political Landslide of 1989, and conclude by exploring the main changes and challenges in the study of the region that have taken place since then.

WHAT IS EASTERN—OR CENTRAL—EUROPE?
The boundaries of Eastern Europe which defined American postwar studies of the area were indeed based on its political features. They thus included all of the European socialist states outside the Soviet Union itself: East Germany, Poland, Czechoslovakia, Hungary, Romania, Bulgaria, Yugoslavia, and Albania. Greece was conveniently placed in Western Europe—despite its social and historical affinities with the rest of the Balkan peninsula—while Austria, the center of many of the cultural characteristics and continuities nowadays considered classically "central" European, was typically treated in isolation from its former hinterland. As for the Baltic states, they were confided to Soviet studies, again reflecting political realities. While such a division of the region surely created difficulties for historians and students of the arts, it raised few problems for the core social science disciplines of sociology, political science, or economics.

As for the notion of Central Europe, it had certainly enjoyed some currency in the interwar period. Yet even then, it carried no less political baggage than the postwar definition of the area. On the one hand, there was Friedrich Naumann's "Mitteleuropa," in which the area's defining characteristic was its ties to Germany, whether through settlement, trade, hegemony, or conquest.[3] On the other, there was the central Europe Tomas Masaryk looked to: a region of small states, from which Germany and Germans were excluded.[4] Both conceptualizations captured important aspects of this "problem" area, and each led to diametrically opposite political conclusions. Yet in classically East/Central European fashion, what nominally appeared to be identities totally at odds with each other turned out to be entirely complementary. It was precisely the Central Europe of small states, each competing with the other and allying against its neighbor in pursuit of its "national" interest that provided the opportunity for the economic and then political hegemony a newly aggressive Germany was able to establish for itself in the area as World War II approached.[5]

Nor was the convergence of the two prewar incarnations of the Central European idea accidental. Both stemmed from the same basic premise: that people had a unique "national identity" and therefore deserved a "national territory" in which they could express it, preferably without other peoples getting in their way. It was this premise that dropped out of the 1980s discourse on Central Europe, a discussion which highlighted the region's cultural interactions and shared sensibilities.[6] Yet the notion of Central Europe in its new incarnation was also a Central Europe of political aspirations, this time of the intellectuals who loosely made up the political opposition. From their point of view, Central Europe became "the eastern border of the West," whereas Russia was a "foreign" civilization.

The "West" to which Central Europe now belonged was a peculiarly reconstructed one, its colonial empires, nasty flirtations with various forms of dictatorship, and periodic indulgences in religious persecution, not to mention its shattering wars or crass materialism, omitted. It was a West moving towards an ever more convinced affirmation of liberalism, respect for the individual, and reciprocal cooperation, a civilization that has always been inherently pluralistic, tolerant of differences, and open to experimentation and change. It was a Europe whose political tradition was founded on the limitation of power and at the heart of whose "value system is the proposition that society is creative and the state is reactive."[7] Or, as Mihaly Vajda puts it, "The leading value of Europe is *freedom*, conceived—more and more—in a very simple and understandable way: namely as the freedom of the individual limited only by that of others."[8]

That westerners, peering over mountains of consumer goods while speeding along six-lane highways on their holidays, might not recognize themselves in this rather flattering picture is quite irrelevant. For the historical and cultural tradition ascribed to Europe is not necessarily the one apprehended by those who enjoy its benefits, but on the contrary, the one appreciated by those who have been deprived of them. Thus, the features attributed to Europe are less a realistic account of the characteristics belonging to it than a selected and idealized listing of properties perceived as antithetical to the Soviet Union and all the Soviet system had come to represent by the mid-1980s. In such circumstances, Central Europe was not—and could not—be a political entity. Rather, it was above all a cultural one, with its boundaries varying according to the cultural and "spiritual" affinities said to link it with the West.

For some, the religious divide was the key. Where Central Europe was distinguished by its adherence to western Christianity, be it Catholic or Protestant, Eastern Europe remained faithful to Orthodoxy despite—or, in the Balkans, even because of—the strong Islamic pressures generated by Ottoman influence. Unlike the West, where religious institutions limited secular authority, in the East they were a means through which the state penetrated and controlled the underlying society—much as Leninism was to do with its own version of sacred doctrine in the twentieth century. [9]

For others, Central Europe had far more secular roots, planted in its historic oscillation between and amalgamation of elements derived from a "West" that stopped in Germany and an "East" that began at the Russian frontier. As Jeno Szucs notes, Central Europe's medieval development followed lines roughly similar to those of the West—with feudal institutions, nobles powerful enough to constrain the monarch, estate-based representation, commercial towns with German charters. Yet the unfortunate combination of new external military pressures and changed economic conditions after the discovery of the New World saw "defensive" structures acquire an "eastern" cast: peasants fell into serfdom, trade languished, and kingdoms became absorbed into centralizing dynastic empires.[10] In this version, Central Europe is less the eastern border of the West than a less successful appendix to it.

A third variant of this approach nominally relies on geography, defining Central Europe as a "Danubian" region in the "heart" of the continent. In practice, this is a view that roots central Europe in the Habsburg Empire and the cultural tradition it is seen as embodying, whether it be the architecture of opera houses and railroad stations, the *kavehaz* as a locus of intellectual life, the distinctive mixing of ideas and talents emanating from all the small nations colliding within its borders, or a monarchy that sought to centralize and ensure uniformity within its domains but never quite managed to do so as thoroughly as its neighbors.[11] If state domination of society and illiberal institutions are the hallmarks of "Eastern" Europe in the first two characterizations, intolerance is its leading characteristic in this one.

The accounts described above by no means exhaust the field. Yet what is quite fascinating about them is how a history long despaired of has been recast and re-edited to reflect the aspirations of late socialist and early post-socialist intellectual elites. For example, the historical forces that for most of the twentieth century were commonly accepted as the source of the region's social, political, and economic problems—the Catholic Church, the local nobilities determined to preserve their "rights" (a.k.a. privileges), the Habsburg "prison of nations"—are now reclaimed to show the area's ties to the west and the key to its progress. Nor is the selective reviving of past memory to argue that "we deserve something better" a phenomenon unique to the past decade; it was quite typical in the national movements at the turn of the century and a not insignificant factor in the appeal (now forgotten) that socialism drew on in the 1940s.[12]

Like any discussion seeking to define a region—even one of the spirit—this one, too, distinguishes between the "ins" and the "outs." Clearly, all accounts converge in excluding the Soviet Union (and Russia in particular) from Central Europe. Austria, in contrast, is "in" now—despite recent electoral showings indicating that Central Europe is not an area its population wishes to have all that much to do with. And unlike the interwar vision of Central Europe, Germany, too, is included, albeit only, to quote Vaclav Havel, "with one leg"—and it is presumably the western, not the eastern, one.[13] By the same token, the Baltic states, lying on the periphery of even Cold War Eastern Europe, have now gravitated close to the continent's center, together with, of course, the core members of Poland, Hungary, the Czech Republic and Slovakia.

Far more ambiguous is the status of the Balkans. For Szucs,

Byzantium may well have been the heir to the Roman tradition, but the territory it included quickly dropped into a peculiar no man's land, not even a "historical region of Europe" at all once "swallowed up by the Seljuk advance." The peninsula fares equally poorly if the religious divide is the boundary, with only Catholic Slovenia and Croatia qualifying as "Central" European. The "Danubian" definition turns out to be more forgiving: after all, more of current day Serbia, Romania, and the Ukraine than of Poland came under Habsburg rule—not to mention all of Bosnia. But finding Galicia once again as "the end of the world,"[14] sharply reminds us that imperial pretensions and Great Power ambitions did not pause to consider cultural sensibilities in the past any more than today. With this in mind, serious questions can be raised about the fundamental assumption underlying the current "rediscovery" of Central Europe—namely, that cultural identities trump political ones.

That is, once we realize that cultures are fluid and dynamic and that influences from one direction by no means preclude equally strong influences from others, it is hardly a surprise that boundaries defined by cultural attributes constantly shift. Centralized rule in Russia may well have been a response to specifically Russian conditions, but it also reflected the influence of France and Prussia as models for state building. Katherine the Great was, after all, a German princess, engaged in extensive dialogue with Voltaire.[15] So it is not clear that even Russia can be written off on account of its lack of exposure to western intellectual and political currents.

Nor does history do a very good job of establishing clear and fast distinctions that define a new Central Europe taking in only a privileged segment of postwar Eastern Europe. For here, one must immediately ask, "which history? And what about the other one?" in an area marked by historical discontinuities and abrupt turnarounds. Thus, whatever similarities the area north of the Sava River shared with the western Roman Empire prior to 1500, it is quite unclear why those features should be more important in defining a regional identity today than the many dissimilarities that emerged after that time, as Szucs is also careful to note. That Bulgaria's recent economic reforms were as radical and neo-liberally inspired as Poland's is perhaps a graphic reminder that history is no more destiny for states and nations than anatomy is for individuals.

Religion is equally problematic as basis for distinguishing the eastern border of the west from the western border of the east. If the Catholic Church allied with and sheltered the opposition in socialist Poland, it also collaborated with fascist regimes in Slovakia and Croatia in the 1940s. Jews survived the holocaust in the Soviet Union, but not in Bohemia or Moravia with their liberal traditions and large middle classes. And Bulgaria, with its eastern Orthodox church and Ottoman background, was the only state in the region to reject German pressures to deport its native Jewish population.

The selective account of culture, religion, and history supplied by the Central European discourse highlighted above makes somewhat more sense attached to an explicitly political program. As described by Jacques Rupnik, it is a program that calls on "societies in the Soviet bloc . . . to think of themselves as subjects, not merely objects of history" and which combines a rejection of an "imposed ideological identity . . . with a critical reassessment of the limitations of nationalism."[16] In the 1980s, it meant "living in truth," "antipolitics," and "self-limiting revolution," a political program fashioned along classically liberal lines whose essence was to deny it had a political content at all.[17] Its most articulate and well-known exponents were in Poland, Hungary, and, in a more muted mode, Czechoslovakia, and for them, the Central European umbrella provided a convenient rubric for cross-border communication and coordination. As a result, Central Europe necessarily included their societies yet also had to be defined in the purely cultural, non-political terms a nominally anti-political program required. But what rendered the concept of Central Europe both plausible and attractive was its political subtext more than the empirical or intellectual validity of the distinctions it sought to capture.

But if the Central European idea essentially originates in a political—or anti-political—program, then adhesion to it is presumably voluntary, the same way adherence to any set of ideas should be. As Egon Schwartz proposes, one can support Central Europe as a utopian program ("universalism, antiracism, sympathy for all ethnic, linguistic, and religious differences, the right to criticize, the renunciation of aggression, " etc. etc.) even while openly acknowledging that there is no such definable region in fact. In that sense, anyone can be a Central European. So it would seem to follow that a priori exclusion due to an inappropriate historical, cultural, or religious pedigree is quite inconsistent with the effort to establish a Central European regional identity—unless the explicit "search for an alternative to the partition of Europe" is actually an implicit search to repartition it along new lines, as those outside the magic circle fear.[18]

Nevertheless, if one cannot define a Central European "identity," one can outline a Central European geography that recognizes the area's many commonalities as well as its distinctive contrasts. Such a Central Europe, ironically, turns out to be remarkably similar to the "Eastern Europe" that marked postwar American scholarship on the area.

One might begin with Milan Kundera's original posing of the question. He writes: "What is Central Europe? An uncertain zone of small nations between Russia and Germany. I underscore the works: *small nation.* . . . Central Europe longed to be . . . a reduced model of Europe conceived according to one rule: the greatest variety within the smallest space."[19] Far from the Balkans being outside the pale, then, pre-1990 Yugoslavia was arguably the most Central European political entity on the continent, and the Baltic states are part of the region not despite but because of their Russian, Polish, and Ukrainian populations.

Moreover, if we look at the "small nations between Germany and Russia," one can define the geographical boundaries of Central Europe fairly precisely. In the north, it is bounded by the Baltic Sea, in the south, by the Aegean; in the west, central Europe begins at the Elbe River, while in the East, it more or less peters out at the Dniestr. What makes such boundaries intellectually meaningful is less a common cultural sensibility or homogeneous "longing" to join "western civilization" than three major historical problems all of the "small nations" within this area have shared. Significantly, those problems long predated the arrival of Leninism in the area, and they persist even as it disappears.

The first problem was that of state formation, a process which followed a trajectory quite different from the one in Western Europe or Russia. Certainly, medieval kingdoms were as common in this area as in the west. Even within the Byzantine Empire, there were Bulgarian and Serbian kingdoms, Bosnia enjoyed a short period of sovereignty, and Croatian nobles on the empire's edge had a crown they were able to offer the Hungarian king in 1100. Bohemia/Moravia had its own monarch, and more spectacularly, so did Hungary and Poland, controlling large expanses of territory in their respective heydays. Yet as medieval kingdoms were being refashioned into modern states under centralized forms of rule and, more importantly, with centralized militaries, in the west of Europe, the more decentralized and noble-dominated kingdoms of the East were being absorbed into larger empires, a process that ended only when Poland was completely partitioned by Prussia, Russia, and Austria in 1795.[20]

Thus, unlike Western Europe, populations east of the Elbe River entered the nineteenth century from within large, multinational imperial orders. As a result, national consciousness emerged prior to state formation, the opposite of the French and English experience .[21] Even then, it was not until national states arose to homogenize populations that nationalism assumed genuinely exclusive forms. The process thus began earlier in the Balkans, spreading north only after World War I. And if national identities were in large part the creation of urban intellectuals, they were often rooted in the peasant traditions of the countryside.

The relationship between urban and rural populations in the east was also different from the west. Certainly, in both regions cities were sites of commercial, and later industrial, development. But in Central Eastern Europe, urban areas prior to industrialization were dominated by groups invited to the area by early monarchs for the specific purpose of engaging in trade and crafts. Commerce and urban life in such a context easily came to be seen as the preserve of "foreigners"—for the most part, Germans and Jews—a factor explaining why nationalist movements in the area often took an anti-modern and anti-Semitic form.

This brings us to the second longstanding problem that makes the area distinct, namely its "lagged" economic development. Nowadays, it is popular to attribute differences in living standards between Western and Central/Eastern Europe to the peculiar features of state socialism. Yet with the exception of Bohemia, Central East Europe lagged behind Western Europe in the traditional indices of economic development throughout the period following the discovery of the New World. Indeed, one of the initial appeals of socialism in the region was precisely the hope that it would be a viable catch up strategy in an area where modern development had always been state-led. [22]

In fact, economic development on the European continent as a whole moved broadly from northwest to southeast, [23] marking relationships between Central European powers as well as within them. Germany was more developed than Austria-Hungary, with Russia following third and the Ottoman territories lagging significantly behind all three. Yet within post-1871 Germany, the Polish areas in the east were less developed than the German areas in the west, while the more industrialized parts of the Romanov Empire were in western areas with a Polish population. In the Habsburg realm, too, industrialization began in Bohemia and Austria, gradually spreading east and south in the last half of the nineteenth century. The Ottoman Empire, in contrast, never succeeded in modernizing its administration or adapting its economic policies to achieve modern economic growth, creating the basis for the Balkan exceptionalism so characteristic of the Central European discourse described earlier.[24] As a result, modern economic development began only when nation-states emerged in the Balkans, in contrast to the area to the north, where development was initiated under imperial auspices.[25]

Nevertheless, even as modern economic growth began to make itself felt, it was never robust enough to absorb excess labor from the countryside, and the persistence of a peasantry mired in poverty and engaged in subsistence agriculture was characteristic everywhere.[26] The disruption of trade links that came after World War I hardly helped, as industries built to serve large imperial markets suddenly found themselves producing for much smaller domestic economies and facing protectionist barriers to their previous outlets.[27] The large proportion of the population remaining in agriculture meant the Great Depression—characterized above all by a huge drop in the price of agricultural commodities—hit the area especially hard. In this context, the offer of a newly aggressive Germany to purchase agricultural goods at above world market prices in exchange for the export of Germany industrial goods turned out to be too good to refuse, and the region moved increasingly within the German sphere of influence in the 1930s. [28]

This brings us to the third problem that has historically characterized Central East Europe, namely, the position of the small nations within it as takers rather than makers of the international order around them. It is this feature, not cultural attributes, that disqualifies both Russia and Germany from Central Europe. As Great Powers, their internal and external dynamics were necessarily different from those of the territories between them and over whose control they competed—or colluded, as the case may be.

In fact, rivalries between major powers have been at least as important in shaping the area as have the aspirations of the domestic populations within it. This is not to say that domestic forces were unable to use those rivalries in their own interests, but it is to say that competition between domestic actors was often a proxy for the external powers backing them. The story of state formation in the Balkans is exemplary, as what began as peasant uprisings or local conspiracies against Ottoman authorities became defined as national movements by major powers seeking to counter each others' influence in the peninsula.[29]

World War I was fought as much on the political as the military front, as each belligerent attempted to utilize the other's minorities on behalf of its own efforts. Thus, Germany could sponsor an independent Poland on Russian territory and support Irish struggles in Britain, while the Western allies gave sanctuary and support to nationalist leaders in Austria-Hungary; that the Balfour declaration was issued in 1917 indicates that even the Jews were not overlooked in these efforts.

Interwar arrangements reflected these trends as well, as the creation of national states was designed as much to fashion a *cordon sanitaire* between Germany and a now Bolshevik Soviet Union as to satisfy notions of national serf-determination.[30] On the domestic front, new states initially sought to adapt institutions modeled on those of the victorious European powers, England and France. But once Germany reasserted itself as the regional hegemon in the 1930s, a new model rapidly presented itself and authoritarian regimes quickly became the norm.[31] Viewed over the *longue duree,* then, the region's entrance into the Soviet sphere of influence after World War II is hardly as inconsistent with previous trends as those despairing of the Yalta accords would have us believe.

Problems of state formation, lagged economic development, and dependence on the power relations and rivalries of major powers based outside the area itself thus define a region, which we can call "Central East Europe," that existed well before the Yalta accords. Its boundaries are quite similar with those of Cold War Eastern Europe, and the main adjustments that can legitimately be made now is simply to extend them southwards to include Greece and northeast to take in the Baltic states. In that context, Austria in the West and Belarus, Ukraine, and Moldava in the East become the borderlands. And as for Russia, if its size and Great Power status exclude it from Central East Europe, they by no means exclude it from Europe as such—either geographically or culturally.

Certainly, such a region is far from homogeneous. If the entire area shared the experience of being absorbed into empires, *which* empire one came to be included in had, to put it mildly, non-trivial consequences for everything from literary production and economic development to the social composition and platform of nationalist movements. Regional heterogeneity continued into the era of nation-state creation, as distinctive national traditions and institutions came to be superimposed on former imperial ones, and each country sought to distinguish itself above all from the states and societies with which it shared a common border.

Thus, while we can define a coherent region in terms of Kundera's "small nation" paradigm and the three longstanding historical problems described above, virtually any other generalization has at least one exception. For example, even as one of the area's leading journals runs under the title *Slavic Studies,* neither Romanian, Hungarian, Albanian nor the Baltic tongues are Slavic languages. In religious terms, it may be convenient to think of the region as split between Roman Catholicism and Orthodoxy, but to do so would be to ignore the Uniate Churches, the Moslem population, the Protestant confessions, and the historic importance of the Jewish population. Nobles may have led the national movements in Hungary and

Poland, but not in Serbia or Czechoslovakia. The "proletariat" was small throughout the area, but the Czech working class made its interwar Communist Party one of the largest parties in the country.

The post-World War II socialist interlude by no means eliminated these differences, although it did see the imposition of a common set of political and economic institutions creating a kind of uniformity in the area. Even then, Greece fell outside the fold, the Baltic nations were within the Soviet Union, and both Albania and Yugoslavia developed very different models out of a shared Leninist commitment. Yet leaving Greece aside, it was precisely the distinctiveness of socialist institutions and the variations between them that created an extremely fertile field for comparative research: in effect, one could follow a kind of controlled experiment conducted in conditions that varied over time and place. It was in this context that East European area studies in the United States was given its initial impetus. We now turn to how the field evolved until the experiment came to what—with the disastrous exception of Yugoslavia—was a surprisingly peaceful conclusion.

"EAST" EUROPEAN STUDIES IN THE STATE SOCIALIST PERIOD

A review of postwar East European area studies should probably begin with the problem of access to the area itself. Similar to the situation in the Soviet Union, conducting primary research in post-1948 Eastern Europe often faced insurmountable political hurdles, especially prior to the 1960s. Even afterwards, however, receptiveness to foreign scholars could vary widely, both by place and time. Yugoslavia and Poland were perhaps the first to support scholarly exchanges; they were followed by Hungary, Romania and the rest of the Warsaw Pact countries.[32] Albania, in contrast, was always quite closed, a prime cause for the paucity of scholarship and knowledge about its society. Czechoslovakia enjoyed a brief period of openness before the Prague spring; after 1968, exchanges continued but politically sensitive topics rarely pursued, as intellectuals of all types came under a cloud. Likewise, Romania's decision to follow a more independent course in the late 1960s was accompanied by a flurry of attention, especially in the social sciences. The contacts formed in those years allowed established scholars to continue their work even as "socialism in one family" assumed its pathological forms, but under deteriorating and increasingly constrained conditions.

Openness to foreign scholars and to the creation of networks among intellectuals and academics was a major factor explaining why some countries were more fully studied than others. The availability of language instruction was another. Polish, Serbo-Croatian, and of course, German, were the most widely offered languages in American universities; other languages were either unavailable altogether, or taught only at the few institutions with a critical mass of area experts on their faculties. Both limited funding and a lack of economies of scale were responsible for the situation: for an area consisting of eight small countries with at least 13 distinct languages spoken in various parts of them, enrollments in language courses were inevitably small and instructional resources difficult to come by. Language training, as we shall see, remains a critical problem, despite recent attempts to organize it in a way accessible to the wider scholarly community.

The size of emigrant communities in the United States also influenced language availability and the degree of attention devoted to a particular state or nation. At the same time, émigrés also made extremely important contributions to scholarship on the region. Unlike the Soviet field, East European studies did not have to wait for substantial numbers to arrive in the United States. Starting with the establishment of full-fledged "People's Democracies" in 1948, each crisis in the area (Hungary in 1956, Czechoslovakia in 1968, Poland in 1981) saw a fresh "East Europeanization" of the scholarly community concerned with the region.

Access to primary research sources in Eastern Europe, the availability of language training, and the presence of an émigré community well represented in academic circles in the United States were all factors affecting the relatively extensive intellectual attention accorded Yugoslavia, Poland, Hungary, and Romania. Equally important was the size, intellectual integrity, and sophistication of the academic and research community within them, a reflection of both larger official cultural policy (from control over intellectual discourse to willingness to engage with the West in a wide variety of spheres) and long established intellectual strengths. For example, while the expansion of institutions of higher education and research occurred throughout the socialist bloc, in Poland and

Hungary it took place on the basis of already distinguished traditions in sociology and economics. As a result, American scholars working in such areas found that, far from having to reinvent the wheel, they could rely on a rich set of domestic analyses, debates, and secondary sources within which to seat their own research. Formal collaboration in the form of joint projects or coordinated studies in several countries around common problems remained limited prior to 1990, partly due to political constraints and partly because the structure of funding in both East and West favored a country-by-country approach. Nevertheless, the growth of these types of efforts in the past decade is integrally related to the research ties that had already been established in previous years.

Finally, the interaction between disciplinary priorities and developments within Eastern Europe itself had a deep impact on which areas and topics came to the attention of American scholars. Particularly in the post-World War II social sciences, how societies changed was a major focus of intellectual inquiry, and the peculiar features of the Leninist order offered a distinctive contrast to the logic of "modernization" in societies less subject to wholesale social engineering. Understanding that logic was necessarily an interdisciplinary effort, given that in Eastern Europe, everything from the structure of society to the organization of economic activity and subtexts of literary and artistic production was in one way or another related to political priorities adopted at the highest levels of the state and party. Moreover, it was an international effort as well, as East European intellectuals often contributed some of the most penetrating analyses of both the logic of change—and the logic of stagnation—in their respective countries.

Typically, coming to terms with postwar Eastern Europe involved elucidating the distinctive structural features of the Leninist order, i.e., those characteristics without which it could not be considered "socialist," and then analyzing how and why change could and was produced, accommodated, and experienced within those constraints. The first task—defining the key structures of rule—invariably brought East Europeanists closer to their colleagues in the Soviet field, partly because postwar regimes in Eastern Europe were smaller scale adaptation of the larger Leninist model and partly because

Soviet policies and priorities were so important in maintaining these structures within Eastern Europe itself. The second task, however, was what made East European studies distinct, insofar as changes and adaptation to local conditions and pressures that were absent in the USSR (e.g., the limited role of collectivized agriculture in Poland, the Hungarian economic reforms) were common outside Soviet borders. Moreover, it was within this second realm of analysis that disciplinary oriented research had its greatest intellectual payoffs. If political scientists had a comparative advantage in exploring patterns of cleavage and consensus within the elite and between it and the opposition, economists shed great light on the causes and consequences of the resulting decisions on patterns of production, investment, employment and trade, while sociologists and anthropologists were well positioned to examine the impact of such processes on social development and interaction at macro and micro levels.

The result of these efforts was, over the years, a quite nuanced and accurate picture of the basic features of the East European socialist systems, the variations they were capable of, and the ways in which they adapted to the distinct societies in which they were seated. There was considerable consensus on the key structural features of "actually existing" socialism. Politically, its hallmark was a single, hegemonic party organized hierarchically along Leninist lines. It faced no electoral constraints, operated according to democratic centralism, and claimed an exclusive right to monopolize the means of collective action, be they lower units of government and administration, the media, or mass organizations and secondary associations. Construed in principal-agent terms, the party was invariably the principal; the state, the mass organizations, and even the population to varying degrees, its agents.[33]

The economic trademark of the socialist economy, in turn, was a distinctive set of property rights, whereby the ownership of assets by private individuals was severely restricted and the dominant share of property is owned *de facto* or *de jure* by the state or "society." As such, socialism was first and foremost an ownership system, one that was invariably accompanied by a low degree of differentiation between the state and the economy As a result, economic units were unable to fully internalize either the costs or the risks of their activities, both of which were born by the state. Budget constraints were "soft," such that enterprises were able to compromise on the achievement of economic objectives for the sake of accomplishing the political priorities of their communal owner. And since prices did not—and indeed could not—govern the allocation of resources, a key task of the party was managing the shortages created by uncontrolled demand—be it for capital, labor, or other inputs.[34]

The "leading role" of the party and the lack of differentiation between state and economy were characteristics East European variants of socialism shared with other socialist systems in different parts of the world. In Eastern Europe itself, however, a third "core" characteristic was specific to the area and was critical to maintaining the first two: namely, the dominant role of the Soviet Union. Certainly, how Soviet influence was exerted varied considerably over time and place, but Soviet actions and preferences—both manifest and anticipated—were invariably a major factor conditioning even purely domestic decisions within Warsaw Pact members and, albeit far less directly, Yugoslavia. Much of the homogeneity between states and societies which, left to their own devices, would have differed substantially from one another was explained by the Soviet military, political, and economic role in the area.

Nevertheless, the core structures of socialist rule were necessarily found in specific states, whose practices could not help but reflect the national context in which governing occurred and economies functioned. Thus, there were important differences between states and societies in the region, and documenting and accounting for them were important contributions area studies made to our understanding of how state socialism functioned in practice and how it was experienced by individuals and social groups. Yugoslavia, for example, quickly revealed itself as a deviant, with a foreign policy that played off West against East, a peculiar adaptation of consociationalism that saw a "leading role" played by eight parties, each hegemonic within its own republic, and a "self-managed" economy that relied on market mechanisms enough to lead even investment planning to be abandoned after 1965. If state or social ownership was the norm throughout the region, tolerance for the private sector varied considerably; neither Yugoslavia nor Poland collectivized agriculture to a significant degree while small scale private ventures became common in Hungary by the 1980s. The degree to which markets could be used to guide resource allocation within an economy based on public ownership had long been a major theoretical debate in economics; by the 1960s, it became a practical one in East European studies, as several states experimented with economic reforms devolving substantial discretion to individual enterprises, often with quite different and unexpected results. [35]

Political differences were no less important. Most parties followed the Soviet Union into "collective leadership" after 1956, but Romania returned to the "cult of personality" by the 1970s along with a more independent, yet strongly nationalistic, foreign policy agenda. Likewise, parties were often more hegemonic in theory than in practice, as the important political role Poland's Catholic Church came to play indicated.

Relations with the Soviet Party also came to be quite differentiated, both politically and economically.[36] In foreign trade, the Soviet Union may have been the single most important trading partner of every state within CMEA, but the terms of trade changed quite dramatically over the years. The immediate postwar period saw resources flowing out of Eastern Europe to the USSR; by 1980, a major debate arose around the degree to which the Soviet Union was subsidizing its East European trading partners by supplying them with oil at below world market prices.[37] Meanwhile, borrowing patterns differed greatly, with Poland, Hungary, Yugoslavia, Romania and, to a lesser extent, Bulgaria running up large hard currency debts in the 1970s—while Czechoslovakia chose to stay out of credit markets entirely.

The differences noted above give only a flavor of the variety possible within a common structural format. Meanwhile, however, the 'core' characteristics of East European socialism made societies, economies, and states there distinctly different from non-socialist counterparts in other regions and at similar levels of development; inevitably, they also imparted a distinct quality to area studies as well. In particular, the applicability of disciplinary tools and frameworks developed in the context of non-socialist societies was often highly problematic. For economists, the dilemma was particularly acute, since the absence of *bona fide* markets made i t impossible to employ many of the most sophisticated econometric and modeling techniques that came to be at the mainstream of the discipline. Similar problems arose throughout the social sciences and even the humanities. On the one hand, phenomena central to disciplinary discussions—such as electoral behavior in political science—were utterly uninteresting in the socialist context. On the other, activities and texts which would be of marginal significance or of second rate quality elsewhere were of great interest to East Europeanists because of the political alternative or challenge they represented to the dominant regime discourse. In addition, even where the study of East European socialist regimes proved amenable to the use of models and frameworks developed in other contexts, the choice of which framework to employ was often complicated by underlying normative and political dimensions. For example, utilizing hypotheses about socialist systems drawn from studies of Nazi Germany clearly implied a very different evaluation of the systems themselves than, say, analyses applying pluralist theory to the same material.

Another set of problems in the relationship between students of Eastern Europe and their disciplines concerned generalizing research findings. That is, even as concepts and methodologies imported into area studies from the disciplines increasingly came to be employed, findings based on them seemed to apply only to other socialist countries.[38] While this presented fewer difficulties in the humanities, in the social sciences it could easily lead to a kind of ghettoization. Intellectually, the compromise was to seat area studies within a larger theoretical discourse on "communist systems," such that more light could often be shed on, say, Hungary by comparing it with China than with its geographically and culturally more compatible neighbor, Austria.[39] As we shall see, the collapse of socialism in 1989 did not so much put an end to this tradition as renew it under the rubric of "societies in transition."

The rise and decline of the various models and frameworks employed in East European area studies reflected these conflicting political and disciplinary pressures, as well as changes within Eastern Europe itself which shifted attention to new actors and new phenomena, the analysis of which required fresh approaches. Thus, the earliest approach to inform analysis of the region was to view it as an example (or examples) of totalitarianism.[40] The heyday of this approach was in the early 1950s, when it captured important realities about the area as it underwent the rapid transformation that marked its entrance into the Soviet bloc. Yet the school's emphasis on the centrality of terror caused it to be brought into question after 1956, as regimes routinized and local parties brought the police under control. Likewise, the adoption of "collective leadership" and the "stability of cadres" policy that came with it, the relative "demobilization" of society, and the waning of "campaign methods" of economic management and social change also suggested that the applicability of the model was limited.[41]

Yet even as totalitarianism fell into disfavor among Western social scientists, the term gained new currency among opposition movements in Eastern Europe.[42] In this context, the term acquired the same mythic value in domestic politics that it had attained earlier on the international level at the height of the Cold War; analogous to Sorel's vision of the general strike, it proved to be a potent mobilizer of a mass public.

Reconciling a theory of totalitarianism with the existence of a domestic opposition able to apply it required no small sleight of hand. Totalitarianism was consequently redefined from a description of the actual political order into a tendency that Leninist parties aspired to but were necessarily unable to realize in practice. Political life in Eastern Europe could thus be described as a process in which an organization with a totalitarian ideology adapted to a nontotalitarian situation. As such, it consisted of a series of skirmishes and battles between a party-state seeking to maximize its control over a society bent on expressing its incipient pluralism.

As a theory, the "new" totalitarianism provided a far more nuanced interpretation of life in Eastern Europe than did the older version. It could accommodate and explain changes in the pattern of rule (from "terror" to "socialist legality"), the rise of social movements, the impulse for and frustration of attempts at economic reform, the switch from "moral" to "material" incentives and the consequent emphasis on improving supplies of consumer goods that took place in the 1970s. At the same time, it highlighted the ideological barriers to the party's relinquishing its claim to control state and society even as the reality of that control began to decline substantially in the 1980s.

The rise of the "new" totalitarian analysis coincided with the decline of another form of theorizing that enjoyed some currency among "left" intellectual circles on both sides of the Elbe, namely, analyses based on Marxist theory which made class its central category.[43] In this account, socialism differed from capitalism in that its class lines were drawn not on the basis of property ownership, but on political control. Accordingly, political power defined class lines in socialism, such that the political leadership (also defined as the "bureaucracy") emerged as a "ruling class" with a set of interests of its own, distinct from and in contradiction with those of subordinate groups in the society.

Politically, using Marxism to unmask Marxism-Leninism was a popular project. On the right, it allowed hypocrisy to be added to the vices of socialism, while on the left, if allowed acknowledging the more unpleasant and authoritarian features of the East European regimes without having to abandon Marxism itself. For the social scientist, the contributions of "ruling class" paradigms were also significant, insofar as they drew attention to what were rather rigid limits to economic and political change in Eastern Europe and to rather striking and well-institutionalized political and social inequalities there.[44] And unlike totalitarian theories, ruling class analyses suggested that authoritarianism did not grow out of a comprehensive ideology, but rather from the power generated by bureaucratic coordination of economic activity, control of which was easily captured by "partial" (i.e., ruling class) interests who then utilized ideology as a rationalization for continued rule.

Yet ruling class analyses had several problems as well. First, though such analyses posited the political leadership as a class, they often failed to specify a class mission, leaving us in the dark as to what leaders would do with the power they have. Given the frequency with which policies would be reversed under the same "class" leadership, it was unclear what exactly was gained from calling socialist political elites a "class." Alternatively, some theories defined a class mission in ways that reality seemed to contradict; "state capitalist" theories, for example, typically failed to explain how leaders bent on maximizing accumulation or the extraction of surplus routinely selected such inefficient economic strategies. Likewise, characterizing elites as "intellectuals" dedicated to "rational redistribution" ran up against the relative paucity of intellectuals in the leadership—and their overabundance in the opposition.

Finally, if class analyses have had some utility in explaining major regime changes, their ability to account for incremental and nonrevolutionary change was always rather weak. Yet it was precisely such incremental changes, varying from state to state and from society to society, that characterized the evolution of the socialist systems in Eastern Europe after the initial period of wholesale "socialist transformation." Explaining these kinds of changes required some theory of intraclass cleavages and coalitions, and for this, social scientists again turned to frameworks and methods of analysis initially articulated in the context of liberal capitalist systems.

In political science, two paradigms came to dominate the field for some time: group politics and organizational-bureaucratic politics. Let us deal with each in turn.

Theories based on group politics rested heavily on the "behavioral revolution" and the work done on interest groups in western systems.[45] They called attention to the cleavages and conflicts within the various political elites of socialist states, suggesting that these conflicts were related in some systematic way to the social differentiation present in the society such elites governed. For example, the various welfare state features common even the least developed socialist systems, and especially their job security/full employment guarantees, were explained by positing an implicit "social compact" between the regime and the population or at least between the regime and its industrial working class. Likewise, decisions to raise purchasing prices for agricultural goods while subsidizing the sale of foodstuffs to households was seen to be a way of juggling pressures from peasants and collective farms against those of urban consumers.

The main problem with this form of theorizing, however, was a serious lack of empirical support for its key assumption, namely that social groups had either the autonomy or political resources needed to press their claims on political leaders effectively or hold them accountable for decisions.[46]Yet if group politics could not explain political and economic decisions in socialism, it proved to be an enormously fruitful framework for research, simply because it pushed scholars to examine aspects of life in socialism that were wider than the top bodies of the party and state. Moreover, once Solidarity made its entrance onto the East European political scene, a new, indigenous version of the group politics approach emerged, this time under the rubric of "civil society versus the state." Popular among sociologists and East European opposition movement, the scholarly impulse behind this approach lay in a healthy reaction to what was felt to be too exclusive an emphasis on the "high politics" of the leadership and the established organizations and an underestimation of significant developments and changes in the larger society.

Unlike the earlier group politics approach, however, the issue in "civil society" studies was not so much whether groups could influence policy but how they were able to form and operate regardless of the will of the elite and whatever prevailing policy happened to be. The framework thus placed heavy emphasis on the unintended consequences of central decisions, pointing to real limits to the control political leaders were thought to have and showing a great deal of social ferment occurring beneath the surface of a population that appeared outwardly passive and apathetic. The growth of the second economy, the rise in nominally apolitical associational activity (from rock groups to environmental discussion clubs), the shop floor activities of workers, the circulation of samizdat manuscripts, and changing patterns of social stratification and attitudinal behavior among youth were all topics explored by a view anxious to "bring Society back" into our understanding of Eastern Europe.[47]

Politically, the "civil society" approach was the natural complement to the new totalitarianism paradigm. If the political elite's instinctive tendency was totalitarian, society's impulse was pluralistic. If the political elite's ideal was the One Big Factory of the centrally planned economy, society's counter was to insist on creating "private spaces" for itself which the political elite could restrict only at great cost to its own control, the second economy being a case in point. The result of efforts to create a self-governing sphere outside the established order, it was hoped, would be the emergence of a full fledged "civil society" that "totalitarian" elites could no longer suppress.

The civil society paradigm proved both intellectually and politically powerful, and shed an enormous amount of light on the activism throughout Eastern Europe that gathered steam in the 1980s. While this line of thinking was closely associated with the "Central European" idea, grass roots activism was far from absent in the Balkans as well. As a tale of the triumph of pluralism and democracy over monolithic tyranny, of the "people" taking their fate into their own hands, it became the standard version of the collapse of socialism that occurred everywhere by 1990. How complete an account it was, however, must be weighed against other explanations, to which we now turn.

The second influential paradigm drawn from the western literature on policymaking was the bureaucratic-organizational model. Here, rather than stress social groups in the decision-making process, the importance of established organizations as political actors was highlighted. Accordingly, conflicts among institutional interests for survival and expansion and among organizational elites representing these interests were considered the central factors in policy choices and changes.[48]

The bureaucratic politics approach proved a powerful tool for unraveling the complexities of "cryptopolitics" in socialist systems, leading to a wealth of rather sophisticated and illuminating case studies. Empirically, bargaining and haggling were endemic to socialism; indeed, the lack of an active price mechanism itself meant that they were often the only techniques available for allocating resources among competing claimants in a socialist economy. Moreover, with the routinization of the East European regimes that came in the 1960s, bureaucracy seemed all pervasive and its well-known dysfunctions seemed to explain many of the contradictory qualities of East European life and the ways in which the population adapted to its exigencies.

Yet to the degree the bureaucratic/organization politics approach focussed almost entirely on the bargaining process, it gave short shrift to the constraints within which the process occurred That is, not only were the arenas within which bargaining went on strictly limited, but even the issues up for discussion were tightly restricted. Nor did the bargaining partners (e.g., enterprises and ministries) themselves determine those limits and restrictions; rather the political leaders outside and above them did.

For example, if one asked why the president of the Academy of Sciences in, say, Czechoslovakia lobbied for improved vacation resorts for research workers, the bureaucratic politics approach not only had an explanation but could even predict what strategy he was likely to use to achieve such goals. But were one to ask why the same figure did not seek greater intellectual freedom and an end to censorship—clearly a benefit for an academy of sciences—the bureaucratic politics paradigm had no ready answer. Likewise, organization politics accurately told us that the Hungarian steel industry would lobby ferociously to minimize the size of investment cutbacks in a period of austerity; it could not, however, explain why the industry did not seek to reduce employment or wages instead. It thus proved difficult to explain how "strong" ministries, industries, or mass organizations ever "lost" if political changes were simply the outcome of organizational competition. Yet enterprise associations (VVBs) did lost their autonomy in East Germany, the Ministry of Industry was cut back and reorganized in Hungary, and even the Polish Party saw its apparatus reduced and streamlined in the 1970s.

Hence, bureaucratic politics came to be supplemented by a focus on patterns of political conflict and cleavage within the leadership itself, where conflict was partly over power (in Lenin's terms, "*kto-kovo*") but equally over how power was to be wielded and for what ends (Lenin's "*shto djelat'{hrs}*"). In those conflicts, organizations and constituencies did not so much 'choose' among leaders as they were invited into the policymaking process by leaders seeking to buttress their own positions. The *nomenklatura* was thus a critical means by which leaders defined the interests of organizations (as opposed to those interests being 'given' by the nature of the organization), and was simultaneously a source of allies in making policy and a way of controlling its implementation.[49]

Such competition among purely political actors over the direction of change and adaptation was most transparent in Yugoslavia, but it was present in other countries as well. In Poland, both policy and personal rivalries were behind the various succession crises that occurred after 1970, and the disagreements in the leadership over how to respond to a g rowing economic crisis plus the propensities of individuals to use the threat of spontaneous group protest to protect their own claims were critical in the rise of Solidarity. In Hungary, too, if the 1956 trauma taught political leaders the importance of managing internal conflicts within their own ranks, splits over the pace and scope of economic reform were nonetheless common. In Czechoslovakia, the post-1968 purges kept the range of disagreements narrow, while in East Germany, close Soviet supervision and what seemed to be relatively satisfactory economic performance also confined the scope of disagreement. Only in Romania were such internal debates avoided entirely by jettisoning "collective leadership" altogether—with the result that policy in the Ceaucescu years became increasingly arbitrary.

Focussing on internal conflicts within the political elite proved quite illuminating in explaining both the domestic factors that led to political and economic reform in Poland, Hungary, and Yugoslavia as well as the absence of such factors in Romania, East Germany, and Czechoslovakia. In effect, just as economic competition lowers the cost of commodities, political competition came to reduce the cost of political involvement. Thus, the secular trend in the parties that followed the Soviet example of "collective leadership" even before the 1980s was to widen the circle of political consultation, as experts, bureaucracies, territorial officials, and the like were deployed as political resources by rival factions.

What kept the circle relatively narrow, however, was basic agreement among top elites that the party should resolve conflicts within its own ranks and thereby monopolize the all important "last say." In Poland, that consensus broke down when the party proved unable to extract the country from its prolonged economic crisis; in Hungary, it broke down as leaders split on the desirability of retaining the party's political monopoly; in Yugoslavia, leaders disagreed more and more openly not only on a strategy for economic adjustment but also on how the federation should be altered to pursue one in the 1980s. In these cases, the regime collapses of 1989–90 followed a dynamic quite similar to that of Latin America: the ruling group split, and society entered the political arena. Perhaps ironically, it was precisely those states that had been in the forefront of economic reform and liberalization that had the most serious macroeconomic imbalances—and consequently, the greatest internal divisions within the elite over how to stabilize the situation. In effect, "society's" activation prior to the winter of 1989 was at least partially politically induced from above.

In East Germany, Czechoslovakia, and Bulgaria, however, no such split occurred in the political leadership, and so leaders did not by themselves seek to mobilize support in the larger society for the path they favored. The economic situation in these countries in 1989 was not nearly so serious as in the heavily indebted others, nor was the top leadership of East Germany or Czechoslovakia seriously divided over the undesirability of liberalization. Accordingly, the dynamics of regime change in those states were cases of "external push" rather than "domestic pull," and if a split in the elite was to come, it had to be engineered from outside. It was here that Mikhail Gorbachev provided the spark—whether by supporting the Hungarian decision to allow East German vacationers to go to Austria and then pushing a deeply conservative party to replace Erich Honecker with a more "progressive" leader, or by pushing the Czech party to permit the student demonstration that started the opposition ball rolling and, once it was in motion, suddenly publishing Soviet apologies for the 1968 invasion.

Thus, while there is no denying the importance of broad social forces in sweeping away the *ancien regime,* forces within the communist parties also played key roles in eliciting and channeling those pressures. Bulgaria was perhaps the extreme case: there, the Communist party literally abandoned its "leading role" even before the opposition requested it to do so. In this sense, the decision of the Soviet Union to relinquish its hegemony over the area and the repercussions that decision had for the power structure's ability to maintain itself was as important as the ability of political oppositions to articulate social claims. That East Europeanists were as surprised as others when the final collapse came is not because they had a weak grasp of social, political, or economic conditions in Eastern Europe. Rather their failure to predict these events is traceable ultimately to their inability to anticipate what was essentially a Soviet decision to abandon its longstanding security concern with the political contours of the area.[50]

FROM EAST EUROPEAN TO CENTRAL EAST EUROPEAN STUDIES: POST-COMMUNISM AND AREA STUDIES

Area studies inevitably reflect their region, and the political earthquake that occurred in Eastern Europe with the collapse of socialism had its aftershocks in area studies as well as in the area itself. Whereas previously, East Europeanists had struggled along at the margin of their disciplines, the unprecedented novelty of the "transition from socialism" and the end of the Cold War suddenly made the area into a focal point of all the social sciences. Indeed, one of the major questions the change raised was whether or not the scholars who had labored long and hard to acquire a deep understanding of the area under socialism still had skills relevant in the new situation, especially at a time when policymakers and intellectuals alike were rushing to repudiate precisely the experience with which they had been so familiar.

Scholarship on Eastern Europe thus became the purview of a far wider community of academics than had been the case for the previous 40 years. The influx was facilitated by English becoming the second language *de rigeur* of university graduates throughout the region, by the collection and publication of statistical information in formats accessible to academics trained in western quantitative techniques, and by the search by local scholars to train themselves in the methods and frameworks popular in West European and American social science.

The benefits of this sudden burst of intellectual interest were not negligible for the area studies community. The insight of major theorists observing the area "from outside" were often extremely valuable in informing the work of those analyzing it from within.[51] Since many of the newcomers relied on the work of area experts for their factual information, the careful, on-the-ground analyses the field had so heavily relied on in the past received a much wider readership as well. Indeed, the number of publications dealing with Eastern Europe appearing in non-area, purely disciplinary journals rose tremendously. A survey of articles dealing with Eastern Europe appearing in non-area social science journals (e.g., *American Economic Review, American Political Science Review, American Journal of Sociology,* etc.) gives a quantitative indicator of the change. Whereas a total of 27 articles dealing with Eastern Europe were published in such mainstream journals during the 5 year period 1983–8, 87 articles appeared in the same journals between 1991–6, a threefold increase. Finally, graduate student interest also increased, and departments in all fields—even in universities without traditionally strong area programs—often found their most promising applicants planning to specialize in East European affairs. The establishment of the Central European University in Budapest also provided training for students from the area itself, many of whom went on to pursue programs in the United States, as well as a new source of colleagues able to collaborate with American and West European counterparts in teaching and research..

At the same time, there were also some significant costs to area experts as they suddenly found their region catapulted into the limelight, not the least of which was the identity crisis described at the start of this essay. Symptomatic here was the renaming process not only of the region itself, but also of the major journals devoted to it: *Soviet Studies* was transformed into *Europe-Asia Studies, Studies in Comparative Communism* turned into *Communist and Post-Communist Studies,* and *Problems of Communism* into *Problems of Post-Communism.* More problematic for the integrity of East European area studies itself were pressures to merge it entirely into a more general "European" framework within universities, efforts which rarely came to fruition in the end, largely because it (quite predictably) turned out that the problems that characterized the region—including eastern Germany—after 1990 remained quite different from those in Western Europe.

Thus, the three historical problems that had long defined the region continued to do so in the 1990s. The problems of state formation reappeared as democratization studies and analyses of nationalism, lagged economic development as how state socialist economies would be transformed into competitive markets—and with what effects on social structures, labor relations, income distribution, and social welfare. And the problem of the dependency of small states on richer and more powerful states on their borders reappeared as rivalries over who would "join" Europe—and what this entailed for traditional notions of sovereignty, international alliance behavior, trade relations, and cultural norms.

In what follows, we briefly review the main debates and themes that emerged around each of the three main area problems. As we shall see, scholarship continued to reflect both the particularities and similarities of the Central East European states. At the same time, insofar as states and societies were now responding to changes and processes that were occurring throughout the world, the thrust of comparisons broadened from states within the area or within the "socialist community" to allow Central East European studies to be seated within a global context.

The study of democratization actually emerged before the collapse of socialism, and had focussed on regime changes in Southern Europe, Latin America, and finally Asia. Hence, there was already a significant body of theory that could migrate to East Central Europe in search of an application. The question, of course, was whether expectations about party competition, the establishment of the rule of law, the protection of civil liberties, and the stability of newly elected governments drawn from the experiences of countries outside the area could also be generalized to East Central European states.

A lively debate over the appropriateness of inter-regional comparisons ensued.[52] In practice, the issue was resolved pragmatically.[53] In some ways, the authoritarian experience in East Central Europe was quite different from that in Latin America. For one thing, it was "transitioning" from a Leninist one-party system rather than a military regime, such that the former ruling party not only remained a competitive political force in the emerging political order but its electoral strategy and positioning was a key factor affecting the entire political spectrum. For another, the difference between economies that combined capitalism with a large state sector and those in Eastern Europe meant the latter's transformation was not only a quantitatively greater task but also a qualitatively different one. The socio-demographic characteristics of the populations were also different: on average, Central East Europeans were better educated, more urbanized, accustomed to a rather extensive network of social services, and even ten years into the transition, characterized by a higher degree of economic and social equality. Finally, what the post-socialist states were transition to was different, reflecting their geographical position on the European continent and the revival of geopolitical relationships that had characterized the area in the first half of the twentieth century. In political-institutional terms, this difference was reflected in the tendency of the Central East European states to opt for basically parliamentary systems, in contrast with Latin American countries, which typically returned to relatively powerful, directly elected chief executives as the head of government.

At the same time, however, the exchange of comparisons and contrasts between East Europeanists and Latin Americanists showed there were indeed some critical similarities between the two regions in the 1990s. If the creation of property rights guarantees was, for the most part, unique to Eastern Europe's abandonment of socialism, the processes of liberalization and stabilization were not. While privatization of state-owned firms may have been more extensive in Eastern Europe, such events were common enough in Latin America as well: debtor governments all over the world sold assets in the 1990s. Explaining why populations and governments in Eastern Europe reacted differently to "de-statizing" the economy from populations in Latin America came to form an intriguing line of research for area experts in both regions, and showed that "globalization" could have quite different political and economic local ramifications.

If one major change in the research agenda was opening up East European studies to comparison with other areas outside the advanced industrial world, another major debate concerned the impact of the socialist experience on the new political order. This debate coincided with an emerging trend in the social sciences stressing the importance of institutions in explaining political, social, and economic behavior. On the area expert side, Kenneth Jowitt made a strong case—then picked up by others—that the "legacies" of socialism meant that establishing democracy in any other than the most formal sense of the term was likely to be a long and difficult process for societies that had little experience or memory of an open and competitive political order from which to work. Others—often, but far from exclusively, those "trespassing" in the region from the realm of general disciplinary theories—stressed the importance of new institutions and rules in eliciting and motivating behavior consistent with democratic norms.[54]

Again, the issue was resolved pragmatically. Clearly, in many ways, social and political patterns of behavior did not undergo a radical alteration even as political institutions changed; in other ways, behavior changed, but in a distinctly undemocratic direction; and yet in other ways, the new formally democratic institutional arrangement did have the effect of creating significant social and political forces with strong interests in preserving them. Thus, even a decade after the socialist regimes collapsed, the jury is still out on the Legacies v. Institutions question. It does appear that formal procedural democracy is now fairly well institutionalized everywhere in the region with, of course, the exception of the ex-Yugoslav states involved in wars. Elections occur regularly, they are relatively fair, the media is lively and alternative sources of information available, parties peacefully alternate in office, laws are passed by legislatures and (more or less) enforced by authorized administrative agencies and courts, oppositions are able to organize and propagate their views. That even this procedural democracy has survived an economic downturn at least as serious as that of the Great Depression is no insignificant accomplishment, and explaining how such institutions stabilized under adverse circumstances has been a major topic of area and non-area analysts alike. Nevertheless, how deeply democratic norms have penetrated the population as a whole and the degree to which support for the new institutions and actors in governments is based on non-democratic impulses or simply the lack of a viable alternatives is still unclear.[55] Thus, while political parties appear extremely active, the non-party secondary associations that engage in interest-based politics in western systems appear weak and fragmented, while electoral turnout has generally been much lower than expected. Likewise, the frequency of corruption scandals suggests that at the elite level, too, politics is not simply about serving the public interest or even broad partisan constituencies.

The "thinness" of democratic norms brings us to another major theme of post-socialist studies in Eastern Europe, namely, studies of nationalism and national identity. Eastern Europe has historically been a major source for theorists of nationalism, and some of the

classic studies of the phenomenon have been based on the rise of
"nations" in this area. In the post-socialist period, the violence that
accompanied (and continues to accompany!) the disintegration of
Titoist Yugoslavia was a dramatic reminder that the mobilization of
ascriptive forms of identity remains very much with us, and of how
democratization could as easily unleash the forces of exclusive
nationalism as produce idyllic multiethnic cooperation. In this
regard, it was symptomatic that the smoothest regime changes to
date tend to have occurred in ethnically homogeneous states.

The distintegration of Yugoslavia itself created a cottage industry
exploring the relationship between democratization and
nationalism. In examining the roots of conflict there, area experts
played a critical role; frequently, they were virtually the only source
of reliable information in a context in which elites and intellectuals
of all types set about embellishing history to provide a basis for
claims that were often weakly founded in reality and were difficult
for newcomers to evaluate.[56] Nor was Yugoslavia the only source of
new states emerging in the area: the Soviet Union dissolved into its
component republics and in 1992, Czechoslovakia passed through its
velvet divorce. Comparisons between the three helped to highlight
the importance of federal structures in facilitating the mobilization
of ethnic bias in periods of economic downturn, the discrediting of
class-based popular organizations, and the weakening of the
political center.[57]

Studies of nationalism and national identity were not limited to
the more spectacular cases of state dissolution and emergence.
Appeals to national loyalty were part and parcel of partisan
mobilizations throughout Central East Europe, even if building such
support occurred at the expense of minority populations. Moreover,
perceptions of national identity were often colored by religious
overtones, as confessional institutions assumed new positions of
prominence. Scholarship on the ramifications of these developments
for minorities (national and religious), regions, and social groups was
thus common even among scholars dealing with Poland, Hungary,
Romania, and Bulgaria—not to mention the Baltic states with
significant Russian-speaking minorities. Such work both drew on as
well as making critical contributions to the larger literature dealing

with the "construction" of identities more broadly.[58]

Yet the attention given to nationalism and cultural identity may have exaggerated the "dangers" such loyalties posed. In many ways, what was most interesting about East Central Europe in the 1990s was how relatively weak the tendency toward ethnic exclusivity tended to be—especially compared with the resurgence of "national" pressures in the nominally more cosmopolitan and tolerant "civil societies" of western Europe. Even in Latvia and Estonia, external pressures from Russia and the European Union pushed reluctant, multiparty but monoethnic national governments to work out some means of accommodating large "non-titular" Slavic minorities.

The second dimension of prominence in post-socialist East European studies was, of course, the massive economic changes that occurred. Analyses tended to run along two lines: prescriptive (what should be done) and descriptive (what policies were adopted, why they were chosen, and with what consequences for economic performance and welfare). Both were heavily colored by a great deal of initial skepticism that the twin transformations—from authoritarianism to competitive politics and from socialism to capitalism—could be accomplished simultaneously.

Among the prescriptions, the most important early debate concerned the pace and scope of economic reform, dubbed as "big bang" v. gradualism.[59] Analogous to the Institutions v. Legacies debate, this one also saw non-area and area experts on different sides. Viewed with hindsight, experience proved both sides could be wrong and right at the same time, perhaps symptomatic of just how unprecedented the situation was. Thus, one of the strongest arguments for immediate, rapid and wide ranging economic reform urged moving quickly during the "honeymoon" period before political opposition could block major change. On the other side, "gradualism" was defended on the grounds that a private sector could only emerge in the context of a functioning economy, and since radical reform necessarily entailed massive output losses, high interest rates, and diminished purchasing power, its impact would be to undercut exactly the objectives it was striving to achieve.

Experience—especially in Poland—indicated that the consequences of the "big bang" strategy initiated in 1990 were precisely what produced political opposition, as the Polish Sejm fragmented into competing proto-parties unable to find common ground. It did, however, greatly facilitate the creation of a vibrant private sector, with new start ups leading the recovery that began in 1993. In contrast, experience elsewhere—Romania and Bulgaria being the major examples—indicated that delaying reforms and seeking to find a gradual method that avoided severe and sharp austerity measures resulted in continued budgetary outlays to state-owned enterprises that quickly came to be a major burden and obstacle to private sector expansion. Yet unlike shock therapy, it allowed ruling parties to be re-elected and govern, at least until economic problems became so large reforms literally could no longer be put off.

Meanwhile, close country studies of economic policy in individual states indicated that the theoretical debate among strategies corresponded only weakly to what states in the region actually did, since once the rhetoric was stripped away, strategies claimed to be "gradual" actually turned out to have quite a number of the elements (e.g., opening borders to trade, liberalizing prices, maintaining a balanced budget) "radical" strategies included, while policies initially adopted as "radical" measures would quickly be modified back to a "gradualist" model.[60]

Descriptive accounts of the policy process focussed much more on explaining why policymakers chose the strategies they used and what the consequences were. The major surprise here was a fairly robust finding that far from competitive politics being undermined even in the face of draconian measures—such as Poland's initial "Big Bang" reforms, Hungary's Bokros Plan, and Bulgaria's establishment of a currency board—the vitality of representative systems seemed to be the main condition allowing such reforms to be made and implemented.[61] The theoretical ramifications of such findings actually went far beyond East European area studies, as they confirmed much of the newer work in institutional economics that stressed the establishment of efficient property rights as the key to economic performance—and explained the evolution of such rights as directly related to the bargaining power of constituents.

Legalizing private ownership, liberalizing prices and foreign trade, bringing budgets into balance, and establishing relatively independent central banks were the norm throughout the region; major differences, however, characterized privatization strategies and the pace and scope of social service reform. Not surprisingly, a great deal of creative work was done in seeking to explain the differences. Critical variables include the relative positions management and labor had carved out for themselves in enterprises during the last phase of socialism, the level of indebtedness of the state, and the commitments of the political leadership that came to power in the immediate aftermath of the regime change.[62]

How labor and management adapted to the new economic conditions—and with what consequences for microeconomic performance—was another important theme in East European studies. While abstract models positing rational actors making choices under a variety of incentive structures proved important in providing a set of hypotheses and expectations, the on-the-ground observations of area experts turned out to be the only means to empirically test these models. The result was a plethora of rich case studies of state and privatized enterprises, labor relations, sectoral adjustment patterns, and, of course, of new private sector start ups and greenfield foreign ventures that burgeoned in the area.[63]

Nor were manufacturing activities the only object of attention. The reorganization of agriculture in a region in which close to a third of the population was typically employed in that sector was also a major field of study, showing that the rural-urban division that had always been so prominent in the region as a whole was far from disappearing.[64] Moreover, such studies revealed the often ambiguous benefits of privatizing land and equipment in a context in which subsidies were removed and domestic markets were invaded by western exports.

The impact of new economic relations on non-economic groups was also of great concern to many in the area. Women's and gender studies more broadly came into their own as altered family relations, the possibility of female engagement in at-home private businesses, the increase in joblessness among both males and females, and the crumbling of many of the social services important for working mothers began to reshape gender relations throughout the region.[65] Likewise, the end of socialist *uravnilovka* and the tendency for economic activities to site themselves on the basis of comparative advantage suddenly made regional differentiation, both within and between the various states in the region, a major problem. Corresponding to this emphasis came a new stress on emerging patterns of social stratification and the growth of poverty. One of the key issues that emerged here was again, how determinative one's position in the old order was for one's position in the new. [66]

Much of the theory used in these inquiries was imported from the discipline in which a scholar worked, whether it was economics, political science, sociology, or anthropology. At the same time, empirical work was often theory generating as well, since the parameters of post-socialism were so unprecedented there was often little in the way of existing theory that could guide inquiries. New journals (e.g., *The Economics of Transition, East European Constitutional Review*) and new sources of information (e.g., the Economist Intelligence Unit's country studies, analyses commissioned by international organizations like the OECD, the World Bank, or the IMF) also appeared, facilitating intra-regional comparisons as well as providing new venues in which scholars of the area could air their findings. Interestingly enough, much of this academic activity was either privately funded or funded by agencies (governmental or non-profit) outside the traditional research funding community. Ironically, such developments coincided with a trend in the disciplines that moved them in exactly the opposite direction: towards increasingly narrowly specialized work employing highly esoteric mathematical techniques and towards an emphasis on theory and lawlike generalization at the expense of more applied and contextual work. The paradoxical result was that just as the demand for area skills grew outside universities and governments, the disciplines that dominated training seemed to be less and less interested in generating a supply with which to satisfy it. From this perspective, the earlier insulation of East European studies within the "communist studies" project may well have been what preserved its integrity in the 1990s, as the internal logic of the transition as viewed in the field continued to offer a compelling set of intellectual puzzles to which the mainstream of many disciplines spoke only tangentially.

This brings us to the third dimension of East European area studies in the 1990s, a dimension which again, turned on the region's "historic" problem: namely, what was to be the relationship of a now increased number of states and societies in the region to the major powers outside its borders. Economic conditions provided an immediate answer, as the collapse of CMEA forced all the states in the region to reorient their foreign trade westward. It was no small irony here that the radial pattern of trade that had characterized East European-Soviet arrangements under socialism now reproduced itself—but with Germany at the hub of the wheel.[67] Affiliation with western institutions became a sought after commodity, too, with membership in the European Union being the ultimate target. At the same time, much of this orientation and activity reflected the traditional tendency of the small states in the area to gravitate towards and imitate the leading power of the day. With the dissolution of the Soviet Union and the collapse of first the Soviet and then the Russian economy, there was little choice about "joining Europe," regardless of whether a given state was "Central," "Southern" or "Eastern" European.

Thus, integration of Eastern and Western Europe, together with its economic, political, and cultural ramifications forms another major thread of inquiry in East European studies in the 1990s. At the same time that western influence has stabilized representative forms of government, pushed leaders to observe minority rights, and provided substantial amounts of aid to facilitate changes in everything from infrastructure, environmental protection, curricula, military organization, and property rights, it has also had major cultural implications that have, on occasion, been greeted with some unease. Intellectuals, traditionally the repository of national cultural life, have found themselves struggling as universities cut back budgets, and media—from newspapers to film—cater to mass markets in search of profits. Significantly, western imports have come to compete on cultural as well as capital and commodity markets. Equally important, elected political leaders now compete with the intelligentsia as articulators of the national will, and the "opposition" is no longer a province inhabited by intellectuals writing sophisticated critiques of the existing order but of professional politicians seeking to be elected to office. One suspects here that a longstanding theme in area studies of the area in the last two centuries, namely, the role of intellectuals as a distinct group in cultural and political life, may well be receding in importance.

Last, but certainly not least, what security arrangements would look like in the area once the Warsaw Pact dissolved became an issue debated by area and international security specialists alike. Newly elected governments were quick to announce their hopes to join NATO, and began shifting forces from their western to eastern borders—despite the absence of any real threat on either. Interestingly enough, while a "Scandinavian model" a la Sweden or Finland was floated as a possible target of domestic reform efforts, it was never given any serious consideration as a security option. The opportunities for expansion and leverage such requests presented to an organization whose mission had been made, in the eyes of many, quite obsolete in a post-Cold War world proved irresistible. Within a few years, the "Partnership for Peace" was launched; by 1999, Hungary, Poland, and the Czech Republic were admitted to NATO, and within a month of their accession, NATO was engaged in its first war.

Debating the implication of NATO expansion for the region as a whole has, perhaps unfortunately, fallen outside the area studies community; rather, it tends to be a much more central concern of security studies experts and even post-Soviet studies scholarship. In that context, whether NATO's new life as the nominal upholder of human rights on the European continent and the United States' willingness to extend a nuclear umbrella up to the borders of the former Soviet Union are actions likely to deter threats and avoid international conflict or create threats and produce international conflict is still a very open question. Yet at the time of this writing, the pattern of alliance adhesion and action suggests very much that the assertion of a "Central European" identity is no longer a purely cultural phenomenon.

With this, we return full circle to the "What is Eastern Europe?" question with which we began. As indicated, renaming the area has not by any means eliminated its distinctive regional identity any more than calling it "Eastern Europe" in the socialist days eliminated major differences within and between the states and societies that made it up. Intellectually, the vibrancy of work in the area studies tradition during the past decade and the need non-area scholars have had to become acquainted with it is some evidence here. Certainly, the collapse of socialism opened Central East Europe to new forms of inquiry and topics for analysis—at the same time making other debates obsolescent. Equally important, it has made i t possible for specialists in the area to place their work in the center of their disciplines, both as consumers and contributors, far more than in the past. In fact, the end of the Soviet bloc has allowed comparative work, be it in economics, political science, sociology, anthropology or the humanities, to broaden its focus beyond the socialist group of countries to include other states—be they in Latin America, the former Soviet Union, or southern Europe—undergoing related, if less dramatic, changes. The result is not that there is no longer a need for area experts, but simply that area experts need no longer be *only* area experts, since their research now sheds light on democratization, nationalism, economic stabilization and transformation, the impact of cultural competition and change, and the nature of sovereignty not only within Central East Europe, but in the world at large.

Such work could not be done had Central Eastern Europe been prematurely merged within West European studies, as many proposed in 1990. Nor has the area's past or present given it a trajectory similar to that of Russia: East Central Europe—from the Baltic to the Adriatic—remains the land in between, and must be approached as such. Institutionally, then, the recognition of the area as a distinct region remains critical to the field, yet funding for area-based centers continues to be problematic. Initially, Central East European studies were relatively fortunate, being in the unusual position of being able to draw from many West European as well as its traditional "East European" funding sources. While such possibilities may remain for the five states on the "fast track" accession to EU, it is unclear where funds will come to support work dealing with the states in less fortunate positions—which are nevertheless critical to comparisons and the understanding of the "fast track" states themselves. The barriers created by "Yalta" were widely resented even if they were not nearly so ahistorical as asserted; it would be a shame were the integrity of the region as an object of scholarship to be divided again by the European Union and NATO—equally "artificial" lines drawn by major powers.

The limited availability of language instruction remains a major obstacle to training future scholars, and the emergence of a large number of small, independent states in the region has certainly not helped. Whereas knowledge of Serbo-Croatian was once (more or less) sufficient for field work in Slovenia or Macedonia, this is no longer the case; nor is knowledge of Czech adequate for work in Slovakia, or Russian or Polish for study in Lithuania. The difficulty of finding adequate instruction in the languages of states with small populations remains substantial, and it is critical that access to these languages be improved in an efficient and hopefully cost-effective way, whether in the United States itself or in the host country.

Further, there is great interest and need for collaborative research between scholars based in American institutions and colleagues in Central East Europe. As should be clear from the work already cited, East European area studies has always been characterized by reciprocal influences on both sides of the Atlantic. But the decade of the 1990s has created much greater opportunities for open and long term research collaboration, and it is important that funding sources recognize such possibilities.

In addition, while significant funding from both governmental and private sources has been devoted to training younger East European scholars in the norms and methodologies of western social science, similar efforts have not been devoted to funding American graduate students and researchers seeking to embark on research in the field. Title VIII funds, critical to academic research, have gradually been cut back, and "project funding" is no replacement. Symptomatic here is the change in the activities of the International Research and Exchange Board (IREX). Once primarily an administrator of academic exchanges, the bulk of IREX's activities are now as an administrator of USIA and USAID programs in Eastern Europe and the former Soviet Union, with only a small budget devoted to its earlier foci.

Finally, how area experts relate to their individual disciplines is also a challenge confronting the field. Although in some institutions, area studies has been considered a field for the humanities only, simply the brief summary of recent work given above indicates that the social sciences are central to the understanding of Central East Europe today. Certainly, the thrust of area studies, with its focus on the particular and distinct, runs somewhat against the grain of much contemporary social science, with its stress on quantification, highly abstract and decontextualized models, and a search for general "laws." Yet social science cannot rely on theory alone. Every good hypothesis needs a test, and for this, only empirical work will do: one cannot use Slovakia as a case unless one knows what it is a case of, and only the dirty empirical details can tell a theorist whether a case is appropriate for the theory at hand. The widespread use of game theory in political science is a good example; highly stylized games of strategic interaction lead to accurate predictions and expectations only if the stylized description fits the empirical context. While it is thus quite correct for area experts working on, say, ethnic conflict to be trained in the tools of their discipline appropriate for studying it, methodology is not a substitute by itself for substance. Yet if departments marginalize their area specialists—or eliminate such positions altogether, as is already the case in economics—it means that area studies will be doomed to being completely atheoretical, while the disciplines become incapable of shedding light on empirically important problems.

All in all then, the changes caused by the collapse of socialism in Eastern Europe have indeed changed its name—but not its distinctive characteristics or longstanding historical problematique. As a result, the area studies tradition in East Central European studies is alive, well, and thriving, although its continued health will clearly depend heavily on whether funding sources match the high level of interest in the area its transformation has engendered in so many fields of inquiry and practical endeavor.

Ellen Comisso is a Professor of Political Science at the University of California, San Diego. Brad Gutierrez is a Ph. D. candidate in Political Science at the University of California, San Diego.

Notes

1. See Gordon Turner, "The Joint Committee on Slavic Studies, 1948–71," in ACLS Newsletter 23 (Spring 1972):6–25.

2. See Milan Kundera, "The Tragedy of Central Europe," *The New York Review of Books*, April 26 1984: 34–8; Ferenc Feher, "Eastern Europe's Long Revolution Against Yalta," *East European Politics and Societies* 2 (No. 1, Winter 1988): 20–41.

3. See Friedrich Naumann, *Central Europe*, trans. By Christabel Meredith (New York: Knopf, 1917); Henry Meyer, *Mitteleuropa in German Thought and*

Action, 1815–1945 (The Hague: Njihoff, 1955); Egon Schwartz, "Central Europe—What It Is and What It Is Not," in George Schopflin and Nancy Wood, eds., *In Search of Central Europe* (Cambridge: Polity Press, 1989), pp. 143–56.

4. See Thomas Masaryk, *The New Europe (The Slav Standpoint)*, Lewisburg: Bucknell University Press, 1972); Roman Szporluk, *The Political Thought of Thomas G. Masaryk* (New York: Columbia University Press, 1981).

5. See Joseph Rothschild, *East Central Europe Between the Two World Wars* (Seattle: Washington University Press, 1974).

6. See essays in Schopflin and Wood, eds., *In Search of Central Europe;* Timothy Garton Ash, *The Uses of Adversity: Essays on the Fate of Central Europe* (Cambridge: Penguin, 1989); Ferenc Feher, "On Making Central Europe," *East European Politics and Societies* 3 (No. 3, Fall 1989),:412–448. Gyorgy Konrad's portrayal of Eastern v. Central Europe is typical in this regard: when discussing nationalism, it is a phenomenon which occurs in Eastern Europe, when discussing democracy, it takes place in Central Europe. See *The Melancholy of Rebirth* (New York: Harcourt Brace, 1994).

7. See his "Central Europe: Definitions Old and New," in Schopflin and Wood, eds. *In Search of Central Europe,* p. 23.

8. In "Who Excluded Russia From Europe?" in Schopflin and Woods, eds., *In Search of Central Europe,* p. 148.

9. See Gale Stokes, *Three Eras of Political Change in Eastern Europe* (New York: Oxford, 1997); Hugh Seton-Watson, "What is Europe, Where is Europe? From Mystique to Politique," in Schopflin and Woods, eds., *In Search of Central Europe.* pp. 30–46; Michaly Vajda, "East Central European Perspectives," in John Keane, ed., *Civil Society and the State* (London: Verso, 1988), pp. 291–333. The theme is also taken up in the non-area studies literature; see Samuel Huntington, *The Clash of Civilizations?* (Cambridge: John M. Olin Institute for Strategic Studies, 1993).

10. See Jeno Szucs, "Three Historical Regions of Europe," in John Keane, ed., *Civil Society and the State* (London: Verso, 1988), pp. 291–333; Ivan Berend, "The historical evolution of Eastern Europe as a region," *International Organization* 40 (No. 2, Spring 1986): 279–99; Istvan Bibo, *Democracy, Revolution, Self-Determination,* ed. by Karoly Nagy (New York: Columbia University Press, 1991).

11. See "The Return of the Habsburgs," *The Economist,* November 18, 1995; Jacques Rupnik, *The Other Europe* (New York: Pantheon, 1988); Dan Chirot, "Ideology, Reality, and Competing Models of Development in Eastern Europe Between the Two World Wars," *East European Politics and Societies* 3 (No. 3, Fall 1989): 378–412..

12. See Marci Shore, "Engineering in the Age of Innocence: A Genealogy of Discourse Inside the Czechoslovak Writers' Union, 1949–67," *East European Politics and Societies* 12 (No. 3, Fall 1998):397–429; Czeslaw Milosz, *The Captive Mind,* trans. by Jane Zielonko (New York: Knopf, 1953)' Katherine Verdery, *National Ideology Under Socialism* (Berkeley: University of California Press, 1995).

13. Cited in Timothy Garton Ash, "The Puzzle of Central Europe," *New York Review of Books*, March 18, 1999, p. 18.

14. Joseph Roth, *The Radetsky March*, trans. Eva Tucker (Woodstock: Overlook Press, 1974).

15. See Larry Wolff, *Inventing Easter Europe: The Map of civilization on the Mind of the Enightenment* (Stanford: Stanford University Press, 1994).

16. Jacques Rupnik, *The Other Europe* (New York: Pantheon, 1989), pp. 4–6.

17. See Adam Michnik, *Letters from Prison and Other Essays* (Berkeley: UC Press, 1985); Gyorgy Konrad, *Antipolitics* (New York: Harcourt Brace, 1984); Vaclav Havel, *The Power of the Powerless* (London: Hutchinson, 1985); Tony Judt, "The Dilemmas of Dissidence: The Politics of Opposition in East-Central Europe," *East European Politics and Societies* 2 (No. 3, Spring 1988: 221–245. See also the essays contained in the special issue of *Daedalus* 119 (no. 1, Winter 1990), "Eastern Europe . . . Central Europe . . . Europe."

18. Rupnik, for example, explicitly sees the "Central European idea" as a way of detaching intellectuals in Zagreb and Ljubljana from the "southeastern, backward, orthodox part" of Yugoslavia. In *Other Europe*, p. 8. For the rebuttal, see Maria Todorova, *Imagining the Balkans* (New York: Oxford University Press, 1997).

19. Kundera, "Tragedy," p. 35. Ernest Gellner describes a "third zone" of Europe in similar terms. See *Conditions of Liberty: Civil Society and Its Rivals* (London: Penguin, 1994), esp. pp. 119–25.

20. On the turbulent pattern of state formation in Eastern Europe, see Jelavich, *History of the Balkans;* Norman Davies, *God's Playground: A History of Poland*, 2 vols. (New York: Columbia University Press, 1984), Piotr Wandycz, *The Price of Freedom* (London: Routledge, 1992); R. W. Seton Watson, *A History of the Czechs and Slovaks* (London: 1947), among many other fine histories. On the early Balkan kingdoms, see John A. Fine, *The Early Medieval Balkans* and *The Late Medieval Balkans* (Ann Arbor: University of Michigan Press, 1987).. The non-area state building literature also deals, albeit peripherally, with Eastern European examples. See Perry Anderson, *Lineages of the Absolutist State* (London: Verso, 1974); Brian Downing, *The Military Revolution and Political Change* (Princeton: Princeton University Press, 1992); Thomas Ertman, *Birth of the Leviathan* (Cambridge: Cambridge University Press, 1997). The way in which the territories of the region came to be absorbed into empires is also, of course, dealt with in the various imperial histories; of particular interest is Robert A. Kann's *A History of the Habsburg Empire, 1526–1918* (Berkeley: UC Press, 1974), but it can be supplemented by the many histories of Prussia/Germany and Russia in the seventeenth through twentieth centuries.

Note that "states" are distinguished from "empires" first and foremost by their governance structure and only secondarily by the homogeneity of their populations or the geographic contiguity of their territories. In a state, individual subjects and subnational units (e.g., provinces, departments, states) bear a uniform relationship to the central sovereign—a legal and political status which, of course, facilitates (but may not necessitate) cultural homogenization. The legal and political status of various subgroups and/or provinces in an empire, in contrast, often varies quite widely and individual provinces may well have rather different rights and responsibilities vis-à-vis the central sovereign, depending on the terms of their incorporation and other factors. The difference between the two political forms is thus institutional, not simply one of "discourse," as has been argued.

21. Compare, for example, Miroslav Hroch, *The Social Preconditions of National Revival* (Cambridge: Cambridge University Press, 1985) with Rogers Brubaker, *Citizenship and Nationhood in France and Germany* (Cambridge: Harvard University Press, 1992) or Eugene Weber, *From Peasants into Frenchman* (Stanford: Stanford University Press, 1976). See also Peter Sugar and Ivo Lederer, eds., *Nationalism in Eastern Europe* (Seattle: University of Washington Press, 1969); Ivo Banac, *The National Question in Yugoslavia: Origins, History, Politics* (Ithaca: Cornell University Press, 1988); Oscar Jaszi, *The Dissolution of the Habsburg Monarchy* (Chicago: University of Chicago press, 1929).

22. While the "lag" in economic development is widely recognized, there is little consensus on its causes. Not surprisingly, disagreements are informed as much by political concerns as by scholarly ones. For some, the lag is due to unequal terms of trade between Central Eastern Europe and more advanced economies, reinforcing the area's "peripheral" status; for others, the problem has been a paucity of trade on whatever terms were available. For some, the state (whether Imperial or national) was so strong it choked off economic initiative from below, while for others, it was only the rise of a political authority able to maintain order and build infrastructure that allowed development to take place at all. One cannot do justice to the variety of perspectives in a brief essay, but they parallel many of the analyses proposed. for the less developed world more generally. See Andrew Janos, *The Politics of Backwardness in Hungary* (Princeton: Princeton University Press, 1982); Kenneth Jowitt, *The Leninist Response to National Dependency* (Berkeley: Institute of International Studies, 1978); Michael Palairet, "Fiscal Pressure and Peasant Impoverishment in Serbia before World War I," *Jrnl. of Economic History* 39 (1979):719–40; Ivan Berend, *Decades of Crisis* (Berkeley: UC Press, 1997), as well as sources cited below..

23. See David Good, *The Economic Rise of the Habsburg Empire, 1750–1914* (Berkeley: UC Press, 1984).

24. How "exceptional" the Balkan states actually were is sharply contested by Diana Mishkova, "Modernization and Political Elites in the Balkans Before the First World War," *East European Politics and Societies* 9 (No. 1, Winter 1995): 63–90. See also N. Mouzelis, *Politics in the Semi-Periphery* (London, 1986).

25. See John Lampe and Marvin Jackson, *Balkan Economic History, 1550–1950* (Bloomington: Indiana University Press, 1982); John Lampe, "Imperial Borderlands or Capitalist Periphery? Redefining Balkan

Backwardness, 1520–1914," in Daniel Chirot, ed., *The Origins of Backwardness in Eastern Europe* (Berkeley: UC Press, 1989), pp. 177–210. Lampe, however, suggests that industrialization actually made little progress in the Balkan territories of the Habsburg Empire also prior to World War I.

26. See Rothschild, *East-Central Europe;* Hugh Seton-Watson, *Eastern Europe Between the Wars*, 1918–1941 (Hamdon: Archon Books, 1962); Ferenc Donath, *Reform and Revolution: Transformation of Hungarian Agriculture, 1945–70* (Budapest: Corvina Press, 1980); David Mitrany, *The Land and the Peasant in Rumania* (New York: Greenwood Press, 1968); Jozo Tomasevich, *Peasants, Politics and Economic change in Yugoslavia* (Stanford: Stanford University Press, 1955).

27. See Ivan T. Berend and Gyorgy Ranki, *Economic Development in East Central Europe in the Nineteenth and Twentieth Centuries* (New York: Columbia University Press, 1974).

28. Rothschild, *East Central Europe;* Berend and Ranki, *Economic Development;* Albert Hirschman, *National Power and the Structure of Foreign Trade* (Berkeley: UC Press, 1945).

29. See Jelavich, *History of the Balkans;* for a more general over view, see Joseph Held, ed., *The Columbia History of Eastern Europe in the Twentieth Century* (New York: Columbia University Press, 1992); John Lukacs, *The Great powers and Eastern Europe* (Chicago: Regnery, 1953)..

30. See Rothschild, *East Central Europe;* Katherine Verdery and Ivo Banac, eds. *National character and national ideology in interwar Easter Europe* (New Haven: Yale University Press, 1995); Michael Kaser and Hugo Radice, *Interwar Policy, the War and Reconstruction* (New York: Oxford, 1986).

31. See Rothschild, *East Central Europe;* Andres Janos, *The Politics of Backwardness* (Princeton: Princeton University Press, 1987);Stephen Fischer-Galati, *Twentieth Century Romania* (New York: Columbia University Press, 1970); Peter Sugar, ed., *Native Fascism in the Successor States 1918–45* (Santa Barbara: ABC-Clio, 1971).

32. See Yale Richmond, *U.S.-Soviet Cultural Exchanges, 1958–86: Who Wins?* (Boulder: Westview, 1987).

33. On the role of the party, see among others Stephen Fischer-Galati, ed. *The Communist Parties of Eastern Europe* (New York: Columbia University Press, 1971), Karel Kaplan, *The Communist Party in Power: A Profile of Party Politics in Czechoslovakia* (Boulder: Westview, 1987); M. K. Dziewanowski, *The Communist Party of Poland* (Cambridge: Harvard University Press, 1976); April Carter, *Democratic Reform in Yugoslavia: The Changing Role of the Party* (London: Pinter, 1982); Kenneth Jowitt, *Revolutionary Breakthroughs and National Development* (Berkeley: UC Press, 1971); Paul Lewis, *Political Authority and Party Secretaries in Poland, 1975–86* (New York: Cambridge University Press, 1989).

34. The "shortage economy" model was pioneered by Janos Kornai and adopted widely in the area. See Janos Kornai, *The Economics of Shortage* (Amsterdam; North Holland Publishing, 1981); idem, *The Socialist Economy*

(Princeton: Princeton University Press, 1992).

35. The original debate between Ludwig von Mises and Oskar Lange on whether or not socialism and competitive markets are compatible is reproduced in Morris D. Bornstein, ed., *Comparative Economic Systems* (Homewood, Ill.: Irwin, 1974), pp. 119–160. The literature on economic reform, especially in Hungary and Yugoslavia is too extensive to be cited here; a good early summary of the considerations involved appears in Deborah Milenkovitch, *Plan and Market in Yugoslav Economic Thought* (New Haven: Yale University Press, 1971); a "final" summary of the issues and experiences is contained in the essays in J.M. Kovacs and M. Tardos, eds., *Reform and Transformation in Eastern Europe* (London: Routledge, 1992). An interesting discussion of the issues is also contained in Wldodzimierz Brus, *Socialist Ownership and Political Systems* (London: Routledge, 1971).

36. See Zbigniew Brzezinski, *The Soviet Bloc* (Cambridge: Harvard University Press, 1960, 1967); Ronald Lindon, *Bear and Foxes: The International Relations of the East European States* (New York: Columbia University press, 1979) Christopher D. Jones, *Soviet Influence in Eastern Europe* (New York: Praeger, 1981); Paul Marer, *Soviet and East European Foreign Trade, 1946–79* (Bloomington: Indiana University Press, 1982); William Reisginer, "East European Military Expenditures in the 1970s: Collective Goods or Bargaining Offer," *International Organization* 37 (Winter 1983): 137–55; David Holloway and Jane Sharp, eds., *The Warsaw Pact: Alliance in Transition?* (Ithaca: Cornell University Press, 1984); Willima Zimmerman, "Hierarchical Regional Systems and the Politics of System Boundaries *International Organization* 24 (Sprig 1972): 18–36.

37. See Michael Marrese and Jan Vanous, *Soviet Susidization of Trade with Eastern Europe* (Berkeley: Institute of International Studies, 1983); for some rejoinders, see Josef Brada, "Soviet Subsidization of Easter Europe: The Primacy of Economics over Politics?" *Journal of Comparative Economics* 9 (March 1985): 80–92; Paul Marer, "The Political Economy of Soviet Relations with Eastern Europe," in Sarah M. Terry, ed., *Soviet Policy in Eastern Europe* (New Haven: Yale University Press, 1984); idem and Kazimierz Posnanski, "Costs of Domination, Benefits of Subordination," in Jan Triska, ed., *Dominant Powers and Subordinate States* (Durham; Duke University Press, 1986), pp. 371–400.

38. Nevertheless, a significant literature comparing capitalist and socialist systems developed. See, for example, Frederick Pryor, *Public Expenditures in Communist and Capitalist Nations* (London: Allen and Unwin, 1968); idem, *Property and Industrial Organization in Communist and Capitalist Nations* (Bloomington: Indiana University press, 1973); Peter Wiles and Stefan Markowski, "Income Distribution under Communism and Capitalism," *Soviet Studies* 22 (Jan. 1971):344–70; Paul Gregory and Bert Leptin, "Similar Societies under Differing Economic Systems: The Case of the Two Germanies," *Soviet Studies* 29 (Oct. 1977): 519–43.

39. See Andrew Walder, ed., *The Waning of the Communist State* (Berkeley: UC Press, 1995); David Stark and Victor Nee, eds., *Remaking the Economic*

Institutions of Socialism (Stanford: Stanford University press, 1989).

40. See Carl Friedrich, ed., *Totalitarianism* (Cambridge: Harvard University Press, 1954); idem and Brzezinski, *Totalitarian Dictatorship and Autocracy* (Cambridge: Harvard University Press, 1956); Hannah Arendt, *The Origins of Totalitarianism* (Chicago: University of Chicago Press, 1951); Bertram Wolfe, *Communist Totalitarianism* (Boston; Beacon Press, 1961)..

41. See, for example, Richard Lowenthal, "Development v. Utopia in Communist Policy, In Chalmers Johnson, ed., *Change in Communist Systems* (Stanford: Stanford University press, 1970);Kenneth Jowitt, "Inclusion and Mobilization in European Leninist Regimes," in J. Triska and P. Cocks, *Political Development in Eastern Europe* (New York: Praeger, 1977), pp. 119–47.

42. See Ferenc Feher and Agnes Heller, *Dictatorship Over Needs* (Oxford: Blackwell, 1983); Vaclav Havel, "Anti-Political Politics," in Keane, ed., *Civil Society*, pp. 361–81; Leszek Kolakowski, "Hope and Hopelessness," *Survey* 17 (1971)..

43. See Milovan Djilas, *The New Class* (New York; Praeger, 1958); Charles Bettelheim, *The Transition to Socialist Economy* (Sussex: Harvester, 1975); Rudolf Bahro, *The Alternative in Eastern Europe* London: New Left Books, 1973); Gyorgy Konrad and Ivan Szelenyi, *The Intellectuals on the Road to Class Power* (Sussex: Harvester, 1979).

44. A large literature on various forms of inequality exists. See, among others, K. Slomczynski and Tadeusz Krause, *Class Structure and Social Mobility in Poland* (White Plains: Sharpe, 1978); A. Matjko, *Social change and stratification in Eastern Europe* (Praeger, 1974); T. Kolosi and E. Wnuk-Lipinski, *Equality and inequality under socialism* (Beverly Hills: Sage, 1983); Walter Conner *Socialism, politics and inequality* (Mew York: Columbia University Press, 1979).

45. The pathbreaking essay here is H. Gordon Skilling's "Interest Groups and Communist Politics," *World Politics* 18 (1988): 435–61; see also Roger Kanet, ed., *The Behavioral Revolution and Communist Studies* (New York: Free Press, 1971); idem, "Political Groupings and Their Role in the Process of Change in Eastern Europe," in Andrew Gyorgy and James Kuhlmann, eds., *Innovation in Communist Societies* (Boulder: Westview, 1978), pp. 41–58; Alex Pravda, "East-West Interdependence and the Social Compact in Eastern Europe," in M. Bornstein, Z. Gitelman, and W. Zimmerman, eds., *East-West Relations and the Future of Eastern Europe* (London: Allen & Unwin), pp. 162–91; Jan Triska, "Citizen Participation in Community Decisions in Yugoslavia, Romania, Hungary and Poland," in Jan Triska and Paul Cocks, eds. *Political Development in Eastern Europe* (New York: Praeger, 1977).

46. See Andrew Janos, "Group Politics in Communist Society: A Second Look at the Pluralist Model, " in S. Huntington and C. Moore, eds., *Authoritarian Politics in Modern Society: The Dynamics of One-Party Systems* (New York: Basic Books, 1970).

47. See David Ost, *Solidarity and the Politics of Anti-Politics* (Philadelphia: Temple University Press, 1990); David Stark, "Rethinking internal labor markets—new insights from a comparative perspective," *American Sociological*

Review 51 (1986): 492–504; Ivan Szelenyi, et. al., *Socialist Entrepreneurs: Embourgeoisement in Rural Hungary* (Madison: University of Wisconsin press, 1988); Jadwiga Staniszkis, *Poland's Self-Limiting Revolution* (Princeton: Princeton University Press, 1984); Christopher Hann, *A Village without Solidarity* (New Haven: Yale University Press, 1985); Sharon Wolchik and Alfred Meyer, ed., *Women, State and Party in Eastern Europe* (Durham: Duke University Press, 1985); Gale Kligman, *The Wedding of the Dead* (Berkeley: UC Press, 1988); Rudolf Tokes, ed., *Opposition in Eastern Europe* (Johns Hopkins University Press, 1979); Jane Curry, ed., *Dissent in Eastern Europe* (New York: Praeger, 1988).

48. See, for example, T. H. Rigby, "Politics in the Mono-Organizational Society," in Andrew Janos, ed., *Authoritarian Politics in Communist Europe* (Berkeley: Institute of International Studies, 1976); Jiri Valenta, *Soviet Intervention in Czechoslovakia 1968: Anatomy of a Decision* (Baltimore: Johns Hopkins University Press, 1979); Terez Laky, "Enterprises in Bargaining Position,' *Acta Oeconomica* 22 (No. 3–4, 1979): 227–46; Jean Woodall, *The Socialist Corporation and Technocratic* (New York: Cambridge University Press, 1982). Attempts to apply corporatist theory to the policy-making process represented an adaptation of the approach; see Valerie Bunce, "The Political Economy of the Brezhnev Era: the Rise and Fall of Corporatist," *British Jrnl of Political Science* 13 (1983):129–48; David Ost, "Towards a Corporatist Solution in Eastern Europe: The Case of Poland," *East European Politics and Society* 3 (1989): 152–74.

49. See essays in Ellen Comisso and Laura Tyson, eds., *Power, purpose, and Collective Choice* (Ithaca: Cornell University Press, 1986); Carl Beck, et. al., *Political Succession in Eastern Europe* (Pittsburgh: Center for International Studies, 1976); Judy Batt, *Economic Reform and Political Change in Eastern Europe* (Houndsmills: Macmillan 1988); Paul Lewis, "Political consequences of the change in party-state structures under Gierek," in J. Woodall, ed., *Policy and Politics in Contemporary Poland* (London: Pinter, 1982).

50. Accounts of the collapse of socialism are numerous. See Ivo Banac, ed., *Eastern Europe in Revolution* (Ithaca: Cornell University Press, 1992); Gale Stokes *The Walls Came Tumbling Down* (New York: Oxford, 1993) for two of the better accounts.

51. See, for example, Adam Przeworski, *Democracy and the Market* (New York: Cambridge University Press, 1991); Juan Linz and Alfred Stepan, *Problems of Democratic Transition* (Baltimore: Johns Hopkins University Press, 1996); Claus Offe, *Varieties of Transition* (Cambridge: MIT Press, 1997); Arend Lijphart, "Democratization and Constitutional Choices in Czechoslovakia, Hungary, and Poland, 198991," *Journal of Theoretical politics* 4 (April, 1992): 207–223.

52. See Philippe Schmitter and Terry Karl, "The conceptual Travels of Transitologists and Consolidologists: How Far to the East Should They Attempt to Go?" *Slavic Review* 53 (Spring 1994): 173–85; Valerie Bunce,

"Should Transitologists Be Grounded?" *Slavic Review* 54 (Spring 1995): 111–127; Sarah Terry, "Thinking about post-Communist transitions: How Different are they? *Slavic Review* 52 1993): 333–337..

53. See, for example, Arend Lijphart and Carlos Waisman, eds., *Institutional Design in New Democracies* (Boulder: Westview, 1996); Adam Przeworski, *Democracy and the Market* (New York: Cambridge University Press, 1991); L. Bresser-Pereira, J.M. Maravall, and A. Przeworski, *Economic Reforms in new Democracies* (New York: Cambridge University Press, 1993); Joan Nelson, et. Al., *Intricate Links: Democratization and Market Reforms in Eastern Europe and Latin America* (New York: Transaction Press, 1994); Bela Greskovits, *The Political Economy of Protest and Patience* (Budapest: Central European University Press, 1998). The East European transitions have also been compared with the establishment of democratic governments in postwar Europe; see, for example, Geoffrey Pridham and Paul G. Lewis, eds. *Stabilising Fragile Democracies* (London: Routledge, 1996).

54. See Kenneth Jowitt, *New World Disorder: The Leninist Extinction* (Berkeley: UC Press, 1992);. Daniel Chirot, "National Liberations and Nationalist Nightmares The consequences of the End of Empires in the Twentieth Century," in Beverly Crawford, ed., *Market, States, and Democracy* (Boulder: Westview, 1995), pp. 43–71. For a rejoinder, see Giuseppe Di Palma, "Why democracy can work in Eastern Europe," *Journal of Democracy* 2 (No. 1, 1991): 21–31; Barbara Geddes, "A Comparative Perspective on the Leninist Legacy in Eastern Europe," *Comparative Political Studies* 28 (July 1995): 239–75.

55. See G. M. Tamas, "Victory Defeated," *Journal of Democracy 10 (January 1999)*:3–8; V. Tismaneanu, ed., *The Revolutions of 1989* London: Routledge, 1999); W. L. Miller, S. White, P. Heywood, *Values and Change in Post-Communist Europe* (London: St. Martins, 1998); Ralf Dahrendorf, *After 1989: morals, revolution, and civil society* (New York: St. Martins, 1998); Richard Rose, William Mishler, and Christian Haerpfer, *Democracy and its Alternatives: Understanding Post-Communist Societies* (Baltimore: Johns Hopkins University Press, 1998).

56. See Susan Woodward, *Balkan Tragedy* (Washington: Brookings, 1995); Leonard Cohen, *Broken Bonds* (Boulder: Westview, 1993, 1995, 1997); John Lampe, *Yugoslavia as History* (New York: Cambridge University Press, 1996); Branka Magas, *The Destruction of Yugoslavia* (London: Verso, 1993; Bogdan Denitch, *Ethnic Nationalism* (Minneapolis: University of Minnesota Press, 1994); this is, of course, only a small sampling of the literature appearing in the past decade.

57. See, for example, Valerie Bunce, *Subversive Institutions* (New York: Cambridge University Press, 1999); Veljko Vujacic, "Historical Legacies, Nationalist Mobilization and Political Outcomes in Russia and Serbia: A Weberian View," *Theory and Society* 25 (December 1996): 763–81; Ellen Comisso, "Federalism and Nationalism in Post-Socialist Eastern Europe," *New Europe Law Review* 1 (spring 1993): 489–503.

58. See, for example, Katherine Verdery, "Nationalism and National Sentiment in Post-socialist Romania," *Slavic Review* 52 (Summer 1991):179–203; Michael Kennedy, ed., *Envisioning Eastern Europe: Postcommunist Cultural Studies* (Ann Arbor: University of Michigan press, 1994); Christopher Hann, "Postsocialist Nationalism: Rediscovering the Past in Southeast Poland," *Slavic Review* 57 (Winter 1998): 840–64; Sharon Wolchik, "The Politics of Ethnicity in Post-Communist Czechoslovakia," *East European Politics and Society* 8 (Winter 1994): 153–89; Laszlo Kurti and Juliet Langman, eds., *Beyond Borders: Remaking Cultural Identities in the new East and Central Europe* (Boulder: Westview, 1997).

59. See David Lipton and Jeffrey Sachs, "Privatization in Eastern Europe—The Case of Poland," *Brookings papers in Economic Activity* 2 (1990):293–3441; Peter Murrell, "{hrs}'Big Bang' versus Evolution: East European Economic Reforms in the Light of Recent Economic History," *Plan-Econ Report* 6 (No. 26, June, 1990):1–11; idem, "What is Shock Therapy and What did it do in Poland and Russia," *Post-Soviet Affairs* 9 (April-June 1993):111–40.

60. See David Bartlett, *The Political Economy of Dual Transformation* (Ann Arbor: University of Michigan Press, 1997); Kazimierz Poznanski, *Poland's Protracted Transition* (New York: Cambridge University Press, 1997).

61. See M. Steven Fish, "The Determinant of Economic Reform in the Post-Communist World," *East European Politics and Societies* 12 (Winter 1998):31–790;Joan Nelson, "Linkages between Politics and Economics," *Journal of Democracy* 5–4 (October 1994): 50–1.

62. The literature on privatization is huge. Some major works include Roman Frydman and Adam Rapaczynski, *Privatization in Eastern Europe; Is the State Withering Away* (New York: Oxford University Press, 1994); M. Ernst, M. Alexeev, and Paul Marer, *Transforming the Core* (Boulder: Westview, 1996); Ivan Major, *Privatization in Eastern Europe* (Aldershot, U.K.: Elgar, 1993); Jozef Brada, "Privatization is Transition—or Is It?" *Journal of Economic Perspectives* 10(Spring 1996):67–85. David Stark, "Privatization in Hungary: From Plan to Market or From Plan to Clan?" *East European Politics and Societies* 4 (Fall 1990):351–93.

63. See for example, S. Estrin, J. Brada, et. Al., *Restructuring and privatization in Central Eastern Europe: Case Studies of Firms in Transition* (Armonk: M. E. Sharpe, 1995); Simon Johnson and Gary Loveman, *Starting Over in Eastern Europe* (Boston: Harvard Business School Press, 1995);; Saul Estrin, ed., *Foreign Direct Investment in Central Eastern Europe: Case Studies of Firms in Transition* (Armonk: Sharpe, 1999); Yudit Kiss, *The Defence Industry in East Central Europe* (New York: Osford, 1997). David Stark and Laszlo Bruszt, *Post-Socialist Pathways: Transforming Politics and property in East Central Europe* (New York: Cambridge University Press, 1997); Wendy Carlin, John van Reenen, and Toby Wolfe, "Enterprise Restructuring in Early Transition: the case study evidence from Central and Eastern Europe," *Economics of Transition*

3 (December 1995): 435–60.

64. See Ivan Szelenyi, ed., Privatizing the Land: Rural Political Economy in Post-socialist Societies (London; Routledge, 1998); G. W. Creed, Domesticating Reform: From socialist reform to ambivalent transition in a Bulgarian village (Pennsylvania State University Press, 1998); Peter and Sandor Agocs, "{hrs}'The Change Was but an Unfulfilled promise': Agriculture and Rural Population in Post-Communist Hungary," East European Politics and Society 8 (Winter 1994): 32–58; J. Davis, "Understanding the process of decollectivisation and agricultural privatisation in transition economies: the distribution of collective and state farm assets in Latvia and Lithuania," Europe-Asia-Studies 49 (December 1997): 1209–32.

65. See Tanya Renne, ed. Ana's Land: Sisterhood in Eastern Europe (Boulder: Westwood, 1997); Nanette Funk and Magda Mueller, ed., Gender Politics and Post-Communism (Routledge, 1993); Ellen Berry, ed., Postcommunism and the Body Politics (New York: NYU Press, 1995); Susan Gal and Gale Kligman, eds., Reproducing Gender: Politics, Publics, and Everyday Life After Socialism (Princeton: Princeton University Press, 2000).

66. See, for example, Sue Bridges and Frances Pine, eds., Surviving Post-Socialism: Local Strategies and Regional Responses in Eastern Europe and the Former Soviet Union (London: Routledge, 1998); Michael Buraoy and Katherine Verdery, Uncertain Transitions (Lanham MD: Rowman and Littlefield, 1999).

67. The impact of the massive reorientation of trade is examined in the essays in John Zysman and Andrew Schwartz, eds., Enlarging Europe: The Industrial Foundations of a New Political Economy (Berkeley: Institute for International Studies, 1998); see also Andras Koves, Central and East European Economies in Transition; The International Dimension (Boulder: Westview Press, 1992); F. Stolze, "Changing foreign trade patterns in post-reform Czech industry," Europe-Asia Studies 49 (November 1997): 1209–35; Laszlo Csaba, "A decade of transformation in Hungarian economic policy," Europe-Asia Studies 50 (December 1998): 1381–91.

Chapter 7

The Transformation of Contemporary China Studies, 1977–2002

Andrew G. Walder

The central focus of this chapter is a distinct subfield within the broader field of "China Studies": the study of the polity, society, and economy of the People's Republic of China. For the most part—although this is changing rapidly—I take this to mean scholarship by "China specialists" in the disciplines of political science, sociology, and economics. I select this narrow definition of the field for several reasons: it is the one in which I have worked for some 25 years, and that I know intimately; it has experienced remarkable growth, transformation, and intellectual reorientation over the past two decades; and this transformation embodies all of the dilemmas and controversies about the meaning of area studies within social science fields that have been cause for so much recent concern. It also shows remarkable progress in the integration of area and disciplinary concerns.

For two reasons, I exclude from this definition the fields of history and anthropology, both integral parts of "the China field". The first is temporal and geographic focus: historians have not written about post-1949 China until very recently, and anthropological research on China long focused upon Taiwan and Hong Kong. Second, and more importantly, the tension between "area studies" and the disciplines, if it existed at all, was markedly less in these disciplines than in sociology, economics, and political science. In both history and anthropology it is expected that someone have a strong research competence, necessarily focused on an area. To be sure, the intellectual evolution of anthropology and history in the past 30 years has raised important issues for China specialists, but these tensions are properly viewed as internal to the disciplines themselves, rather than a tension between "area studies" and disciplines.

To a considerable extent, my portrayal of this field's transformation, and its implications for the meaning of area studies within social science disciplines, is based on personal reflection, and draws on my own intellectual biography—my experience in graduate school, as a scholar in search of an intellectual identity, and as a teacher of graduate students. When I first entered graduate school in sociology in 1976, already committed to the study of China, my teachers at the University of Michigan made very clear that I would be judged primarily by the extent to which my work met disciplinary standards of rigor and theoretical relevance; on the job market, the same hurdles loomed large; for every submission to a professional journal, the rejections came back with the same incantation; and at tenure time, the same skeptical scrutiny of my record by people with no devotion to the study of China. This personal experience conditioned my immediate reaction to the rationale of the recent questioning of the usefulness of "area studies", and the related anxiety evident among some of its practitioners: *"So what else is new?"*

This essay will make clear that I do not perceive any crisis in China area studies. To the contrary, I believe that the perennial tension between area specialization and disciplinary scholarship is much reduced from 25 years ago, and has virtually disappeared in some topic areas. Indeed, some scholarship on contemporary China has not only moved to the mainstream of these disciplines, but has served in some ways to define subfields within them. Area studies is succeeding within disciplines in ways unimaginable to me when I entered the field in the mid-1970s. At the same time, traditional area scholarship of the kind published in the pages of such journals as *The China Quarterly, The China Journal,* and *Modern China* continues to thrive.

So I state my biases at the outset. I come to this subject encouraged by recent gains in political science, sociology, and economics, and skeptical about claims that area studies are now beseiged by attacks from social scientists hostile to area knowledge. *So what's all the anxiety about?* In the remainder of this essay, I will review the past 20 plus years in my subfield, explain why I am encouraged by recent developments, and then provide my brief and optimistic interpretation of recent debates within the comparative politics section of the American Political Science Association, which appear to be the cause of much recent anxiety among some area specialists.

WHAT'S AN AREA SPECIALIST, ANYWAY?

The proper definition of an area specialist is a minimalist one: someone who *at least* is able to speak and read the language of the country sufficiently well to do extensive research in and about the country, using primary sources. For a language like Chinese, where after 4 full years of instruction one is able to read a newspaper with the aid of a dictionary, and usually one is able to write Chinese prose at the 6th grade level, actual linguistic competence varies enormously. The ideal of practical fluency in spoken Chinese is less common than we care to admit, and fluency in reading and writing rarer still. Many area specialists in the social science fields are able to hold only rudimentary conversations in Chinese, and are semi-literate outside of the kinds of documents they read for their research. Higher levels of linguistic competence are more commonly attained in the humanistic fields and in anthropology (although in anthropology this is usually in spoken Chinese and its regional dialects, rather than the written language). Of course, the second part of this minimalist definition is that the person actually *does* work primarily, if not exclusively, on the geographically defined area, using primary sources.

When people discuss area specialists, however, they inevitably mean much more than this minimalist definition. The vision articulated in this country in the 1950s, when the "social science" approach sought to free itself of the scholarly demands of traditional European sinology,[1] implied much more. The ideal area specialist was someone who, in addition to language courses, would take a battery of courses in history and perhaps anthropology that would permit them to understand the "culture" of the region. In the 1950s, 1960s, and even early 1970s, given the extreme provincialism of American higher education, this process usually began in graduate school. And it should be emphasized that this ideal was not realistically attainable: mastering a punishingly difficult language, familiarizing oneself with a history and culture of extraordinary subtlety, variability, and historical depth, *while at the same time* learning the canon of theory and research in one's discipline and the skills necessary to pose significant questions and design research. More often than we care to admit, those of us educated as area specialists during that period emerged from the process with only rudimentary language skills, a stereotyped set of cultural traits of "the Chinese" or of China's "modern historical dilemmas", and little sense of, or interest in, the core intellectual problems of social science disciplines.[2] I emphasize these uncomfortable realities because too often discussions about "area studies" are about the *ideals* rather than the less inspiring realities of actual area competence of area specialists in the social sciences.

What we *did* have, however, was a ferocious interest in specific areas of competence about China that we chose as our own, a finely developed sense of the limits of our knowledge about China (based in large part on the country's inaccessibility), and a relentless approach to gathering available evidence through emigre interviews or limited documentary sources. This was a major world revolution, and for intellectual as well as geopolitical reasons it was essential to understand the kind of polity, society, and economy that was emerging from this process.[3] The field of contemporary China studies initially was relatively small, tightly knit, centered on the superb journal *The China Quarterly*, in which disciplinary boundaries were unimportant. In this setting, political scientists, economists, and sociologists could speak to one another and learn a great deal from one another. If a political scientist could unravel the workings of the People's Communes during the Great Leap Forward of 1958–60, scholars in all fields would benefit. If a sociologist could describe accurately the system of grass roots social organization in urban China, the economist could learn something important about scarcity and rationing, while the political scientist could draw important inferences about the sources of political order in the new regime.

From the outside, however, we were viewed as an insular and narrow lot, and we have to admit that this was not entirely unjustified. We usually did not read much about countries other than China, and often were completely uninterested in any other region (except sometimes, for obvious reasons the Soviet Union and eastern Europe, although this too was resisted strongly by many). We rarely read our disciplinary journals, often could not understand the articles in them, and never published in them. If we were aware of the core concerns of theory and research in our disciplines, and were interested in them, we usually had no idea how to relate our research to these concerns, and almost never had the kind of data that would permit us to do so. From the perspectives of our respective disciplines, we were not at all engaged in *interdisciplinary* research, as we liked to tell ourselves, we were in fact engaged in *nondisciplinary* research. Commonly heard from some of us was the refrain that "theories developed in western contexts do not apply in nonwestern settings"—a statement that entirely misses the point about theory: *most "western" social science theories do not apply to the "West" either!* All theories are contested, no matter who contrives them and where they attempt to apply them. The only intellectually defensible response is to offer an alternative theory and to show how it is better supported by the evidence.[4] Our scholarship was almost never involved in theoretical projects in any case, because we surely were not testing "western" theories, nor were we devising new ones of our own. I strongly believe that the scholarship of this earlier era was often superb and worthy of respect on its own terms. There was something extremely important going on in China that was well worth studying, and it was virtually impossible at that time to study it while simultaneously meeting the scholarly standards of the disciplines. But what they said about us in the disciplines was often justified.

The issue is more complicated than this, however, for the 1950s ideal of the "area specialist" in the social sciences, while hardly attainable, contained intellectual traps to which area specialists were often blind. *The insistence on the cultural and historical situatedness of what we observed and analyzed led too easily to fallacious arguments.* The problem here was twofold. First, area specialists who took their knowledge of history and culture from textbooks rarely had the depth of knowledge necessary to appreciate this situatedness beyond stereotypical statements (historians and anthropologists, however, often did, and often viewed our forays in these directions with justified skepticism). Yet the traditional model of the China specialist obligated us to point out the Chineseness of what we observed by referring to alleged Chinese cultural universals or to parallels in earlier Chinese times or other Chinese settings. And this led to a second kind of problem: our area-focused training left us with insufficient knowledge about parallel institutions or behaviors in other societies. The default position was an unwitting "occidentalism", an orientation that led us *implicitly* to compare what we observed in China with a stereotyped textbook image of "the West"—our bureaucracies are models of Weberian impersonalism, our political systems actually operate according to the principles of our written constitutions, people advance primarily according to merit, objectively judged, and we are a society of rugged, self-reliant, socially isolated individualists. When we detect organizations that operate according to personal loyalties, political behavior at variance with written regulations, nepotism and corruption, and reliance on friends and family to accomplish things, the temptation was to move to quickly to our list of Chinese cultural traits to explain these "divergences" from western institutions and behavior. Unfortunately, we were not equipped with enough knowledge about other countries to be able to identify the generic and universal from the distinctive and the Chinese. This was one of the complaints lodged against us as area specialists by scholars in our disciplines, and it was not unjustified.

SO WHAT DO THE "DISCIPLINES" EXPECT FROM US?

What do the disciplines of political science, sociology, and economics demand from us as scholars? On the surface, not much, really. All they ask is that we analyze China as a social scientist in our discipline would analyze any country, including our own—as someone who works on a generic intellectual *problem*. The ideal of the social science disciplines is simply stated: that we are social scientists *who happen to be doing research on China*. This sounds disarmingly simple, but it is an ideal that was almost impossible to attain so long as scholars and students were "area specialists" by education and orientation, and so long as information about China was so scarce.

The contradictions between area and discipline were not uniform across social science fields. Economics as a discipline is notoriously hostile not only to area studies but seemingly to the historically situated analysis of *any* real world economy. Theory in that discipline has been heavily oriented toward working out in mathematical form intriguing anomalies in the general equilibrium model. Empirical work in econometrics demands large sets of data and advanced modelling techniques. Economists who worked on China were trying to describe the economic institutions formed after the Chinese revolution, and to glean data on their performance. The general equililbrium model had little to do with any of this, and econometricians were not impressed by painstakingly assembled descriptive series of data on, for example, grain harvests in China. It was therefore almost impossible for China area specialists to survive in professional economics departments, and very few did. If it were not for the Ford Foundation's endowment of a handful of specialized chairs in the 1960s at such universities as Michigan and Harvard, departments of applied (eg. agricultural) economics, and schools of international studies that hired area specialists in economics, and such agencies as the World Bank and Asian Development Bank, the species *sinologus economicus* might well have become extinct.

The environment in sociology was not so hostile, yet it was still harsh. The mainstream of the discipline clearly shared the scientific aspirations of economics, yet the discipline had no single dominant theoretical model, and in fact was divided into several competing camps. More importantly, the idea of quantitative analysis as the ideal was a contested one, with strong and outspoken proponents of field work and historical approaches providing ample shelter for the unorthodox. Nonetheless, China studies of the variety published in the *China Quarterly* had no legitimate intellectual standing within the discipline. A scholar who painstakingly assembled evidence about patterns of social inequality in China might be celebrated by the readers of the *Quarterly,* and receive praise from China specialists across the disciplines. Yet colleagues in sociology departments would ask: *So what? What does your study of China tell us about generic processes of social stratification in all societies; what are the implications of your research for theories about processes of inequality?* It was a challenging and intimidating question of a kind few China specialists were able to address. And it meant that in the competition for jobs in a discipline that only rarely set aside jobs for "comparativists" in world regions,[5] and in the daunting process of tenure review, few China area specialists survived.

Political science contrasted markedly with sociology and

economics, and for this reason the discipline contained the vast majority of China area specialists across these three fields. The field of "comparative politics" grew rapidly in the 1950s and 1960s, and set aside numerous jobs for specialists on various world regions. While the China specialists often were viewed critically by their more discipline-oriented colleagues, especially those with strong theoretical or quantitative orientations, they were tolerated within the discipline and prospered within their protected niches. The political science departments at leading universities with major centers for China studies—Harvard, Berkeley, Stanford, Michigan, Columbia, for example—have long set aside two or even three positions for China specialists. To a considerable extent, the *China Quarterly* was their organ; it was the journal that defined their field and it was the primarily journal outlet for their published work. The field of Chinese politics attained critical mass and was fairly self-contained; while it made occasional nods in the direction of Soviet politics, and borrowed ideas periodically from other political science subfields, it operated largely in isolation from the discipline as a whole.

I suspect that this sketch of the position of area studies in economics, sociology, and political science would hold true across regional areas, and am confident that this is so for Soviet and East European studies (a similarly self-contained and thriving field with such excellent journals as *Soviet Studies* and *Problems of Communism*). Unlike economics and sociology, where China scholars were constantly exposed to critical scrutiny and were never able to establish a disciplinary niche or a self-sustaining intellectual community, political scientists *were* (the primary audience for the few active sociologists and economists was in fact the political scientists who subscribed to the *Quarterly*). It is not surprising that as the boundaries between area studies and the disciplines have broken down over the past decade, this has caused much more anxiety among political scientists than in the other two disciplines. For sociologists and economists have no vested interests, or related intellectual identities, to defend. They have been exposed to the harsh critical scrutiny of their disciplinary colleagues from the beginning, while the political scientists who study world regions like China are feeling the heat for the first time. This is why the recent debates within the comparative politics subfield have little resonance in sociology and economics, fields that have in many ways already transcended the perennial divide between area studies and social science.

THE "CHINA FIELD" IN 1977

I have already referred to the transformation of China studies in the social sciences; now it is time to sketch its outlines. The China field in 1977 was a thriving international enterprise that was nonetheless intellectually isolated and marginal within the disciplines, the study of China was not seen as a promising research site for the analysis of generic social science issues. This has changed fundamentally in the past 25 years, and the reasons for this transformation are the equally fundamental transformations of China itself, and of its place in the world.

In 1977 China was still an internationally isolated and remarkably obscure country. Mao had died only the year before and the country's new leadership had arrested the top officials who had supported and benefited from the Cultural Revolution, but the reforms of Deng Xiaoping would not begin until 1979. Few Chinese citizens could travel abroad, U.S. citizens could not freely travel to China. Research by foreigners was impossible; collaborative research was out of the question; scholarly exchanges had yet to begin. The country's publishing industry had yet to recover from the effects of the Cultural Revolution; only a handful of leading national party newspapers could be obtained abroad; even regional and local party newspapers were off limits to foreigners and were scarce. Government documents that found their way outside China through obscure means were pored over by scholars; the open press was painstakingly read and analyzed; english-language transcriptions of radio broadcasts published by the BBC World Service and the U.S. Foreign Broadcast Information Service were important sources. Interviews of emigres in Hong Kong was a major component of one's "field" research.

The above implies, of course, something that seems remarkable in retrospect, but which we took very much for granted at the time: *almost none of us had ever been to the People's Republic of China.* Some of our teachers had, in carefully orchestrated tours that had followed on the heels of Nixon's visit to China in the early 1970s, and some students with left-wing orientations had participated in similar "friendship society" tours that began in the mid-1970s. I still recall the excitement at the University of Michigan when the Political Science department admitted a Canadian graduate student in 1976 *who had actually studied at Beijing University for two whole years!* The student was accorded near-celebrity status, gave a major colloqium presentation about what he had seen and observed, and soon published in the *China Quarterly* a long analysis of a political campaign he observed as a student. Our sense of isolation from the object of our study was much more than our colleagues who studied the USSR. China was not quite as isolated as North Korea today, but the feeling was similar.

Some of the students who entered graduate departments with an interest in China already had some exposure to the history and language of China. Some liberal arts colleges like Oberlin and Yale maintained programs for their undergraduates in Taiwan and Hong Kong, respectively, and were an important source of students with prior language training. But for the most part students did not begin serious language and area training until they enrolled in such Master's Degree programs as Harvard's venerable M.A. in Regional Studies-East Asia and similar programs at Columbia, Michigan, Berkeley, Stanford, Washington, and elsewhere. For the most part graduate students, whether European-American or Asian American, were still working on their language courses as they began their social science Ph.D. programs.

Students who entered Ph.D. programs in political science, economics, and sociology found that China just did not fit with the focus of the mainstream of their disciplines, nor did their teachers and colleagues have much interest in China of a scholarly nature. The country seemed so obscure and arcane that it did not appear to be relevant to the mainstream concerns of any of the disciplines, with the partial exception only of political science. The late 1960s were an era of widespread questioning of the earlier (and much caricatured) "totalitarian model" in the field of Soviet and East European politics, and research on China quickly joined in the spirited search for valid models of interest group politics, tendencies of articulation, bureaucratic politics, incipient pluralism, and later corporatism and clientelism as institutional descriptions and as images of the pursuit of interest or the policy-making process. At least in political science it was possible to partake in a scholarly dialogue that spanned across areas, and to speak to general conceptual and theoretical questions. Yet the field of "comparative communism" was often neglected by students of China and was itself marginal to mainstream political science.

Students of the Chinese economy were the most marginal of all: there was no place in the discipline for descriptions of economic institutions or analysis of China's economic policy. To the extent that economists took Chinese economic data seriously, their efforts were likely to be dismissed as arcane accounting exercises employing data of highly questionable accuracy. The prospect of relating the operations of the Chinese economy to theoretical issues that derived from marginal analysis and the general equilibrium model seemed hopeless. Under Mao the Chinese were so hostile to market *and* bureaucratic allocation that they denounced even the Soviet Union as revisionist. Under such circumstances, and given the almost complete paucity of reliable economic data, the study of the Chinese economy was often a special branch of the study of China's institutions, political campaigns, policy making, and policy implementation.

The position of the sociologist was somewhat better. Potentially, the Maoist anti-bureaucratic efforts, the attempt to further level income and other social differences, and the red guard and other protest movements of the period were all potentially topics of great sociological interest. But to the vast majority of sociologists China was still a great enigma, and to the extent that these subjects were known, they were viewed as arcane curiosities whose relevance to the core intellectual concerns of scholars in the fields of social stratification, complex organizations, or social movements was far from clear. And even if budding China scholars were able to frame questions about China that paralleled the kind of questions asked in the mainstream of the discipline, the extreme paucity of reliable evidence prevented them from providing plausible (i.e., publishable) answers.

Despite these barriers to full participation in the intellectual conversations of their disciplines, students gravitated to the thriving if self-contained and somewhat isolated field of contemporary China studies, centered on the *China Quarterly*. Unable to state the implications of inequality under Mao for general theories about the causes of social inequality? No matter; China scholars will warmly welcome your description of the different life chances of students from different family backgrounds, or the importance of party membership in building a career. Unclear about what, if anything, your analysis of the production failures of the People's Communes has to teach the discipline of economics? Don't worry, the readers of the *China Quarterly* will eagerly welcome your description and analysis, especially the political scientists. The contemporary China field was active and growing, already with a clearly developed sense of scholarly subfields (especially in political science), and with a growing literature and emerging debates of real intellectual substance. One such debate in economics was about the extent to which China's economic system redistributed resources across provinces, versus the extent to which each province was left to rely on its own resources. Another such debate, in the field of domestic Chinese central-level politics, was about the extent to which policy-making was dominated by Mao, or the extent to which various functional bureaucracies limited the room for maneuver for Mao or any other central-level politician. While students of Chinese foreign policy or the Chinese military might share little of interest with students of Chinese secondary education or of the rural family, there was nonethless a sense that China scholarship was equally accessible to all scholars, regardless of disciplinary training. The divisions among China specialists were primarily due to differences in substantive interest, not disciplinary orientations or methods.

REMAKING CONTEMPORARY CHINA STUDIES: THE FORCES FOR CHANGE

This all seems so long ago. The forces for change were initiated in 1979, with the rise of Deng Xiaoping as China's paramount leader, the beginnings of what would become a remarkable policy of economic reform, political liberalization, and opening up to the outside world, and the restoration of formal diplomatic ties between the US and

China. There is no need to rehearse here the subsequent economic and political history of the region, and later the geopolitical map of the world, since that date. We need only point to the rise of industrial east Asia and the emergence of China as a major market and trading nation, and the collapse of the Soviet Union and the rapid demise of its military might, all of which have moved a resurgent and increasingly comprehensible China more to the center of attention. The end of communism in eastern Europe and the USSR, the attendant trend toward political democratization and the attempted transformations of these countries into market economies have captured the attention of all three social science disciplines and have raised fundamental questions about how polities, societies, and economies are organized and how they change. No longer is China viewed as a marginal and arcane subject. It has moved to center stage.

As part of this transformation of China and the world since 1979, a number of specific trends have had a direct and major impact on the field of Chinese studies, transforming the field I have just described almost beyond recognition.

Access to Information and Research Opportunities
The opening of China, coupled with extensive internal political liberalization, completely transformed the research environment. Students of contemporary China, used to gleaning evidence from a small number of cryptic sources, eventually found themselves buried in an avalanche of new newspapers and periodicals, books, and published regulations, and the trickle of more valuable "internal" documents and books also grew to a steady stream, as regulations on the control of publications broke down by the late 1980s. (Students of the Soviet Union might appreciate the magnitude of this change if we point out that it telescoped within a 10 year period all of the liberalizations that took place in the USSR from the death of Stalin to Gorbachev's early years.) Now the problem was how to select the most useful and digest it. The life of East Asia librarians was transformed utterly, as large backlogs of new publications laid uncatalogued for years.

Research opportunities in China grew more slowly, but steadily.

The first official exchanges were "from above", through a central board not unlike the International Research Exchanges Board, which placed U.S. students and scholars in the Soviet Union and eastern Europe. The Committee on Scholarly Communication with the People's Republic of China, sponsored jointly by the National Academy of Sciences, SSRC, and ACLS, began exchanges in fall of 1979, initally sending only language students. Shortly thereafter the Committee sought to place researchers with universities and academies of social science; within two years scholars were sent to China for field research, and there followed a long struggle to gain research access to archives and villages. Early on, one anthropology graduate student was expelled from the country and charged with spying, leading to a ban on field research for several years. Despite these setbacks and frequent frustrations, the program grew steadily and indeed prospered, hitting its stride by the late 1980s, by which time the bulk of new research published on China was based at least in part on research done in the country.

By 1984 research in Hong Kong, the traditional base for scholarship on contemporary China, was languishing. The Universities Service Centre, for most of the period since its founding in 1963 with funding from the Ford Foundation, and later administered by the ACLS until its demise in the 1980s, had served two generations of China specialists. Located in a moldering villa on the approach to Kai Tak airport in northern Kowloon, the Centre maintained a small but outstanding research library of Chinese language newspapers and periodicals and translation series from various government agencies. (Much of the translation work, except for the radio broadcast series, was done at the U.S. Consulate in Hong Kong.) More importantly, the Centre had been the place where recent emigres from China were contacted and interviewed, often passed from scholar to scholar and sometimes became long-term research assistants and occasionally researchers in their own right. Each year since the mid-1960s, the Centre hosted a new cohort of Ph.D. students and faculty members for a year of research; from the late 1960s to the late 1970s the Centre was bursting at the seams, unable to find sufficient office space. By 1982, however, there was a rapid decline in demand, and offices went unoccupied as scholars flocked to Beijing and elsewhere to take advantage of the new opportunities. The era of emigre interviewing was over, and the Centre shifted its emphasis to enlarging its Chinese-language library collection. In 1988 the old Centre was closed and it moved to the Chinese University of Hong Kong, where it has grown into one of the finest libraries on contemporary China in the world. But for the past 15 years the rite of scholarly passage has occurred in Beijing, not Hong Kong.

As contact between scholars in China and the U.S. grew, other routes to archives and field research opened up that bypassed the centrally-administered programs of the Committee on Scholarly Communication. Universities established relationships and exchange programs, and many Chinese language programs opened their doors and welcomed students from abroad. Many of these programs were organized or run jointly beween U.S. and Chinese universities. By the mid-1980s, despite the initially low quality of language instruction available in China, students were ignoring the long established and outstanding language programs in Taiwan, like the Inter-University Consortium ("Stanford") Program in Taipei. Universities themselves began to arrange research visits for their students and faculty through both official and unofficial ties, and eventually the most effective routes to archives and the field proved to be paved by personal relationships between faculty who shared research interests. For social scientists in the old China field, the well worn path from language study in Taipei to dissertation research in Hong Kong was no longer travelled. After the early 1980s, students and faculty went directly to Beijing and points beyond.

During the first decade of such access to China, the model employed was primarily that of the lone U.S. China scholar "placed" in some Chinese university or research institute in the social science academy network. The researcher was funded by the Committee on Scholarly Communication, and the institution that served as host was obligated to arrange access to the relevant archives, to field sites, or to arrange interviews in relevant organizations (for example, among factory mangers or government economic planners). This was an extraordinarily burdensome obligation for the host institution, which almost never received anything directly in return, and it could lead to considerable frustration for both the visiting scholar (who often complained about the denial of full access, not realizing that they were often getting better treatment than their Chinese colleagues), and the host institution (for whom the guest could be a constant and complaining burden). But gradually, somehow, the "exchange" began to yield fruit for the foreign researchers.

The Revival of China's Social Sciences and the Rise of Collaborative Research

The opening up of China to U.S. researchers was simultaneously a period of revival for the social sciences in China, which had been virtually abolished in the 1950s and 1960s. Initially, the revived economics departments were filled with surviving political economists of the Marxist school, whose orthodox Soviet training had been considered revisionist since the late 1960s. Some of them had been highly influenced by reformist thinking in the 1950s of the kind encouraged by the writings of the early Soviet reformer Liberman, and by echoes in Hungary, Poland, and Yugoslavia. But they were not equipped for full engagement with modern neoclassical economics. Senior sociologists were typically trained in Marxist philosophy, the best of them in "dialectical materialism" that came out of 1930s Soviet textbooks. Only a few very senior figures survived from the once-proud tradition of Chinese sociology from the 1930s and 1940s; the field was abolished as bourgeois after the anti-rightist campaign of 1957. Political science has yet to be revived fully; it is still a marginal discipline in China.

Despite the courtesy and genuine curiosity displayed by many of these senior figures, it would take a while before real scholarly collaboration was possible. During the 1980s most of these senior figures gradually retired or were promoted into university administration or government service, helping their successors build the foundations for further contact and cooperation. There was no successor cohort just below them in age, because the social science departments had been closed since the 1950s (sociology and political science) or since 1966 (all universities closed from 1966 to 1972, and reopened only with skeleton crews and smaller student bodies from 1972 to 1977). As a result, generational succession was very rapid. Younger faculty and graduate students avidly immersed themselves in western, primarily American, social science, translating enormous numbers of monographs, recent articles, and textbooks. After the early 1980s, traditional Marxist economics and dialectical materialism had no credibility among those below age 40. Some attended summer institutes and guest lectures given by visiting U.S. scholars, others made visits to U.S. campuses or enrolled for degree programs. By the early 1990s, beginning to receive reinforcement from scholars returned from abroad, the younger generation moved into departmental and institute headships and paved the way for a new development: collaborative research.

Since 1988, with a 2-year interruption due to the military suppression of the 1989 protests and the diplomatic reaction to this, collaborative research has perhaps been the modal form of research in these social science fields. Typically, these now involve jointly planned and administered sample surveys or field research projects, in which Chinese and foreign researchers jointly analyze and publish the resulting data. Important sample surveys have been completed in the past ten years on political participation and political attitudes, rural household incomes, health and nutrition, mate choice and marriage patterns, social stratification and mobility, and other subjects. The collaborative projects are only a tiny fraction of the hundreds of projects carried out each year on every conceivable subject connected with China's economic growth and rapid social transformation. Because these projects are conceived and planned jointly by academics, they do not need prior approval and clearances by higher level government bodies as part of bilateral national level exchange agreements. As a result, a far greater range of research subjects and forms of collaboration are possible, even those subjects and forms of research that are formally proscribed by various national agencies. And the incentives and rewards for Chinese scholars, and the intellectual benefits for both sides, are much greater than is usually the case for the lone scholar placed in an institution by a government to government exchange program. The output of these research projects is fueling the rise of disciplinary scholarship about China increasingly published in social science journals, a subject to which I will return below.

The Transformation of Student Demographics

Above I have touched upon two subjects that have had a major impact on the study of China in the social science disciplines. I mention them again to emphasize their importance. In many ways the transformation of the characteristics of students entering Ph.D. programs with an interest in the study of China has been the key change in transforming the intellectual contours of the field. And its impact is still working its way through the system.

The first change is the direct result of the opening of China and the increased prominence of China in America's perception of the world. Most students who embark upon a Ph.D. in these fields today are already fluent in Chinese and have spent one or more years studying or working in China. It is not uncommon for entering students to have spent one or two years in a language program and then work for up to five years for a Chinese or foreign organization in China. What this means is that the typical student, unlike 20 years ago, is already able to do research in the Chinese language and needs no introduction to the country and its people. Students of this type are far better prepared to spend time mastering their disciplinary core subjects than their peers two decades ago. Increasingly over the past decade, large numbers of highly motivated students come from Chinese family backgrounds. The rise of Asian-American students to plurality status on many major U.S. campuses has provided a larger reservoir of highly motivated potential recruits for social science Ph.D. programs, even though the language training is often just as large a barrier for them as for their peers who do not have a Chinese heritage.

A second change has had an even greater impact, and has more than anything else challenged our traditional notions of area scholarship: the rise of the graduate student/scholar from the People's Republic of China. From the first few graduate students to arrive in the early 1980s, the PRC graduate student has become an important fixture in social science departments across these three fields. This is an immense and seemingly inexhaustible national pool of talent; its impact on such fields as physics and chemistry is already legendary in this country. The effect has not been so dramatic in the social sciences, but the impact is highly magnified in the study of contemporary China. My rough impression is that more than half of the graduate students in these disciplines who specialize in research on China received their B.A. level degrees from Chinese institutions. I have personally directed the dissertations of nine sociology students since 1982 on subjects related to contemporary China: seven of them are from China (four of them from Beijing University).

Our 1950s ideal of the "area specialist" obviously was not devised with this kind of student in mind. And generally speaking, students from the PRC want nothing to do with this conception of "China scholarship". They did not surmount enormous odds to gain fellowships in leading North American universities in order to learn nondisciplinary scholarship that amounted to looking at China from a foreign perspective. They come to our universities in order to learn the theory and methods of the contemporary social sciences. These students, whether they were interested in dissertation research on China or not (they sometimes were not), often bypassed the area specialists to work with theorists and methodologists. A good many of them ignored the area specialists altogether, putting them on their dissertation committees as an afterthought.

The great strength of student-scholars from the PRC has been their single-minded focus on the discipline. I have to admit that this was not the strength that I and many of my area specialist colleagues would have predicted when graduate students first began arriving in the early 1980s. From our area studies perspective, we would have expected such students to excel at intensive documentary research of the kind we commonly practiced ourselves, enjoying a massive linguistic advantage. Instead, students from China gravitated quickly to models that predominated in the core of the disciplines: theoretically engaged empirical research, often highly mathematical and statistical in orientation. I recall my first encounter with a Chinese scholar who earned his Ph.D. in economics from the University of Chicago: he seemed to have a purer faith in the general equilibrium model than Milton Friedman himself, and he felt that the scholarly output of

"China specialists" who worked on the economy was trivial nonsense. This was an extreme version of a sobering experience that would recur over the years.

This single-minded dedication to disciplinary canons has served these students well in the competition for elite faculty positions during the past 15 years. Near the end of the 1980s it was becoming apparent that students from China were out-competing students trained in the traditional "area studies" approach in the job market. In the 1990s, the most highly coveted jobs in Political Science have been filled by Ph.D.'s who came originally from China: Yale, Princeton, Chicago, Duke, and Michigan. In sociology, students from the PRC have been offered similar entry-level jobs at Harvard, Chicago, Cornell, Duke, Minnesota, Michigan, and California-Irvine (these are partial lists, based on my personal familiarity with these scholars and their work; I exclude an equally large group of scholars of PRC origin who do not specialize in research on their own country).

THE RISE OF DISCIPLINARY CHINA SCHOLARSHIP

The forces for change that I have described above have rapidly brought into being a new kind of scholarship on China that did not exist in 1977: research motivated by the core concerns of their respective disciplines, whose questions are framed as part of a disciplinary dialogue, whose theoretical orientation and methods of analysis are a recognized part of the mainstream of these disciplines. In part, this new China scholarship addressed longstanding questions within the disciplines with data that became available for the first time. In part, the new scholarship addressed issues raised by China's recent transformation against the backdrop of the collapse of communist regimes elsewhere. Some of this new work has been pushed forward by longstanding area specialists taking advantage of new research opportunities. Some has been pushed forward by established social scientists without prior research interest in China, and who have been attracted to the study of China for the first time.[6] Much of this work has been the product of collaboration between China specialists and nonspecialists, and this new work has enormously enriched the quality of research on China—while helping China area specialists address the mainstream of their disciplines.

Economics: The Analysis of "Economies in Transition"

The debate over economic policy in the "economies in transition" has put China at center stage. Neoliberal advice to the new post-communist governments of Russia, the former Soviet Republics, and east-central Europe, urged a policy of monetary stabilization and rapid privatization that would have involved massive social dislocation. This advice was controversial within the economics profession, and has been heatedly refuted by area specialists of the region. China has been drawn into the policy debates because by the early 1990s people began to notice that its economy was making enormous progress without deflating its currency and making it convertible, without cutting subsidies to unprofitable firms, and without systematically privatizing its massive public sector. This led first to a debate about the extent to which China's economic reforms really had been successful, second to a debate over whether China's experience was at all relevant to eastern Europe's problems anyway, and third, over how one explains the positive economic performance of many sectors of the Chinese economy.[7] Relevant publications have been carried in a series of World Bank and Asian Development Bank publications, in the annual "proceedings" issue of the *American Economic Review* (published each May with short papers from the annual convention), in shorter articles in the AEA's *Journal of Economic Perspectives*, in the *Oxford Review of Economic Policy, Cambridge Journal of Economics*, and in a long review essay in the *Journal of Economic Literature*.

A more scholarly literature has engaged the theoretical and empirical issues raised by China's economic transformation. One area of inquiry and debate is about the causes of the massive productivity increases in Chinese agriculture that followed the disbanding of collective agriculture. One school argues that almost all resultant productivity gains were due to incentive and monitoring advantages of family farms. Another school claims that sustained increases in state grain prices and freeing of peasants from ill-advised bureaucratic cropping decisions explain large parts of the productivity increases. Just beneath the surface is the issue of the presumed superiority of private property as a form of economic organization: the main contributions to the debate have appeared in the *Journal of Political Economy,* the *American Economic Review,* and *Economic Development and Cultural Change.* Other areas of inquiry are about the extent to which productivity improvements have been observed in Chinese state sector firms and therefore whether privatization is necessary for improved economic incentives; about the nature of ownership and agency relationships in China's rural industrial sector, with related new explorations of the theory of the firm, agency theory, and the economics of property rights. One of the main outlets for these articles, in addition to the journals mentioned above, has been published in the *Quarterly Journal of Economics* and especially in the *Journal of Comparative Economics,* which in recent years has become the leading outlet for academic work on the Chinese economy (see Table 1).

Sociology: Stratification and Economic Organization in Former Command Economies

In sociology, a much smaller field, the new disciplinary scholarship has been concentrated to a surprising degree the two leading journals of the discipline, the *American Sociological Review* and the *American Journal of Sociology.* It has also begun to trickle back into the venerable *China Quarterly,* as articles from sociologists more commonly bring the questions and methods of their discipline back to their area audiences. These articles have been concentrated into two broad areas: social stratification and economic sociology. The former area has focused heavily on the impact of the post-1980 reforms on social inequality and opportunity, especially the relative advantages of the politically connected and the impact on the rural household economy on the status of women, although some studies have sought to identify the distinctive attributes of inequality and social mobility in the earlier planned economy. The latter area, economic sociology, has sought to identify the features of Chinese firms and their environments that have permitted many to prosper and grow while still under public ownership (this literature also extends to publications by sociologists in the *Administrative Science Quarterly* and *Economic Development and Cultural Change).* As Table 1 suggests, scholarship on contemporary

China did not appear in either of the major sociology journals before 1988, but after 1992 it has become relatively common.

Political Science: Regime Transformations and Market Reform

Disciplinary scholarship in political science has not been so focused topically as work in sociology, but two identifiable areas of concentration are the political impact of economic reform, and the role of the state in fostering market-oriented growth. These are, however, nascent foci, and the published papers tend to look like more disciplinary versions of traditional area studies papers, rather than focused attacks on general theoretical questions posed by the collapse of communism and the evolution of China. These papers as a group do not have the coherence and focus of work in economics and sociology. Instead, they cover areas of topical interest, but with a disciplinary twist: for example, on the political implications on increased migration to cities; on the causes and consequences of corruption, on the implications of local elections in rural areas; the role of government in economic reform, or on political attitudes and political participation. While some of these publications have begun to appear in the *American Political Science Review*, the bulk of them have been published in the two leading journals in comparative politics: *World Politics* and *Comparative Politics* (see Table 1). Compared to economics and sociology, the rise of disciplinary scholarship in political science has been slow, with arguably only small changes from 10–15 years ago.

CONCLUSION: OPPORTUNITIES AND FEARS

What I find most striking about the transformation of contemporary China studies over the past twenty five years is that it has not occurred as part of any clearly articulated plan. The initial establishment of the "China field" in the 1950s and 1960s was a deliberate creation, and resulted from the coordinated efforts of various "Joint Committees" of Chinese Studies of the Social Science Research Council and the American Council of Learned Societies, in which major senior figures at the large centers for Chinese Studies—Harvard, Yale, Michigan, Columbia, Berkeley, Stanford, Washington, Chicago—plotted the development of a new field. With the help of major infusions of funding from the Ford Foundation and the federal government (primarily through Fulbright and "National Defense" fellowships), a new and thriving field of study was created very much by design. That field was highly specialized, insular, and nondisciplinary in nature. Scholars from all disciplines shared a common set of interests, found little barrier to communication, and indeed felt themselves part of a broader community that also included non-academics from the world of journalism to intelligence agencies.

That field still exists, and in many ways it is th   riving as neve r before. But it is being rivaled and in some respects (especially in economics) supplanted by the rise of disciplinary scholarship on China. Some of the best work on the Chinese economy is now published in *Journal of Comparative Economics* and the *Quarterly Journal of Economics;* some of the best work on Chinese society in *American Sociological Review;* on Chinese politics in *World Politics.* Scholars who are widely respected in their social science fields, but who are not China specialists, are beginning to make significant contributions to the study of China, often in collaboration with China specialists in their own disciplines. Especially in economics and sociology, this disciplinary scholarship employs a theoretical language or a methodology that is opaque to most area specialists educated before the 1980s. The 1970s community of China specialists has become fragmented, with scholars more insulated in their respective disciplines, their work increasingly inaccessible to those without specialized training.

No committee o r agency willed this result; no one planned fo r it. It has occurred without senior China specialists encouraging it (indeed, many are not enthusiastic about it). True, the Social Science Research Council established a fellowship program more than a decade ago to reinforce the combination of area and social science competence among graduate students. This program certainly helped push matters in this direction, but it is tiny compared to earlier efforts in the 1950s and 1960s, and its impact on China studies has not been large. The train was already in motion, the SSRC has simply joined in to help push. This transformation is rather the result of grass-roots efforts in graduate social science departments throughout the country. The longstanding demand of the disciplines for a certain kind of scholarship has gradually had an effect. Geopolitical changes in the past twenty five years have brought China more to the center of the concerns of various disciplines, and have made it easier for students to conceive of the relevance of their China research to core problems in their disciplines. These same changes have helped attract a student body, both from China and North America, much better prepared, linguistically and otherwise, to combine area knowledge with disciplinary competence. Ph.D. requirements and the dictates of publication and the job market have finished the job.

These changes do indeed require us to rethink area studies, for in the China field they have occurred so rapidly, without planning and sustained reflection, that our intellectual environment has become transformed with very little by way of commentary. But the first step in rethinking area studies is the realization that, to a considerable degree, "area studies" have *already* been re-thought by scores of scholars, working quietly on their own. These people feel that their disciplines are their primary intellectual homes; they are social scientists who are contributing to their disciplines through their research on China. The interesting thing about the debate in the pages of the newsletter of the Comparative Politics Section of the American Political Science Association is that it is *not* an attack on area studies from a disciplinary perspective; it is about how to incorporate research on areas into the mainstream of theory and research in comparative politics. That process has already advanced considerably, and I interpret that debate as an *internal* one *within* political science, a symptom of the changes of recent years. Some may find this dialogue threatening; indeed the area specialists within political science may find it so because they have been insulated from such critical scrutiny for so long. Perhaps there are unsuspected dangers for area studies that are lurking in these trends, but I see these debates as evidence of falling barriers between the area and the disciplines, something that promises to further enrich both in the years ahead.

Table 1. Publication of Articles on China in Disciplinary Journals, 1978–2002

Discipline/Journal	1978–82	1983–87	1988–92	1992–97	1998–2002
American Sociological Review	0	0	3	7	4
American Journal of Sociology	0	0	2	8	7
Total, Sociology	**0**	**0**	**5**	**15**	**11**
World Politics	6	8	3	7	2
Comparative Politics	0	3	5	7	8
Total, Political Science	**6**	**11**	**8**	**14**	**10**
Journal of Comparative Economics	4	24	16	32	67

Note: Numbers for 2002 include issues through June only.

Andrew G. Walder is a Professor of Sociology at Stanford University.

Notes

1. The sinological tradition is a formidable one that would preclude serious social science work of any kind. The sinologist must immerse him or herself in Chinese (high) culture, thought, and history, mastering (primarily written) modern as well as classical Chinese, developing a deep understanding of history and literature. This would equip the sinologist with the tools to study *any* subject having to do with China, on whatever period or subject; it is an approach that idealizes total mastery of all available written sources on a subject and detailed and lengthy explication of the texts. To the traditional sinologist, what passes for China scholarship in our modern "area studies" is not serious, and can only with charity be termed scholarship.

2. This is the kind of U.S. social science area specialist searingly portrayed in Graham Greene's *The Quiet American*. The protagonist, a C.I.A. operative and recent product of Harvard's M.A. program in East Asian Studies, has a smattering of Vietnamese language, a head filled with untested social science theories, and a textbook understanding of culture and history that made him oblivious to the people and events around him.

3. Lest one be tempted by the tired old caricature of a government-funded cold war machine that sought to train intelligence specialists for purposes of empire, we should remember that many, if not most students attracted to China studies in the decade after 1966 were initially motivated by opposition to the Vietnam war and ideological fascination with China under Mao.

4. Too often these debates about "theory" are about the adjectives one applies to them ("euro-centric", "orientalist", "functionalist", "bourgeois", the accusations change with the years) or the presumed motives of the people who offer them (which usually amounts to the same thing). In the three social science disciplines about which I write, the only valid criterion for judging the validity of a theory is whether it fits with existing evidence better than the alternatives. Therefore the burden is to offer a clear alternative and re-examine existing evidence in the light of it. Mainstream social scientists suspect that scholars who limit themselves to deconstructing the "assumptions" of theories to which they object are either not prepared to offer a clear alternative, are trying to shield themselves from critical intellectual scrutiny, or both.

5. For example, Berkeley, Harvard, and Michigan, where chairs were created as a legacy of the Ford Foundation.

6. This is an important development that deserves more space than I am able to devote to it here, and it would have been unthinkable in 1977. Within my own discipline of sociology, one example of this trend is the career pattern of Nan Lin, a graduate of a Taiwan university who received his Ph.D. in sociology in the US, and who became a widely respected quantitative analyst of social networks and social stratification before moving almost exclusively into China research in the early 1980s. Other examples are such leading sociologists as Peter Blau, Phyllis Moen, Nancy Tuma, Anthony Oberschal, John Logan, Donald Treiman, and Barbara Entwistle, who became involved in collaborative research projects in China with senior China specialists or PRC students. Yet another example is Craig Calhoun, theorist, historical sociologist, analyst of social movements, and now President of the Social Science Research Council, who has written an outstanding book on the 1989 Beijing student movement, having observed it from beginning to end as a visiting lecturer in Beijing.

7. See, e.g., Andrew G. Walder, "China's Transitional Economy: Interpreting its Significance," in Andrew G. Walder, ed., *China's Transitional Economy* (Oxford: Oxford University Press, 1996), pp. 1–17.

Chapter 8

South Asian Studies
Futures Past

Nicholas B. Dirks

ORIGINS

South Asian studies in the United States began in the conjuncture between Sanskritic scholarship and the strategic concerns and contexts of World War II. [1] This conjuncture has had vast importance in the shaping of South Asian area studies, which in its early years was dominated by concerns having to do on the one hand with ancient Indic civilization and on the other with contemporary society, politics, and economy. Only in recent years, in the wake first of the critique of Orientalism, and subsequently of the rise of Subaltern Studies, have the fields of colonial and postcolonial studies, modern history, and contemporary cultural studies emerged as a new conjunctural foundation for the study of South Asia, albeit one still unevenly represented in some of the principal area centers. It is the aim of this paper to tell the story of this transition, and to speculate in preliminary ways about the larger implications of this transition as we look towards the next century.

The person at the heart of the original conjuncture was W. Norman Brown, [2] founder of the University of Pennsylvania's Department of South Asia Regional Studies and Professor of Sanskrit at Penn between 1926, when Franklin Edgerton vacated the Sanskrit Chair and moved to Yale, and 1966, when Brown retired. Along with several specialists of the Near East, Brown founded the Oriental Studies Department in 1931, and he played a key role in initial discussions in the 1930s, some of them sponsored by the Committee on Indic and Iranian Studies of the American Council of Learned Societies. But it was the war, and the dearth of personnel trained to deal with issues in contemporary Asia, that crystallized these discussions, both for South Asia and other area studies initiatives. The University of Pennsylvania was the only University conducting

341

any courses of intensive language and area study during the war, and it was at the University of Pennsylvania that South Asian studies was to be born soon after the war was over.

In 1944 Brown advocated the serious development and funding of Oriental Studies in a draft document in which he wrote: "During the course of the war the US govt. agencies have needed information about the Orient to a degree far beyond anticipation... Our nation must never again be caught so ill-equipped with knowledge and specialists on the Orient as it was at the end of 1941. The postwar Orient will also probably be freer than before to engage in trade with the Occident... To meet this new situation America will need to acquire information and develop personel able to handle the increased political, business, and cultural relations."[3] In 1947 he revised this draft and expanded his vision of Oriental Studies: "It is... possible for us in the West to view the Orient as a large area with a certain number of problems and cultural movements common throughout its major divisions. This has been the condition in the Orient throughout 5000 years... Today the whole Orient has a common political problem of reaction against occidental colonialism; it has a general economic problem of developing its natural and human resources to produce an industrial civilization which can exist beside that of the West; it is bound to expand trade relations between its different divisions; it has inner social and cultural adjustments to make between its own great divisions, and then with the West."[4] It was with this intellectual argument and rhetorical justification that Brown advocated Asian studies. The context for interdisciplinary regional studies was in large part the result of this broad based sense of world civilizational areas in which the present—however embedded in the historical experience of colonialism and no matter how quickly drawn into the spiral of modernization and technological transformation—could not be understood without taking into account the great sweep of the civilizational past.[5] The broad contours of Edward Said's critique of "Orientalism" fit the case precisely.[6]

Soon after rewriting this draft document, Brown abandoned the idea of regional Oriental studies and argued instead for the development of a more bounded version of South Asian regional studies. No doubt this decision correlated with the announcement of India's independence in the summer of 1947, the very summer that the University of Pennsylvania offered a summer school in Indian studies for the first time. This summer session, funded by the ACLS among other sources, served as the basis for the establishment of the Department of South Asia Regional Studies in 1948, an institutional development that was funded by the Carnegie, Rockefeller, and Ford Foundations.[7] Brown recruited a number of scholars who had worked with him first during the war in Washington, where they furnished South Asian expertise for military and strategic purposes, initially in the Research and Analysis Division, later in the planning staff of the Office of Strategic Services: Holden Furber, a British imperial historian, Daniel Thorner, an economist who was later fired by Penn as a result of McCarthy's red scare, and Dorothy Spencer, an anthropologist. By the academic year 1949–50, a complete program for South Asia Regional Studies, both at the undergraduate and graduate levels, had been established under Brown's leadership, and an affiliated faculty of twenty one scholars, covering such fields as geography, linguistics, Hindustani, sociology, and other affiliated fields in Asian studies, were listed in the catalog.

The Department of South Asian Studies (and the area center that subsequently developed out of this initiative once federal funding was established for area studies in the 1950s) at Penn both trained many of the first generation of U.S. South Asianists and provided a model for and a set of institutional and intellectual concerns critical to the development of South Asian studies across the United States. Additionally, graduate students interested in South Asia but working at other Universities often went to the summer sessions at Penn and established ideas and contacts that carried Penn's influence far and wide. In the summer of 1948, according to the reminiscences of Robert Crane,[8] four scholars who went on to play major roles in South Asian studies all attended the summer session and began close professional and personal associations that were to last for some thirty years and affect developments at Universities as various as Chicago, Michigan, and Duke, as well as at Penn. One of these was Richard Lambert, a prominent sociologist who later succeeded Brown as Chair of the Penn Department in 1966, and was one of the chief advocates for South Asian studies in the 1960s and 70s. Also in Philadelphia that summer was Richard Park, a political scientist who earned a Ph.D. from Harvard in 1951 for work on India before joining the faculty at Berkeley that same year, later becoming the first Director of the Berkeley South Asia Program where he also created the Modern India Project, which was sponsored by the Ford Foundation and ran between 1954 and 1957. In 1959 Park moved to the University of Michigan, where Crane had begun teaching Indian history in 1956. According to Crane, the South Asia Program at Michigan was "designed as a multi-disciplinary program, a format already well established. . . in the Center for Japanese Studies. The Asian Studies Committee of the University was creating a new, multidisciplinary undergraduate core course in comparative Asian civilizations. This new core course received Foundation and University support and this enhanced our need for qualified South Asianists on the faculty. That facilitated a challenging offer to Richard Park who, in 1959, became an Associate Professor of Political Science and Director of the new Center for Southern Asian Studies."[9] Park not only continued to play a major role in the development of South Asian studies at Michigan and elsewhere (ultimately becoming President of the Association for Asian Studies in 1978), he soon became one of Norman Brown's key collaborators in the establishment of the American Institute for Indian Studies in 1961.

In many ways, then, W. Norman Brown set the tone and the most prominent institutional context and agenda for the early development of South Asian studies in the United States, both through his intellectual vision and his institutional investments. His legacy continues to be seen at Penn, and perhaps even more importantly in the American Institute of Indian Studies which since its origins has been the primary funding agent for U.S. doctoral and postdoctoral research on South Asia. Given his preeminent importance in the establishment of South Asian studies, it is worth dwelling for a moment on Brown's own scholarly interests and commitments.. Brown was classically trained as a Sanskritist, earning his Ph.D. in 1916 under Maurice Bloomfield at Johns Hopkins (six years after his father, who had been a missionary in India, also attained a Ph.D. in Sanskrit under Bloomfield at Hopkins for a thesis on the human body in the Upanisads).[10] Norman's thesis had been on the relationship between the Pancatantra and modern Indian folklore, and was part of a broader collaboration that included Franklin Edgerton's more philologically based work on the classical text. Brown's own work bridged philological and contemporary issues, demonstrating, according to Rosane Rocher, "a basic interest in studying the Indian tradition from its most ancient sources to its most recent manifestations."[11] Rocher also notes that this mix of interests seemed based in part on the fact that Brown had spent a number of years in India as a young boy with his missionary father, and could never completely adapt to the European based philological classicism of Sanskrit studies as it existed in the U.S. at the time. Although he established a formidable reputation as a classical scholar, he was interested in addressing contemporary issues from an early stage in his career. During the 1930s he wrote a manuscript entitled, "Why Conflict in India," which described political developments in the Indian subcontinent and, according to Rocher, "evinced strong sympathies for the nationalist movement." Doubtless it was because of this interest that he was called to Washington during the war, at which time he was assigned the task of collecting information and preparing reports on various aspects of the contemporary Indian scene by regional area.

It was on the basis both of the unpublished manuscript prepared before the war, and his wartime experience in Washington, that Brown ultimately wrote a book entitled *The United States and India and Pakistan*, published in 1953 in the American Foreign Policy Library by Harvard University Press. In 1954 it was awarded the Watamull prize, given by the American Historical Association, for the best book in the history of India, a sad commentary on state of Indian historiography at the time given its general textbook character. The book provided a basic summary of Indian history, from the Indus Valley, through British colonial history, to partition, and presented a great deal of material about contemporary politics, economic development, and relations between the United States and both India and Pakistan. However, Brown's scholarly background and interests emerge at various points in the narrative. For example, he writes early on in the book, "The greatest achievements of characteristic Indian civilization are in religion and philosophy[12]." And for him, these achievements are not only Hindu, they refer in particular to an abstract form of monistic philosophy associated with the term advaita and the thinker Sankara. Brown's Orientalist perspective also shows through when he discusses language groups in India. He calls Sanskrit the "cement that bound together diverse linguistic groups in a cultural unity, and though the Aryan language complex is an immigrant in India, we commonly call the country's culture Aryan. . ."[13] He goes on to say that, "the preeminence of Sanskrit as a medium of educated communication throughout India was impaired by the Muslims as they spread over the country. . . In the period of their power the position of Sanskrit declined."[14] In the wake of partition and within the context of major tensions both between India and Pakistan and between Muslims and Hindus within India, such scholarly statements are simultaneously unexceptional and deeply problematic. In fact, it would be difficult to claim that Sanskrit was ever a cement of the kind adumbrated by Brown. It would further be simultaneously wrong and politically dangerous to suggest that "Muslims" as a community "impaired" the preeminence of Sanskrit. And although Brown was sympathetic with the cause of Indian nationalism, his fundamental lack of suspicion and critique about the role played by colonial power in the prelude to partition allows him to follow up his pronouncements about the role of Muslims in disrupting the cultural unity of India with the following, even more problematic, statement: "By far the most effective force in separating Indian communities from one another and so producing national disunity has been religion. At the same time religion, at least in the case of Hinduism, contributed to the formation, growth, and power of nationalism."[15] In the aftermath of the destruction of the mosque in Ayodhya, these are precisely the kinds of statements that are being actively contested for political and scholarly reasons by intellectuals, activists, and scholars in India as well as the West.

While Brown's intentions were framed within his own larger goals to increase understanding and exchange between India (and Pakistan) and the United States, it seems obvious now that his sense of modern Indian history was profoundly shaped by his disciplinary concern with issues of religion and classical Sanskritic (and in his terms "Hindu") civilization. Given his founding role in South Asian studies, as well as his own popular writings about South Asia, these views both established their authority on the weight of colonialist and Indological knowledge and worked to further establish, within the context of postwar/cold-war American liberalism, a whole set of fundamental "truths" about the essential nature of religious identity and ontology in the Indian subcontinent. In his book, Brown explains the partition of India as "a direct result of communalism... The Muslims in pre-partition India disliked the beliefs and ways of the Hindus, distrusted them, and as a minority feared for their treatment if they should have to live in a state where the Hindu majority had power. The Hindus in their turn disliked the ways of the Muslims, and, though a majority, feared the rise to power of the Muslims under whom they had experienced centuries of oppression... The basis of Hindu-Muslim communalism lies in cultural differences."[16] Brown goes on to give potted versions of Islam and Hinduism, in which Islam is represented as requiring a strident form of monotheistic uniformity, whereas Hinduism is open to an endlessly proliferating array of diverse possibilities.

In promulgating these views of religion, and of the implications of religious life for political and cultural outcomes and convictions, Brown, with the greatest of authority, naturalized the partition of India even as he recognized it as a disaster and a source of perilous insecurity for the subcontinent. Brown purveyed similarly Orientalist constructions of India with equal conviction and authority in the remaining pages of the book, averring that Hindus had no theory of the state and precious little in the way of a history of the state outside of standard assumptions about oriental despotism, that caste was an ironclad social fact destined to influence politics in much the way as predicted by the colonial ethnographer H. H. Risley[17] and that women were horribly backward. All this served as the frame for Brown's review of the depressing condition of agricultural production, oppressive poverty both in the countryside and the cities, and the many problems confronting the establishment of democratic politics across the subcontinent. Nevertheless, Brown was convinced that greater knowledge about the subcontinent, as well as cultural exchange between its nations and the United States, would lead to a happier and more prosperous world. He was tireless in his criticisms of those Americans who out of ignorance or malice (or both) had contributed to negative images of the subcontinent, and convinced that the natural, though frequently difficult, friendship between the United States and India would be furthered significantly by educational and cultural developments. Thus he saw his work with University programs, as well as in the solicitation of foundation support for the development of South Asia (and other) area studies, the constant lobbying for government support for programs in education and culture, as a life work that was simultaneously political and academic. And in this endeavor, the establishment of the American Institute of Indian Studies, financed principally by Indian rupee repayment for loans to India from the U.S.[18] and by a start-up grant from Ford, and dedicated to the support of American academic research in South Asian studies, was his crowning achievement.

Norman Brown's life not only documents many of the most important aspects of the early formation of South Asian studies in the United States, it also helps to explain why area studies at the University of Pennsylvania, and elsewhere, privileged a combination of classical Indological scholarship and modern political and economic concern in the early history of the field. Penn was soon joined by a number of other institutions that sought to introduce the serious study of South Asia into their programs of research and teaching during the postwar academic boom years, among them Berkeley, Michigan, Chicago, Columbia, and Wisconsin. In the early years, the most important institutional developments outside Penn took place at the University of Chicago, where the study of South Asia emerged principally out of the efforts of Robert Redfield and Milton Singer to introduce a comprehensive program in the comparative study of civilizations. Singer, who began teaching social science core courses in the college at Chicago after completing his Ph.D. under Rudolph Carnap in philosophy, became a close associate of Robert Redfield's in the late 1940s, just as Redfield was attempting to develop an integrated plan for the study of culture and civilization. At that time, Redfield was a major figure in social science and in anthropology at Chicago, having served as dean and principal advisor to Robert Maynard Hutchins for many years, and having written important work on folk cultures, the folk-urban continuum, and the civilizational contexts for understanding local communities.[19] In the late 1940s, Redfield drafted a plan for an Institute in Cultural Studies that he saw as the basis for a comprehensive and "comparative study of the principal systems of values of the societies that have mattered most in history."[20] Upon hearing that the Ford Foundation would support his project in 1951,[21] he recruited a number of colleagues to help him run the program; most important among these was Singer.

Milton Singer had first become a close intellectual colleague of Redfield's when he wrote a paper on the study of American civilization in 1949 titled "How the American got his Character,"[22] and, by the fall of 1951, was co-teaching courses with him in cultural anthropology. In large part through this association, Singer came to see himself as an anthropologist, and in 1955 accepted a formal position within the department of anthropology at Chicago. In the early 1950s, Redfield and Singer used their grant money to sponsor a series of conferences in "civilizational studies," collecting the proceedings in a book series entitled, "Comparative Studies of Cultures and Civilizations" published by the University of Chicago Press. During this time Redfield worked out many of his earlier ideas about great and little traditions, civilizational process, and the role of anthropology in investigating folk cultures within a larger civilizational context. Singer worked with Redfield in the preparation of a methodological treatise, never finally published, that began to chart out a set of disciplinary procedures privileging context based anthropological fieldwork and local study for little traditions and the text based study of language, literature, philosophy, cultural history and the history of civilizations for understanding great traditions. In the early phase, they were especially influential in the field of Chinese studies. But soon Singer turned his attention to the study of India, and he became primarily interested in the development of South Asian civilizational studies.

In the academic year 1953–54, Singer engaged in a year long postdoctoral study of India, spending the fall term at Penn studying with Brown, and the winter term at Berkeley working with the anthropologist David Mandelbaum.[23] While at Berkeley, Singer was especially influenced by the work of M.N. Srinivas, an Oxford trained anthropologist who had published his *Religion and Society under the Coorgs of South India* in 1952. Singer quickly grasped that

Srinivas' idea of sanskritization, in which notions of Brahmanic Hinduism spread in part through a process of status emulation, could be seen as an illustration of Redfield's ideas about the interactions of great and little traditions. Inspired by Redfield and Srinivas, Singer committed himself to a plan for field studies in India that led to many years of sustained research and publication on India. At Chicago he began immediately to orient the Chicago civilizations project toward the study of India. Singer and Redfield planned a symposium on the Indian village that brought eight social anthropologists to work with graduate students in Chicago, leading to the volume edited by McKim Marriott entitled *Village India: Studies in the Little Community* (Chicago, 1955). The papers all argued that villages in India were not self sufficient units, isolated in conventional anthropological terms from larger civilizational forms and processes, and established India as a primary site for the working out of Redfield's and Singer's programmatic agenda. Marriott's paper argued that classical and folk forms, and by implication civilizational and village sites, were vitally connected, through processes he labelled particularization and universalization. Shortly after the volume's publication, Marriott was recruited back to Chicago, where he had done his Ph.D., from Berkeley, and once there he went on to advocate the importance of empirically based long term field work studies in India.

If the University of Pennsylvania was dominated by Brown's combination of Indological scholarship and current events, and Berkeley's South Asia initiatives were activated principally through the work of the anthropologist David Mandelbaum,[24] Chicago's history reveals a combination of these two tendencies in the working out of Redfield's and Singer's civilizational agenda for the study of South Asia. Anthropological concerns and fieldwork methods were linked to the textual concerns first of Sanskritists and then, increasingly, specialists in modern languages, to provide a particular disciplinary framing for South Asian studies.[25] As for other areas, political science played an important role in the first postwar decades (before methodological concerns in the discipline began to challenge the importance of comparative politics). Indeed, among Asianists in the United States, anthropology played a more

significant role for South Asian studies than any other sub-area with
the exception of Southeast Asia. And it is noteworthy that when the
University of Chicago decided to hire a tenured historian of South
Asia to develop a serious graduate program in this field, it recruited
an anthropologist with historical interests rather than an historian
who would have been, as was the case with Holden Furber at Penn,
initially trained in the history of the British empire. Bernard Cohn,
an anthropologist trained at Cornell[26] and later the chair of the
department at University of Rochester (he had been one of the
contributors to the volume *Village India*), was invited to Chicago in
1963, and he soon became the pioneer for the development of the
social history of India in the U.S. Although Cohn has introduced a
powerful note of critique to the position of anthropology in area
studies, he has also maintained a close interdisciplinary
relationship throughout the years between developments and projects
in history and anthropology.

This review of historical and disciplinary origins has suggested
ways in which South Asian studies has been produced in the United
States out of a curious conjuncture between Indology and anthropology,
in the context of a recognition of the strategic importance of South
Asia and the growing need to educate Americans, academics and
others alike, about a place that was populous but poor, largely
democratic but politically fragile, and likely to be of growing
military and political significance in a postcolonial cold-war world
system. These conjunctures both reflect and were in large part
responsible for installing a set of dominant tropes for the
representation of South Asia, perpetuating colonial and Orientalist
forms of knowledge and producing new American ones. Specifically,
serious academic study in the U.S. of the contemporary political,
social, and economic predicament of the new postcolonial nations of
South Asia was initially mediated by forms of knowledge focussing
either on ancient India or its most remote hinterlands. It is hard to
imagine a group of Hellenic scholars being called together with
fieldworkers experienced for the most part only in the village life of
peasant societies to found, say, a modern European studies program.
But there was a long history of representing India in ways that made
this history seem unexceptional, and current political and economic
dilemmas were accordingly approached in part through assumptions

about India predicated principally on readings of classic texts and
backwater contexts. Thus it was that essential statements about the
nature of Hinduism and Islam could be accepted as either true or
relevant in regard to understanding contemporary South Asia; and
thus it was that questions about the political stability of a nation
and the economic viability of a society could be evaluated in relation
to timeless truths about Indian culture. Further, this history reveals
how many components of colonial knowledge about India could be
appropriated with only minor modifications in the formation of a
new postcolonial academic orthodoxy.

THE MIDDLE PERIOD

The establishment of federal funding for area studies programs in
1959 (the National Defence Education Act, Title VI allocation, was
passed in late 1958), and the steady increase in support for the study
of foreign area languages and cultures (in the late 1950s and 60s the
Ford Foundation played a critical role in providing this support), [27]
provided a great boon to the development of South Asian studies
during the 1960s' and 70s'. The University of Pennsylvania continued
to be an important center for South Asian studies and expanded in a
number of disciplinary directions, though like other Universities
with separate departments for South Asian studies (e.g. Chicago and
Berkeley) it was able to hire an unusual concentration of language and
literature specialists. Penn became known for its powerful group of
Sanskritists (including linguists and textualists) at the same time
that it continued to be strong in social science fields such as history,
sociology, and economics. Berkeley became an important player in a
wide range of fields. Wisconsin emerged as another center for South
Asian studies with faculty appointed in fields such as political
science, sociology, and history, as well as across the humanities.
Programs of various sizes developed during these decades in places as
various as the Universities of Michigan, Washington, Minnesota,
Virginia, and Texas. Columbia had a small but well placed group of
South Asianists led by figures such as Ainslee Embree in history and
Howard Wriggens in Political Science. And Chicago grew rapidly to
become what perhaps was the most active center during these years,
certainly in the social sciences. As can be noted even in this

incomplete inventory, these were years when social science disciplines across the board discovered the importance of South Asian studies; although today it is difficult to locate South Asianists in disciplines such as sociology and economics, and indeed even, increasingly, in political science, these were years when figures such as Richard Lambert, Richard Park, Joseph Elder, and Leo Rose played central roles.

Perhaps the most important contribution of the NDEA funding of South Asian studies was the growing stress on language study during this period, in large part because of the direct linking of graduate funding to serious language learning. Many of the great early figures of South Asian studies, with the exception of the Sanskritists, had little if any knowledge of South Asian languages, and engaged in research on South Asia using either English or local interpreters. Often this was because these scholars had been "re-tooled" as South Asianists after initial training in other fields, as well as because research in areas such as election analysis involved a combination of statistical methods and interviews with high level officials, usually in English. Increasingly a new generation of scholars were trained specifically in South Asian studies with language skills and cultural expertise. At Universities such as Penn, Chicago, and Berkeley, faculty were hired during these years to teach Hindi and other Indian languages, sometimes in conjunction with other disciplinary interests. While language skills never became as important for South Asian Studies as they did for East Asian Studies, the sense of South Asia as a region that could be approached solely through English (with the occasional Sanskritist) changed dramatically during these years.

The 1960s witnessed the growing seriousness and quality of work on South Asia in a number of different regards. Amateurish prognostications about India's democratic viability were increasingly supplanted by serious analyses of political and social change. Lloyd and Susanne Rudolph, who had been hired by Chicago to teach political science, published an important study in 1967 entitled *The Modernity of Tradition* that complicated social scientific conceptions of "modernization" as well as of the constituent categories of modernity and tradition, at the same time that it built powerfully on the work of other scholars (some completing their doctoral work on

South Asia under the Rudolphs, as for example Robert Hardgrave) on subjects as various as caste politics and legal change. Bernard Cohn developed a history program at Chicago rooted in interdisciplinary methods and serious attention to language and culture. In 1970 he published an essay reviewing the state of the art in South Asian history, and noted that "the historian's contribution has largely been a negative one. The historian sensitive to social components in South Asian history has contributed to a questioning of the timeless view which social scientists have used in their discussion of modern South Asia. The historian has pointed to the complexity of the process of political change, especially in the study of the nationalist movement, by pointing to regional and caste differences in participation in the movement."[28] However, he suggested a bright and powerful future for South Asian history, based both on his assumption of fruitful interchange among social science disciplines, and the recent and promising work of younger scholars in the field, including J.H. Broomfield, Eugene Irschick, S.N. Mukherjee, John Leonard, Peter Marshall, David Kopf, Ronald Inden, and Tom Kessinger (some of whom were or had been his students).[29] Cohn was as excited by the discovery of new kinds of sources for the writing of Indian history as he was by the new historical writing itself.

Bernard Cohn's work and influence on the field more generally was innovative and highly significant not only because of his enterprising rethinking and dramatic expansion of the sources, methods, and questions of historical work, but for two other, though related, reasons. First, as mentioned before, he had been trained as an anthropologist and thus brought to his historical sensibility a lively sense of social theory as well as direct experience of village fieldwork. Indeed, many of his writings over the years have argued for new collaborations between history and anthropology, with the aim of making history more adventurous in theoretical as well as empirical terms, and of making anthropology grapple with the essential change*ful*ness of South Asian society. Second, Cohn early on developed a critical sense of British colonial rule. In a set of early papers he wrote about the history of western knowledge about India, and began to subject western social science to serious criticism. He noted in 1970 that not only was the idea of an autonomous village world in India a myth, it was a myth specifically created by the British.[30] In his early writing he focussed more on the creation of new institutions by innovations in areas such as land policy; in later writing he focused increasingly on British colonialism and its forms of knowledge. Indeed, long before the powerful critical work of Edward Said and the new field of postcolonial studies, Bernard Cohn had suggested ways in which colonial rule would not have been possible without the development of certain forms of colonial knowledge, at the same time that he critiqued the implication of western social scientific knowledge about India in the maintenance of basic colonial categories and assumptions.

Cohn's inventive sense of how to study different aspects of colonial history not only anticipated many recent theoretical developments well outside South Asian studies, it has also directly inspired a great deal of historical and anthropological work on the character of the colonial state. In Cohn's own writing, colonialism is no longer an historical irruption that has to be stripped away to get down to the real subject of anthropology, but rather the focus of the study of social transformation in all societies touched by world systems of colonial rule. For Cohn, colonialism played a critical role in the constitution of the metropole—in the formation of the state and in the development of its basic forms of knowledge—even as it shaped, through its cultural technologies of domination, much of the modern history of colonized places and peoples. Cohn has consistently written brilliant and innovative articles on various aspects of his research, ranging in focus from the massively orchestrated darbars in Delhi to the enumerative technologies of power deployed by the census, from the specific careers of terms like "village," "tribe," and "caste" to the anthropology of the colonizers as well as the colonized. Beyond his writing, Cohn has also exerted important influence on the shaping of South Asian studies through his students, his role in teaching and research at the University of Chicago, as well as through professional networks and scholarly collaboration, as for example in his early recognition of and participation in the Subaltern Studies history project. Cohn also participated in the 1983 Subaltern Studies Conference in Canberra, subsequently publishing his paper, "The Command of Grammar and the Grammar of Command," in the fourth volume of the publications of the Subaltern Studies Collective.[31]

If Cohn's critique of western social science led both to wide ranging critiques and an intense interrogation of colonial genealogies of knowledge, it for a time seemed that it was also part of an allied movement based principally in Chicago that attained a great deal of influence, particularly in anthropology, during the decade of the 1970s. I refer here to a new set of proposals made under the banner of an "ethnosociology of India." The principal architects of these new ideas were McKim Marriott and Ronald Inden. After Marriott's work convening new scholarship on village India and expanding the insights of Redfield, Singer, and Srinivas in relation to his own intensive fieldwork experience, first in Uttar Pradesh and later in Maharashtra, Marriott had become interested in the question of how to understand the nature of hierarchy in caste society. After focussing on the question of caste ranking, and the relationship of attributional statements concerning status to empirical practices in the domain of food exchange, Marriott became increasingly intrigued by cultural questions around the meaning of caste. In one sense, he built on the generally accepted understanding of the goal of social anthropological research, at least at Chicago, that Singer articulated in the following passage: "The understanding of another culture or civilization, as social and cultural anthropology rightly teaches, requires that the foreign traveler rid himself of ethnocentrism and look at another culture in its own terms. Malinowski's axiom that a major aim of ethnology is to understand the "native" from his point of view, his relation to his world, has been accepted by anthropology since the 1920's."[32] Marriott worried about how this might be accomplished with unusual intensity. Influenced in part by his colleague David Schneider that cultural domains had to be identified and described in terms consistent with the cultural object of study, Marriott began to collaborate with the historian Ronald Inden, whose 1972 Chicago dissertation had established an innovative model for the cultural analysis of early Indian texts. Deriving "native" terms and categories from classical sources such as the *Manu Dharma Sastras* (Hindu prescriptive texts about social duties and orders), Inden and Marriott wrote a series of papers in the early 1970s which argued that Indian society could be properly understood in relation to a monistic world view. Their papers combined a rigorous critique of prevailing social scientific theories and procedures—ranging from American empiricism to French idealism—with a programmatic set of recommendations for a new kind of cultural analysis, to be pursued both in textual analysis and contextual fieldwork. The primary emphasis was to be on "native" terms and categories. Ethnosociology was to mean "Indian" sociology, rather than western.

The ethnosociology project was in ascendency for quite some time, propelling many a graduate dissertation at Chicago and elsewhere, and defining a number of important conferences organized by the Social Science Research Council and other research organizations.[33] Ethnosociology was certainly an outgrowth, at least in part, of serious language study, and it was a consequence of serious frustration with a social scientific inheritance—from Weber to Durkheim, and from colonial ethnography to comparative social stratification studies—that offered little genuine guidance in the quest to understand the complex social and cultural realities of a much mystified subcontinent. However, it soon became clear that Cohn's initial support gave way to greater and greater qualification, that the Rudolphs among many others had residual commitments to comparative social science that they did not wish to relinguish, and that scholars outside of Chicago, even in nearby Michigan, failed to accept the "Indianness" of this new endeavor. In a review of a book on Bengali kinship by Ronald Inden and Ralph Nicholas,[34] Tom Trautmann, an historian of ancient India at the University of Michigan, asked whether anyone outside of Chicago believed any of this.[35] And although some scholars in India were intrigued by this new work, including T.N. Madan and Veena Das, most "Indian" social scientists were unclear why these Chicago anthropologists were informing them of the realities of Indian social science. In retrospect, ethnosociology was a peculiar product of a certain strand of American liberal social theory (which stressed cultural relativism as the antidote to historical and political issues of power) that in some ways was more of the same: a heady stew made of equal parts Indology and cultural anthropology. And while ethnosociology took advantage of, and further encouraged, serious language study, encouraging full immersion in classical texts and ethnographic contexts, it represented a retreat from earlier area studies agendas. For example, there was no room within ethnosociology for a critical

engagement with "modernity", since all modern forms were signs of
the contamination of the west; likewise, there was no interest within
the project in contemporary politics or social-economic dilemmas.
And, ethnosociology involved an essentialization of India which
rendered Indian cultural truth both timeless (i.e. ancient) and
religious (i.e. Hindu). Viewed today, ethnosociology appears,
despite its many claims, not only as another mainstream
manifestation of western social science, but as an academic movement
that ignored modern India not least in its steadfast refusal to consider
how it collaborated in the naturalization of India as a Hindu land
devoid of history.

At the same time that ethnosociology played such an important
role in Chicago, a number of scholars in the U.S. were engaged in
serious study of Islamic history, institutions, and identities in South
Asia. Among many other examples, Barbara Metcalf, who taught at
Penn for much of the decade, wrote a study of the Deoband revival
movement;[36] John Richards, who taught at Wisconsin before moving to
Duke, wrote on Mughal rule in Golkonda in southern India,[37] Richard
Eaton of the University of Arizona published an account of Sufism in
Bijapur,[38] Richard Barnett published his work on the history of
Awadh in the seventeenth and early eighteenth centuries,[39] and
David Lelyveld of the University of Minnesota finished his own
study of Sir Sayyid Ahmad Khan and the making of Aligarh Muslim
University.[40]

There were other scholarly voices engaged in very different kinds
of research and teaching during these years. Burton Stein, an
historian of ancient south India who taught at the University of
Hawaii but was a visiting Professor at places such as Penn and
Chicago, inspired a group of students who worked on different aspects
of the social, cultural, and economic history of southern India,
especially in the Tamil country.[41] Stein, who like Cohn had interests
that bridged history and anthropology, never completely shed his
interest in material determinations (even when he failed to identify
them in much of his own work on medieval south Indian peasant state
and society), also attempted for a number of years to establish a
dialogue with a group of historians trained at Cambridge, among
them Chris Bayly and David Washbrook. Stein shared with Bayly

a Braudelian interest in long term change, with Washbrook a concern to chart the history of capitalism in India. He was more patient with Cambridge suspicion of Indian nationalist ideology than most other American historians of India, most notably Leonard Gordon, Eugene Irschick, and Stanley Wolpert, despite his extremely non-Cambridge interest in the subject of community. Stein's interest in the longue duree, and his fascination with the connection of cultural questions and material logics, exercised an important corrective for a number of scholars given the dominance of abstract cultural analysis brought about by the institutional centrality of certain people at the University of Chicago and the continued weight of Indological interest. He provided the basis for important connections between American and British scholarship after moving from Hawaii to London, while playing a continuously innovative role in the development of workshop ideas and research projects. He also inspired a great deal of work on Southern India, the Tamil country in particular, and gave rise to a number of studies that attempted to link premodern and modern questions. Not only did Stein influence my own attempt to write about political authority in Tamil Nadu between the seventh and the nineteenth centuries, he also influenced the work of David Ludden, a Penn trained historian[42] who focussed on agrarian issues and wrote a powerful study of peasant society and institutions in the southern Tamil region. Stein also encouraged the economic historian Sanjay Subramanian—who later collaborated with the religious and literary scholars David Shulman and V. Narayana Rao in a study of Nayaka cultural history[43]—to think about cultural issues.

South Asian studies in the United States in its first thirty years was for the most part a very American affair. There were multiple relations with England, not only because of the close relationship of academic institutions and disciplines between the two nations, but because South Asian studies was more firmly rooted in British history than it was in the U.S., where Asia typically means East Asia. However, in the early decades, very few scholars from South Asia were actually hired to teach in North American Universities. Granted, the study of India meant that certain Indian scholarly interlocutors became particularly important (e.g. M.N. Srinivas in anthropology, Rajni Kothari in political science, Romila Thapar in history, and a whole host of distinguished development economists) at the same time that increasing levels of exchange, collaboration, and institutional participation led to closer and closer intellectual and social ties among academics. Although as time went on there was steady growth in the numbers of South Asians who secured positions in the U.S. academy, in the early years many of these examples figured in language study rather than the mainline social sciences and humanities. And many of the debates held by American academics—over the significance and impact of green revolution technologies, over questions about the relationship of agricultural and industrial development, about social redistributive policies, about levels of state control over economic growth, over the stability of the Indian state and the future of democracy, and over the perdurance of caste, untouchability, and communal tensions in Indian society and political life—were also held with and in close relationship to debates within India itself. But these debates were frequently characterized by various tensions: over the relationship of American academics to U.S. state policies (e.g. at the time of the Bangladesh war), over the relationship between academics in India and the U.S. to the emergency called by Prime Minister Indira Gandhi between 1975 and 1977, in relation to the place of Marxism in the Indian academy and the resilient concern about the role of U.S. cultural, political, and economic imperialism, and over the role of development and its perceived connections to U.S. interests, international markets, and the continued commitments of Indian state socialism. There was still a marked divide between knowledge in situ and in the academy. For most American academics, it was as it had been both for Milton Singer and for McKim Marriott: the key questions in the social science of India were still motivated by the general problematic of how do "we" understand "them?"

I have so far said little about some of the fields that played extremely important roles in the history of South Asian studies in the U.S. The largest percentage of active academics, according to statistics maintained by the Association for Asian Studies in 1991, were in religion and philosophy. In earlier years, these fields were dominated by missionary connections and backgrounds. The Divinity School at the University of Chicago, for example, regularly trained

missionaries about to go off to do church work in India, at least up to
the point that missionary activity in India began to be controlled and
then curtailed after Indian independence. But in later years the
fields of religion and philosophy maintained a strong interest in
things Indian. It requires only a casual survey of departments in recent
years to realize that when religion departments think of hiring a
"non-Western" position they often turn to India—or at least to
Hinduism and Buddhism—before turning to most other areas/world-
religions. The concentration of these kinds of positions are skewed in
part by the complex history of institutional relations between the
church and the university; Divinity Schools are sometimes set off
from other academic departments, and public institutions such as
Michigan have no religion departments. Additionally, few
philosophy departments hire in non-Western areas, and Sanskritists
are usually hired in departments in one aspect or another of Asian
studies, or in religion, rather than in classics or comparative
literature. But the study of Indian religion is alive and well, though
frequently partitioned in the sense that Islamists tend to be
specialists in the Middle East rather than South Asia (which has
many more Muslims), and South Asia religionists tend to be
specialists in Hinduism. Happily, there are exceptions in this last
regard, for example in the concentration of South Asia scholars at
Duke and the University of North Carolina.

While much important scholarship and teaching has been done in
areas defined in one way or another by religion, there are obvious
problems with the disproportionate attention paid to religion rather
than, say, contemporary politics. And given the fact that
contemporary politics in South Asia has problematized, and
politicized, the study of religion to an unprecedented extent, the
disciplinary concentrations and divisions have all too often
exacerbated basic problems of knowledge. If it is the case that the
most likely exposure of students in U.S. Universities to the
subcontinent would be in courses on world religions, it is also the case
that South Asianists have played important roles in stressing the
need for curriculum reform around, for example, the requirements in
Western Civilization, long before multiculturalism and identity
politics inaugurated culture wars on American campuses. At
Universities such as Chicago, where Singer concentrated his early

attention not just on conferences but on the development of a year long course in South Asian Civilization, and Columbia, which produced the famous source books for the study of both East Asian and South Asian traditions, some of the first requirements for study in areas outside the west concerned South Asia.

Despite the classicism of much South Asianist scholarship, there was widespread recognition from the start that academics had to address questions of modernity. W. Norman Brown's recruitment to South Asian studies was mediated in important ways by the security considerations of the U.S. state during the war and in the cold war era. But it is also the case that nationalism in India, and the long heroic struggle against British colonial rule, fell on sympathetic ears in the U.S., from the reporting of William Shirer for the Chicago Tribune, to W. Norman Brown's own predilections, to Martin Luther King's admiration for and use of the non violent methods of Mahatma Gandhi. Historians in the United States for many years focussed on issues around the nationalist movement, and tended to take serious issue with British academic trends that worked to disparage the integrity of nationalist mobilization. And academics from a variety of disciplines took particular interest in the lives and works of Gandhi and Nehru. An inventory of works on Gandhi over the last fifty years would touch every discipline and betray a steady fascination with the man who still appears to many as emblematic of the best of modern India. Interestingly enough, however, only recently has Gandhi once again become central to debates over political theory and cultural history within contemporary India itself.

MODERN TIMES

The modern era of South Asian studies might be said to have begun in 1978, with the publication of Edward Said's *Orientalism.* Although Said wrote principally about the Middle East, and from the disciplinary position of literary studies, his critique could be directly transposed onto South Asian studies, both in relation to the colonial past and the scholarly present (and the myriad relations between the two). In the early years after the publication of this magisterial work, a number of South Asianists reacted sharply against Said's critique,[44] but it soon became clear that there was no going back to an age of pre-Orientalism innocence. Although there were many contentious arguments about the status of the Saidian critique and its relevance for South Asian studies, as for example at the year long seminar held at the University of Pennsylvania in 1988–89 entitled "Orientalism and Beyond: Perspectives from South Asia," Said's extraordinary intervention has now become a canonical prelude to most contemporary writing in the U.S. about South Asia.[45]

In an essay I published in 1992,[46] I wrote that, "During the last decade, it has been impossible to engage in the study of the colonial world without either explicit or implicit reference to [Said's] charge that not only our sources but also our basic categories and assumptions have been shaped by colonial rule." The power of the Saidian critique was precisely that it linked colonial knowledge with contemporary scholarship, and that it did so with far more polemical fervor and historiographical range than even the earlier suggestions of Bernard Cohn. Orientalism, in the paraphrase I gave back in 1992, "whether in the guise of colonial cultures of belief or of more specialized subcultures of scholarship, shared fundamental premises about the East, serving to denigrate the present, deny history, and repress any sensibility regarding contemporary political, social, or cultural autonomy and potential in the colonized world. The result has been the relentless Orientalization of the Orient, the constant reiteration of tropes conferring inferiority and subordination. . ."[47] In a review essay first published in 1990 considering the question of what a post-Orientalist history would look like, Gyan Prakash wrote that, "The attention to the historicity of knowledge demanded by the invitation to chart post-Orientalist historiography, therefore, runs counter to those procedures that ground the third world in essences and see history as determined by those essential elements. It requires the rejection of those modes of thinking which configure the third world in such irreducible essences as religiosity, underdevelopment, poverty, nationhood, non-Westerness; and it asks that we repudiate attempts to see third-world histories in terms of these quintessential principles."[48] Prakash went on to propose what he called a post-foundationalist history, in which attempts to grapple with the fundamental historicity of modernity in South Asia would necessarily be combined with critical attention to the historical formation of basic categories for the representation of South Asia.

Prakash's critique both echoed and advanced a critical consideration of a great deal of writing on South Asia, in the U.S., in Europe, and in India. Part of the specific merit of the paper was his sympathetic review of various genres of nationalist and Marxist history in India, which worked against Orientalism both as a structure of rule and a source of authority but found itself implicated nevertheless in some of the key categories of Orientalist thought.[49] The paper also worked to place the contributions of Subaltern Studies history in relation to historiographical events and questions both in India and in the American academy. Prakash also invoked my own critique of scholarly literatures on caste in the context of an attempt to rethink what a history of caste (through a study of political authority and social relations in the Tamil countryside from the seventeenth century to the present) might imply about dominant assumptions in the field. From the standpoint of *Orientalism*, it was even clearer than before that the proposals by Louis Dumont in his classic anthropological treatise, *Homo Hierarchicus*, were virtual parodies of Orientalist knowledge, even within Dumont's claim that he was critiquing notions of individualism and egalitarianism in the West.[50] And it became equally clear in retrospect that the entire ethnosociological project was deeply problematic in precisely the registers laid out by Said.[51] Ronald Inden wrote an ambitious book in 1990 in which he debunked the Indological essentialization of India, claiming that he wished "to make possible studies of 'ancient' India that would restore the agency that those histories have stripped from its people and institutions. Scholars did this by imagining an India kept eternally ancient by various Essences attributed to it, most notably that of caste."[52] Given Inden's pre-eminent importance in mapping an ethnosociological project in which caste, defined first and foremost by Manu,[53] was the distinctive feature of Indian civilization, it is hard to read this book without the sneaking suspicion that it was written at least in part as a fervent attempt at self-exculpation.[54]

Prakash's critique was not universally admired, even by those who accepted the force of Edward Said's critical intervention. Two English historians of India, David Washbrook and Rosalind O'Hanlon, wrote a spirited reply to Prakash,[55] sparking off a debate on such matters as the importance of Subaltern Studies, the status of Marxism in Indian historiography, the place of cultural analysis and reflection in the American academy, and the implications of poststructuralist theory and postmodernist dispositions in the writing of history and anthropology.[56] O'Hanlon, whose about-face on matters of theoretical perspective and historiographical sympathy seemed bewildering to many given her earlier sympathetic review of Subaltern Studies history, and Washbrook, one of the earliest polemicists of the Cambridge school, pilloried Prakash's advocacy of post-foundational history for the theoretical and political entailments of poststructuralism, declared Prakash's approval of Ranajit Guha and Subaltern Studies history to be contradictory given his/their primordial and exclusionary commitment to the foundational category of the nation, and argued that even Prakash's use of the work of historians such as Bernard Cohn and myself was flawed because of our interest in the relationship between culture and power rather than on questions concerning class and wealth. Washbrook and O'Hanlon took glee in pointing out what they identified as the myriad contradictions and confusions of Prakash's position, arguing that Derrida is really a closet essentialist, that neither postmodernism nor identity politics—assuming that these characterizations are at base what Prakash is really all about—has claim to anything like an emancipatory political project, that Said's use of Foucault is undermined by his residual commitment to a humanist critique, and that Prakash's historiographical position is an expression of the same tendencies displayed by James Clifford and other anthropological critics who displace the true domain of politics into the American academic theater of self-representation. Instead, we are told that politics can be preserved only by taking class, and historical materialist analysis, as foundational for any historical project, and that postcolonial critics such as Prakash ignore class so as to disguise their own position as victors rather than victims in a world capitalist system that produces, *inter alia*, the ideological underpinnings of American academic political culture.

Washbrook and O'Hanlon were ostensibly most concerned by Prakash's sense of inadequacy in the work of Marxist historiography on the political economy of India, though they seemed especially defensive of the work of the Cambridge School, and used the work of

C.A. Bayly, a reputed historian of South Asia who is no more a Marxist than he is a Subalternist, to exemplify their own sense of what should be done. Without going further into the thicket of argumentation over politics and postmodernism, what really seems to be at stake in this debate is the place of colonialism in the historical representation of South Asia. Washbrook and O'Hanlon only referred to British colonialism once, to disparage James Clifford and the operations of liberal ideology. In this single reference it becomes clear that while the great sin of colonialism was to develop the idea of culture to argue for cultural difference, the great sin of the American academy is to accept "culture" in any sense, even inverted and transformed through nationalist struggle, as anything more than a mystification. Historiographical attention to colonialism, rather than identifying key political dynamics behind the exercise of capitalist domination by England of India, instead merely licenses postcolonial anxiety about cultural rather than core economic matters. In turn, a history focussing on world capitalism belies the possibility of such difference under the weight of global forces that differentiate among peoples based on access to the means of production rather than the epiphenomenal questions of ethnicity, nationality, and race. The problem then with the historical anthropology of Cohn, Dirks, and Prakash or the historical rhetoric of Subaltern historians is that colonialism—and questions precisely of ethnicity, nationality, and race—becomes the primary category of modern historical analysis. And here is where a foundational Marxism blends seamlessly with Cambridge School history, for the latter—whether in the hands of Anil Seal, John Gallagher, or David Washbrook [57]—used networks of material interest and "class" analysis to disparage nationalism and ultimately deny the historical reality of colonialism (which in this view was just another ruse to justify and disguise the world operations of capitalist exploitation).

Prakash replied to his critics in equally polemical terms, suggesting not only that it was unfair to place his views in a relation of "strange resemblance to colonial strategies of knowledge," but that if anything, there was a strange resemblance between the downplaying of the historical significance of colonialism and the insistence on one kind of totalizing historical mastery.[58] More to the point, Prakash[59] wrote that "The Cambridge School's long dormant historiography of India, which sought in the 1970s to delegitimize nationalism's challenge to colonialism by portraying the former as nothing but an ideological cover for the elite's manipulation of power and profit, comes roaring back once again to salvage colonialism, this time by subordinating colonialism to the logic of unfolding capitalism."[60] And while Washbrook and O'Hanlon tried to oppose both colonial history and culture as a category of analysis (or of history) to questions of material reality and class formation, it is certainly the case that Cambridge School history in its origins was neither Marxist in the sense that it was allied to a politically emancipatory project nor self-conscious in any sense about its own uncritical relationship to colonial sources and assumptions. Cambridge school history saw Indian elites as British collaborators, Indian nationalism as elite self-interest, and Indian politics as something that British colonial administration was justified in treating as illegimate at best.

In fact, the antinomies of the above debate hardly capture the range of attempts to integrate analyses of culture and political economy over the course of the past twenty years. Additionally, whatever else is involved in the return of interest in colonialism, it provides a rubric for exchange and collaboration among many new players in South Asian studies, without the invidious subordination of the "East" (now always in quotation marks) that was part of earlier interests in imperial history (or imperial literature). The recognition that colonialism has been the historical vector both for world domination and for the South Asian encounter with modernity (as well as with modern forms of capitalism) has opened South Asian studies to theoretical and substantive issues that have taken South Asianist scholars far away from the initial agendas, and commitments, of area studies. It has also become part of a theoretically sophisticated interrogation of the fundamental nature of modernity, and what happens to the categories of the modern when introduced as part of a structure of colonial power.[61]

These reflections can be traced by a cursory look at the workshops and conferences sponsored by the South Asia joint committee of the Social Science Research Council over the last two decades. The South

Asia Political Economy Project (SAPE),[62] organized by scholars such as Michelle McAlpin, an economic historian, Veena Das, an anthropologist from Delhi University, Paul Brass, a political scientist, among others, attempted to link critical political economy concerns with cultural analysis. A similar venture on agricultural terminology was organized by Arjun Appadurai, an anthropologist then at Penn, and Pranab Bardhan, an economist at Berkeley. Barbara Stoler Miller, a Sanskritist, organized a conference on patronage with art historians, historians, and anthropologists. Susan Wadley, an anthropologist, collaborated with Pranab Bardhan on a workshop concerning, "Differential Mortality and Female Healthcare in South Asia." Appadurai, along with fellow scholar Carol Breckenridge, historian and founding editor of the journal *Public Culture,* organized a series of conferences in the late 80s and early 90s around questions concerning the transformations of modernity in South Asia in relation to global developments and influences.[63] A series of conferences linking feminist scholarship and activism began to introduce serious feminist concerns into areas as diverse as anthropological research on violence to historical research on migration and political change to women's political participation in and recruitment to Hindu fundamentalist movements. Humanist scholars (among them, the Sanskritist Sheldon Pollack of the University of Chicago) concerned with South Asian languages, classical as well as modern, organized workshops that attempted to stimulate new forms of research in literary history, the sociology of literature, and the implications of critical theory in the humanities for the study of South Asian literatures. Historians, anthropologists, art historians, political scientists, and others collaborated in efforts to understand the transformations affecting debates over and sentiments relating to the history and future of nationalist ideology and institutions. Other leading scholars arranged for collaborations between medical practitioners and a range of social scientists to investigate questions concerning disease and epidemic, health care and international medical crises. In recent years, the committee has begun to organize an ambitious project on the study of industrialization, and its social effects, in South Asia, at the same time it inaugurated a project on the oral history of partition and war in Bangladesh. More recently, the committee has begun a long term project on the question of governance in South Asia.

Part of the success and excitement of SSRC sponsored workshops and research initiatives has been their necessarily interdisciplinary character. The joint committee, which has aimed to represent different disciplines as well as different regions related to the study of South Asia, typically has approved no project that has not had interdisciplinary framing and ambition. The interdisciplinary character of area studies has had much to do with the history of social science funding, from Ford interest in interdisciplinary program development in the 50s' and 60s' to SSRC commitments ever since the joint committee was formed in the 70s'. This interdisciplinary context has more often than not been responsible for the innovative and exciting work done in areas such as South Asian studies. Recent assaults on area studies from the disciplines, and the hard social science disciplines in particular, have represented area studies as devoid of theoretical engagement and innovation. Such views are only possible from within autonomous and confined disciplinary spaces, spaces that have been increasingly isolated in terms of theory, even as they have turned more and more to the study of the modern West itself (and increasingly the global extension of the West through world capitalism). It is worrisome indeed that despite decades of interdisciplinary programming and rhetoric, the disciplines seem stronger, and more defensive, than ever. In the leading departments of political science and economics it is becoming almost impossible to think of hiring someone whose primary research interests are locatable in a particular area of the "third" world, despite the rhetoric about the need for comparison.

Perhaps the most important change in area studies activities in the U.S. over the last few years, now clearly visible in the SSRC, has been the recognition that area studies can no longer be a solely U.S. based institutional or intellectual activity. Only in the last few years did the SSRC include more than one South Asia based scholar, and last year for the first time the annual SSRC area committee meeting was held in South Asia itself. These developments in part reflect significant changes in the way in which knowledge is organized, but they also highlight the need for formal changes at a variety of different levels. It should no longer possible to think of

U.S. based area studies as either autonomous or privileged (except perhaps still at the level of resources), and comfortable academic communities of reference and rhetorics of relevance have had to change or be betrayed for the provinciality they exhibit (and in retrospect have always exhibited). "Us" and "them", "we" and "they", have finally become italicized and problematic, and there are new levels of concern about why the trajectories, stakes, and politics of knowledge shift fundamentally across areas, as well as about what might be the implications of breaking down first world communities of scholarship. On the one hand, the Indological and anthropological trajectories of South Asian scholarship in the U.S. have been seen to provide support for the development of fundamentalist politics in South Asia; on the other hand, new intellectual and political movements in South Asia are challenging, sometimes fundamentally reworking, academic positions that had previously been evaluated solely in terms of their meaning for debates within the U.S. academy. And of course, the more things break down, the more the limits of globalism—the continuing disparities between resources available to academics within South Asia and the west, the relentless entailments of academic disciplines in the dominance of western knowledge, the residual ambivalences inherent in a western academy that still reveals its hegemony when sponsoring precisely the right kinds of collaborations and exchanges—become clear. There is no doubt that the current attack on area studies is at least in part an attempt to restore the unchallenged ascendency of American social science.

Some aspects of the above story can be seen in the career of Subaltern Studies. Ranajit Guha, who had turned to a major study of peasant rebellion in colonial India after completing his magnificent study of the Bengal permanent settlement,[64] convened a group of promising young historians working on their dissertation research in various Universities in Britain while teaching at Sussex in the 1970s; among these students were Gyanendra Pandey, Shahid Amin, David Hardiman, and David Arnold. Dipesh Chakrabarty, Partha Chatterjee, and Gautam Bhadra were soon recruited to the collective, which began publishing volumes of essays in 1982. The volumes began with a straightforward charge, to combat elitism—both colonialist elitism and bourgeois-nationalist elitism—in the writing of Indian history. This movement, which as Prakash noted challenged various institutionally dominant modes of Indian historiography, both in India and in Britain, quickly emerged as a major intervention, combining excellent examples of the writing of Indian history "from below" with an increasingly theoretically self-conscious exploration of the implications of taking "subalternity" as the principal object/problematic of historical analysis. When Gayatri Chakravarty Spivak, a poststructuralist literary critic known for her translations of Derrida, began writing in the pages of Subaltern Studies, an historical movement—seen within India as a dangerous anti-nationalist enterprise, within Britain as an attempt to oppose Cambridge historiography, and within the United States as a model for a progressive social history of nationalism—became increasingly recognized as a political intervention in fields as diverse as cultural studies, comparative history, and the emerging field of postcolonial studies. And while Subaltern Studies has become within some U.S. circles an ambivalent symbol of the way identity politics can challenge conventions of history writing, the movement has both stimulated enormous interest in South Asian studies and facilitated further connections between disciplines in the humanities and the social sciences.

The career of Subaltern Studies confronts us again with the limits of globalism. Within South Asia, Subaltern Studies has become an active site for debate about the nature of modernity, the failure of the enlightenment, the violence of the state, and the place of "traditional" culture in contemporary political theory. Within the United States, Subaltern Studies continues either to mean new kinds of authentic histories from below or even newer kinds of postmodern excesses in the representation of history and society from above. Whatever the differences, Subaltern Studies has exercised growing influence on research and teaching here. Nevertheless, as many of the practitioners of Subaltern Studies spend increasing amounts of time in the United States, and as their intellectual influence increases here, their political credentials for waging certain kinds of battles within India weaken. Interestingly, recent tensions within the community of Subalternists reflects a growing shift in South Asian studies in the U.S., namely over the level of attention to pay to the question of the diaspora. While this question seems somewhat removed to some scholars who still locate their intellectual commitments, if not their only professional affiliations, within South Asia, it is increasingly clear to "South Asianists" in the U.S. that the diaspora is working to fundamentally change the nature of South Asian studies, in terms of research, new pedagogical constituencies, and even new political affiliations.

Indeed, perhaps the single most important development on U.S. campuses in South Asian studies is not the growing intellectual exchange and collaboration among scholars but rather the growing numbers of students in language, civilization, and area studies courses who come from South Asian backgrounds, most of them children of immigrants who moved here from India after the change in the immigration act of 1965. The success of most South Asia programs in ensuring regular funding for the teaching of Hindi and Urdu is the direct result now not of pressure from graduate programs but rather from undergraduates who are overwhelmingly South Asian American. The experience I had of teaching South Asian Civilization at the University of Michigan, where in the last few years 80 percent of the students who took this course came from immigrant backgrounds, is no longer exceptional. As South Asian students are both more numerous and more active on campuses across the country, regularly claiming significant proportions of student activity funds for South Asia related programing, and increasingly advocating South Asia courses in terms of the rhetorics of multiculturalism and identity representation, colleges and Universities are paying a different kind of attention to South Asian studies. Where once arguments for courses and faculty were made for strategic reasons combined with the goal of international understanding, arguments are now made through constituency representation on the part of a vocal and talented community. And funding for South Asia related activities is increasingly coming from community gifts and endowment projects. In the last few years new programs have begun to spring up on campuses such as the University of California at Santa Cruz, Rutgers, and the State University of New York at Stony Brook; funds have been raised for chairs in Sikh and Tamil Studies as well as Indian studies more generally; and the politics of nation, community, and culture have begun to erupt at Universities such as the University of British Columbia, Berkeley, Michigan, and Columbia.

The growing relationship between South Asian Studies and South Asian Americans has been a great boon to the field, and has provided both a constituency and an urgency to a field that had previously been restricted for the most part to graduate studies and undergraduate courses in religion and philosophy. However, the new situation has also introduced new tensions and questions for the field. While the "us" and "them" distinction has been further eroded (to be replaced by a sense of panic on the part of many non-South Asian students about whether they can keep up in undergraduate classes), there have already been elements of identity politics that raise questions about who can teach South Asia (beginning with the categories of Americans on the one hand and South Asians on the other, but also introducing categories of nation, e.g. Pakistan and India, as well as religion, e.g. Hindu and Muslim). Additionally, the question as to whether South Asian Americans should be included within the field of South Asian Studies—whether for example linkages should be forged with Asian American studies more generally—have been raised both within Universities and in funding agencies. While South Asian Americans have typically maintained very close relations with South Asia itself, reflecting a new kind of immigration and a very different situation than has applied, for example, in the relations between African and African-American studies, the American experience is not merely a continuation of the middle class experience in South Asia. Indeed, one of the consequences of these new collaborations has been a tendency to focus even more on some of the cultural questions noted above than economic ones, let alone questions concerning the poor in South Asia, whether in the cities or the countryside. And the politics of middle class India, for example in the domain of rising communalist tensions and the strong role played by organizations such as the VHP in the United States, have begun to play themselves out very powerfully in the American context where the immediate stakes of these tensions—as in proximity to riot situations or palpable communal conflict—are largely invisible. Additionally, disagreements emerge between donor communities and Universities, as happened at the University of Michigan when the first occupant of the Chair in Sikh Studies was declared by many devout Sikhs as blasphemous because of his doctoral dissertation work in which he subjected the Sikh scripture to historical hermeneutics. The endowment to Columbia University by the Hinduja family for an Institute focussing on ancient Hindu belief systems and medicine produced serious tension both within the University and across the greater New York City area.

Communal tensions both in South Asia and by extension among South Asians in the United States are also reflected in a growing transnational form of nationalism. For many years it has seemed necessary in the United States to label the subcontinent South Asia rather than India to encompass Pakistan and later Bangladesh, as well as Nepal and Sri Lanka. On occasion in the current climate, fundraising for South Asia seems suspicious, and fundraising for India a cover for something other than Pakistan. Coming back to the question of South Asian studies, it is in fact frequently the case that academic studies privilege India, and for that matter Hinduism, despite the fact that two of the most populous Muslim nations are in South Asia, given that Islam is a world religion with deep roots in South Asian culture and history. Because of its political instability, Pakistan has attracted particular interest among political scientists;[65] and because of its poverty, Bangladesh has been a special province for development economists. Sri Lanka has been entirely left out of my discussion above, despite deep ties between southern India and the island, both historically through Buddhism and the Tamil migrations. For reasons that are not entirely clear, Sri Lanka has produced four of the finest anthropologists currently teaching in U.S. Universities,[66] and has occasioned more interest within anthropology generally than has been the case for other disciplines, tied as many of them are to the importance of the nation-state as an object of study. Nepal has also been a site for important anthropological work,[67] though increasingly it is attracting interest on the part of development students and applied social scientists in areas such as forestry and water management. Once again, smaller nations tend to attract more attention from anthropology than they do from history, though there are even fewer historians working on Nepal than on Sri Lanka or Bangladesh.

These problems notwithstanding, South Asian Studies is in some ways in better shape today in the U.S. than it has ever been before. Thanks to Subaltern Studies and trends in comparative history, South Asian history is thriving; and thanks to postcolonial studies, South Asia has become important in the humanities well outside the traditional Indological niches of earlier years. While South Asia is not faring very well in the hard social sciences, neither are other areas outside North America and Europe. Although the growing population and interest of South Asian Americans has led to new issues and problems in the field, there is little doubt that this new constituency will continue to grow and demand greater representation for South Asia in University life. South Asian cultural studies—in areas such as film, music, the arts, and popular culture—will grow in part because of this kind of connection.

Nevertheless, all is not well. It is peculiar, for example, that even recent economic expansion and liberalization in India have had little impact on the academy. The problems of area studies in disciplines such as economics, political science, and sociology, have further rendered many aspects of the study of South Asia in the United States relatively insignificant. At the same time, although the teaching of Hindi and Urdu has received support from new students, the teaching of most other South Asian languages has steadily succumbed to budgetary pressures. Funds for research in and about South Asia have been cut back due to the dimunition of federal funding for area studies and the loss of PL 480 funds for AIIS and Fulbright Hays. Without ample research funds for graduate students and scholars, all fields that require serious empirical work will begin to atrophy. And in an age of academic downsizing, South Asianists are often the first to go, or at least not be replaced. New appointments, outside of the few growth areas mentioned above, are rare.

FUTURES PRESENT
While in 1990, the Universities of Chicago, Pennsylvania, and California at Berkeley had what many observers believe to be leading programs in South Asian studies, the situation is rather different now. This is both because of some the trends just mentioned (the rising importance of undergraduate programs, the spread of South Asian studies to fields like colonial and postcolonial studies,

the general vitality of South Asian studies across many campuses, but also the growing marginalization of Indological studies vis a vis other developments in the field) and because the big three are not equally strong in all disciplines (e.g. Penn had some key departures, Chicago some significant retirements, and Berkeley unfortunately retrenchments) Wisconsin continues to have a strong program, and hosts an annual conference on South Asia that has become the major academic venue for many South Asianists rather than the Annual Meeting of the Association for Asian Studies. Texas has become a leading player in recent years, with strengths in Sanskrit, linguistics, and language study, among other fields. Michigan has once again become very strong, particularly in history and anthropology, and was recently awarded NRC status for the first time. Columbia has once again become a major center despite a relative paucity of full time faculty; it is also the leading center for postcolonial studies. Cornell has strengths in applied social science as well as in studies of Nepal, Bangladesh, and Sri Lanka. Virginia has become an undergraduate center, and the Triangle Consortium made up of Duke, North Carolina, and North Carolina State have impressive strength in a number of areas, among them the historical, textual, and ethnographic study of Islam in South Asia.

In thinking ahead to the future, it is likely that South Asian Area studies will continue to prosper even if they will be vulnerable to a variety of factors, ranging from disciplinary trends to the continued perception of South Asia's marginality in the world. There will be many challenges—both new and old—in the years ahead. In conclusion, I will address these challenges by making some suggestions regarding potential institutional mechanisms and research areas for future attention.

Institutionally, it is likely that those area centers that draw strength not only from their local institution but also their metropolitan constituencies—including other colleges and universities (and institutions such as museums) as well as the growing numbers and interests of South Asian Americans—will do particularly well, both in maintaining interest for separate programming in South Asian studies and for persuading University administrators to invest resources. Of course, these centers must continue to argue for strong support for top faculty, for regular support for a full menu of areas classes in fields such as history, culture, politics, literature, and language, and for support for graduate students, especially South Asian students who are not U.S. citizens. There are obvious possibilities for fundraising in these arenas, but the problem is that there are typically too few faculty, with limited administrative time, to engage usefully in fundraising; faculty need foundation support, both for funds, and for help in community endowment, a very tricky business as mentioned above. Additionally, I would recommend that centers should become increasingly connected to institutions within South Asia, working to collaborate on research projects among faculty and students, establishing mechanisms for regular exchange, identifying both issues and individuals worthy of support.

Increasing connections between scholars in South Asia and the United States will continue to provide urgency to questions around nationalism, modernity, the politics of culture, and the character of tradition. It seems necessary to anticipate a future in which the terms of these debates will be set as significantly in South Asia as they are in the U.S. academy, though there will continue to be tensions and differences, not to mention continued problems of U.S. academic hegemony. Given current disciplinary configurations and interests, it is likely that the fields of history, anthropology, comparative literature, and art history will continue to provide important opportunities for South Asianist research and participation. It will be important to work against the usual boundaries between Asian language and literature departments and comparative literature departments, even if the existence of separate departments has traditionally protected Asian subjects. Art historians will have to realize that some of the most important and interesting work in the field now concerns modern art—the participation of art in the formation of the national modern, the rise of new forms of contemporary aesthetic expression[68]—rather than assume that Indian art history can only mean early Hindu and Buddhist art; by the same token there is a pressing need to work against the usual periodizations of art historical time, divided as it is among "Hindu", "Islamic", and "British" times. Other art forms should also be included in a menu for projected growth, most importantly music, given the salience of South Asian musical systems and their implication in the history of modernity and the nation. There will also be opportunities for expansion in what might be called "comparative cultural studies." Some wonderful scholarship on Indian cinema has been produced in recent years,[69] and it is likely that some of the most interesting work on South Asia will continue to concern questions around popular/public culture, television and the media, global culture and social change. Massive technological and cultural changes are taking place through a variety of cultural media that are currently being studied in arresting ways in South Asia. Of course, cultural studies can only be done if language skills continue to occupy pride of place in the agendas of area programs. It is becoming increasingly clear that cultural homogenization cannot be assumed even when cultural images, whether in soap operas or fashion advertising, seem to have become global; as always, research that is exclusively in English misses much of the story.

Despite the abdication of fields such as economics and political science, it is also urgent to maintain serious research interests in areas around political theory and political institutions, the effects of economic liberalization on political, social, as well as local economic phenomena, and the implications of new state forms and ideologies for other aspects of contemporary life in the subcontinent. Areas of increasing interest include questions having to do with governance, with rethinking the relationship of state and society, state and nation, nation and inter-nation. At the same time, no study of contemporary politics can be done without looking as well at global forces such as the IMF and the World Bank, U.S. foreign policy, the U.N. and issues on the flip side of world legitimacy that have to do with the role of international "mafia" groups in the underworld economy of currency smuggling, illegal weapons trades, drugs, etc. Unfortunately, the hard social science disciplines that would seem particularly relevant here have not only lost interest, they have so far been largely impervious to foundation attempts to encourage "area" study through special grant initiatives. It is likely that the kind of work envisaged here will increasingly be done by historians, sociologists, and anthropologists, as well as perhaps in departments of communication, geography, or even business.

If the picture I paint is not particularly dire, the fact remains that the kinds of research projects, exchange programs, and collaborative enterprises alluded to above are expensive and typically beyond the reach of single Universities, no matter what their historical commitment to South Asian Studies. I would encourage the development of a fund for the development of a new kind of South Asian Studies in the twenty-first century. It is time to go beyond the originary visions of W. Norman Brown, Milton Singer, and Richard Lambert, to set up an organization that would complement but by no means duplicate the American Institute for Indian Studies. This organization would provide mechanisms for genuine collaborations, exchanges, and reciprocal research, as well as providing seed money for seminars and workshops. And the organization would be genuinely international, made up of scholars from North America and Europe as well as India, Pakistan, Bangladesh, Sri Lanka and Nepal, hosting events in North America, Europe, and South Asia. If such an entity—an International Institute of South Asian Studies—could in fact be launched in the next few years, and then funded at levels that would give it scope for impacting teaching and scholarship across multiple sites and institutions, it is likely that South Asia could play an even greater role in establishing new models for the rethinking of area studies more generally in the century to come.

Nicholas B. Dirks is a Professor of History and Anthropology at Columbia University.

Notes

The subject of this paper is South Asian Studies in the United States, and thus the story told here is incomplete. The paper was written for a conference on "Rethinking Area Studies," organized by David Szanton and funded by the Ford Foundation, held at New York University on April 24–26 1998. It is because of this context that I conclude the paper with some institutional recommendations.

1. Any review of dominant trends in a field as complex and differentiated as South Asian studies is bound to be partial, to focus on certain players at the expense of others, to critique certain configurations of knowledge while leaving others out of the picture altogether. Besides, this review is intended to highlight

certain moments in the formation and working out of the field and not to provide a complete account. Nevertheless, I apologize in advance both to those who feel their work is unfairly singled out and subjected to symptomatic critique, and to those who feel neglected by this highly personal and specific review.

2. For information about Brown, see Rosane Rocher's introductory essay in Rocher, ed., *India and Indology: Selected Articles,* by W. Norman Brown. Delhi: Motilal Banarsidass, 1978; see also Richard J. Cohen, "Historical Notes: W. Norman Brown," in *South Asia News,* the bulletin of the South Asia Center at the University of Pennsylvania, Spring 1992, pp. 16–18; and Jerome Bauer and Richard Cohen, "Historical Notes: Insight into the Origin of 'South Asia Regional Studies' at the University of Pennsylvania," *in South Asia News,* Autumn 1991, p. 14. I am grateful to Bob Nichols for the references.

3. Cited in Bauer and Cohen, ibid.

4. Ibid. p.14.

5. Indeed, despite the manifestly salutory character both of area studies and interdisciplinarity, it is important to remember the extent to which both activities seem rooted in a particular colonial moment and mentality.

6. Edward Said, *Orientalism,* New York: Vintage, 1978. See my edited, *Colonialism and Culture,* Ann Arbor: University of Michigan Press, 1993.

7. See the *University of Pennsylvania Bulletin,* South Asia Regional Studies, Announcement for the Academic Year 1949–50 and Summer Session, 1949.

8. Although he also notes that this was the first summer session, so perhaps he was thinking of the summer of 1947. See Robert Crane, "Preface on Richard L. Park," in Paul Wallace, ed., *Region and Nation in India,* New Delhi: Oxford and IBH Publishing Co., 1985.

9. Ibid., p. 7.

10. See Rocher, "Biographical Sketch," in Rocher, ed., *India and Indology..*

11. Ibid., p. xviii.

12. The United States and India and Pakistan, p. 24.

13. Ibid., p. 29.

14. Ibid.

15. Ibid., p. 30.

16. Ibid., p. 130.

17. Ibid., p. 316.

18. The reference here is to Public Law 480, which even more significantly used loan repayment in the non-convertible rupee currency for the development of library resources on South Asia in twelve participating U.S. libraries, including 10 University libraries, the New York Public Library, and the Library of Congress.

19. Redfield had done his Ph.D. under Robert Park, the great Chicago sociologist, and had taught in the anthropology department since 1928. For a thorough study of the life and career of Robert Redfield, see Clifford D. Wilcox, *Encounters with Modernity: Robert Redfield and the Problem of Social Change,* Doctoral Dissertation in History, the University of Michigan, 1997.

20. Cited in Wilcox, p. 210.

21. Largely because Hutchins left the University of Chicago at that point and became Associate Director of the Ford Foundation.

22. In *Ethics* v. 60, October 1949.

23. Mandelbaum was the first American social scientist to do field research in India. Patterson, 2.8 For an account of his career, see Milton Singer, "David Mandelbaum and the Rise of South Asian Studies: A Reminiscence," pp. 1–9, in Paul Hockings, ed., *Dimensions of Social Life: Essays in Honor of David G. Mandelbaum.* Amsterdam: Mouton de Gruyter, 1987.

24. As at Penn, Yale, Columbia, Hopkins, and Chicago, Sanskritists arrived long before South Asian Area Studies. Arthur W. Ryder was appointed to a chair in Sanskrit at Berkeley in 1905 in the classics department. Murray Emeneau succeeded him as Sanskritist in 1940, and went on to become the key person in the establishment of the Linguistics Department at Berkeley in 1953. Emeneau, who did fieldwork in the Nilgiris of Southern India and studied Dravidian philology, collaborated with Mandelbaum in the establishment of a Center for South Asian Studies in 1957, along with Richard Park, as mentioned above.

25. While in 1991, the average percentage of anthropologists among all disciplinary specialists in Asian studies was only 9.6 [and only 5.0 for China and inner Asia and 6.5 for Northeastern Asia], the percentage of anthropologists for South Asia was 14, surpassed only by Southeast Asianists where anthropology was even more dominant, at 25 percent. For Eastern Asian studies overall, history was the dominant discipline; for South Asia, religion and philosophy claimed greater proportions of scholars than anywhere else, followed closely by history, political science, and anthropology.

26. Where he studied under Morris Opler, who ran a village studies project and trained a number of the early postwar anthropologists in the U.S., including Pauline Kolenda, John Hitchcock, and Michael Mahar.

27. The Ford Foundation gave the University of Chicago 5.4 million dollars for area studies in the 1960s, including 1,786,000 specifically earmarked for South Asia.

28. "Society and Social Change under the Raj" in Bernard Cohn, *An Anthropologist Among the Historians and Other Essays.* Delhi and New York:Oxford University Press, 1987, p. 195.

29. See for example J. H. Broomfield, *Elite Conflict in a Plural Society: Twentieth Century Bengal.* Berkeley: University of California Press, 1968; Eugene Irschick, *Politics and Social Conflict in South India: The Non-Brahmin Movement and Tamil Separatism, 1916–1929.* Berkeley: University of California Press, 1969; S.N. Mukherjee, *Calcutta: Essays in Urban History.* Cambridge: Cambridge University Press, 1970; John Greenfield Leonard, *Kandukuri Viresalingam, 1848–1919: A Biography of an Indian Social Reformer.* Ph.d. Dissertation, University of Wisconsin-Madison, 1970; Peter James Marshall, *Problems of Empire: Britian and India, 1757–1813.* London: Allen and Unwin, 1968; David Kopf, *British Orientalism and the Bengal Renaissance: The*

Dynamics of Indian Modernization, 1773–1835. Calcutta: Firma K.L. Mukhopadhyay, 1969; Ronald Inden, *Marriage and Rank in Bengali Culture: A History of Caste and Clan in Middle Period Bengal.* Berkeley: University of California Press, 1976; and, Tom Kessinger, *Vilayatpur, 1848–1968: Social and Economic Change in a North Indian Village.* Berkeley: University of California Press, 1974.

30. Cohn, "Society and Social Change under the Raj," p. 195.

31. Cohn's major works include *An Anthropologist among Historians* (1987) and his more recent *Colonialism and its Forms of Knowledge: The British in India.* Princeton: Princeton University Press, 1996; see also "The Command of Grammar and the Grammar of Command," Ranajit Guha, ed., Subaltern Studies, Vol IV. Delhi: Oxford University Press, 1985, pp. 276–329.

32. Introduction to *When a Great Tradition Modernizes.* Chicago: University of Chicago, 1972, p. 3.

33. Four of the first workshops to be sponsored by the Social Science Research Council, beginning a long tradition of conferences, seminars, and workshops, were organized around Marriott's ethnosociology project. On the one hand, Marriott worked to diagram the major dimensions of a Hindu ethnosociology; on the other, philosophers such as Karl Potter sought to explore the philosophical dimensions of major Hindu themes, for example the question of Karma.

34. *Kinship in Bengali Culture.* Chicago: University of Chicago Press, 1977.

35. "Marriage and Rank in Bengali Culture" in *Journal of Asian Studies,* v. 39, no. 3, 1980, pp. 519–521.

36. *Islamic Revival in British India, Deoband, 1860–1900.* Princeton: Princeton University Press, 1982.

37. *Mughal Administration in Golconda.* London: Oxford University Press, 1975.

38. *Sufis of Bijapur, 1300–1700, Social Roles of Sufis in Medieval India.* Princeton: Princton University Press, 1978.

39. *North India between Empires: Awadh, the Mughals, and the British. 1720–1801.* Berkeley: University of California Press, 1980.

40. *Aligarh's First Generation: Muslim Solidarity in British India.* Princeton: Princeton University Press, 1978.

41. Among Stein's own works see, for example, *Peasant State and Society in Medieval South India.* Delhi: Oxford University Press, 1980; *Thomas Munro: The Origins of the Colonial State and His Vision of Empire.* Delhi and New York: Oxford University Press, 1985; and, *Vijayanagar.* Cambridge and New York: Cambridge University Press, 1989.

42. Ludden's advisor was Tom Kessinger, an anthropological historian who had been trained by Bernard Cohn at Chicago, and who had written an ethnohistorical study of social relations within a north Indian village between the mid nineteenth and mid twentieth centuries, titled, *Vilayatpur, 1848–1968: Social and Economic Change in a North Indian Village.* Berkeley: University of California Press, 1974.

43. *Symbols of Substance, Court, and State in Nayaka Period, Tamilnadu.* Delhi: Oxford University Press, 1992.

44. See for example David Kopf's "Hermeneutics versus History" in the *Journal of Asian Studies,* v. 89, no. 3, 1980, pp. 495–506.

45. The volume that ultimately came out of this seminar was edited by Carol Breckenridge and Peter van der Veer, *Orientalism and the Postcolonial Predicament: Perspectives on South Asia,* University of Pennsylvania Press, 1993.

46. "Introduction: Colonialism and Culture," in Dirks, ed., *Colonialism and Culture.* Ann Arbor: University of Michigan Press, 1992, p. 9

47. Ibid., pp. 9–10.

48. "Writing Post-Orientalist Histories of the Third World: Perspectives from Indian Historiography" in Comparative Studies in Society and History, v. 32, April 1990, p. 384.

49. As pointed out by Partha Chatterjee in his provocative book *Nationalist Thought and the Colonial World: A Derivative Discourse?* London: Zed Books, 1986.

50. Louis Dumont, Homo Hierarchicus: The Caste System and its Implications. Chicago: University of Chicago Press, 1970.

51. See the new preface to the second edition of my book, *The Hollow Crown: Ethnohistory of an Indian Kingdom,* University of Michigan Press, 1994, where I wrote, "Edward Said's revolutionary critique of Orientalism worked to problematize both colonialism and the anthropological conceit that one could get around colonial epistemology by constructing the essential categories and meanings of the 'other'. Reading Said was like reading a direct refutation of ethnosociology; the ethnosociological inattention to the politics and procedures of interpretation and representation could now be seen as genealogically predicated in colonial forms of Western knowledge. We had not been decolonizing the epistemology of India after all. I came increasingly to realize that colonialism was not just a historical stage and an epistemological problem but the crucible in which the category of 'culture' itself had been formed." (p. xvii).

52. *Imagining India.* Oxford and Cambridge: Basil Blackwell, 1990, p. 1.

53. See McKim Marriott and Ronald Inden, "Caste Systems," *Encyclopaedia Britannica,* 15th edn, III, 982–91.

54. He does say, "I, too, was lured in earlier research by the siren of caste (p. 82)." Now, however, he uses the historiographical charter of R.G. Collingwood, and his own research on a text concerning Hindu kingship, to restore Indian agency, albeit solely of a Hindu kind (Islam is said to be another region of the world, like Africa or Eastern Europe, on p. 3), and articulated in the classic anthropological terms of a totalizing view of kingship and an emphasis on cosmological baths and cosmogonic time. Inden, *Imagining India,* Oxford University Press.

55. See "After Orientalism: Culture, Criticism, and Politics in the Third World" in *Comparative Studies in Society and History,* v. 34, Jan. 1992, pp. 141–67.

56. Thus joining a growing number of vitriolic debates over the politics of history, whether in relationship to postcolonial writing, as in the interventions of Aijaz Ahmed in *In Theory: Classes, Nations, Literatures.* (Oxford 1985), and Arif Dirlik in "Postcolonial Aura: Third World Criticism in the Age of Global Capitalism" in *Critical Inquiry,* v.20, Winter 1994, pp. 328–56; or more generally in contests between old left/Marxist commitments to historical truth and the contention that such a commitment is the only way to ground any genuine political activism. For a variation on the latter see the Sokal debates, specifically Allan Sokal, "What the Social Text Affair does and does not prove" in *Critical Quarterly,* v. 40, no. 2, Summer 98, pp.3–18. For a review of some of these debates, see my, "The Politics of Location" unpublished manuscript.

57. See for example Anil Seal, *The Emergence of Indian Nationalism: Competition and Collaboration in the Later Nineteenth Century.* London: Cambridge University Press, 1968; John Gallagher, Gordon Johnson, & Anil Seal, *Locality, Province, and Nation: Essays on Indian Politics, 1870–1940,* Cambridge: Cambridge University Press, 1973; and David Washbrook, *The Emergence of Provincial Politics: The Madras Presidency 1870–1920,* Cambridge: Cambridge University Press, 1976.

58. "Can the 'Subaltern' Ride? A Reply to O'Hanlon and Washbrook" in *Comparative Studies in Society and History,* v. 34, no. 1, p. 171.

59. Prakash's first book was an anthropological history of bonded labor in Bihar, and emerged out of a long term engagement with Marxist theory and politics stemming back at least to the first phase of his graduate studies in history at Jawaharlal Nehru University in New Delhi. See *Bonded Histories: Genealogies of Labor Servitude in Colonial India.* Cambridge and New York: Cambridge University Press, 1990.

60. Ibid., p. 177–178.

61. I refer here principally to the work of scholars such as Ashis Nandy, Partha Chatterjee, and Dipesh Chakrabarty.

62. Between 1979 and 1986 SAPE held fourteen conferences, some co-sponsored by the Indian Council of Social Science Research and the Ford Foundation with additional support from NSF. According to Maureen Patterson, "With its focus on development in post-Independent India, the SAPE planners wanted to go beyond a purely economic approach and 'envisioned a research alliance' to 'approximate a more contextual understanding of economic processes' (S. Rudolph, p. 2). They looked for 'anthropologically oriented scholars attuned to 'indigenous conceptual systems as bases for understanding, explaining, and interpreting South Asian institutions and behavior'. . . And the planners looked for economists. . .Thus the project assembled anthropologists, economists and political scientists plus a few historians and proceeded to delineate three major areas to work on: . . . relationships between local poer structures and agricultural productivity; . . . problems of health and nutrition at the household and family levels; . . . societal responses to crises, or order and anomie in South Asian history and culture" in "South Asian Studies: Our Increasing Knowledge and Understanding," mimeographed manuscript, January 1988., p.21.

63. Appadurai's early work was on the history of temples in southern India, but in recent years he has made important arguments—basing many of them in relation to South Asia—for the globalization of academic inquiry. See his *Modernity at Large: Cultural Dimensions of Globalization.* Minneapolis: University of Minnesota Press, 1996.

64. Ranajit Guha, *A Rule of Property for Bengal.* Delhi: Orient Longman, 1982 (1963); *Elementary Aspects of Peasant Insurgency in Colonial India,* Delhi: Oxford University Press, 1983.

65. There are, however, significant exceptions. Perhaps the most important historian of Pakistan is Ayesha Jalal, whose book, *Sole Spokesman: Jinnah, the Muslim League and the demand for Pakistan* (Cambridge: Cambridge University Press, 1985) is a major contribution to the rewriting of the history of partition.

66. Stanley Tambiah at Harvard, Gananath Obeyesekere at Princeton, Valentine Daniel at Columbia, and H.L. Seneviratne at Virginia. All of these figures have been known not just for their excellent empirical studies in Sri Lanka, among other places, but also for their theoretical power and influence. For example, Tambiah has made important contributions to political anthropology, the anthropology of Buddhism, and the study of ethnic violence. See his *Sri Lanka: Ethnic Fratricide and the Dismantling of Democracy.* Chicago: University of Chicago Press, 1986; *Buddhism Betrayed? Religion, Politics, and Violence in Sri Lanka.* Chicago: University of Chicago Press, 1992; and, *Leveling Crowds: Ethnonationalist Conflicts and Collective Violence in South Asia.* Berkeley: University of California Press, 1996. Obeyeskere is one of the most creative psychological anthropologists practicing today and raised many eyebrows when he bested Marshall Sahlins in a debate over Captain Cook in *The Apotheosis of Captain Cook: European mythmaking in the Pacific.* Princeton: Princeton University Press, 1992. Valentine Daniel, in addition to his early ethnosociological work and current work on the anthropology of violence among many other things, is a specialist in the philosophy of Charles Saunders Pierce. See in particular his *Charred Lullabies: Chapters in the Anthropology of Violence.* Princeton: Princeton University, 1996.

67. Cornell is a major center for Nepal studies, though students have worked in a number of other institutions, among them Michigan, Washington, Columbia, and Virginia.

68. See for example Tapati Guha-Thakurta, *The Making of a new 'Indian' Art: Artists, Aesthetics, and Nationalism in Bengal, c. 1850–1920.* Cambridge and New York: Cambridge University Press, 1992. Also, Partha Mitter, *Art and Nationalism in Colonial India 1850–1920: Occidental Orientations.* Cambridge and New York: Cambridge University Press, 1994; and, *Much Maligned Monsters: A History of European Reactions to Indian Art.* Chicago: University of Chicago Press, 1992.

69. See, for instance, Sumita Chakravarty *National Identity in Indian Popular Culture.* Austin: University of Texas-Austin, 1993.

Chapter 9

The Contributions Development of Southeast Asian Studies in the United States

John Bowen

The intellectual development of a concept called "Southeast Asia" in the U.S. involved the coming together, under the influence of regional conflicts and the Pacific War, of three streams: island ethnography, contemporary political studies, and classical Indology. This convergence onto a new academic unit produced a particular configuration of subsequent writings, in which anthropology loomed relatively large, and classical texts on power and religion underwrote analyses of nationalist movements and societal modernization. This patched together field of study, of a region with no single dominant power, religion, or language, continues to lead many specialists to reflect questioningly on the identity of the region and the usefulness of "Southeast Asian studies" as a category.

Perhaps all world areas are the object of insecure reflections, but, for better or worse, some areas live under the felt dominance of a country or of a language—India, China; Spanish, Arabic. Regions with these rather strong center-periphery structures may be easier to identify as study areas, and there may arise stronger connections across disciplines on the basis of shared language competence—or, perhaps there arise "high culture" imperialisms that mirror their regional counterparts. One thinks of the resistance of some Middle Eastern specialists to Islamicists who know no Arabic, or the historical marginalization in East Asian Studies of specialists in languages other than Chinese or Japanese.

In the case of Southeast Asia, the decided lack of a single center in the region (or even a half-dozen centers), has allowed the flourishing of disciplinary and areal pluralism. (This decenteredness is ironic in a region where center-periphery relations have provided a major organizing trope for studies of history, politics, culture, and art.) The specialist on upland Burma or Mindanao is not considered peripheral to the effort of producing areal knowledge, as the specialist on Chinese Muslims or Brazilian native populations might once have been. From an institutional perspective, this pluralism may also have been facilitated by the weakness of classical humanities disciplines in U.S. Southeast Asian studies.

DEFINING THE AREA AND DEVELOPING AREA STUDIES

Although some geographical features suggest themselves as the natural foundations for Southeast Asia, none of them imply the region as defined today. The South China sea links southern China with the region, and trade in those waters depended on Malay as a lingua franca, flung Chinese pottery to remote islands, and led some rulers to proclaim fealty to the Emperor. The Indian Ocean brought Hindu, Buddhist, and Islamic ideas of power and salvation, as well as cloth, cuisine, and *dangdut* music. Taking either body of water as definitive of the region would stretch "Southeast Asia" either northward or westward. Alternatively, the very fact of islandness would group Indonesia and the Philippinese with their Polynesian and Melanesian neighbors, and apart from the mainland.

In a less boundary-obsessed way, perhaps we can see (with Wolters 1982) a willingness to adopt and adapt imported ideas as characteristic of the region. Southeast Asia then may be viewed as a geographical and cultural openness, toward all the seas, distributing throughout the archipelago and the mainland a panoply of cultural forms, including quite particular *stupa* constructions, images of Siva, Vishnu and Buddha, Perso-Islamic ideas of governance, and modernist Islamic critiques of ritual. This widespread distribution has been possible only because of the local adaptations of each cultural form: when the T'ang code was brought into Vietnamese law, or the Arthasastra to Java, or Islamic teachings about death to archipelagic societies, these broader traditions were modified to fit local ideas and practices.

One could also highlight cultural contrasts between Southeast Asia and its neighbors. For example, the gender equality of Southeast Asia vis-à-vis East and South Asia plays a central role in Anthony Reid's (1988, 162–72) history of the region, as it also does in Amartya Sen's (1990) contemporary account of cross-regional differences in the survival of women.

Prior to the 1940's scholars were seldom concerned with fixing the region's boundaries. Most U.S. scholarship conducted in the area did not refer to a region called "Southeast Asia," but was part of broader research agendas, especially the ethnological study of Pacific cultures, and the analysis of current events and social problems in Asia. (European colonial powers carried out literary and historical scholarship, but usually limited to their own colonial possessions and not extending to a broad region.)

Early American ethnology was based upon fieldwork in the Americas and in the Pacific. The diversity of Pacific islands suggested the idea of a "natural laboratory" to Boas and his students. Margaret Mead and Gregory Bateson's series of studies in the Pacific, including Bali (Bateson and Mead 1942), were framed as experiments in cultural variability, particularly with respect to gender relations, personality, and life cycles. (Indeed, the Pacific continues to be a favored region for culture and personality studies, from Cora Dubois in Alor to current work on Tahiti, Samoa, and elsewhere.) U.S. possession of the Philippines led to much less research than did the other colonialisms in the region, and most of what was done was limited to uplands areas.

The two anthropologists who most effectively moved from prewar ethnology to postwar area studies were Lauriston Sharp and Raymond Kennedy, whose particular research styles shaped postwar research at Cornell and Yale, respectively. Sharp undertook fieldwork in Arizona and in North Africa after his undergraduate years, and later referred to these experiences in regional contrasts as directing him toward the study of a region as a whole (Skinner and Kirsch 1975:11). After having decided to focus on Southeast Asia for post-graduate study, but realizing that possibilities for area-wide study did not exist in the U.S., on Robert Lowie's advice he studied German and traveled to Vienna to work under the historian Robert Heine-Geldern (Kahin 1994:2). His PhD dissertation, from Harvard in 1937, was based on research in Australia (because funding for Australian research was offered by A. R. Radcliffe-Brown). He took a position at Cornell in 1936 (initially in the Department of Economics), served as assistant chief of the Division of Southeast Asian Affairs in the Department of State in 1945–46, and only began fieldwork in Southeast Asia in 1947, when he began a field project near Bangkok. This project grew to become the site for a succession of studies by students at Cornell and elsewhere on a wide range of topics—Skinner and Kirsch (1975:15) claim fifty doctoral dissertations grew out of the Cornell-Thailand Project! Sharp's combination of regional focus, government service, and multidisciplinary fieldwork established a pattern for subsequent teaching at Cornell and elsewhere. His early association with Harvard (beginning with his undergraduate colleague Clyde Kluckhohn) probably encouraged the development of a social science approach to area studies at Cornell.

Raymond Kennedy was the consummate compiler of ethnographic data. He worked for General Motors in Java and Sumatra from 1929 to 1932, and went to Yale in 1932, where he received a doctorate in 1935 and became Professor of Sociology in 1947. Kennedy took up the East Indies part of George Murdock's ethnographic bibliographic project (Kennedy 1945), and also planned an extensive fieldwork project on acculturation in Indonesia, which he carried out in part before he was murdered in Java in 1950 (Kennedy 1953). His emphasis on long-term, linguistically sophisticated fieldwork aimed at classifying peoples and studying social processes characterized anthropology at Yale, as exemplified by George P. Murdock's Human Relations Area Files, and by the subsequent Philippines fieldwork of Harold Conklin and Charles Frake. Yale Southeast Asian studies also drew on a long tradition of linguistic study of the region, for example, Leonard Bloomfield's (1917) grammatical analysis of Tagalog texts, and Isidore Dyen's (1946) studies of the Malay language.

Other prewar anthropologists could be mentioned whose work might have led to the establishment of later area studies centers. For example, Fred Eggan's Philippine Studies Program brought together Eggan's own work with that of R. F. Barton (1949), Fay-Cooper Cole, and others at Chicago, but never developed into an area center in the postwar mode. Instead, Philippines studies developed at Yale, and emphasized fieldwork in linguistics, law, and economics.

The second line of prewar U.S. research focused on contemporary social issues in the area, and was in large part sponsored by the Institute of Pacific Relations, founded in 1925 in New York. These research projects concerned in particular matters of social welfare, such as labor relations (Tompson 1947) and human bondage (Lasker 1950), and questions of politics and nationalist movements (Emerson, Mills, and Thompson 1942; Thompson and Adloff 1950), all of which were undertaken with a general sense of international crisis and a look toward decolonization. Country studies were also produced (e.g., Thompson 1941 on Thailand), with the same "current issues" emphasis.

Researchers affiliated with the Institute tried to reach a broad public by organizing international conferences, such as the 1931 meeting in China published as *Problems of the Pacific* (Lasker 1932), and by writing books about the area for the non-specialist (Lasker 1944, 1945). The special issue of *The Annals of the American Academy of Political and Social Sciences* devoted to the area (Mills 1943) may have been one of the first collections entitled "Southeast Asia". Karl Pelzer's (1945) active role both in Institute research and later at Yale gave a geographical and ecological dimension to these studies and to later Yale research—and provided an intellectual connection to contemporary French geographical work in Indochina (e.g., Gourou 1939).

European work during the same period had a broader dimension, including studies of prehistory and religion as well as culture and social issues. Of particular importance for later U.S. research was the study of the long historical ties with India, on which the major work was George Coedes's 1944 *Les Etats Hindouisés d'Indochine et d'Indonésie* (1948), which traces "the imprint of the Indian genius" across Southeast Asian countries. This scholarship was as often situated in the colonies as it was in Europe, as in the case of the Vietnam-born Paul Mus, who later was to figure in the French Indochina war, but who in the prewar years argued (1933) for a common substratum in India and Southeast Asia that facilitated Indianization. Robert Heine-Geldern provided a critical link between prewar European and postwar U.S. scholarship through his role at the Institute of Pacific Relations, his writings on the center-periphery structure of early states (1956), and his ancestral status as Sharp's teacher. A counterpoint to "Indianization" was developed by J.C. van Leur, who in 1934 (1955) emphasized local cultural and economic continuities underneath the "thin and flaking glaze" of Indian and Islamic presences. Van Leur's significance for later U.S. work lay both in his use of Weber to construct models of trade and culture, and in his argument for a non-Eurocentric perspective on regional studies (see Smail 1961).

SOUTHEAST ASIAN CENTERS

The first U.S. academic institution bearing the label "Southeast Asia" was the Southeast Asia Institute, formed in 1941 in New York City, and with a branch in Berkeley. The Institute's Board included Margaret Mead, Claire Holt, Raymond Kennedy, Arthur Schiller, and as Research Associate the person who often acted as the group's driving force, Robert Heine-Geldern. In 1946 Institute members edited a special issue of the Far Eastern Quarterly (1946) on the Netherlands Indies.

Although academic work on the region predated World War II, publication and organized research activity flourished in the 1940's, coinciding with the war effort. Efforts to define the region were led by military concerns. In the flurry of wartime map-making, the National Geographic Society decided that Southeast Asia was to be labeled as a distinct region (Emmerson 1984:7). As the by-now standard story continues, it was the creation of the South-East Asia Command (SEAC) under Admiral Lord Mountbatten in 1943 that fixed the idea of the region (Steinberg et al. 1985: 5). But this command did not cover the Philippines or eastern Indonesia until 1945, and it did include Sri Lanka (Emmerson 1984:7–8). Fixing the region's boundaries on military grounds gave a political and strategic cast to subsequent research on the region as a unit—as opposed to research on particular countries, subregions, or problems.

Organizations in the region itself have also been defined around strategic concerns. The creation of the Southeast Asia Treaty Organization (SEATO) in 1954 was directed at containing Communism, though other strategic interests were confused therewith—Pakistan joined the group as part of its own strategy to "contain" India. SEATO died in 1977, succeeded in a fashion by a locally-conceived organization, initially named the Association of Southeast Asia (ASA), consisting of Thailand, the Philippines, and Malaya and lasting from 1961 to 1967, and then the Association of Southeast Asian Nations (ASEAN), which in 1967 added Singapore and Indonesia to the ASA group, and which has since expanded to include the over time Vietnam, Laos, Cambodia, and Burma of the strategically-defined region.

Because many of the most prominent postwar studies of the region in the U.S. were motivated by pro-nationalist and anti-colonial sentiments (Anderson 1973), taking current political boundaries as the basis for defining the region seemed "natural", but had the effect of drawing the attention of scholars and students away from those other linkages—to India, China, and the Islamic world—that had been pursued in Europe but that had not yet been established as central concerns in U.S. scholarship.

Debates about how and where to draw regional boundaries continue to surface in scholarship and in arguments about faculty appointments in the 1990s. Is a Vietnam scholar best situated next to his Indonesianist colleague or his Chinese ones? Funan and Champa are associated with the rest of Southeast Asia on solid scholarly grounds, but Vietnamese rulers borrowed much from China. Should we write histories of "Southeast Asia" as defined above (Reid 1993), or do the mainland states, on the one hand, and the trading parts of the archipelago, on the other, exhibit sufficiently distinct dynamics so as to be best treated separately (Lieberman 1995)?

Only after the war were academic units for the study of the region established at U.S. universities. Southeast Asia Centers appeared in roughly three rounds. First was the period right after World War II, when nervousness about Communism and enthusiasm about nationalism combined to lead foundations and university administrators to support regional studies with emphases on politics, recent history, and other "macrosocial" issues. Centers were created at Yale (1947), Cornell (1950), and Berkeley (1960), with support from the Rockefeller Foundation and the Carnegie Corporation. Cornell's center came to dominate studies of the region more than is the case for any center devoted to any other world region (and is treated at greater length below). Both Cornell and Yale quickly attracted graduate students: in 1952, Cornell had 28 graduate students working on the region; Yale had 25, and each university had four graduate students in the field. Berkeley worked on a more departmentalized basis (Van Niel 1964).

The second round of center creation came during the sharp rise in funding for nearly anything in the mid-1960's (including the creation of NDEA funding for graduate students and greater activity by the Ford Foundation), the public attention to the Vietnam war, and the emergence of a new generation of professors who had been trained at the first-round centers. Southeast Asian studies probably enjoyed their greatest degree of academic visibility then, (marked by the creation of a separate section in the Association for Asian Studies). New centers in Southeast Asian (or South and Southeast Asian) studies developed at Ohio in 1969, Northern Illinois in 1963 as an extension of a Peace Corps program for Malaysia (Van Niel 1964:193), Wisconsin in the late 1960s as a development from the Program in Comparative Tropical History, and Michigan in 1960. These dates may obscure earlier training in de facto center fashion, for example at Hawaii in the History department after about 1964, when Walter Vella and Robert Van Niel joined the department, and at Ohio, where John Cady had been teaching Southeast Asian history for twenty years prior to the creation of a Center for International Studies (William Frederick, personal communication 1998).

By the early 1980's, there were eight centers, five of which were receiving federal (NDEA) funds. They were joined, in a (to date) final round of center-creation in the 1990's, by programs at Arizona State, and at an innovative Regional Consortium for Southeast Asia Studies, which includes the Universities of Oregon, Washington, and British Columbia.

Of course, teaching the languages and literatures of Southeast Asia was not entirely absent from U.S. universities before and outside of Center development—Malay was taught at Cornell in the 1870's and 1880's, for example (Sharp 1976:2). George Kahin (1952) found that between 1943 and 1952, courses exclusively on Southeast Asia in U.S. colleges and universities had increased from 27 to 72, with Malay or Indonesian being the main language taught, and political science and anthropology the two major other disciplines. (However, 413 courses were found that devoted some time to Southeast Asia, overwhelmingly in history departments.) Moreover, collaborative research programs often focused on Southeast Asia without choosing the Center route—the "Modjokuto" project in East Java that provided material for several Harvard PhD students was coordinated by M.I.T.'s Center for International Studies.

Area studies centers usually got their start when an administrator and at least one faculty member agreed that the region was worth close study. Cornell, for example, had Lauriston Sharp and the sympathetic and influential chair of the Far Eastern Studies department, Knight Biggerstaff, plus the agreement by the Rockefeller Foundation to provide grant money (Kahin 1994:3). Yale had Raymond Kennedy, already teaching the civilizations of Indonesia in Sociology during the late 1930's and with field experience in Indonesia and the Philippines, who was influential in recruiting new faculty in the late 1940's (for example, Harold Conklin in 1948.) Wartime linguistics training for G.I.s also may have provided a boost to the postwar efforts: at Yale, for example, both Bloomfield and Dyen were involved in creating suitable teaching materials in Ilocano, Dutch, and Malay. (My first course in conversational Dutch in the 1970's used Bloomfield's wartime tapes.) The addition of the historian Harry Benda, also with extensive Indonesia experience, and the geographer Karl Pelzer, gave the Yale program a high profile despite the eventual loss of internal Center support. Similarly, the loss of one or two key people could effectively disempower a center, as happened at Yale when, early in its history the center suffered the deaths of both Raymond Kennedy and John Embree.

The Centers have had varied degrees of success, gaining or losing funding over the years. Cornell maintained its high level of productivity. Berkeley and Ohio had periods of regional focus, but lost faculty or external support or both. Northern Illinois succeeded in part through a specialization on Burma, but then lost its key Burma historian.

The fragility of Southeast Asia centers is in part due to the most interesting feature of the region itself, namely its cultural diversity. Although a minor region of the world in terms of the numbers of U.S. scholars concentrating their activities there or the number of students taking courses on the region, Southeast Asia has far greater linguistic and cultural diversity than most other regions, with several distinct language families, no one or two of which are dominant in any respect, and with all the world's large-scale religions. Nonetheless, most universities that developed Southeast Asian programs tried to develop capacities for teaching several languages, about several countries, and across several disciplines. There have been concentrations—Berkeley specialized in Thai anthropology, for example—but by and large programs have tried to map onto the political area of Southeast Asia, with more or less effectiveness. Government funding criteria push centers in this direction, and may punish those centers that overly specialize—Ohio, for example, lost its FLAS funding because it had only developed teaching of one language, Indonesian, according to William Frederick (personal communication 1998).

In recognition of the particular demographics of this area of study—cultural diversity but small numbers of specialists—the area centers agreed to pool some federal funds and create a Southeast Asian Summer Studies Institute (SEASSI). The Institute began as a summer program in Indonesian Studies (ISSI) in 1975, but as additional languages were added, SEASSI increasingly came to "stand for" the region as a whole. The Institute rotates among area centers, and includes courses in history, literature, or social sciences, and has held conferences at the end of the session. In the early years, and particularly as ISSI, the conferences attracted a reasonably large sample of senior, junior, and protoscholars of the region. As the compass of the program expanded, and perhaps the pattern experienced fatigue, the conferences came to be put on by and for graduate students. But the cohort-building effect has continued.

The low profile of Southeast Asia in some disciplines has meant less than productive relations between some departments and centers. History seems to be the most difficult discipline in this regard, perhaps because little in the way of theory links specialists in different areas and periods. Berkeley, for example, made several attempts to hire a Southeast Asian historian—at least once in the late 1960's (to hire Harry Benda) and several times in subsequent decades, succeeding only on a third attempt with Luce Foundation support to help convince the History department that Southeast Asianists indeed could do sociopolitical history (as Lauriston Sharp had convinced Rockefeller to do for Cornell in the 1950's [Kahin 1994:4]).

It may be that those centers that initially tried to go their own way, with distinct degree-granting powers, for example, paid for that decision in the coin of little subsequent cooperation from departments. George Kahin (1994:3–4) argues that this early independence at Yale and Berkeley weakened those centers; whereas Cornell's (or rather Sharp's) decision that all students would major in a department and faculty would be hired through departments led to better cooperation and better success at placing students. And yet in the late 1990's this structure allowed certain of Cornell's departments to frustrate the efforts of the older generation of Southeast Asianists to hire those younger scholars they see as best positioned to invigorate (or even reinvent) regional studies.

THE CASE OF CORNELL

The problems noted above for Southeast Asian studies—a high degree of regional diversity, low numbers of specialists and students, difficulties retaining Federal support—certainly have facilitated the current role of Cornell as a kind of meta-center, from which many of the other centers developed and which continues to maintain the best library facilities, the major publications program, and an unmatched set of language and area courses. Although in some disciplines (anthropology, for example), most specialists in the region never studied at Cornell, nearly all have relied on the university's resources.

Sharp (1976) traces the Cornell program's genesis to the 1919 gift of a "South Seas" collection to the library that became the Wason collection. Sharp joined Cornell in 1936, began the program in 1951, and by 1954 had hired George Kahin in government, Frank Golay in economics, John Echols and R.B. Jones in linguistics, giving the program region-wide coverage. In 1954, Ford sponsored the Modern Indonesian Project, Cornell's major subregional enterprise, and the source of the major journal on that country, *Indonesia.* Ford's overall plan had been to undertake a comparative study of Communism in 4 Asian countries headed by noncommunists, but agreed that the Cornell Project would encompass all dimensions of modern social and political life. The 1962–1972 London-Cornell Project allowed Cornell and the various University of London institutions to complement each other's strengths. For example, British experts on Burma and Malaya, such as the historian D.G.E. Hall, taught seminars at Cornell. ("The program with London relieved our guilt at not covering Malaya and Burma; we still had some guilt, mainly about history and the Philippines"; George Kahin, interview, 1997).

Cornell's trick to develop broad regional coverage was to make use of its "upper campus" [directionality in Ithaca is with respect to the flow of water, as it is in Southeast Asia], the public segment of the university dealing with applied topics, where the Rural Sociology department hired Robert Polson, Walter Coward, and Randy Barker. The anthropologist Milton Barnett also worked on development projects (Kahin had brought him from "the field"), and the group as a whole emphasized the Philippines and Malaysia, two countries not represented in the liberal arts segment. Economics, although in the "lower campus", had stronger intellectual ties to the sociologists. Kahin (interview 1997) recalls that upper and lower campus students mixed mainly in country seminars, which took up a different country each semester. All graduate students had to take one such seminar outside their research country, and many took two.

A strong intellectual gap eventually developed between the liberal arts, culturally-oriented faculty housed in the Southeast Asia Program building and the applied faculty. The subregional division of labor also has meant that the "lower campus" students have been mainly of U.S. origin, with interests in history, politics, and anthropology, and working on Vietnam, Thailand, and Java, whereas applied students, who include many Southeast Asians, study topics with little intellectual overlap, such as hydrology and agriculture, and are more widely dispersed across the region.

Cornell's "field" system has promoted interdisciplinary communications by distinguishing between field committees and departmental affiliations. Anthropology graduate students, for example, need only have one member of the anthropology department on their committees; other members may be area specialists from various departments. The historian David Wyatt (interview, 1997) points to these committees as an important site for communication among Southeast Asianist faculty with very different intellectual orientations.

Cornell's first-generation faculty, teaching before Vietnam escalation and before the Indonesian massacres of 1965–66, were more likely to move between government service and university positions (in an role analogous to that of the colonial scholar-bureaucrat), and to encourage both applied and "basic" research. Sharp spent eighteen months after the war in the State Department, where he worked with several other major scholars of the region, including the anthropologist Cora Dubois and the political scientist Rupert Emerson (Kahin 1964: 2; Kirsch 1996:6–7). Stanley O'Connor came to the field of art history from a career in government (where he drew the map of Laos used by President Kennedy in a 1960 television appearance [Kahin 1996: 4]). The Vietnam war soured many scholars on developing any ties to the

U.S. government; Sharp and others received strong criticism for their involvement in the Academic Advisory Council for Thailand during the days of counterinsurgency research (Wakin 1992)

Periods in Cornell research emphases correspond to the general periods I set out below. Kahin (interview 1997) recalls that the baseline for graduate study in the first postwar decade was country history, "including how countries were emerging from colonialism." Comparative seminars stressed current dimensions of religion, treatment of ethnic minorities, Communism, nationalism. By the 1960's the emphasis was economic development in a political context, or modernization, and the research fashion was large-scale comparative studies, into which Southeast Asia was placed—Sharp collaborated with Morris Opler (India) and Allen Holmberg (Peru). Two "waves" of students were produced during these first decades, followed by a decline in job availability after the Vietnam War, and thus fewer students choosing graduate study of the region during the late 1970s and early 1980s, then followed by a surge of enrollments in the late 1980's, leading to a 1990's "third wave" of Cornell PhDs on Southeast Asia, with renewed interest in Vietnam.

As of the late 1990's, Cornell faculty have been searching for new themes to replace those of nationalism and modernization that guided early faculty development.[1]

TRENDS WITHIN AREA STUDIES

It is frequently said that the social sciences have played an unusually dominant role in U.S. Southeast Asian studies, and that this dominance has been at the expense of the humanities. But one must add that the "social science" in question has been of an unusually humanistic sort, in which the public forms of culture—ways of speaking, ritual events, performances—take center stage. The real dominance has been of cultural studies over both textual studies and behavioristic social science.

As of 1970 (reflecting training in the 1950's and 1960's), about 60% of all U.S. Southeast Asian specialists sampled by Richard Lambert (1973:109–110) were social scientists, of whom about half were political scientists and one-quarter anthropologists.[2] [3] The social science percentage was the highest for any world area, with Africa close behind. The region was about in the middle (far below East and South

Asia) regarding the percentage of specialists who worked on the arts, philosophy, or religion, but at the bottom in language, literature, linguistics, and history.

Data on Foreign Area Fellowship Program and Social Science Research Council funding applications between 1951 and 1982 (Szanton 1984)—which include a very broad range of disciplines but nonetheless favor "social science"—show an overall temporal pattern that could be summarized as follows. Political science led in the postwar period, with nationalism and the development of new elites and political structures providing exciting dissertation topics. Anthropology surged ahead in the late 1950's, but with much of its research on topics of modernization closely allied to political science. Political science moved back into lead position during the Vietnam War period, 1962–70, when total numbers of applications peaked. Anthropology dominated the field thereafter, with students less often choosing those lowland communities that were taken as proxies for "new nations" in the 1950's and 1960's, and more often choosing small highland and island communities for their distinct cultural patterns, maintained in the face of state attempts to standardize social life.[4]

These shifts in discipline and topic bring with them shifts in place, from lowlands parts of Thailand, the Philippines, and Indonesia in the 1950's and 1960's, to "marginal" regions, especially in Indonesia, in the 1970's and 1980's. Studies of "Indochina" were of course most affected by the war: of relatively low frequency before 1969, they rose sharply in 1969–1974, and then declined to zero. They began to rise again in the 1990's as field research became possible. The demand for Vietnamese studies by U.S.-born children of Vietnamese parents has meant that at Cornell, Berkeley, and the University of Washington (and perhaps elsewhere) the Vietnamese language program is the largest among Southeast Asian languages.

Differences in emphasis also distinguish country study traditions. Tugby (1968, 1970) asked anthropologists and sociologists in North America, Europe, and Southeast Asia to describe the pressing problems faced in the study of their country (Tugby 1970:50–52). Thai specialists couched their replies in terms of exhaustively describing Thai society and its contemporary developments; Indonesia specialists stressed the relatively uncharted ethnological diversity of the country; Philippines specialists urged studies motivated by anthropological theory rather than comparative or ethnological concerns (perhaps because of the uncertainty some of them expressed as to what "Philippine culture" might be).

What is not revealed in disciplinary data is the rising importance of a cultural approach after 1969. Funding applications from humanists to the SSRC grew, and those from anthropologists (and some others) more often concerned indigenous conceptual systems than had those submitted by earlier generations. Even if "humanities" in the European sense of text study and philology continues to lead a subterranean life in the U.S., "humanities" in other senses, whether as broad as "studying other ways of life" or as specific as "studies of texts, performances, art, and music", arguably has been the central occupation of Southeast Asianists for some time. After all, in what other region would the two best-known political scientists be as oriented toward literature and ethnography as are Benedict Anderson and James Scott?

Some disciplines, such as paleontology and primatology, have had a close relationship with Southeast Asia without any involvment in "Southeast Asian Studies." Conversely, some central fields within Southeast Asian studies have had little impact on their discipline. Southeast Asian linguistics, for example, shed light on early population movement, provided ways to study rituals and everyday lives, made translation a central and culturally sophisticated activity, and, through language teaching, made everyone's work possible. But Southeast Asianists are at best marginal to the discipline, even to the subdiscipline of historical linguistics. John Wolff (interview, 1997) argues that had historical linguistics started in Southeast Asia it would have taken a quite different turn, because language use in the region includes a greater command of different registers and different languages by a single speaker, and a higher frequency of people who speak different languages coming together routinely, and these features of the region imply different patterns of borrowing and language change than those currently occupying subdisciplinary center stage.

U.S. scholarship also has been shaped by what takes place elsewhere. A general division of labor in regional studies can be attributed to historical patterns of scholarship and different contemporary interests. Europeans, especially in Britain, France, and the Netherlands, continue to produce in the traditions of philology and text criticism, even when they draw on current literary theory. The colonial scholar-administrator, with a long residence in the colony and time to gather texts and study languages (see Anderson 1992), lives on in the long periods of residence granted researchers attached to one of the two French Southeast Asianist *equipes* funded by the *Centre National des Recherches Scientifiques* (CNRS) at Paris and Marseilles, and to their counterparts at Leiden's *Koninklijk Instituut voor Taal-, Land- en Volkenkunde* (KITLV), which devotes most of its funding to continued research on and in Indonesia (and other former Dutch colonies). Other Europeans, sometimes located at rival universities, focus on contemporary political-economic issues, as do most Australian researchers—Indonesianists wishing to follow rural as well as national-level economic changes have come to rely on issues of the *Bulletin of Indonesian Economic Studies*, published in Canberra, and on the occasional volumes written and edited by that journal's contributors. Southeast Asians figure increasingly prominently among scholars of the region who write in Western-language publications, and the Singapore-produced *Journal of Southeast Asian Studies* has become a journal of note for regional studies.

Quite distinct from all the above, however, are the traditions of research carried out by Southeast Asians in their home countries and generally published in the country languages. These research complexes are generally segmented off from Western scholars, although this segmentation is changing to some degree as some of these scholars write in English, and as some Western scholars devote some of their time to translating or examining these works. The stakes are not simply the boundaries of collegiality, but access to the most expert scholarship on various topics. Anderson (1992) points out that Thai-language scholarship on literature and history now sets the standard but is inaccessible to all but a few U.S. scholars. Islamic legal scholarship in Malaysia, Indonesia, and the Philippines is enormous, of high quality, and of great interest to those seeking to understand law, politics, and social change in the region, but, again, is generally unread in the U.S. Overall, those sciences with the greatest indigenous purchase—law, literature, religion—are the most de facto closed to U.S. scholars, whereas those whose analytical centers are in Western countries—economics and anthropology, for example—are the most readily available. (History is probably somewhere in between.)

POLITICS, HISTORY, AND CULTURE IN SOUTHEAST ASIAN STUDIES

I have chosen to treat separately the studies of politics, history, and culture, and yet these fields are so closely related that under "politics" I subsume many themes that might have been repeated in subsequent sections (but, I assure you, will not be).

Arguably, two major dynamics have shaped these fields. The first has been the coming together, in anthropology, history, and politics, of European humanistic and historical traditions of study—work by the philologists and literary specialists of Leiden, the epigraphers and archeologists of the French colonial service, and the British gentleman observers of culture and literature in Malaya—with U.S.-centered social sciences. Even by the 1960's, the processes of "Indianization" charter by European scholars had become integrated into U.S. studies of contemporary politics or village rituals.

The rise of the concept of culture facilitated this convergence (as did the vogue of structuralism), but so did the close ties between area studies at Cornell, where long-term history gradually became a more important part of the curriculum, and social sciences elsewhere, especially at Harvard and Chicago. Clifford Geertz, in particular, articulated a Boasian view of culture-as-pattern within a broader social science framework, thereby giving humanistically inclined studies—whether in art history, politics, or anthropology—a certain legitimacy within an otherwise largely behaviorist social science world.

The second overall dynamic (running somewhat counter to, and later than, the first) has been a movement away from uniform notions of "society" and "culture" toward emphases on disunity, conflict, and inequality—a shift that on a theoretical level might be traced to disillusionment with the Parsonian consensus model of society (with its heavy reliance on notions of function and a domestication of both Durkheim and Weber) and a rediscovery of the historical analyses carried out by Marx and Weber.

POLITICS AND POLITICAL ECONOMY

Southeast Asian studies hardly needed to "bring the state back in" (Evans, Rueschemeyer & Skocpol 1985) because the state always has been doubly central: cultural models of statehood were a major part of the intellectual inheritance from the Indologists, and postwar area studies focused on nationalism and political self-fashionings. These two themes were intertwined: even as one moves from the concern with Communism in the immediate postwar period, to the more explicit effort to build political science models in the 1950's and 1960's, to the attention to culture and conflict thereafter, the best writers on politics in the region argued that politics in the region was shaped by some very old ideas, and that this shaping meant that "politics" involved "religion" and "social organization." Even a model-builder like Fred Riggs (1966), avowedly not a specialist in the region, begins his analysis of Thai politics by invoking Robert Heine-Geldern and the importance of macro-microcosmic ideas to understanding political life. And one of the more important accounts of the background to the Vietnamese Revolution published in the U.S. (McAlister and Mus 1970) was coauthored by a man best known for his studies of prehistory and cosmology, Paul Mus.

This general insight, that long-term cultural patterns inform current political behavior, has rested on a handful of interrelated concepts. It is these concepts, and not the behavioristic-attitudinal notion of "political culture", that have most effectively directed Southeast Asian political studies. They include the local power-broker often called *datu*, the *mandala* or "circle of kings", patron-client ties, and the (patrimonial) "bureaucratic polity." Each of the institutions described by these concepts is found throughout the region, thus usefully knitting together its diverse parts, has had a long historical presence, and can be used to explain patterns of behavior not otherwise predicted. The centrality of these institutions to political studies has also facilitated close intellectual and institutional ties between students of politics and students of history and culture.

One can, with the usual trepidation, identify successive emphases within Southeast Asianist political studies. During the first two decades of regional study, an initial focus on nationalist politics was followed by efforts to understand politics as part of general developmental processes in society. Beginning in the 1970's, students of politics refined each of these two lines of analysis. First, the ideas of "power" and "nation" that lay behind the early nationalism and its successor forms were explored. Secondly, what had been taken to be universal processes of modernization were subjected to a more fine-grained, critical, historically-based examination of central and local politics, bringing class analysis back into the picture.

Soon after its creation in 1950, the Cornell center began to produce country studies focused on current political developments, under the direction of George Kahin. These descriptive studies kept the exigencies of nation-building and nationalism very much in mind. A collection that appeared in two editions, in 1959 and 1964 (Kahin 1964), presented accounts of each country in a uniform manner; some of the authors then produced de facto third editions in monographic format.

Anderson (1982) refers to the "Kahinian" approach as historical in method and pro-nationalist in orientation. Some of the orientation of this school may come from George Kahin's own close involvment in the revolution, his acquaintance with the nationalist elite, and his opposition to American neo-colonialism as well as to the older Dutch, British, and French varieties. One feels in many of these works a sense of the excitement of "being at the creation" and a responsibility to give a clear account of events happening fast and furious in the heady days of the anticolonial struggles, revolutions, and efforts to form new independent states. Theory and social science seemed distant concerns. As Kahin said to me in a 1997 interview at Cornell: "we had no paradigms". Even the early work of that very theoretical of social scientists, Clifford Geertz, including *The Religion of Java* and his articles on economic change, are written in this straightforward mode of trying to catch the sense of new and unfamiliar developments in the "new nations."

Of course theories and assumptions did shape these works. In Geertz's case, the Weberian framework set up by Parsons at Harvard, the approach to culture practiced by Franz Boas and Ruth Benedict (and taught at Harvard by Clyde Kluckhohn), and the ways of analyzing civilizations through ethnography just then being mapped out by Robert Redfield and his students at Chicago, all make their appearance, through style and structure rather than footnote and theory, in *The Religion of Java*, a book which has as much to say about the cultural bases of politics as it does about the historical roots of religions.

Most students of the region took for granted the idea that states should, and perhaps were, moving toward secular, liberal constitutional orders. Such was the brunt of Kahin's *Nationalism and*

Revolution in Indonesia, and of the works of the others at Cornell. But that assumption also lay behind Geertz's writings throughout these decades, and behind the general approach adopted by the Committee for the Study of New Nations at Chicago, even as some of those social scientists also tried to move political studies in a more model-building direction.

As Anderson (1982) points out, the early Cornell focus on the heroic efforts of nationalist elites led them to pay less attention to other groups, including the Communists, the army, and, I would add, those Muslim groups not part of the more pro-Western orientation. (This last set of sympathies and dislikes continue to shape the foci and blind spots of regional political studies, such that quite often the same set of Western-oriented, liberal Islamic leaders or regime critics are interviewed for their views, but not those leaders and scholars advocating other types of regimes or laws.) The first, Cornell-dominated set of political studies also paid much more attention to the capital cities, the repositories of "nation", than to regions or towns, and tended to downplay diversity in favor of the one-nation-state model. To support this style of analysis a particular idea of culture was employed.

David Wilson, for example, followed his chapter on Thailand in the two editions of Kahin's collection with a 1962 monograph, in which he justifies studying such a remote country as Thailand by pointing to its power in the region and ultimate importance for U.S. security. His goal is synthesis and overall description of the country, drawing on the field studies carried out after the war at the Cornell Research Center in Bangkok. But Wilson also incorporates, indeed takes as the foundation for his analysis, the long-duration history of Thai culture, from which he extracts in particular two elements: the cosmologically-based relations of center to periphery (based on Heine-Geldern), and the tenet that moral value determines power, from which follow both the idea of a single hierarchy of statuses and the institution of personalized bureaucracy that governs the country. Wilson makes extensive use of Thai-language texts.

In drawing on these elements Wilson's analysis resembles those previous and those to follow. But the nation-state format also leads him to describe Thailand in terms of a uniform culture, in which people accept their fate because of Buddhist teachings, and in terms of a more or less shared ethnic identity. Culture appears as a constant, and society as providing a uniform set of social norms. Political institutions follow from culture and society.

For some authors writing from outside Cornell an even stronger sense of anti-Communism (and pro-democracy) served as the urgent motive for writing their books. Rupert Emerson's *Representative Government in Southeast Asia* is written in the middle of "the desperate eleventh-hour struggle to create a viable non-Communist state in southern Vietnam" (1955:v), and describes the efforts by Westernized elites in Southeast Asia to apply the constitutions of the West to very different societies. Donald Nuechterlein's Berkeley dissertation on foreign policy concerns Thailand's place in "the struggle for survival among the free nations of Southeast Asia" (1965:vii) and, although published by Cornell, makes no attempt to base the study on Thai concepts of power, borders, or other nations, concepts which might have been thought to be of particular importance for this study.

A somewhat later set of studies emphasizes model-building and comparisons, and often draws on the emerging literature about "modernization". Almond, Verba, Colman, Pye and Apter are the demigods of this group (for example, Pye 1962). In describing some of these authors Anderson (1982) emphasizes their opposition to nationalism in the name of a smoother transition to democratic capitalism, but the liberal democratic vision remains unchallenged, only the taste had soured as nationalism showed other sides.

Political studies could still draw on older culture history even as they responded to the theory-consciousness of the 1960's. In his study of the Thai bureaucracy, Fred Riggs (1966) represents himself as a model builder (he had received an SSRC grant for comparative political studies) and not an area specialist, and yet spent considerable time "in country". Although not part of the Cornell program, Riggs benefited from the Cornell Bangkok field station. The Janus-faced nature of his situation—country focus yet analytical drive—troubled him (1966: 3–12), and one ought to read his musings when confronted by the more intolerant versions of this tension thrown up in the 1990s.

Riggs' aim is to produce a model of the "bureaucratic polity" by drawing on his Thai data. He examines at length the macro-microcosmic roots of political life (with due acknowledgement of Heine-Geldern's ideas), but can only use this information after he has inserted it into a comparativist vocabulary. All this cosmos stuff may seem insubstantial, he confesses, but when understood as "the legitimizing or ordering function" (1966:69) it becomes recognizable as "politics." His main concern is typology, and Rigg tells a very Weberian story—but keeps the cultural roots present. Riggs's model was influential because it showed a way to remain true to one's areal sensitivities and yet also write in a comparative-analytic way, as required for respect in political science.

The modernization approach required that social phenomena be sorted into two categories, the primordial and the modern, and here other social sciences were perforce brought into play. The modern side had already been analyzed. On the primordial side were ethnic groups (hill tribes, island cultures) (Leach 1964; Keyes 1979), Chinese and Indian minority communities, and distinctions of religious and cultural orientation within the majority lowland populations on Java, Luzon, the Malay peninsula, in central Thailand, and southern Vietnam (such as Geertz's [1960] *abangan/priyayi/santri* for Java), or the puzzling *absence* of such "structure" in other lowland areas. Of note are the analytical axes not employed here: the Chinese could have been seen as a commercial bourgeoisie with historically-specific roles (Rush 1990); the three-way division in Java could have been seen as a reflection of the balance of power at the time between landowners and landless, and between state agents and others (Hart 1989). (A naive version of "the primordial" survives even after the social scientists have given it up—attacks on Chinese shops in Indonesia in 1997 and 1998 were generally described as motivated either by "ethnic hatred" or "religious tensions", despite the fact that they were directed mainly against property, and that they were in response to specific economic measures or conditions.)

More recent political studies have taken two forms. One explores ideas and institutions of power in a more ethnographic and cultural, rather than comparativist and societal, fashion. Benedict Anderson's (1972) essay on "the Javanese concept of power" and Clifford Geertz's *Negara* (1980) are among the most frequently cited. But in the same vein are other studies on law and politics in Indonesia (Liddle 1997) and elsewhere. For Thailand, one could mention David Engel's (1975) explorations of the Thai *thammasat* legal code, derived from the dharmashastras, as the theoretical basis for King Chulalongkorn's reforms in the late 19th and early 20th centuries, and which gave Engel the foundation for his later (1978) ethnography of a Thai provincial court.

A second set of studies has emphasized the diversity of political ideas, institutions, and processes within a country, thus challenging the universal and implicitly teleological idea of modernity, but also challenging the idea of a unitary, stable political culture. Thus, John Girling begins his textbook on Thailand (1981a) by citing Coedes's history of the Indianized states, starts his analysis of politics with a discussion of Buddhism, and retains Weber as the major analytical source, but then (unlike Wilson in his 1962 study) subjects earlier ideas of political culture and structure to a historical critique. In discussing the Thai status hierarchy, Girling points to local challenges to that order—a line of study further pursued by Craig Reynolds (1987), who translates and analyzes Thai Marxist challenges to the "feudal" order (sakdina), thereby illuminating the field of political contestation within a Thai cultural domain.

Girling (1981b) points out two major problems with Riggs's earlier study, and his criticism can be taken to signal a major shift in political studies. First, by assuming a single set of norms and values, derived from the mandala polities of the past, Riggs missed other norms, those based on ideas of constitutionalism and democracy, that in Thailand came to fruition in 1973. Secondly, the model of bureaucratic polity assumed more consensus across social strata than ought to have been assumed. One might add that Riggs also assumed a single bureaucracy rather than competing ones, a mistake often replicated in studies of "the state" in all these countries.[5]

Similar critiques have been launched regarding other states in the region. For Vietnam, debates about state-society relations are currently in the forefront: is the state bureaucracy the source of all decisions—a model of a powerful bureaucratic polity (Porter 1993)? Or are social forces powerfully causal on their own, with a "penetrating civil society" (Thrift and Forbes 1986) shaping local activities in defiance of state dictates?

Many distinct models of the state have been proposed for the region—indeed, each major political scientist appears to want to have his very own. Debates turn on the extent to which the bureaucracy is shielded from outside influences, or to which a pluralistic model is appropriate, or, rather, a model of "corporatism" such as has been developed for Latin America (for some of the debates regarding Indonesia, see Anderson and Kahin [1982]). (I myself find that "corporatism" captures very well the propensity of Indonesia's government to establish its own authorized interest groups, often called a "single container" [wadah tunggal] for "the people's aspirations").

But most of these models assume that "politics" is mainly about members of the bureaucracy, particularly those living in the capital cities. This idea of politics omits all those who work for the government in some capacity but who can hardly be thought of as part of a single pyramid—religious judges, school teachers, village headmen. These actors are subject to state regulation but also conceive of power, interests, and values in ways not captured by any of these models. A focus on bureaucracy also ignores the "everyday politics" (Kerkvliet 1990) that has more to do with other political bases, such as landowning, control of rice mills, high rank in a local system of rank and prestige, and membership in local associations.

One line of analysis did focus on non-state actors, however; these studies turned on patron-client ties or the "entourage" (Hanks 1966), and may serve as an instance of the second general dynamic I mentioned earlier, namely, the movement away from accepting cultural categories as adequate descriptions of power relations, and toward analyzing them as tokens in highly varied discourses about power and legitimacy.

Patron-client analysis has had several lasting strengths. It ties political studies to historical and cultural studies of authority, including studies of figures Wolters (1982) terms "men of prowess", resembling Melanesian big-men and often referred to as *datu*, the local leaders who amass power through successfully claiming greater proximity to local spirits. It also provides a convincing analytical account of how norms of generalized reciprocity can provide a basis for social order without state intervention (for a theoretical development of this idea, see Taylor 1982). The framework also holds up well as it is translated across levels of society: patron-client ties in agrarian regions involve landholding and laboring; at court they involve status ranking; in bureaucracies they involve mentoring and patronage.

One can probably trace the development of patron-client analysis to those anthropologists of the Philippines (e.g., Lynch 1968) who used Tagalog reciprocity terms as labels for basic cultural values. These values were then used to provide cultural explanations for the acceptance and persistence of patron-client ties, especially in the plains societies of Luzon (Lande 1965). The general theory of patron-client hierarchies was most elegantly set out by Scott (1972), who argues that in the absence of highly developed corporate kin groups, and against the general background of uncertainty and scarcity, patron-client networks naturally develop across Southeast Asia, imbued with and in turn promoting social inequality (see also Hanks 1966).

Patron-client ties and the moral vocabularies of reciprocity were quickly accepted into Southeast Asian studies. Not only did they appear to provide politics with a cultural grounding, they also met a strongly felt need for an analytical framework to study the plains societies of Thailand, Malaysia, and the Philippines. Whereas anthropologists working in highland Thailand and Burma, or east and west Indonesia, could draw on local categories of descent and exchange for instant analyses, scholars interested in social structure in the plains areas found no such home-grown kinship ideas. This apparent vacuum gave rise to ideas such as "loosely structured societies" (Embree 1950) that had little analytical or comparative import. "Patron-client" supplied an attractive new way of studying social life in these areas.

But do these culturally-elaborated ties of reciprocity and patronage indicate a generally-accepted system, or do they mask an imposed, and historically changeable inequality? One example around which these debates unfolded was the phenomenon of "agricultural involution" examined by Clifford Geertz for Java. In the best tradition of social science, the clarity of Geertz's (1963) argument for the ecological symbiosis of rice and sugar and the "shared poverty" ethos in contemporary Java set off a flurry of research projects, both historical and ethnographic. Some scholars argued that labor recruiting and harvesting practices on Java, far from embodying a communitarian ethic, work for the benefit of the better-off (Stoler 1977). Gillian Hart (1986) contends that the redistributive mechanisms described by Geertz appeared only at times when state power was weak (including the period in the 1950s when Geertz did his original fieldwork). At times of greater state control, local elites have built ties to state officials, allowing these elites to reduce their reliance on the poor for economic and political support (Hart 1989). Parallel arguments *(mutatis mutandis)* have been made for the rice plains of Thailand (Turton 1989); Malaysia (Scott 1985), and Luzon (Fegan 1989; Kerkvliet 1990; Wolters 1983).

Moreover, the "clients" in question have often challenged the existing order, sometimes on its own terms and sometimes with concepts taken from alternative moral systems. Ileto (1979) shows how millennial movements in the Philippines fashioned their own ideologies from the same debt-reciprocity ideas that were used by the elites to justify ties of dependency. Furthermore, precisely because the relation of Mary to Christ (and that of Spain to the Filipino people) had been promoted through the cultural vehicle of *utang na loob,* the "debt of gratitude", Filipinos could safely, and effectively, use this term to critique the colonial relationship (Rafael 1988). Scott (1985) has made the same argument for Malaysia: that the very generality of the ideology of reciprocity gives the landless some basis for an effective public critique of the well-off (see also McLellan 1986). Scott contrasts the public statements about social relations (the kind of statements that had once been taken as "reality"), with the "offstage" and often very cutting remarks made by peasants about landlords and vice-versa. The surface appearance of allegiance to a dominant norm (here, patron-client reciprocity), may conceal a great deal of peasant dissatisfaction with the current terms of trade. Ironically, the rich ethnographic studies by Scott and Kerkvliet now place in question Scott's (1976) earlier argument that precapitalist villages were characterized by a generally accepted set of socioeconomic relations. Could it not be that just as much (concealed) subaltern hostility characterized the precapitalist village?

Adding a new dimension to the problem, Kerkvliet (1990) stresses the multiplicity of values available to farmers. Luzon landowners and tenants value vertical ties of clientage and kinship networks, but they also value progress (including the capacity to "rationalize" labor use) and the right to buy and sell property (see also Wolters 1983). Though developing their ideas in complementary fashion, Scott and Kerkvliet present agrarian societies from slightly different angles: Scott, working in Kedah, assigns to "winners and losers" two clear and distinct points of view; Kerkvliet, in Luzon, emphasizes ambivalences and contradictions.

Reciprocity terms are thus better seen as constructing a field for political action rather than transparently revealing widely accepted values. The state also has an interest in the reinterpretation of reciprocity terms. The state may use these terms to mobilize labor or wealth for development programs (Bowen 1986). Laotian Communist officials tried to base collectivization efforts on local traditions of "mutual solidarity and assistance" (Evans 1990, 149). Communist cadres were able to build on existing labor-exchange arrangements in their efforts to restructure labor recruitment, but encountered widespread resistance when they attempted to collectivize land ownership. Yet many Western observers of Laos and Vietnam had confused the two types of programs, arguing that the region already had traditions of collectivism (Evans 1990). Here, as in the Philippines and Indonesia, social science assumptions that cultural categories reflected broad traditions highly internalized by actors unfortunately have converged with state efforts to control labor and dissent.

Political studies have benefited from Southeast Asianist research in a number of closely interrelated ways, including at least the following. First, the long tradition of attention to concepts of power, their religious foundations, spatial display, and ritual reproduction in the region have produced a small number of studies read by political scientists (and others) with no special interest in the region including Clifford Geertz's *Negara* (1980), and Benedict Anderson's (1983) *Imagined Communities,* which sees the idea of nation as the search for a national analogue to the village (perhaps due to a longing for the pre-1965 Javanese village). Secondly, the region is becoming known for a kind of ethnography-based political theory (or theory-based political ethnography?), associated with James Scott's studies of political consciousness. Finally, local texts have become the sources of choice for understanding the history of power. One can mention Tambiah's (1976) analysis of Thai politics, Keith Taylor's (1983) work on Ly Vietnam, and the use by political scientists of literature, cartoons, and popular theatre, and novels. These features not only contribute to political studies generally, but have led to an unusually close intellectual relationship among practitioners of anthropology, history, and political science. The footnotes in Girling's excellent 1981 textbook on Thailand includes far more references to historians and anthropologists than to political scientists: the older, expected references to Coedes, Heine-Geldern and Wales, but also the contemporary ethnographic references to Tambiah, Keyes, and others.

Conversely, many of the key analytical concepts used by anthropologists of Southeast Asia come from students of politics. Surely none are cited more frequently in the 1980's and 1990's than the ideas of "imagined community" from Anderson, "moral economy" and "forms of resistance" from Scott—but so was the case in the previous generation with "patron-client" ties.

The Vietnam War may have changed the direction of political and economic studies most sharply of any field. Some research was carried out on and during the war itself; for example Osborne's (1965) study of the failed strategic hamlet program. The war also gave raise to later, more reflective studies, that drew on area specialist knowledge, such as Hue-Tam Tai's (1992) study of the Vietnamese revolution (Tai 1992) or Ben Kiernan's (1996) attempt to understand the success of the Pol Pot regime, and the continuing effort, now centered at Yale, to document the regime's murderous life.

The war sharply changed an entire generation's attitude toward how one acquired knowledge and what kinds of knowledge were worthy of acquiring. In the 1950's, social scientists could engage in field research while attached to an AID mission, with RAND Corporation support, and discuss their work with State Department personnel with few if any qualms (see the discussion in Halpern 1964: v). The mere involvment in discussions and seminars with government staff was later to haunt some fieldworkers from the first two generations when government minutes of meetings were scrutinized for objections to the Vietnam War or to counterinsurgency research (Wakin 1992). CIA sponsorship of anti-Communist books in the 1960's, and covert military support for journals (*Vietnam Perspectives,* followed, after bombing broadened to include Cambodia, *Southeast Asian Perspectives*) (Kahin 1997: 41–2) added to a general mistrust of research on certain topics.

One result of this suspicion was that any involvment with issues of economic development or foreign aid, much less direct work for hire, now appeared tainted to many specialists. Before the Vietnam War, scholars moved with some ease between government and academia, and engaged in "development administration" as well (see Esman 1972). Thereafter, a sharp division of labor has separated academics, who largely work on the cultural and social side of things, and consultants, most of them economists, who work in the non- or quasi-academic sector. For example, Harvard (as the Development Advisory Service, later the Institute for International Development) has maintained a very visible presence in Indonesia, and to some extent in Malaysia and Thailand, for several decades, and many economists and other social scientists have carried out studies as well as provided advice to the government through HIID's offices. But this research is published in development journals or as in-house reports. (Compare the wealth of studies on development-related issues in Africa or Latin America carried out by academics and published for other academics.)

The war led many U.S. political scientists and economists interested in questions of development or political economy to turn to other world areas for their research. Richard Doner notes "the relatively meager contribution of Southeast Asian studies to the political economy literature" (1991:821), and that most of what there is comes from scholars located in Australia. (Here the international division of labor is particularly important.)

Early work in political economy was dominated by two themes. First, students of the colonial economy emphasized the "dualistic economy" (Furnivall 1956; Geertz 1963). Under this system, natives played only the role of increasingly pressured deliverers of produce and self-sufficient, at best, peasants, while the Europe-oriented export sector—perhaps better named the extractive sector—employed Europeans plus native workers. Chinese served as middlemen, for example holding the monopoly on opium and thereby making it profitable to extend retail marketing well into the countryside (Rush 1990).

Secondly, economists lamented the postcolonial response of economic nationalism, the desire to place economic control in the hands of those natives who had been kept away from the benefits of development for so long. Golay et al. (1969) argued that so long as the new states gave economic nationalism priority over economic development—distribution of product over size of product—then economists had better tailor their policy advice to those priorities or risk having no effect at all on economic policy. Issues of economic nationalism developed most intensely in the Philippines, with its strategies of import substitution (and which thus resembled Latin America), and studies of capitalists and nationalism continued to focus there, and made few if any connections with the rest of Southeast Asian studies. For the rest of the region, interest was in state structures and bureaucrats. As a result, "political economy" approaches, including studies of local entrepreneurs and Chinese capitalists, received little attention (McVey 1992).[6]

By the 1980's an approach stressing "agrarian dynamics" had coalesced (see Hart, Turton, and White 1989), drawing on long-term research into rural agricultural change, and adding more recent studies of multinational factories (Wolf). Business studies promise to expand idea of state power to include groups with independent power bases, such as the textile industry group studied by MacIntyre (1990), that successfully forced the Indonesian government to overturn a monopoly grant for the procurement of materials for the spinning industry.[7]

THE STUDY OF SOUTHEAST ASIAN HISTORY

History contributed to regional study the mandala idea, a "circle of kings", where datu-like claims that one has ties to local spirits become king-like claims that one has ties to Siva or Vishnu, and hence universal power.

But in the first two decades of U.S. historical writing the emphasis was on producing local, nearly-contemporary social histories. At Cornell these dissertations were written for both History and Government departments. Robert Van Niel's 1954 dissertation, the first in History, concerned the modern Indonesian elite, Harry Benda's the following year (in Government) was on Islam during the Japanese occupation of Indonesia (1958), while Taufik Abdullah's (1970, History) examined recent developments in Indonesian Islamic education. John Smail's in 1964 (in History) and Benedict Anderson's in 1967 (in Government) both analyzed the Indonesian revolution on Java. History dissertations about the mainland focused on the late 19th and early 20th centuries, including David Wyatt's (1966) on modern education in Thailand, Milton Osborne's (1968) on Indochina, and Constance Wilson's (1970) on Thailand's King Mongkut.

Some of these historians felt themselves increasingly constrained to focus on their particular research problem and not to venture too widely into study of the region as a whole. Kept busy learning a field language and one or two archival languages, "we were not pushed to do comparative work or to see Southeast Asia in a world context" (Frederick, personal communication 1998). Nor have many historians become regional experts: for obvious practical reasons, few scholars in any discipline learn Thai and Indonesian and Vietnamese (which would also require knowing Dutch and French). The few who have made these linguistic efforts tend to be at regional centers and to see their readerships as not described by a single discipline—the best examples being (again at Cornell) Benedict Anderson, who works on Indonesia, Thailand, and the Philippines, and Oliver Wolters, who moved from early Malay studies to Vietnamese history.[8]

Time focus recedes as the Cornell program ages: dissertations on earlier periods began to appear toward the end of the 1960's: John Whitmore's (1969) on 15th century Vietnam, Leonard Andaya's (1971) on 17th-18th century Johor, and Charnvit Kasetsiri's (1972) on 14th-15th century Ayudhya (Thailand). These backward progressions probably reflect the new appointments of David Wyatt and Oliver Wolters to the History faculty; Wolters was largely responsible for developing research interest in early archipelagic history.

The resurgence in premodern history in the 1970's probably contributed to a general heightened interest in reexamining the analytic categories used in history writing, from "source" to "center" and "state."[9] Indigenous writings about the past have always been mined for information about specific past events, but during the 1970's many historians turned to such local genres for information about the perceptions and perspectives of participants in those events, as well as for insight into ideas about the past that are found in the past or in the present. A number of collections from the 1970's and 1980's emphasize the importance of such "sources", especially for the writing of premodern history (Gesick 1983; Marr and Milner 1986; Wolters 1982; Wyatt and Woodside 1982), and the essays in Reid and Marr (1979) sought to establish a new kind of indigenous historiography for the region. A number of particularly fine examples of this approach regard early Vietnamese history (Taylor 1986; Wolters 1986), perhaps because such sources provide insight into Vietnamese ideas about authority and legitimacy that had been misleadingly overlaid with Chinese-

Confucian terms.

Premodern studies also queried concepts of "center" and "state." Historians and anthropologists have taken up the concept of "Indianization" in various ways: in Tambiah's (1976) study of the "Galactic polity," which links the Asokan figure of the "wheel-rolling ruler," the *cakravartin,* to the *mandala* polity, and to current political ideas; Clifford Geertz's (1980) *Negara;* Paul Wheatley's (1983) study of the early cities, *Nâgara,* Michael Aung-Thwin's (1985) *Pagan.* At the same time, an awareness of problems in "Indianization" as a category (redolent of "Orientalism" to some), led some historians to propose substituting "classical" (see the results in Gesick 1983). Other work has undermined projections of modern centralized states back in time (projections perhaps aided by the mandala idea)—for example, James Siegel (1969) pointed out the relatively independent roles of religious scholars, traders, and rulers in 19th century Aceh.

Other historians wish to deconstruct the notion that current state boundaries describe a single political and cultural entity. Taylor, for example, argues that even the idea that northern Vietnam polities resemble China; southern ones the Theravada neighbors oversimplifies the matter, because kings drew on different features for different purposes, giving locally distinctive forms to Theravada concepts (such as the *sangha*), and incorporating Confucian terms without creating Confucian-style bureaucracies,

Finally, the analytical usefulness of writing about historical developments in "Southeast Asia" as currently defined has become the subject of greater debate since the publication of Anthony Reid's two-volume study (1988, 1993) of the region in the early modern period. Reid saw two kinds of grounds for taking the region as the analytical unit: a single set of cultural materials and norms, and a single regional historical dynamic, as exemplified in the crisis of the 17th century (Reid 1993). Victor Lieberman (1995), among others, disagrees, arguing that the mainland and archipelago experienced the 17th century (and presumably other centuries as well) in significantly different ways, because of the increasing vulnerability of the latter region to fluctuations in overseas commerce.

Other historians (Day 1996; Reynolds 1994) have asked whether the interest in the state and a reliance on Indic models have not obscured the importance of family—a question that suggests a way in which the older anthropology of family and marriage could become reinvigorated as part of historical studies. Day argues that shared problems of competition in families and the demands of controlling one's ancestors are what shaped the development of states in Southeast Asia.

This idea has been developed as a general theory of regional history by Oliver Wolters, who, although he favors subregional analyses on grounds that they better capture distinctive local processes (and thus would probably side with Lieberman in the debate mentioned above), also claims that the region's histories have to be placed on a non-Europeanist footing. Wolters (1982) argues that in the cognatically organized, isolated societies of premodern Southeast Asia, some men ("men of prowess") successfully claimed to possess higher quality "soul stuff". As ancestors they continued to benefit the community, and their veneration would have served as the cultural receptacle for the *devaraja* cult established by the Cambodian ruler Jayavarman II in 802. Cognatic kinship ensured that all Cambodians could benefit from the ruler's prowess, but the operant concept of power also required that the ruler continually validate prowess through achievement. From this perspective, "Indianization" did not mean adopting, whole cloth, a new world view, but rather selecting certain specific ideas that fit with the ideas and interests of the adopters. In this case one such ideas was devotionalism, a powerful closeness to Shiva or Vishnu that depended on personal effort, especially ascetic practices.

This theory accords well with Keith Taylor's (1986) argument that from the Vietnamese perspective it was the moral qualities of the 11th-century Ly rulers that aroused the spiritual powers dwelling in the Viet realm and induced them become protectors of the realm. The role of the Buddhist monkhood then becomes one of urging spirits to conform to the royal order. Taylor argues that although Chinese texts and precepts were employed to explain this new order, its basis was the Southeast Asian idea of a sacred kingship: for example, the actions of "Taoist priests" were similar to those of Japanese Shinto priests, namely, dealing with local spirits (Taylor 1986:149). This line of analysis brings us back to the work in Europe and Southeast Asia of Paul Mus (1933) and others on local religious cults.

Viewed in this way, the passage from "prestate" to "state" is a gradual aggregation of similar powers, not a sharp discontinuity, and does not necessarily involve creating a bureaucracy or a large city. That which later makes the ruler look like the summit of Weber's "patrimonial bureaucracy" (in Angkor, Sriwijaya, Ayudhya, Majapahit, and probably elsewhere) was his role as mediator between spirits and the realm, and among the many client groups that made up his entourage. Southeast Asian classical states thus begin to look more like Hawaiian kingships, where distant siblings were brought into alliance against dangerous siblings, or the court at Versailles, where centralization of power was designed to reduce the power both of regional lords and of close relatives, and less like the Chinese bureaucracy or its European cousin—or for that matter Indian kingships.

THE HUMANITIES AND CULTURE

Have humanities flourished within Southeast Asian studies? Cultural studies surely have; humanities, a different concept, arguably have not. "Humanities," of course, can mean many different things: a set of disciplines or departments (art history, literature), a very specific set of methods (philology), a set of objects of study (paintings, novels), or a certain approach to studying any topic (humanistic). I think that those who find humanities neglected in Southeast Asian studies have the first two meanings in mind. Humanities disciplines indeed have been less well represented for Southeast Asia than for other areas, as I indicated earlier, and those disciplines have been confined to a few area centers, principally Berkeley, Cornell, Michigan and Wisconsin. Classical humanities approaches, centering on the comparative, philological analyses of texts, are not practiced widely even at those centers that do have strong representation of humanities disciplines.[10] By contrast, social scientists concentrating on the region are found in many universities.

Why the relative neglect of the humanities in the study of Southeast Asia? Perhaps a series of contrasts with other regional traditions would help explain the situation. For South Asian studies, the particular emphasis of British colonialism on English-language training and higher education created a relatively large number of superbly trained English-speaking scholars. These scholars then developed a strong critical study of colonialism and an important body of post-colonial fiction and studies of that (and other) fiction. For Southeast Asia it may only be the work of Pramoedya Ananta Toer that could claim a comparable position to that of so many South Asian writers—one lone figure!

The post-colonial studies of South Asianists fit with the current fashions in some comparative literature departments, creating jobs for South Asianists—but not for Southeast Asianists, where the initial training never existed. (The story is complex, of course, because some of the post-colonial interest is itself due to the extraordinary productivity of many of South Asian scholars in the first place!) A similar close relationship between colonial and postcolonial studies and developments in literary studies within the region could be described for the Middle East and Latin America.

Yet, if we take "humanities" in the second and third senses suggested above—as defining certain objects of study and a certain appreciative approach to those objects—then the situation looks very different, and the complaint about neglect is much less true. Consider, first, that studies of Javanese art, music, theater, and literature are on a recent rise (e.g., Florida 1993; Sears 1996), and popular enjoyment of Southeast Asian performing arts, in particular gamelan, has spread across the U.S.. Studies of contemporary art are also enjoying a vogue (e.g., Wright 1994). Perhaps growing regional strength in performing arts and literature departments will follow suit. I suspect, however, that even if Southeast Asia achieved parity with other regions in these disciplines, the complaint about neglect of the humanities would still be heard, because it derives from the sense that given the salience of arts in the region (Bali, Java, etc.), Southeast Asia ought to have proportionally *more* humanities faculty than other regions.

More centrally, as I have said elsewhere (Bowen 1995), the striking feature of Southeast Asianist anthropology, the dominant discipline in U.S. studies of the region, has been its consistent attention to those performance forms that constitute the primary object of study for the humanities. Public cultural performances have been central to the anthropology of the region, from Bateson and Mead's (1942) work on Balinese character, to analyses of culture through dance (Ness 1992), shadow plays (Keeler 1987), and shamanistic healing (Atkinson 1989). Historical and political studies of lowland realms have emphasized the capacity of temples and royal performances to convey power from a sacred center (Geertz 1980; Hall and Whitmore 1976; Heine-Geldern 1956; Tambiah 1976). The study of local ways of speaking has been a critical point of departure for understanding processes of social change (Errington 1989; Kuipers 1990; Luong 1988) and religious debates (Bowen 1993), as has the study of how people read and understand novels (Banks 1987; Sweeney 1987) and enjoy popular music (Yampolsky (1989).

A general appreciation and enjoyment of Southeast Asian literature has also crossed disciplinary lines, such that specialists in all fields read works produced in the region. I would guess that my colleagues in government or social history of Southeast Asia are more likely to have read a novel in Indonesian or Thai than would be the case for their colleagues in African studies and even their colleagues in South Asian studies, if we limit ourselves to indigenous languages.[11]

It may be that when discussing the "fate of the humanities" we ask the wrong questions. Why should the study of art in Southeast Asia look like the study of European art as classically practiced in Europe? The art historian Stanley O'Connor makes the case for "cultural contextualization" in studying art objects, arguing that the gradually learned ability in the U.S. and Europe to encompass art from all parts of the world as "art" has reduced our ability to see that, as he puts it, "the arts of much of the rest of the world, over most of human time, were actions embedded in community; that these works both sustained and disclosed the worlds from which they have now been pried loose" (1995:152).

At the beginning of this century, anthropologists were engaged in a vehement debate over the way to organize museums: were artifacts to be grouped in terms of a presumed universal function, e.g., as a progressive ordering of "the developing arts of warfare," as they had been, or, as Franz Boas and others urged, should they be exhibited as part of the specific cultural complex that gives the objects meaning? The latter position won as far as anthropology was concerned, but, as O'Connor laments (1995), it lost ground in art history. Perhaps the contribution of Southeast Asian art studies will be to resituate art as part of cultural life.[12]

The kind of fieldwork-based study of speech, texts, art, and performance I have been remarking has been particularly effective in cutting across older disciplinary divisions of labor. The study of large-

scale religions provides a good example. At the time when the first
Southeast Asia centers were established, the study of Islam, Buddhism,
and other highly textualized religious traditions (what Robert Redfield
[1956] called the urban "great" traditions) was largely controlled by
historians of religion, while anthropologists limited themselves to the
study of illiterate, rural "little" traditions—"folk" stuff such as cults of
ancestors, saints, and village spirits.

Breaking through this dichotomy was done largely through the
study of how villagers read, recited, and listened to religious texts, and
much of the break-through work was done in Southeast and South
Asia. Stanley Tambiah (1970) showed that northeastern Thai village
monks learned Pali texts as well as vernacular ones, and that ordinary
folk considered it of religious importance to "listen without
understanding" to Pali ritual utterances (1970: 195–214). Tambiah also
turned the tables: it is not just that Buddhism also lives in the village,
but that there is no Buddhism (or Islam or Catholicism) that is
independent of any particular social realization of Buddhism (1976:
402)—although continued use by others of phrases such as "normative
Islam" or "doctrinal Buddhism" implies that there is.

Islam has provided a greater analytical challenge, because Muslims
inherit a tradition that urges them to construct all of their lives around
Islamic norms. In the 1950's and 1960's this tradition itself was of
interest neither to political scientists, for whom Islam was important
only as a set of political forces or movements, nor to anthropologists,
who found it unappealingly homogeneous next to fascinating local
cultural diversities. The initial approaches were through the sociology
of Islamic ideas, as in Clifford Geertz's *Religion of Java* (1960), written
along Redfieldian lines, which convincingly situated "streams" of
religion in the institutional contexts of market, school, and office, or in
Clive Kessler's (1978) analysis of Islamic party politics in eastern
Malaysia. Two studies from the earlier period stand out: Taufik
Abdullah's (1971) history of Islamic education in Sumatra, and James
Siegel's (1969) study of [the Atjeh] religion and society.

Siegel's study perhaps represents the "breakthrough" analogue to
Tambiah's, in that he paid close attention to the ways that poetry,
prayer, and economic life were interpreted through a single lens of
religious reformism. More recent studies have examined the
importance of novels, rural poetry, women's study sessions, and new
religious schools and associations in transforming popular Muslim

consciousness in the twentieth century (Banks 1987; Bowen 1993; Hefner 1994; Peacock 1978).[13]

Redfield's original call for the study of those "culture brokers" who mediate between what he called great and little traditions has in the end born fruit, by way of a closer study of religious texts and their modes of transmission, in effect a cultural contextualization of religious studies.

The diversity of Southeast Asia can be put positively, in terms of the multiplicity of its cultures, religions, islands, and language families, or negatively, in terms of the absence of a single dominant political power or literary tradition. In the context of academic institutions, the negative sense of this diversity often prevails, emerging as a decenteredness, a lack of clear identity, a choice of trying for thin coverage or risking thick partiality. In the context of academic inquiry, both the cultural multiplicity and the absence of a dominating central tradition have, ironically, produced a unifying analytical approach, that of comparative studies of culture in context. Cultural contextualization of politics, religion, language, or art requires attention to the local (how is it meaningful for *these* people?); the historical (what is preserved or transformed over time?); and the comparative (what does *this* place tell me about *that* one?). It sees theories as themselves local, and so facilitates conversations between model-builders and detail-absorbers. It works best when multiplicity, change, and conflict are taken to be the nature of things, rather as the sign of an incomplete research agenda. It has, for all these reasons, come to define the study of Southeast Asia at its best.

John Bowen is the Dunbar-Van Cleve Professor in Arts & Sciences and Professor of Anthropology at Washington University in St. Louis.

Notes

1. In conversations with me in 1997, Kahin hoped his colleagues would study upland peoples before they disappear; to realize that early history is still vastly understudied; and to turn to topics of labor movements and the environment. James Siegel advocated taking current analytical issues such as technological innovation and emphasizing the distinctive contribution of Southeast Asian studies.

2. These data usually concern specialists either born or teaching in the U.S., and not specialists receiving degrees from U.S. universities. The majority of

Southeast Asians receiving advanced degrees in the U.S. do so in applied fields such as education, and although their dissertations nearly always concern their home countries, many of them have little to do with the U.S. area centers.

3. Other developments in the region arguably shaped the direction of research: the 1973 student uprisings in Thailand created a new (Romantic?) strain of anti-state thinking parallel to that created after the Indonesian massacres of 1965-66--both developments probably had their strongest intellectual effects at Cornell, and in particular among students working with Benedict Anderson.

4. In Indonesia, rarely studied but very consequential are the deep rifts between ministries that have strong local effects, such as that between the technocratic Ministry of Finance and the nationalist Ministry of Cooperatives.

5. Of course, economists with no particular areal expertise do write about the region; in general they find great interest in the combination of technocratic policies such as tax reform, devaluations of currencies, bank liberalizations, judicious use of windfall revenues to develop infrastructure, with corrupt and often monopoly-favoring governments, huge disparities in income, and widespread environmental destruction.

6. One would like to see case studies of key political decisions, such as the Indonesian government's decision to withdraw control over import duties from the bureaucracy and give it to a foreign enterprise, which may clarify the international dimensions of state-society relations; such studies would also provide a historical context for the decisions taken by the IMF or the World Bank.

7. Nor, I would suggest, is it clear that a regional focus is always desirable: perhaps developing competencies in Indonesia and Morocco in order to speak comparatively about Islam, as did the Geertzs, or the Philippines and Mexico in order to do so about Spanish colonialism, or Vietnam and Algeria for the French version, are more productive historical research strategies for those with vast energies.

8. Not that studies of colonial history have not also grown, reflecting a new generation's effective use of French and Dutch archives to examine processes of economic change in greater detail, and the cultural contours of colonial rule (Stoler 1985).

9. Because classical humanities approaches have been maintained in Europe (for this region, at Leiden), and Europe produces many of the best young text specialists, there is a resultant lack of fit between the current fashion in U.S. comparative literature programs and the approaches taken by many of the best Southeast Asianist candidates for U.S. literature positions. The problem has plagued Cornell's effort to develop a Southeast Asian strength in literary studies.

10. I make this claim despite the fact that as recently as 1970, Southeast Asianists reported the lowest levels of language competence among regional specialists, and rarely took courses in literature as part of their training

(Lambert 1973:57). I believe that this situation has sharply changed.

11. O'Connor's own career exemplifies the contextualizing approach: it included fieldwork into material culture techniques and the study of metallurgy on Java and Borneo.

12. For the Philippines one would mention recent studies of Catholic imagery and texts in local social history (Ileto 1979; Rafael 1993). Little has yet been done on Protestant movements in the Philippines.

www.ingramcontent.com/pod-product-compliance
Lightning Source LLC
Chambersburg PA
CBHW030634270326
41929CB00007B/66